iOS App Development

FOR DUMMIES®

A Wiley Brand

by Jesse Feiler

FOR DUMMIES®
A Wiley Brand

iOS App Development For Dummies®

Published by: **John Wiley & Sons, Inc.,** 111 River Street, Hoboken, NJ 07030-5774, www.wiley.com

Copyright © 2014 by John Wiley & Sons, Inc., Hoboken, New Jersey

Published simultaneously in Canada

No part of this publication may be reproduced, stored in a retrieval system or transmitted in any form or by any means, electronic, mechanical, photocopying, recording, scanning or otherwise, except as permitted under Sections 107 or 108 of the 1976 United States Copyright Act, without the prior written permission of the Publisher. Requests to the Publisher for permission should be addressed to the Permissions Department, John Wiley & Sons, Inc., 111 River Street, Hoboken, NJ 07030, (201) 748-6011, fax (201) 748-6008, or online at http://www.wiley.com/go/permissions.

Trademarks: Wiley, For Dummies, the Dummies Man logo, Dummies.com, Making Everything Easier, and related trade dress are trademarks or registered trademarks of John Wiley & Sons, Inc. and may not be used without written permission. All other trademarks are the property of their respective owners. John Wiley & Sons, Inc. is not associated with any product or vendor mentioned in this book.

For general information on our other products and services, please contact our Customer Care Department within the U.S. at 877-762-2974, outside the U.S. at 317-572-3993, or fax 317-572-4002. For technical support, please visit www.wiley.com/techsupport.

Wiley publishes in a variety of print and electronic formats and by print-on-demand. Some material included with standard print versions of this book may not be included in e-books or in print-on-demand. If this book refers to media such as a CD or DVD that is not included in the version you purchased, you may download this material at http://booksupport.wiley.com. For more information about Wiley products, visit www.wiley.com.

Library of Congress Control Number: 2013957974

ISBN 978-1-118-87105-8 (pbk); ISBN 978-1-118-87107-2 (ebk); ISBN 978-1-118-87110-2 (ebk)

Manufactured in the United States of America

10 9 8 7 6 5 4 3

Table of Contents

Introduction

*i*OS App Development For Dummies is a beginner's guide to developing iOS apps. And not only do you not need any iOS development experience to get started, but you also don't need any Mac development experience, either. I've written this book as though you are coming to iPhone and iPad app development as a blank slate, ready to be filled with useful information and new ways to do things. Well, almost a blank slate, anyway; see the upcoming "Foolish Assumptions" section for details on what you *do* need to know before using this book.

Because of the nature of the iPhone and iPad, you can create small, bite-sized apps that can be quite powerful. Also, because you can start small and create real applications that do something important for a user, it's relatively easy to transform yourself from an "I know nothing" person into a developer who, though not (yet) a superstar, can still crank out quite a respectable app.

But the iPhone and iPad can be home to some pretty fancy software as well — so I'll take you on a journey through building an industrial-strength app and show you the ropes for developing one on your own.

A Bit of History

It's 6:00 a.m. PST on January 9, 2007. A distressingly long line of nerds wrapped all the way around San Francisco's Moscone Center. Why? To hear Steve Jobs give his MacWorld Expo keynote address. It was nuts to get up so early on a cold morning, but Steve Jobs was rumored to be introducing an Apple phone.

No one knew whether an Apple phone would be any good, but perhaps Steve would show us magic — something that would revolutionize an industry. Perhaps it would be as cool and important as the iPod! A few hours later, Steve told the crowd that "Apple is going to reinvent the phone." Steve was never modest, but he was certainly correct — Apple completely blew away the phone industry that day. The damage was not yet visible to the current phone vendors (Palm, Motorola, Nokia, Sony, Ericsson, RIM, and Microsoft), but they were suddenly left back in the 20th century. The future had arrived.

The iPhone stands alone

The first iPhone shipped in late June 2007. It came with a bunch of Apple's native apps such as Contacts, Maps, Stocks, Safari, and so on. The problem was that only Apple could develop these native apps. The Apple developer "evangelists" told developers that we should be happy writing web apps. This did not make us happy — we wanted to write native Objective-C apps.

Steve Jobs and Apple eventually saw the light (in fact, some people believe that there was always the possibility of releasing tools to let developers write native apps, but getting the iPhone itself launched took a higher priority). Apple released a beta version of the iPhone Software Development Kit (SDK) in the spring of 2008, and it opened the App Store for business in July 2008. At this point, you could develop native apps — but only for the iPhone, because the iPad did not yet exist.

Enter the App Store

The App Store in July 2008 was a far cry from today's App Store. The numbers of apps and the numbers of downloads today are staggering. Search for "App Store" on Wikipedia to get the latest numbers. The billions of dollars that developers have earned directly from the App Store are fantastic.

But beyond these large numbers, there's something about the App Store that I didn't truly appreciate until my first app went on sale. On the first day, more than 20 copies were sold. (My initial advertising was a mass e-mail to friends.) This was very much a niche-of-a-niche product, but it continued to sell a few copies each week. I added a link to the app to my e-mail signature, and, when I saw a few copies had been sold in Great Britain, I assumed that some of my English cousins had pitched in (bless their hearts, as they say in the South).

But I don't have any relatives in Argentina. I'm pretty certain I don't know anyone in Malaysia. Okay, the first couple of sales in Canada might be explained by the fact that I live 20 miles south of the border. But why would someone in China be buying the app? I certainly hope the people in South Africa who have bought the app are using it productively.

Almost all of those people found the app by searching on the App Store. Apple provides a great deal of help and advice for you to put your app's best face forward on the App Store, and they provide tips and continually refine their search algorithms so that if you use good keywords, people can discover your apps. Apple wants to sell hardware, and they want users of their devices to discover apps that enhance their experiences with the devices.

The numbers of iOS devices are so vast that, with good keywords and a good app description, a niche-of-a-niche-of-a-niche app can find a home on the App

Store. You may write the next blockbuster app, but you also may write an app that gets modest results. The highly automated App Store provides the infrastructure to make it all possible.

You can count me among the people who think that the App Store itself may turn out to be a more significant achievement for Apple than the iPhone itself.

The iPad joins the party

Apple released the first iPad in April 2010. In some ways, the iPad was an even more remarkable achievement than the iPhone. The mobile phone existed before iPhone. iPad was the first time that a high-powered computing and communicating device that was truly mobile caught on.

Initially, the iPad ran the iPhone OS. That was a little hard for some people to understand, and before long, the operating system was renamed iOS. We're now at version 7 of iOS. In addition to the renaming, there has been some restructuring of the developer tools and environment so that things fit together very well.

When I look at developer features such as universal apps (they can run on both iPhone and iPad with minimal code changes), support for in-app purchases, and iBeacon integration, I see a full-featured environment that matches and even surpasses some of the most sophisticated development environments I've worked with.

Even though there are many more features today than there were back in 2008, iOS development today is easier than it was a few years ago. The developer tools have matured, and the frameworks themselves have been tweaked with tools such as auto layout that make the placement of interface elements on a screen automatic as devices are rotated and as new screen sizes appear on the devices.

The Plan for This Book

You will build this book's RoadTrip app using the following steps:

1. Create the initial storyboards for both the iPad and iPhone versions, starting with Xcode's Master-Detail project template.

   The template's iPad storyboard is based on using UIKit's `UISplitView Controller`, which uses the same custom `MasterViewController` and custom `DetailViewController` used in the iPhone version. The Master View controller will appear on the left when the iPad is held in landscape orientation, whereas the Detail View controller appears on the right.

2. Build and test the iPad version in the iPad simulator. You should see a Table view embedded in a Navigation controller in the Master view.

   The template's initial iPhone storyboard design begins with a custom `MasterViewController` (a Table view) embedded in a Navigation view. Selecting an item in the Table view displays data managed by a custom `DetailViewController`.

3. Build and test the iPhone version in the iPhone simulator. It should also work perfectly because you haven't had a chance to make any mistakes yet.

4. Add a `TestDriveController` to the iPhone storyboard. Build and test. Add it to the iPad storyboard. Build and test.

5. Add animation and sound to the Test Drive controller. Build and test both the iPhone and iPad versions.

6. Add additional features to each version until done.

iOS and Xcode Game Changers

With iOS 7 and — more importantly — with Xcode 5 (and later versions), the nuts and bolts of iOS app development have changed dramatically. Xcode 5 has added much more functionality to the integrated development environment (IDE) you use to develop iOS applications, especially when it comes to writing syntactically correct (and bug-free) code that's better able to manage memory. The latest versions bring much simpler integration with the App Store as well as newly designed performance-monitoring tools. Of course, the rub is getting the hang of Xcode 5. That's where this book comes in. I carefully take you through Xcode 5, pointing out its features and describing how to best use them. When you set this book aside, you'll have a great understanding of how to take advantage of all those features that will make your life easier.

You find out how to develop a single app that includes features that readers and students of earlier editions have been asking for — including more animation and sound — as well as an infrastructure that people can use to develop more robust applications. The resulting example is an app called RoadTrip, which can send you on your way to developing apps that you can be proud of and that other people will want to have.

This new edition is based on iOS 7 *and* Xcode 5. If you want to find out how to develop applications, the tools discussed in this book are the tools you absolutely need to use to do it the right way.

About This Book

iOS App Development For Dummies distills the hundreds (or even thousands) of pages of Apple documentation (not to mention my own development experience and that of many colleagues and friends) into only what's necessary to start you developing real applications. But this is no recipe book that leaves it up to you to put it all together. Rather, it takes you through the frameworks (the code supplied in the SDK) and iOS architecture in a way that gives you a solid foundation in how applications really work, and also acts as a road map to expand your knowledge as you need to.

I assume that you're in this for the long haul and that you want to master the whole app-development ball of wax. I use real-world applications to show the concepts and give you the background on how things actually work on iOS.

For many people, their first excursion into programming has been the classic Hello World C program. Depending on how you space it, it can be written in anywhere from one to three lines of code. For a long time now, I've thought that this program has long since outlived its usefulness. We just don't write code like that today (and many of us never did). As you'll see in this book, the development process involves typing code, but it also involves drawing an interface with your mouse, choosing options in check boxes to configure your app, and a whole bunch of other activities that are as far as you can get from typing a few lines of code into a blank document.

It's a new world for developers, and I think its excitement and opportunities have barely started.

Conventions Used in This Book

This book guides you through the process of building iOS apps. Throughout the book, you use the classes provided by Apple's iOS frameworks (and create new classes of your own, of course). You code them using the Objective-C programming language.

Code examples in this book appear in a monospaced font so that they stand out a bit better. That means that the code you see will look like this:

```
#import <UIKit/ UIKit.h>
```

Objective-C is based on C, which *is* case-sensitive, so please enter the code that appears in this book *exactly* as it appears in the text. I also use the standard Objective-C naming conventions — for example, class names always start with a capital letter, and the names of methods and instance variables always start with a lowercase letter.

Note that all URLs in this book appear in a monospaced font as well, like this:

```
www.northcountryconsulting.com
```

When I ask you to add code to a program, it will be in bold like this:

```
#import <UIKit/ UIKit.h>
```

You'll notice — starting around Chapter 8 — that you will sometimes be asked to delete some of the code you have in place for your project to make room for some new stuff. When that happens, I comment out the code to make things really clear. I refer to code I want you to delete as commented out, bold, underline, and italic code because said code will show up as commented out, bold, underlined, and italic. Simple enough, as shown in the following example:

```
// Delete this
```

If you're ever uncertain about anything in the code, you can always look at the source code on the companion website. (More on that in the section "Beyond the Book," later in this Introduction.)

Icons Used in This Book

This icon indicates a useful pointer that you shouldn't skip.

This icon represents a friendly reminder. It describes a vital point that you should keep in mind while proceeding through a particular section of the chapter.

This icon signifies that the accompanying explanation may be informative (dare I say interesting?), but it isn't essential to understanding iOS app development. Feel free to skip past these tidbits if you like (though skipping while learning may be tricky).

This icon alerts you to potential problems that you may encounter along the way. Read and obey these blurbs to avoid trouble.

 This icon indicates how to use an important part of Xcode functionality. This helps you wade through Xcode's complexity and focus on how to get specific things done.

Foolish Assumptions

To begin programming your iOS applications, you need an Intel-based Mac with the latest or next-to-latest version of OS X on it. (No, you can't develop iOS applications directly on the iPhone or iPad.) You also need to download the iOS Software Development Kit (SDK) — which is free. And, oh yeah, you need an iPhone and/or iPad. You won't start running your app on it right away — you'll use the iOS Simulator that Apple provides with the iOS SDK during the initial stages of development — but at some point, you'll want to test your app on a real, live iOS device.

This book assumes that you have some programming knowledge and that you have at least a passing acquaintance with object-oriented programming, using some variant of the C language (such as C++, C#, or maybe even Objective-C). In case you don't, I'll point out some resources that can help you get up to speed. The app example in this book is based on the frameworks that come with the SDK; the code is pretty simple (usually) and straightforward. (I don't use this book as a platform to dazzle you with fancy coding techniques.)

I also assume that you're familiar with the iPhone and iPad themselves and that you've at least explored Apple's included applications to get a good working sense of an iOS app's look and feel. It might also help to browse the App Store to see the kinds of applications available there and maybe even download a few free ones (as if I could stop you).

How This Book Is Organized

iOS App Development For Dummies has six main parts, which are described in the following sections.

Part I: Getting Started

Part I introduces you to the iOS world. You find out what makes a great iOS app and see how an iOS app is structured. In Chapter 2, I give an overview of how Xcode 5 works that gets you up to speed on all its features; you can use this chapter as a reference and return to it as needed. You also create your Xcode project in this part — a universal app that can run equally well on an iPad or iPhone — and I take you on a guided tour of what makes up the Xcode project that will become your home away from home.

Part II: Building RoadTrip

In this part of the book, you find out how to create the kind of user interface that will capture someone's imagination. I explain the Interface Builder editor, which is much more than your run-of-the-mill program for building graphical user interfaces. You also discover storyboards, which are the icing on the Interface Builder cake that let you lay out the entire user experience and app flow — saving you a lot of coding, to boot.

You'll also take a brief tour of the RoadTrip app, the app that you build in this book. I show you not only what the app can do but also how it uses the frameworks and SDK to do that.

I also explain how the main components of an iOS app go together. I describe how the iOS applications work from a viewpoint of classes and design patterns, as well as show how the app works at runtime. I spend some time on three very important ideas: how to extend the framework classes to do what you want them to, how to manage memory, and how to take advantage of declared properties. I also explain how everything works together at runtime, which should give you a real feel for how an iOS app works.

Parts I and II give you the fundamental background that you need to develop iOS applications.

Part III: Getting Your Feet Wet: Basic Functionality

Now that you have the foundation in place, Part III starts you on the process of having your app actually *do* something. You start off by determining whether a network is available to support the app functionality that requires Internet access. You find out how to customize the appearance of the controls provided by the framework to make your app a thing of beauty. You finish off by adding animation and sound just to get going. You also see how to connect the elements on your storyboard to your app code to make them do things — such as have a '59 pink Cadillac Eldorado Biarritz convertible drive up and down the screen.

Part IV: The Model and the App Structure

Now you begin to get down to the real work. You find out about the iPad's popovers and Split View controllers, and you also add navigation to the app. Along the way, I really get into showing you how to account for the differences between an iPad and an iPhone, and make sure that the app can run flawlessly on whatever device the user has handy. You also add the app model, which provides both the data and the logic you need to create an app that delivers real value to the user. You then finish the storyboard so that you can see your basic application flow. To wrap it all up, I show you how to package your app with a custom icon and prepare it for the App Store.

Part V: Adding the App Content

Now that you have the application foundation and the user experience architecture in place, Part V takes you into the world of applications that contain major functionality. I show you how to display the weather using a web page right off the Internet, how to allow the user to page through local events as if he were reading a book, how to display a map of where the user is going and where he is right now, how to find a location that he has always wanted to visit and display it on a map, and even how to change where he is going (limited in the RoadTrip app to New York and San Francisco, but it's incredibly easy to add other destinations). I don't go slogging through every detail of every detail, but I demonstrate almost all the technology you need to master if you intend to create a compelling app like this on your own.

Part VI: The Part of Tens

Part VI consists of some tips to help you avoid having to discover everything the hard way. It talks about approaching app development in an "adult" way right from the beginning (without taking the fun out of it). I also revisit the app and explain what else you would need to do to make this app a commercial and critical success.

Beyond the Book

This book has additional content you can access online:

- ✔ **Sample code:** Sample code for each chapter can be found online at www. dummies.com/extras/iosapplicationdevelopment. Note that the posted code represents the code as it is at the end of the chapter. If you want to download code to follow along with as you read, download the code for the previous chapter.

- ✔ **Cheat Sheet:** This book's Cheat Sheet can be found online at www. dummies.com/cheatsheet/iosapplicationdevelopment. See the Cheat Sheet for more on expanding your app with subclassing, target action, and delegation.

- ✔ **Dummies.com online articles:** Companion articles to this book's content can be found online at www.dummies.com/extras/ iosapplicationdevelopment. The topics range from tips on building an interface, using frameworks in iOS app development, and ten ways to make your app-developing life easier, among others.

- ✔ **Updates:** If this book has any Updates after printing, they will be posted to www.dummies.com/extras/iosapplicationdevelopment.

Where to Go from Here

If you're starting from the beginning, I would suggest you start with Chapter 1. However, if you are brushing up your skills, feel free to jump into a chapter that is particularly relevant to your question. Chapters such as Chapter 10, "Adding Animation and Sound to Your App" may be useful to you on their own. The chapters in Part V are relatively independent of one another.

Part I
Getting Started

getting started
with
iOS App
Development

In this part . . .

- Figuring out what makes a great iOS app
- Getting to know the SDK
- Sorting out the parts of an Xcode app

Chapter 1

What Makes a Great iOS App

In This Chapter

▶ Figuring out what makes an insanely great iOS app

▶ Discovering the iOS features that can inspire you

▶ Understanding Apple's expectations for iOS apps

▶ Making a plan for developing iOS software

*J*uly 10, 2008.

That was the day the App Store opened. The next day, Apple launched the iPhone 3G, which came with the brand-new iPhone OS 2.0.1. Owners could choose from the 500 apps in the App Store to expand their phone's power and features. You can find the latest numbers and versions in the App Store article on Wikipedia, which is updated regularly. I think it's fair to say that no one in 2008 envisioned the world of apps that we have today.

This is a world that some people have dreamed of from the dawn of the computer age in the early 1950s. It's a world of computers that are highly portable, that boast terrific connectivity without wires and cables, and that do things that people find useful, such as providing entertainment, education, practical support, and information. Part of that dream was a world in which the ability to program computers is accessible to the largest nations and corporations on almost equal terms as it is to the individual developer or hobbyist.

April 3, 2010.

That was the day the first iPad was shipped. Its operating system was iPhone OS 3.2. iOS 4 was released a few months later, and, today, iOS and its development tools have been substantially rearchitected to make both the user experience and the development process easier.

Today.

Because of the App store and the new development tools, this is a great time to start developing for iOS. Welcome!

Figuring Out What Makes a Great iOS App

A great iOS app can be described simply: It helps people do something that they want to do; it does it well; it does it when and where people want to do it; and it disappears. Because you can leverage the power of the App Store, your app can be successful globally. Yes, that may mean millions of users for your app, but it also may mean that you can find the 100 widely scattered around the world for whom your app may become a necessity.

For the most part, choosing your app's topic and market is beyond the scope of this book, but you can find many articles on the Internet and in books and magazines. You can even study the topic in colleges.

What this book does focus on is the rest of that description — building an app that works well, works when and where people want to use it, and has a user interface that helps people use the app but does not draw attention to itself. If people are thinking about your app when they should be thinking about a plot, a high score, or a trip to a store or another country, your app isn't great.

Making your app work well

The nuts and bolts of making your app work well are described in this book. At the most basic level, they are technical and organizational, but the first step is understanding what your app is going to be and do. Before you write your first line of code, think through the app. Who will the audience be? What will the app look like?

For large app development projects as well as small ones, sketching out a wireframe sequence of your app's screens is a good idea. You may think it's unnecessary in a one-person project, but it may even be more essential there. Show your sketches to friends who will be honest with you. You can search for "ios wireframe" on your favorite search engine to get recommendations for tools to help develop wireframes.

If your app delivers content, make certain that you have the content. If you have expertise in a specific area, that can serve as the basis for an app. If you have access to experts in other areas, see if they will advise you. If you go to the App Store and look at the reviews for apps, you'll see that people quickly provide low ratings for apps that don't work or that don't provide reliable data.

Making your app work well is easier than ever before with Xcode 5. Powerful debugging tools are built in so that you can even watch your app's performance on real-time gauges. Compared to earlier versions of iOS, iOS 7 has a host of improvements for users and simplifications for developers. In my opinion, the milestone was iOS 5. Although significant changes occurred in the later releases, iOS 5 was the first to provide the concept of universal apps where you could write a single code base for both iPhone and iPad. That entailed making some changes to the APIs, but we're over that hump and proceeding full speed ahead.

Handling networking, social media, and location

Networking, social media, and location can make your app great. There certainly are many successful and even great apps that don't use them, but they add additional layers of greatness to your app. Networking means that you can access Internet resources directly from your app. You can display web pages within your app, and you can also access data that you display in your app's interface. The tools to do this are available to you in the APIs.

Today, social media integration scarcely needs promotion: It has become part and parcel of our daily lives. Allowing users to promote your app on Facebook or Twitter with a simple tap is a no-brainer for many developers. iOS lets users enter their sign-in information whenever those taps occur.

Location awareness has opened a wide range of opportunities for apps. The most obvious opportunities involve integration with Maps, but "near me" functionality intrigues developers and users. With iOS 7, developers now have two sets of location tools to use. For traditional mapping, a set of tools uses GPS and cell tower locations to locate the device. Now, iBeacon adds tools to handle low-energy Bluetooth beacons over much shorter distances, such as individual paintings in a museum or specific shelves in a store.

Designing a powerful and intuitive interface that disappears

Designing a disappearing interface is one of the most challenging aspects of app design, and you'll find tips to achieve this throughout the book. A *disappearing interface* is one that works (or as many people say, "just works") without people having to think about it.

When someone looks at your app's interface and notices the interface, you're on the wrong track. What you want to achieve is a situation where someone looks at the screen and immediately sees how to get a weather report, the current temperature, or the prediction for tomorrow's weather in New York City. Users should not notice the interface. Instead, they should notice what the interface can *do*.

Using the iOS Platform to the Fullest

Okay, enough talk about the user experience. Just what exactly is the iOS platform, and what are its features?

Exploiting advantages of the system

One of the keys to creating a great app is taking advantage of what the device offers. In the case of a new platform with new possibilities, exploiting advantages is especially important. The combination of hardware and system software opens up design advantages that depart from the typical design approach for desktop and laptop apps. For example:

- **Multifinger gestures:** Apps respond to multifinger gestures, not mouse clicks. If you design an app that simply uses a single finger tap as if it were a mouse click, you may be missing an opportunity to design a better user experience.

- **Movement and orientation:** iOS devices have a variety of sensors that collect movement and orientation data. The new M7 chip in iPhone 5S, iPad Air, and iPad Mini (second generation) collects sensor information from the integrated accelerometers, gyroscopes, and compasses. This enhances existing location services and takes some of the workload off the main chip.

- **Split views and unique keyboards:** You can use a split view on an iPad to display more than one view onscreen at a time. Both iPad and iPhone provide a special keyboard unique to a task, such as the numbers-and-formulas keyboard that appears in the Numbers app.

- **Internet access:** With quick and easy access, your app doesn't need to store lots of data — all it really needs to do is jump on the Internet and grab what it needs from there. However, to be truly useful, your app needs to be ready to function when the Internet is unavailable to it.

✔ **Television or projection system connection:** Users can connect an iPhone or iPad to an HDTV or projection system to show content to larger audiences. With iOS's AirPlay feature and an Apple TV, users don't even need a physical connection.

✔ **Consistent system environment:** The Home button quits your app, and the volume controls take care of audio, just like you'd expect them to. User preference settings can be made available in the Settings application to avoid cluttering your app's user interface. Your native iOS apps can coexist with web services and apps created in HTML5.

✔ **Breathtaking imagery:** Photos and video already look fantastic on this display, but the artwork you create yourself for your app should be set to 24 bits (8 bits each for red, green, and blue), plus an 8-bit alpha channel to specify how a pixel's color should be merged with another pixel when the two are overlaid one on top of the other. In general, the PNG format is recommended for graphics and artwork that are included as part of your iOS app.

In the following sections, you get to dive into some of the major features, grouped into the following major areas:

✔ Accessing the Internet

✔ Tracking location

✔ Tracking motion

✔ Supporting multifinger gestures and touches

✔ Playing content

✔ Accessing the content of Apple's supplied apps (such as Contacts and Photos)

✔ Taking advantage of the display

Accessing the Internet

An iOS device can access websites and servers on the Internet through Wi-Fi or optional data services from the same carriers that support the iPhone's voice communication. This Internet access gives you the capability to create apps that can provide real-time information. An app can tell a user, for example, that the next tour at the Tate Modern in London is at 3 p.m, how to get there, and how long the line for the tour is.

This kind of access also allows you, as the developer, to go beyond the limited memory and processing power of the device and access large amounts of data stored on servers, or even offload the processing. You don't need all the information for every city in the world stored on the device, nor do you have to strain the device processor to compute the best way to get someplace on the Tube. You can send the request to a server for all that information, especially information that changes often.

Knowing the location of the user

You can create an app that can determine the device's current location or even be notified when that location changes, using iOS location services. As people move, it may make sense for your app to tailor itself to where the user is, moment by moment.

Many iPad and iPhone apps use location information to tell you where the nearest coffeehouse is or even where your friends are.

When you know the user's location, you can even put it on a map, along with other places she may be interested in. You find out how easy it is to add a map to your app in Chapter 17.

Tracking orientation and motion

All iOS devices contain an *accelerometer with three-dimensional data* — a component that detects changes in movement. The accelerometer measures change along one of the primary axes in three-dimensional space. An app can, for example, know when the user has turned the device from vertical to horizontal orientation, and it can change the orientation from Portrait to Landscape if doing so makes for a better user experience. Newer devices add a gyroscope and — together with the accelerometer — improve the ability of the device to measure in the direction you are moving it in space.

You can also determine other types of motion such as a sudden start or stop in movement (think of a car accident or a fall) or the user shaking the device back and forth. It makes some way-cool features easy to implement — for example, the Etch A Sketch metaphor of shaking the device to undo an operation. You can even control a game by moving the iPhone or iPad like a controller.

Tracking users' fingers on the screen

People use their fingers to select and manipulate objects on the device screen. The moves that do the work, called *gestures,* give the user a heightened sense of control and intimacy with the device. Several standard gestures — tap, double-tap, pinch-close, pinch-open, flick, and drag — are used in the apps supplied with iOS.

You may want to stick with the standard gestures in your app just because folks are already aware of (and comfortable with) the current pool, but iOS Multi-Touch gesture support lets you go beyond standard gestures when appropriate. Because you can monitor the movement of each finger to detect gestures, you can create your own.

Playing content

Your iOS app can easily play audio and video. You can play sound effects or take advantage of the multichannel audio and mixing capabilities available. You can even create your own music player that has access to all the audio synced to the device from the user's iTunes Library, or from Apple's iCloud service. You can also play back many standard movie file formats, configure the aspect ratio, and specify whether controls are displayed. You can put up pages that look like web pages or book pages if you want, and you can easily mix content for an immersive experience.

Accessing information from Apple's apps

Your app can access the user's information in the Contacts app and display that information in a different way or use it as information in your app. For example, a user could enter the name and address of a hotel, and the app would file it in the user's Contacts database. Then, when the user arrives in New York City, for example, the app can retrieve the address from the Contacts app and display directions. What's more, your app can also present standard interfaces for picking and creating contacts.

What you can do with Contacts, you can do in a similar fashion with the Calendar app. Your app can remind a user when to leave for the airport or create calendar events based on what's happening this week in New York. These events show up in the Calendar app and in other apps that support that framework.

Your app can also access the Photo library in the Photos app, not only to display photos but also to use or even modify them. For example, Apple's Photos app lets you add a photo to a contact, and many apps enable you to edit your photos on the device itself. You can develop your own photo-editing app for the iPhone or iPad using, for example, Apple's Core Image framework.

Copying, cutting, and pasting between apps

iOS provides support for Copy, Cut, and Paste operations within and between apps. It also provides a context-sensitive Edit menu that can display the Copy, Cut, Paste, Select, Select All, and Delete system commands. That means that although each iOS app is generally expected to play only in its own sandbox, you actually do have ways to send small amounts of data between apps.

Multitasking, background processing, and notifications

Recent releases of iOS have implemented and improved background processing for apps. (This has been made possible by new hardware as well as software.) As you will see throughout this book, a lot of iOS development takes place in an *asynchronous* environment. In older software, programs typically executed in a linear (or *synchronous*) manner — one line of code after the other. From time to time, this linear process was interrupted with conditional statements and branches such as *if* and *switch* statements, but the overall flow was linear.

With asynchronous processing, you can execute a section of code (often in the form of what is called a *block*) and not continue on to another line of code. When the block finishes executing, it notifies the app that it is done, and, at that point, the app executes some other code. You basically never know when you will receive such notifications, but iOS makes it easy to manage them. This architecture provides for a peppy user experience.

iOS also offers *push* notifications for receiving alerts from your remote servers even when your app isn't running, and *local* notifications that you can use in your app to alert users of scheduled events and alarms in the background (no servers required). You can use local notifications to get a user's attention; for example, a driver navigation app running in the background can use local notifications to alert the user when it's time to make a turn. Applications can also schedule the delivery of local notifications for a future date and time and have those notifications delivered even if the app isn't running.

Living large on the big screen

The iPad display offers enough space to show a laptop-style app (which is one reason why web pages look so great). You can organize your app with a master list and detailed list of menu choices, or in a layout for Landscape orientation with a source column on the left and a view on the right — similar to the OS X versions of iTunes and iPhoto and exemplified by the Contacts app on the iPad.

Note: Although the iPhone screen is smaller than the iPad screen, don't think of the iPhone screen as being tiny. The iPhone 5 screen, for example, at 1136 x 640 pixels, displays more pixels (on a smaller physical screen) than the original Macintosh screen (512 x 342 pixels). The first Mac had a 0.18-megapixel monochrome display. The iPhone 5 clocks in at a 0.73-megapixel (four times larger) dazzling full-color display. Progress is a wonderful thing, eh?

For example, to crop and mask out parts of an image in Apple's Keynote app for iPad (the app that lets you create slide shows), you don't have to select a photo and then hunt for the cropping tool or select a menu item — just double-tap the image, and a mask slider appears. In Apple's Numbers app for the iPad, if you double-tap a numeric formula, the app displays a special numeric-and-function keyboard rather than a full-text keyboard — and the app can recognize what you're doing and finish the function (such as a Sum function) for you.

These are examples of redesigning a known type of app to get rid of (or at least minimize) that modal experience of using a smartphone app — that sinking feeling of having only one path of communication to perform a task or supply a response. iOS apps should allow people to interact with them in nonlinear ways. Modality prevents this freedom by interrupting a user's workflow and forcing the user to choose a particular path.

 Lists are a common way to efficiently display large amounts of information in iPhone apps. Lists are very useful in iPad apps, too, but you should take this opportunity to investigate whether you can present the same information in a richer way on the larger display.

Embracing Device Limitations

Along with all those features, however, the iPhone, and even the iPad, have some limitations. The key to successful app development — and to not making yourself too crazy — is to understand those limitations, live and program within them, and even learn to love them. (It can be done. Honest.) These constraints help you understand the kinds of apps that are right for this device.

Often, it's likely that if you *can't* do something (easily, anyway) because of device limitations, maybe you shouldn't.

- ✔ **Users have fat fingers.** You may think that the iPad's larger display makes that relatively easy to deal with, but keep in mind that you may want to design a multiuser app for the iPad that takes into account multiple fingers. (Anyone for a nice game of Touch Hockey?)

- ✔ **Memory and battery power are limited.** This limitation may or may not be a decisive factor, depending on what kind of app you want to create, but smaller apps generally perform better.

The next sections help get you closer to a state of iOS enlightenment.

Designing for fingers

Although the Multi-Touch interface is a feature of the iPad, iPhone, and iPod touch, it brings with it some limitations.

First of all, fingers aren't as precise as a mouse pointer, which makes some operations even more difficult on an iPhone or iPod touch than on an iPad (text selection, for example). Still, due to fat fingers, user-interface elements need to be large enough and spaced far enough apart so that users' fingers can find their way around the interface comfortably. Apple recommends that anything a user has to select or manipulate with a finger be a minimum of 44 x 44 points in size.

Because it's so much easier to make a mistake using fingers, you also need to ensure that you implement a robust — yet unobtrusive — Undo mechanism. You don't want to have your users confirm every action (it makes using the app tedious), but on the other hand, you don't want your app to let anybody mistakenly delete a page without asking, "Are you *sure* this is what you *really* want to do?" Lost work is worse than tediousness.

Balancing memory and battery life

As an app designer, you have several balancing acts to keep in mind:

- ✔ **Limited memory:** When compared to the original Macintosh's standards, the computer power and amount of memory on the iPad may seem significant . . . but that is so yesterday. No ifs, ands, or buts; the computer power and amount of memory on the iPhone and iPad are limited. But this is an issue much more with older devices. The newer iPhones and iPads do have fairly large amounts of memory. However, as experienced developers know, the actual amount of memory is pretty much irrelevant: there is never enough for you to relax.

✔ **Limited battery power:** Access to the Internet can mitigate the device's power and memory limitations by storing data and (sometimes) offloading processing to a server, but those Internet operations eat up the battery faster.

Although it's true that the iOS power-management system conserves power by shutting down any hardware features that aren't currently being used, a developer must manage the trade-off between all those busy features and a shorter battery life. Any app that takes advantage of Internet access, core location, and the accelerometer is going to eat up the batteries.

As with memory, there is never enough power that you can afford not to think about it.

iOS devices are particularly unforgiving when it comes to memory usage. If you run out of memory, in order to prevent corruption of other apps and memory, the system will simply shut down your app.

Why Develop iOS Apps?

Because you can. Because it's fun. And because the time has come (today!). iOS apps are busting out all over, and developers have been very successful.

Developing iOS apps can be the most fun you've had in years, with very little investment of time and money (compared with developing for platforms like Windows). Here's why:

✔ **iOS apps are usually bite-sized, which means that they're small enough to get your head around.** A single developer — or one with a partner and some graphics support — can do them. You don't need a 20-person project team with endless procedures and processes and meetings to create something valuable.

✔ **The apps tend to be crisp and clean, focusing on what the user wants to do at a particular time and/or place.** They're simple but not simplistic. This makes app design (and subsequent implementation) much easier and faster.

✔ **The apps use the most innovative platform available for mobile computing.** It's completely changing the Internet as a publishing medium, the software industry with regard to applications, and the mobile device industry with regard to the overall digital media experience.

✔ **The free iOS Software Development Kit (SDK) makes development as easy as possible.** This book reveals the SDK in all its splendor and glory in Chapter 2. If you can't stand waiting, you *could* register as an iOS developer, and download the SDK . . . but (fair warning) jumping the gun leads to extra hassle. It's worth getting a handle on the ins and outs of iOS app development beforehand.

iOS has these two other advantages that are important to you as a developer:

✔ **You can distribute your app through the App Store.** Apple will list your app in the App Store in the category you specify, and the store takes care of credit-card processing (if you charge for your app), hosting, downloading, notifying users of updates, and all those things that most developers hate doing. Developers name their own prices for their creations or distribute them free; Apple gets 30 percent of the sales price of commercial apps, with the developer getting the rest. However, keep in mind that Apple must approve your app before it appears in the App Store.

✔ **Apple has a robust yet inexpensive developer program.** To place your app in the store and manage it, you have to pay $99 per year to join the Individual or Company version of the iOS Developer Program (which includes iPhone and iPad development support). (Apple also offers an Enterprise version for $299 per year to develop proprietary, in-house iOS apps that you can distribute to employees or members of your organization, and a free University version for educational institutions to include iOS development as part of a curriculum.) But that's it. You don't find any of the infamous hidden charges that you often encounter, especially when dealing with credit card companies. Go to the Apple iOS Developer site (`http://developer.apple.com/programs/ios`) and click the Enroll Now button to get started.

Developing with Apple's Expectations in Mind

Just as the iPhone and iPad can extend the reach of the user, the device possibilities and the development environment can extend your reach as a developer. To make sure that you're reaching in the right direction, it helps to understand Apple's perspective on what iOS apps should be — the company clearly has done some serious thinking about it, far longer than anybody else out there, having taken years to bring iOS devices to market under a veil of secrecy.

So what does Apple think? Spokespeople often talk about three different app styles:

✔ **Productivity apps use and manipulate information.** The RoadTrip sample app that I show in this book is an example, and so are my own Minutes Machine app as well as FileMaker Go (FileMaker), and Apple's iWork apps — Keynote, Pages, and Numbers. Common to all these apps is the use and manipulation of multiple types of information.

✔ **Utility apps perform simple, highly defined tasks.** Google's YouTube app is an example — it deals only with the YouTube videos. The Brushes app for painting (by Steve Sprang) is considered a utility because it performs a simple, highly defined task.

✔ **Immersive apps are focused on delivering — and having the user interact with — content in a visually rich environment.** A game is a typical example of an immersive app.

Although these categories help you understand how Apple thinks about iOS apps (at least publicly), don't let them get in the way of your creativity. You've probably heard *ad nauseam* about thinking outside the box. But hold on to your lunch; the iOS "box" isn't even a box yet. So here's a more extreme metaphor: Try diving into the abyss and coming up with something really new.

Thinking About You, Apps, and Money

This book focuses on technology, and you can find many books and articles about the business side of apps. Nevertheless, it's worth spending a moment to review the financial world of apps as it has developed over the last few years.

First of all, consider the fact that it is likely that most apps are given away. They may be given away under various circumstances:

✔ They may be used as cross-promotion for products that are priced (think of Apple's iWork apps, which became free with the release of iOS 7). People who have iOS 7 (or any other version) have bought at least one iOS device.

✔ They may be used to provide added value for services that are priced. Think of the free apps for many banks and the free apps from hotels, airlines, and tour companies.

✔ They may be given away, but they support in-app purchases, whereby you can add more advanced game levels or additional functionality to the basic free app.

Beyond the question of the app's price, you may be wondering if you can be paid for building apps. Although it's hard to find accurate numbers, it is also likely that most developers are not paid. These include students (and remember that only a few years ago everyone was a student when it comes to iOS) as well as would-be professional app developers who are building a portfolio — often with free work for friends or non-profit organizations.

Organizations that are building apps to give away often hire developers (and graphic designers and marketers) as do organizations that are selling apps.

Then there are individual developers or small groups thereof who attempt to do one of the hardest things of all: They attempt to make money from selling the apps they have written.

This is a broad overview of you, apps, and money. You don't have to decide where you're going to land as you become a proficient app developer; you can wait and see what you like to do most. In addition, be aware that many developers today mix and match roles. They may work for free for a non-profit and for pay for an app developer as well as for themselves. (Does every app developer have at least one "skunkworks" project to work on in his free time? Probably.)

Two things are important for you right now:

- ✔ Learn iOS with this book.
- ✔ Look for groups of app developers near you or online. (Meetup is a good resource.) Many developers share their experiences.

Enter the Cloud

Apple, of course, created a great deal of excitement when it announced iCloud. However, iCloud is more than just an integral part of the built-in applications; it can also be used by developers to implement new functionality for their apps.

iCloud lets you create apps that share data among all of a user's devices. For example, you could create a RoadTrip app that allowed the user to plan a trip on an iPad, and then access and even update that data on an iPhone.

iCloud is available on iOS as well as on the Mac's operating system, OS X. This means that sharing iCloud data among all of a user's devices can mean iPad, iPod touch, iPhone, MacBook Pro, Mac Pro, and the remarkable new device that's still under wraps in Cupertino at Apple's headquarters. (It doesn't matter when you read this: there will always be a remarkable new device under wraps. And, if the past is any indication, we'll all try to figure out how we ever lived without it.) All of this sharing relies on one simple fact: You must use the same (free) Apple ID on all of your devices that you want to share.

Because this book deals only with iOS, I look at iCloud only from that side, but remember that you can make a round trip from iOS to OS X and back again.

Developing an App the Right Way Using the Example App in This Book

As I mention in the Introduction, the point of this book isn't to find out how to program in Objective-C using the iOS frameworks. Instead, the point is to discover how to build apps, and that's what you'll be doing — finding out the *right way* to develop iOS apps.

The best way I can think of to show you how to build an app is to build one, and I take you through doing that throughout this book. The app you build is called RoadTrip. It allows you to plan a trip, check the weather along the way, find the events happening at your destination, and display the destination, sights, and your current location on a map, as well as display any other location by entering the address or the name of a point of interest. You can also choose between destinations.

As simple as it is, RoadTrip shows you how to do many of the tasks that are common to iOS apps. You add animation and sound, display views and navigate through them, and use controls such as buttons, as well as use the Navigation controllers like the kind you find on the iPhone and the split screen on the iPad that allows you to see two views side by side, or one view with another in a popover window.

As you build the RoadTrip app, you even find out how to display a web page and navigate its links (and return) from inside the app. You also download and display data from the Internet.

In addition, I have you build a *universal app* — one that can run either on the iPad or iPhone. Let's get started!

What's Next

You must be raring to go by now and probably can't wait to download the Software Development Kit (SDK). That's exactly what many new developers do — and later are sorry that they didn't spend more time up front understanding the iOS user experience, how apps work in the iOS environment, and the guidelines that Apple enforces for apps to be approved for the App Store.

The following chapters cover all the aspects of development you need to know before you spend time coding. Then, I promise, it's off to the stars.

Chapter 2

Getting to Know the SDK

· ·

In This Chapter

▶ Understanding what's in the SDK

▶ Getting an overview of how programmers use Xcode for app development

▶ Taking a detailed tour of the Workspace window

· ·

Xcode is the integrated development environment (IDE) that you use to build your iOS apps. In addition to building iOS apps, it can be used to build OS X apps. It is used to build Apple's own apps such as the iWorks suite. And to top it all off, it's used to build iOS and OS X themselves. Over its history, it has gotten even more powerful. In its most recent versions (4 and 5), it has also been given a modern and easy-to-use interface. It also has served as a test bed for user interface technologies that Apple later brings to its consumer apps.

In this chapter, I take you on a guided tour of the features you'll find in Xcode — giving you the view from 30,000 feet. I go through it all in detail as you use it throughout this book until your feet are firmly planted on *terra firma* — at least when it comes to Xcode. The point of this chapter is to provide a frame of reference as you move forward, and a complete reference for you to look back on.

Developing Using the SDK

The iOS Software Development Kit (SDK) provides support for developing iOS apps and includes the complete set of Xcode tools, compilers, and frameworks for creating apps for iOS and Mac OS X. These tools include the Xcode IDE (its integrated development environment) and the Instruments performance analysis tool, among many others.

Xcode 5 (the latest version) is an app that you simply download from the Mac App store. You need the current or first prior version of OS X installed to use Xcode. You should also become a registered developer. To do that, first go to `http://developer.apple.com/devcenter/ios`, look for (and then click) the link to become a registered developer, fill out some registration information, and then start reaping the benefits of being a registered developer, starting with access to tons of documentation sample code and a lot of other useful information. ***Note:*** If you want to actually run your app on your iPhone or iPad and submit it to the App Store, you need to join an official iOS Developer Program, which you can do right after you become a registered developer.

Apple links do change from time to time, so if a link I provide in this book doesn't work, you can always start at `http://developer.apple.com` and navigate to the iOS Dev Center from there.

Xcode is the latest iteration of Apple's IDE, a complete toolset for building Mac OS X and iOS apps. With Xcode 5, you can develop apps that run on any iPhone, iPad, or iPod touch running iOS. You can also test your apps using the included iOS Simulator, which supports iOS 6 and iOS 7.

The Xcode IDE includes a powerful source editor, a sophisticated graphical user interface editor, and many other features, including source code repository management. Moreover, as you code, Xcode can identify mistakes in both syntax and logic, and even suggest fixes.

To start with, I give you an overview of Xcode and how you'll use it to develop your app. As you move from step to step, I provide more detail on how to use Xcode to specifically do what you need to do in any given step.

Using Xcode to Develop an App

To develop an iPhone, iPod touch, or iPad app, you have to work within the context of an *Xcode project*. Xcode supports the following activities that are parts of developing your app:

- Creating an Xcode project
- Developing the app (designing the user interface using a storyboard, coding, and running and debugging the code)
- Tuning app performance
- Distributing the app

It supports many more activities as well, such as automated testing, but these are the activities I focus on in this book. The following sections tell you more about each of these tasks.

Creating an Xcode project

To develop an iOS app, you start by creating an Xcode project. A project contains all the elements needed to create an app, including the source files, a graphical representation of the user interface, and build settings needed to build your app. You work on your project in the *Workspace window,* which allows you to create all of these elements as well as build, run, debug, and submit your app to the App Store.

Developing the app

You have a lot to do to develop an app. You need to design the user experience and then implement what you came up with as a user interface. You need to write code to implement the features of the app. You also need to test and debug the app.

Designing the user interface using a storyboard

Xcode's Interface Builder is the editor you use to assemble your app's user interface with the help of preconfigured objects found in the Library. The objects include windows, controls (such as switches, text fields, and buttons), and the views you'll use, such as Image, Web, and Table views. The Interface Builder editor allows you to add objects, configure their properties, and create connections not only between user interface objects, but also between user interface objects and your code.

When you use a storyboard (which you do in this book), most of if not all your screens end up being displayed in the storyboard, and Interface Builder saves your storyboard in a storyboard file (with the `.storyboard` extension). When you don't use a storyboard, each screen is saved separately as a nib file (with the `.xib` extension). Either way, these files contain all the information iOS needs to reconstitute the user interface objects in your app at runtime.

Interface Builder saves you time and effort when it comes to creating your app's user interface. You don't have to code each object (which saves you a lot of work), and what's more, because Interface Builder is a visual editor, you get to see what your app's user interface will look like at runtime.

Coding

To code, you use the Source Code editor, which supports features such as code completion, syntax-aware indentation, and source code folding (to hide "code blocks" temporarily). You can get context-based help to assist you, and if you need information about a particular symbol, you can either get a summary of a symbol's documentation directly in the editor, or you can opt for more extensive documentation.

Xcode's Live Issues and Fix-it features work together to point out mistakes as you enter your code and offer to fix those mistakes for you.

Running and debugging

When you run your app to debug or test it, you can run it in the iOS Simulator on your Mac and then on an iOS-based device (if you're in the developer program). Using the simulator, you can make sure your app behaves the way you want. You can also get debugging information — as you run — in the Debug area. By running your app on a device connected to your Mac (still using the debugger, if you like), you can observe the actual user experience and see how the app will perform.

Tuning app performance

As you are running your app, gauges show you the amount of memory you're using, what's happening in your app's iCloud sandbox, how you're doing on energy consumption (a critical issue for mobile devices), network activity, and more. The clear, graphical interface of the gauges is a major new feature of Xcode 5.

Distributing the app

Xcode provides various kinds of app distribution, including

- ✔ Ad hoc distribution for testing on up to 100 iOS devices.
- ✔ The App Store for distributing to hundreds of millions of iOS device users. You can give your apps away for free or let Apple sell them for you.
- ✔ Custom B2B Apps for distributing business-to-business apps directly to your business customers who have a Volume Purchase Program account.

You create an archive of your app that contains debugging information, making it easier to track down bugs reported by testers (and users) of your app. When your app is ready to go, you submit it to the App Store. (Before you submit your app to the store, you even run some of the same software-validation procedures on your app that Apple does — passing these tests makes your app's approval process as fast as possible.)

The Workspace Window

Command central for Xcode is the Workspace window, where you'll do almost all the things you need to do to develop your app.

In this section, I present only an overview — more or less the map of what's in the Workspace window and what each bar and button is and does. I came up with this as a way to provide a quick reference to the Workspace window so you can see all its elements, including the various bars and buttons and what they do.

Figure 2-1 shows the window. (If you like, bookmark this page so you can refer to this figure at any time when reading the book.) At first glance, it may seem overwhelming, but take a deep breath and don't worry: I explain each part. As I take you through using Xcode to develop your app, I go into more detail as needed. So for now, take a quick read through the upcoming sections just to familiarize yourself with the lay of the land and then return to Figure 2-1 as needed for quick reference.

Figure 2-1: The Xcode Workspace window.

Although I have added shadings to the Workspace window components in this chapter for easy reference, figures in the remainder of the book show the components as they appear on your screen.

The Workspace window consists of

✔ Workspace areas

✔ The toolbar

✔ An optional tab bar

The following sections describe each of these elements — the heart of Xcode.

Workspace areas

The Workspace is divided into four *areas,* as follows:

✔ Editor area (always shown)

✔ Navigator area

✔ Utility area

✔ Debug area

You can configure the Workspace area in a number of ways. Right off the bat, you can choose to hide and/or show various areas in various combinations. (Note that the Editor area is always present.) The Debug and Utility areas are already configured with panes, but in the Debug area, you can select the pane configuration.

Editor area (always present)

The Editor area is always present. You can choose any of the various content editors to be shown within the Editor area; you do so using the Editor selector, the group of buttons in the toolbar you can see in the following figure.

The content editors you have available are as follows:

 ✔ **Standard editor:** The button for this editor is on the left side of the Editor selector. The Standard editor displays a single pane for editing. You have probably worked with standard editors in many environments and IDEs.

✔ **Assistant editor:** Select this editor using the center button. This adds an additional pane to the Editor area so that you can view two files at the same time. You can also split one of the panes so that you can work with three, four, or more files at the same time (the size of your monitor limits the number you can work with at the same time). The Assistant editor has some navigation features that I explain in Chapters 7 and 9.

✔ **Version editor:** Open this editor using the right button on the Editor selector. This enables you to compare two different versions of a file.

I later explain the tasks you can perform within these areas.

Additional areas to view as needed

You use the View selector (see the following figure) to toggle between showing and hiding any of the optional areas. These optional areas are as follows:

✔ **Navigator area** (left button): This area can display any of a number of navigators that let you navigate through your project, through breakpoints, and other items. It is described in the following section ("Displaying an area's content").

✔ **Debug area** (center button): Displays either or both of two panes depending on what you choose to see. You change panes using the Debug area Scope bar, shown in the following figure.

The Debug area Scope bar toggles each pane's visibility. You can choose either or both of them:

- *Debug pane:* This shows you the values for variables as they are set and changed while the app runs.

- *Console pane:* This shows you messages generated by the app for the console (including debugging messages you can insert).

You can control the visibility of each pane, but you can't reorder them. If the Variables pane is shown, it is always on the left, and if the Console pane is shown, it's on the right. If only one pane is shown, it takes up the entire width of the Debug area.

> ✔ **Utility area** (right button): Is further configured with two panes (either can be expanded to hide some or all of the other):
>
> • *Inspector pane*
>
> • *Library pane*

I explain what you see in each of those panes when I explain the Utility area section, later in the chapter.

When you hover your mouse pointer over a toolbar button, a tooltip describes its function.

Displaying an area's content

Each area displays certain content, and each area has its own way of displaying its content:

✔ **The Navigator area** has navigators.

✔ **The Editor area** has content editors.

✔ **The Utility area** has

• *Quick Help* or *Inspectors* in the Inspector/Quick Help pane.

• *Libraries* in the Library pane.

✔ **The Debug area** has

• *Debugger variables* in the Variables pane.

• *Debugger output* in the Console pane.

The following sections tell you about these areas in more detail.

Navigator area navigators

The Navigator area contains a host of navigators that organize the tasks and components you use within your Xcode project. You use a Navigator selector bar to select the navigator you need. The following figure shows the various navigators you can choose from. The navigators you most frequently use are described in this book. Here is a summary of them:

✔ **Project navigator:** Here's where you manage all the files in your project. You can add files, delete files, and even organize your files by placing them into groups. Selecting a file in the Project navigator launches the appropriate editor in the Editor area.

 ✔ **Symbol navigator:** Lets you zero in on a particular *symbol* — an element such as a variable, method, or function name — in your project. Selecting a symbol highlights it in the editor.

 ✔ **Find navigator:** Finds any string within your projects and frameworks.

 ✔ **Issue navigator:** Displays issues such as diagnostics, warnings, and errors that arise when you're coding and building your project.

The following navigators are beyond the scope of this book:

 ✔ **Test navigator:** Xcode 5 allows you to integrate automated test suites into your project. Unfortunately, the Test navigator and automated test suites are beyond the scope of this book, but don't worry: You can still build great apps and test them manually.

 ✔ **Debug navigator:** Displays the *call stack* — information about what method has called what method — during program execution.

 ✔ **Breakpoint navigator:** Manages and edits the *breakpoints* — markers you add to your code that stop program execution at a certain point in your program — in your project or Workspace.

✔ **Log navigator:** Examines the logs that Xcode generates when you run and debug your app.

Editor area content editors

The Editor area has a number of editors you use to edit specific content. Content editors are context based where the context is determined by the type of file you are editing. This means that the selection you make in a Navigator or Editor *jump bar* — the toolbar that appears at the top of each Editor area pane and is used to navigate through the files and symbols in your project — determines the Content editor. The following bullet list names each Content editor that is described in this book and outlines the tasks associated with each one (note that not all tasks are applicable to iOS app development):

✔ **Source editor:** Write and edit your Objective-C source code; set, enable, or disable breakpoints; and control program execution.

✔ **Project editor:** View and edit settings such as build options, target architectures, and code signing.

✔ **Interface Builder:** Graphically create and edit user interface files in storyboards (and XIB files if you are not using a storyboard).

✔ **Property list editor:** View and edit various types of small, highly structured property lists (plists). (You'll use one for some of your program's data.)

✔ **Viewer:** Display files for which there is no editor (some audio, video, and graphics files, for example) using the same Quick Look facility used by the Finder.

For the sake of completeness, the other content areas that are beyond the scope of this book are briefly described here:

✔ **Core Data model editor:** Implement or modify a Core Data model.

✔ **Mapping model editor:** Graphically create and edit a mapping between an old Core Data store and a new one.

✔ **Script editor:** Create and edit AppleScript script files.

✔ **Scripting dictionary editor:** Create and edit the scripting definition (.sdef) file — used by AppleScript — for your app.

✔ **Rich text editor:** View and edit rich text (.rtf) files, much as you would with Text Edit.

Utility area

The Utility area has two panes: the Inspector pane and the Library pane. Part of the Inspector pane is always visible, but you can totally collapse the Library pane if you want by dragging it to the bottom of the Utility area.

When working within the Inspector pane, you click a button in the Inspector selector (shown in the following figure) to select a particular inspector. (Note that a previous navigator selection or Content editor selection may determine which inspectors are available.) Your choices are as follows:

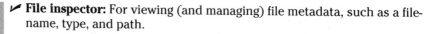

  ✔ **File inspector:** For viewing (and managing) file metadata, such as a filename, type, and path.

✔ **Quick Help (second button):** For viewing (applicable) details about what has been selected in an editor, such as an abstract or concise description, where and how it is declared, and selection-based information such as an element's scope, the parameters it takes, its platform and architecture availability, references, sample code, and so on. The following selections are supported:

- *Symbols,* in the Source editor
- *Interface objects,* in Interface Builder
- *Build settings,* in the Project editor

Additional inspectors are available in some editors; for example, Interface Builder offers the following:

 ✔ **Identity inspector:** For viewing (and managing) object metadata such as an object's class, runtime attributes, label, and so forth.

 ✔ **Attributes inspector:** For configuring the attributes specific to the selected interface object. For example, some text field attributes include text alignment and color, border type, and editability.

 ✔ **Size inspector:** For specifying characteristics such as the initial size and position of an interface object, its minimum and maximum sizes, and various autosizing rules for the object.

 ✔ **Connections inspector:** View the outlets and actions for an interface object, make new connections, and delete existing connections. (Connections "connect" your program code to user interface objects you create in Interface Builder.)

When working within the Library pane, you click a button in the Library selector bar (shown in the following figure) to select a library of resources you can use in your project. The following libraries are available:

 ✔ **File templates:** These templates are for the common types of files listed as choices in the New File menu. To add a file of that type to your project, drag it from the library to the Project navigator.

 ✔ **Code snippets:** These are short pieces of source code for use in your app. To use one, drag it directly into your source code file.

 ✔ **Objects:** This library contains the kinds of interface objects you'd use to make up your user interface. To add one to a view, drag it directly into your storyboard or nib file in the Interface Builder editor.

 ✔ **Media library:** This library contains a whole slew of graphics, icons, and sound files. To use one, drag it directly to your storyboard or nib file in the Interface Builder editor.

Debug area

The Debug area is where you'd try to track down the bugs in your code and squash them. A selection in the Debug area Scope bar determines the information the debugger displays as described previously in this section.

The pop-up menu in the Variables Pane Scope bar lets you display in the following ways:

✔ **Auto:** Display recently accessed variables

✔ **Local:** Display local variables

✔ **All:** Display all variables and registers

```
✓ Auto
  Local Variables
  All Variables, Registers, Globals and Statics
```

The pop-up menu in the Console Pane Scope bar lets you display

✔ **All Output:** Target and debugger output

✔ **Debugger Output:** Debugger output only

✔ **Target Output:** Target output only

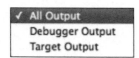

```
✓ All Output
  Debugger Output
  Target Output
```

You also find other controls and filters for what is displayed; explore them on your own.

Xcode has extensive contextual help articles that you can view by Control-clicking in the Workspace window on the item you need help on.

The toolbar and Tab bar

The *toolbar* (see the following figure) includes Workspace-level tools for managing and running *schemes* (instructions on how to build your app), viewing the progress of (executing) tasks, and configuring the Workspace window.

That's a lot of tools, so to keep things straight, it's best to think of the toolbar as actually having three parts: A Flow control part, an Activity Viewer part, and a Workspace Configuration part.

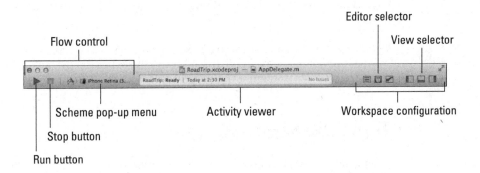

Flow control   Editor selector   View selector

Run button   Stop button   Scheme pop-up menu   Activity viewer   Workspace configuration

Flow controls are for defining, choosing, running, and stopping projects. A *scheme* defines characteristics such as build targets, build configurations, and the executable environment for the product to be built in.

The Flow controls are as follows:

- ✔ **Run button:** Clicking the Run button builds and runs the targets. (A *target,* in this context, is the product you want to build as well as the instructions for building that product from a set of files in a project or Workspace for the currently selected scheme.) Pressing and holding the mouse button opens a menu (which is also available in the Product menu) that allows you to run, test, profile, or analyze your app.

- ✔ **Stop button:** Terminates your executing app in either the Simulator or the device.

- ✔ **Scheme menu:** Lets you select the scheme and build destination to use.

The Activity Viewer part of the toolbar shows the progress of tasks currently executing. This viewer displays status messages, build progress, and other information about your project. Click the Issues icon in the Activity viewer to open the Issue navigator (explained earlier in this chapter, in the "Navigator area navigators" section).

You use the final part of the toolbar — the Workspace Configuration part — to configure the Xcode Workspace window to suit your needs. You can use these controls to select an editor type, show or hide optional view areas, and open the Organizer window. (See the "Displaying an area's content" section, earlier in the chapter, for more on your choices here.)

The Tab bar is great for keeping track of where you've been and what you might want to go back to. Note, however, that showing the Tab bar is optional. If you decide that the Tab bar is something you just can't do without, choose View➪Show Tab Bar from Xcode's main menu. You can reorder tabs, close them individually, or drag them out of the bar to create a new window.

If you lose the toolbar (or Tab bar), you can always add it back to any window by selecting View➪Show Toolbar (or View➪Show Tab Bar). The View menu also allows you to configure the Workspace window.

The Organizer window

The Organizer window (see Figure 2-2) enables you to do supplemental tasks such as accessing documentation and managing devices, archives, and project-related metadata.

Figure 2-2:
The
Organizer
window.

To display the Organizer window, choose Window⇨Organizer from Xcode's main menu. The Organizer window includes three individual organizers, which enable you to do the following:

- ✔ **Devices organizer:** Provision a device, manage your developer profile, install iOS on the device, and manage your app and data on a device.
- ✔ **Projects organizer:** Lets you locate your projects without having to remember where they are in the file system and offers *snapshots* — a Save feature that enables you to save different versions of your projects.
- ✔ **Archives organizer:** Submit your app to the App Store or testers and manage your product archives.

As you can see in Figure 2-2, the Projects organizer shows a list of projects at the left. When you select a project, you can see its location on disk, snapshots that you may have taken or that Xcode has taken, and perhaps most importantly, derived data that has been generated by Xcode.

To create a snapshot, choose File⇨Create Snapshot. To revert to a snapshot, choose File⇨Restore Snapshot. This will take you back to that version of your project. This provides similar functionality to the Source Control menu that lets you work with Git or Subversion.

Derived data is a feature to remember. Xcode caches some intermediate values during its build process. It actually caches two sets of values. When you make modifications to your project, you can use Product⇨Clean to remove many of the cached values. (In fact, some developers routinely use the key combinations to Clean and Build their projects all at once. They are Control+Shift+K and Control+B.)

In addition to cleaning your project, you can remove the second cache of values — the derived data you see in Figure 2-2. If you make a change to your project and don't see anything different, clean and purge derived data: Often that will do the trick.

Chapter 3

The Nuts and Bolts of an Xcode Project

*T*o use Xcode to create an app, you need to create an Xcode project. An Xcode project includes all the files, resources, and information required to build your application. It's your partner in creating your application, and the sooner you make friends with it, the easier your life will become.

In this chapter, I show you how to create an Xcode project and then build and run your app in the Simulator.

Creating Your Project

Because developing an iPhone and/or an iPad app requires you to work in an Xcode project, it's time to create one. The app you'll be building is called RoadTrip (and will also be the name of the project). The app, as I mention in the Introduction to this book, is like a travel guide on your iOS device. Here's how you get your RoadTrip project off the ground:

1. **Launch Xcode.**

   Simply go the Mac App Store, search for Xcode 5, click the Free button, and then click the Install App button that the Free button transmogrifies into, and you are done. After the download, you'll find Xcode in your Applications folder. Double-click to launch it.

Here are a couple of hints to make Xcode handier and more efficient right from the start:

- *Create a shortcut.* Control-click the Xcode icon that appears in the Dock and then choose Options⇨Keep in Dock. You'll be using Xcode a lot, so it wouldn't hurt to be able to launch it from the Dock.

- *Nix the Welcome to Xcode screen if you'd like.* When you first launch Xcode, you see the Welcome to Xcode screen with several links. (After you use Xcode to create projects, your Welcome screen lists all your most recent projects in the right column.) If you don't want to be bothered with the Welcome screen in the future, deselect the Show This Window When Xcode Launches check box.

You can also just click Cancel to close the Welcome screen.

If you ever want to see the Welcome screen again, you can access it through the Window menu or by pressing Shift+⌘+1.

2. **Click the Create a New Xcode Project link on the left side of the Welcome screen, or choose File⇨New⇨Project to create a new project.**

Alternatively, you can just press Shift+⌘+N.

No matter how you decide to start a new project, you're greeted by the Choose a Template for Your New Project sheet (a "sheet" is also known as a "document-modal dialog"). Its purpose in life is pretty clear: It's there to let you choose a new template for your new project. Note that the leftmost pane has two sections: one for iOS and the other for OS X (Apple's name for the Macintosh operating system).

3. **In the upper-left corner of the Choose a Template dialog, select Application under the iOS heading (if it isn't already selected).**

After clicking Application, the main pane of the Choose a Template sheet refreshes, revealing several choices. (See Figure 3-1.) Each choice is actually a template that, when chosen, generates code to get you started.

4. **Select Master-Detail Application from the template choices displayed (as I have in Figure 3-1) and then click Next.**

After you click Next, the Choose Options for Your New Project sheet appears.

This Master-Detail Application template provides a starting point for the appropriately named Master-Detail application. What you get is a skeleton app with a split view. (I explain all about split views in the "The iPad's Split views" section, later in this chapter.) A Split view is what you see in the Mail application. In Landscape orientation on the left is a *Master view,* and on the right is a *Detail view.* In Portrait orientation, you see the Detail view with a button that enables you to display the Master view in a popover.

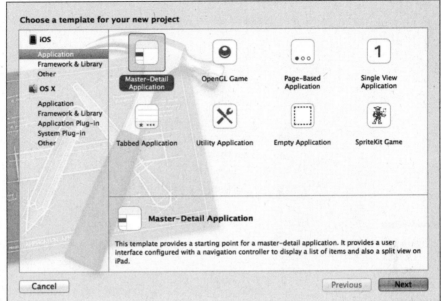

Figure 3-1:
Choose a
template
first.

Note that when you select a template, a brief description of the template is displayed underneath the main pane. (Again, refer to Figure 3-1 to see a description of the Master-Detail Application template.) In fact, go ahead and click some of the other template choices just to see how they're described as well. Just be sure to click the Master-Detail Application template again when you're done, and then click Next, to follow along with developing the RoadTrip app.

These template names do change from time to time, so don't be surprised if yours are a little different from the ones I refer to in this book. For the most part, the kinds of application they build tend to stay the same.

5. **In the Choose Options for Your New Project sheet (see Figure 3-2), enter a name for your new project in the Product Name field, and add a company name (or your name) in the Organization Name field. For the Company Identifier, use your reverse domain name (com.yourdomain) if you have one.**

   If you don't have one, you can make one up as long as you are not going to be submitting the app to the App Store.

   I named this project *RoadTrip*. (You should do the same if you're following along with developing RoadTrip.)

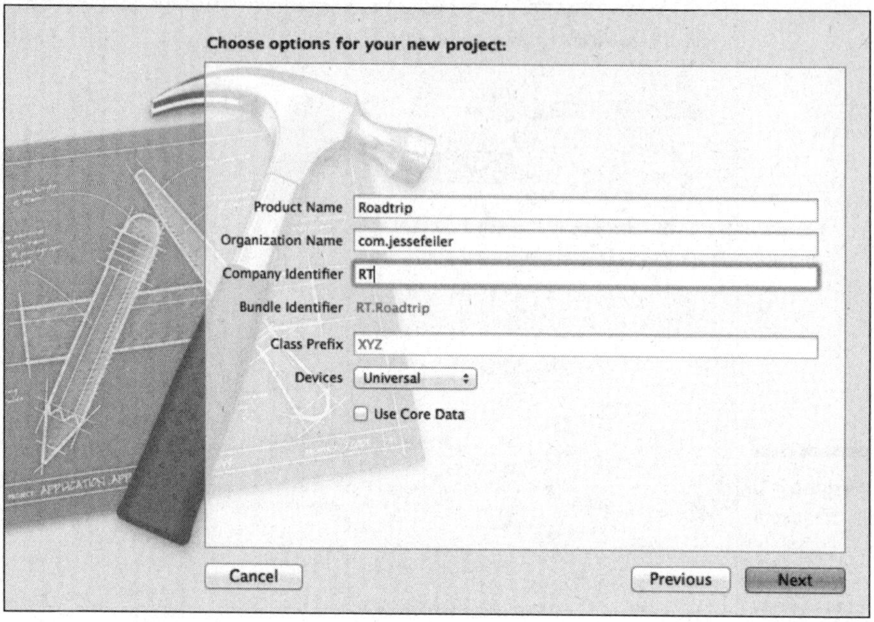

Choose options for your new project:

Product Name	Roadtrip
Organization Name	com.jessefeiler
Company Identifier	RT
Bundle Identifier	RT.Roadtrip
Class Prefix	XYZ
Devices	Universal
	☐ Use Core Data

Cancel   Previous   **Next**

Figure 3-2:
Choose
project
options.

Class prefix is something that will get prepended to the classes the template will generate, so enter **RT** (for RoadTrip) in the Class Prefix field. Prefixes are most often used to distinguish classes created by different teams so that if they are combined into a single project at a later date, duplicate names are avoided. (These are called *namespace collisions*.)

6. **Select Universal from the Devices Family pop-up menu (if it isn't already selected).**

   Doing so creates a skeleton app that will be configured to run on the iPad, iPhone, or iPod touch.

   By choosing Universal, you're creating an app that can run on iPhone (and iPod touch) and iPad.

   Any iPhone application will run on the iPad, but it doesn't work the other way around unless you create a Universal application.

   I have you select Universal because, with the introduction of storyboards in iOS 5 and Xcode 4.2, creating a universal application has become much easier.

   Do not select the Use Core Data check box. (Core Data is not covered in this book.)

7. **Click Next and choose a location to save the project (the Desktop or any folder works just fine), do not select the Source Control: Create Local Git Repository check box, and then click Create.**

Git is a software control management (SCM) system that keeps track of changes in the code and saves multiple versions of each file on your hard drive. Git can be used as a local repository — thus the Create Local Git Repository for This Project option — or you can install a Git server on a remote machine to share files among team members. Git is beyond the scope of this book — but if you want to find out more about it, check out the Xcode 5 User Guide (choose Help➪Xcode User Guide).

After you click Create, Xcode creates the project and opens the Workspace window for the project — which should look like what you see in Figure 3-3.

Xcode will remember your choices for your next project.

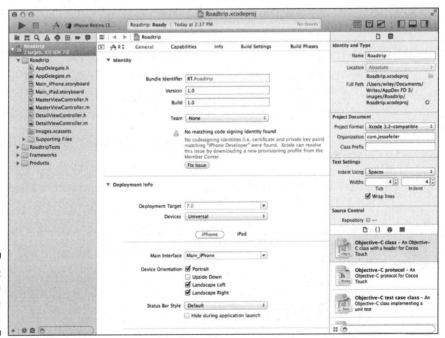

Figure 3-3: The Xcode Workspace window.

Exploring Your Project

Not to sound like a broken record, but to develop an iOS app, you have to work within the context of an Xcode project, very much like the one shown in Figure 3-3. This is, in effect, Command Central for developing your app; it displays and organizes your projects, source files, and the other resources needed to build your apps.

The project

If the project isn't open, go ahead and open it in Xcode by tracking down the project file — on the Desktop, in a folder, wherever — and double-clicking it. When your project is launched in Xcode, the Navigator area appears on the left side of the Workspace window. When using the Master-Detail Application template — you did select the Master-Detail Application template when you created your project, right? — the following options may be selected for you by default:

- ✔ The Utility and Debug areas are hidden.
- ✔ The Navigator area is shown, with the Project navigator selected by default in the Navigator selector.
- ✔ The project (RoadTrip, in this case) is selected in the Project navigator.

And as a result, the Project editor displays the RoadTrip project information in the Standard editor.

Long story short, when you launch your RoadTrip project in Xcode, what you see in the editor is the Project editor displaying the RoadTrip project.

When I refer to (or ask you to select) the *RoadTrip project in the Project Navigator,* I am referring to the RoadTrip project that you see selected in Figure 3-3.

The Project editor

Having your RoadTrip project selected in the Navigator area's Project navigator (refer to Figure 3-3) sets a couple of balls rolling. In the first column of the Project editor, under the Project heading, you see the project itself. (A workspace can actually have more than one project, but you won't be doing that in this book. One common use for a multi-project workspace is one that contains an iOS project, an OS X project, and some shared files.) A bit below the Project heading, you see the Targets heading. (Yes, there's room for more than one target here as well.) Any project you create defines the default build settings for all the targets in that particular project. (Note that each target can also specify its own build settings, which could potentially override the project build settings.)

A *target* is really just the *app* (the product you are building) and includes the information that Xcode requires to build the product from a set of files in a project or workspace — stuff like the build settings and build phases which you can see and edit in the Xcode project editor. A target inherits the build settings for the project, but you can override one or more of them by specifying different settings at the target level. There is one active target at a time, with the Xcode scheme (iPad Simulator for example) specifying the target.

The Project editor shows tabs across the top; clicking these tabs opens panes that enable you to examine and change project settings. Most of the default settings will work for your needs. The tabs are as follows:

- ✔ **General:** There are five sections in General. Each can be opened and closed with the disclosure triangle next to its name. Most of the time all start opened. Here they are:

  - *Identity:* This section is filled in automatically, but each value can be changed. For now, leave the defaults. It contains your app's *bundle identifier,* which is a unique identifier built from your organization name and project name, a version (1.0 to start) and a build (1.0 to start). You can select a development team (there's more on this later in this chapter in the section "Setting Your Xcode Preferences"). You may see a warning saying "No matching code signing identity found" or a similar warning with regarding to provisioning profiles. You can safely ignore it for now.

  - *Deployment Info:* This is the deployment target (the minimum iOS version you're writing for) as well as which devices you support (the default is Universal). For each device, you can specify the interface, which orientations you support, and the status bar style. For starters, simply leave the default values.

  - *App Icons:* This section lets you specify where the icons are. Before Xcode 5, the names determined which icon was which. Now, *asset catalogs* let you provide your own names even as you place the images in a structured interface. Asset catalogs are discussed in "Using Asset Catalogs" later in this chapter. You can still provide individual images, but the asset catalogs are easier for newcomers as well as experienced developers.

- *Launch Images:* These are the images that are shown as the app is launching. They, too, can be stored in asset catalogs.

- *Linked Frameworks and Libraries:* These are the iOS frameworks that you need to use. The Master-Detail Application template automatically includes CoreGraphics, UIKit, and Foundation. Don't worry about these for now: just leave them there.

✔ **Capabilities:** This is where you turn various features on and off. Each one can be opened or closed with a disclosure triangle. An on-off switch at the right controls each capability. Most have a description of the capability along with a notice about what will happen if you turn the capability on. In this book, I focus on the common features do not use any of the advanced capabilities.

✔ **Info:** If you actually created the RoadTrip project earlier in this chapter and were then to open the disclosure triangle next to the Supporting Files folder in the Project navigator, you'd see a file called `RoadTrip-Info.plist`. The Info tab contains more or less the same information as that file. An *information property list file* contains essential configuration information for a *bundled executable* (the executable code and the accompanying resources, such as the storyboard, nibs, images, sounds, and so on). The system uses these keys and values to obtain information about your application and how it's configured. As a result, all bundled executables (plug-ins, frameworks, and applications) are expected to have an information property list file.

There also are sections where you can specify the types of documents your app can read and write. RoadTrip doesn't use documents, so you don't need to worry about the settings on this section.

✔ **Build Settings:** Most developers can get by with the default build settings, but if you have special requirements — ones that require anything from tweaking a setting or two to creating an entirely new build configuration — you'll take care of them in this tab.

✔ **Build Phases:** This tab has a number of sections that control how Xcode builds your products. For example, Xcode detects when one of your products is dependent on another and automatically builds those products in the correct order. However, if you need to tweak the order in which Xcode builds your products, you can use the Build Phases tab to create explicit target dependencies.

✔ **Build Rules:** Xcode processes your source files according to file type using a set of built-in rules. For example, property list (`plist`) files are copied into the product using the CopyPlistFile script located in the Xcode directory. Because the built-in rules are fine for almost all circumstances, you won't need to mess with this particular tab for a long time — and if you're lucky, never.

The Project navigator

After your project is created, the Xcode workspace displays the Project navigator. I introduce the Project navigator in Chapter 2, but give you a full tour here.

Xcode has a lot of context-based help. Whenever you're curious about what something does, try Control-clicking on it, and you'll likely find a menu with relevant commands including Help. In Figure 3-4, for example, I Control-clicked in the Project navigator to bring up a shortcut menu from which I can choose the Project Navigator Help menu.

Figure 3-4:
Project
navigator
help.

The Navigator area is an optional area on the left side of the Workspace window where you can load different navigators — including the Project navigator — with the help of the Navigator selector. To hide or show the Navigator area, click the left View selector button in the workspace toolbar, shown in Figure 3-5.

Click to view the Navigator area.

Figure 3-5:
The View
selec-
tor in the
workspace
toolbar.

The Navigator area includes the Navigator selector bar, the Content area, and the Filter bar. It can also include other features specific to the selected navigator.

 The Project navigator enables you to do things like add, delete, group, and otherwise manage files in your project or choose a file to view or edit in the Editor area. (Depending on which file you choose, you'll see the appropriate editor.) In Figure 3-6, for example, you can see that I've decided to open all the disclosure triangles so that the Project navigator displays all the files in the project.

The *Filter bar* lets you restrict the content that's displayed — such as recently edited files, unsaved files, or filenames.

Making your way down the group structure shown in the Project navigator (refer to Figure 3-6), the first group listed is labeled RoadTrip.

 "What?" you may be saying. I see folders just like in the Finder. "What are these groups?" In the Project navigator, you can group files together. They are shown using folder icons just as in the Finder, but they are Xcode groups. The files may be in different folders on disk.

The RoadTrip group contains all the source elements for the project, including source code, resource files, graphics, and a number of other pieces that will remain unmentioned for now (but I get to those in due course). Although each template organizes these source elements in different ways, the Master-Detail Application template organizes the interface header and implementation code files (along with the Storyboard file(s) and a Supporting Files folder) inside the RoadTrip group. (For good measure, the RoadTrip group also includes a Frameworks folder and a Products folder.)

Here's the kind of stuff that gets tossed into groups for projects like the RoadTrip project:

✔ **AppDelegate files:** The `AppDelegate.h` and `AppDelegate.m` files contain the code for app-specific behavior that customizes the behavior of a framework object (so that you don't have to subclass it — as I describe in Chapter 6). A behavior-rich framework object (used as-is) delegates the task of implementing one of its responsibilities to an application delegate for a very specific behavior. The *delegation* pattern of adding behaviors to objects is described in more detail in Chapter 6.

✔ **Storyboard:** The storyboard files live in your project as the `Main_iPad.storyboard` file and the `Main_iPhone.storyboard` file (for a universal app), or just as a lone `Main_whatever.storyboard` file (for a device-specific app). With a storyboard, you can create and implement an overall view of the flow of your application and the user interface elements. I go into great detail on storyboards in Chapter 4. Soon you'll like the `.storyboard` files as much as I do.

✔ **View controllers:** The `MasterViewController.h` and `MasterViewController.m` files contain the code to control the initial view of the RoadTrip (based on the Master-Detail Application template). You'll do a lot more with view controllers in later chapters.

✔ **Supporting Files:** In this folder, you typically find the precompiled headers (header files that are compiled to reduce your application compilation time) of the frameworks you'll be using — such as `RoadTrip_Prefix.pch` — as well as the property list (`RoadTrip-Info.plist`) and `main.m`, your application's `main` function. You may even find images and other media files, and some data files. The `InfoPlist.strings` file is used for localization (translating the text in your app to the user's language preference). Default values are provided in your `Info.plist` file for items such as the copyright and the app name; `InfoPlist.strings` then provides language-specific versions of the values in `<yourApp>-Info.plist`. Each language has its own `InfoPlist.strings` in a folder for that language.

✔ **Frameworks:** This folder holds the code libraries that act a lot like prefab building blocks for your app. (I talk about frameworks in Chapter 4.) By choosing the Master-Detail Application template, you let Xcode know that it should add the `UIKit`, `Foundation`, and `CoreGraphics` frameworks to your project, because it expects that you'll need them in this kind of application.

You'll be adding more frameworks yourself in addition to these three in developing RoadTrip. You find out how to add more frameworks in Chapter 8.

✔ **Products:** The Products folder is a bit different from the others. In it, you'll find the final `RoadTrip.app` file — not the source code of the app, but rather the *built* version of the app, which means that it has been translated from the source code into the object code for the iOS device's processor to execute. At the moment, this file is listed in red because the file can't be found.

When a filename appears in red, this means that Xcode can't find the underlying physical file. And because you've never compiled the RoadTrip app, it makes sense that the `RoadTrip.app` file (the app itself) is missing.

Setting Your Xcode Preferences

Xcode gives you options galore. I'm guessing that you won't change any of them until you have a bit more programming experience under your belt, but a few options are actually worth thinking about now — so in this section, I show you how to set some of the preferences you might be interested in.

Follow these steps to set some of the preferences you'll find useful:

1. **With Xcode open, choose Xcode⇨Preferences from the main menu.**

2. **Click the Behaviors tab at the top of the Preferences window to show the Behaviors pane.**

   The Xcode Preferences window refreshes to show the Behaviors pane.

   The left side of the pane shows the Events pane (the check marks indicate events for which settings are set), while the right side shows the possible actions for an event.

3. **Select (Running) Generates output in the left column and then choose the Show, Hide, or If No Output Hide option from the Debug area pop-up menu to the left of the debugger in the right pane.**

   This step controls what appears while you run your app. By default, you'll find that the check box for showing the debugger in the Debug area is selected. (See Chapter 8 for more about debugging.)

4. **Select other options from the left column — perhaps (Build) Starts, (Build) Generates new issues, (Build) Succeeds, and (Build) Fails — and experiment with the options available.**

   You can link an event with playing a sound (something I like to do) or have an event trigger the Xcode icon bouncing up and down in the Dock. You can change many options in the Behaviors pane — too many to cover in this chapter! But take a look through them and experiment — they can make your life much easier.

Figure 3-7 shows the behaviors I have chosen if the run pauses. (By *pause*, I mean the run hits, say, a breakpoint; I cover breakpoints in Chapter 8.) I like to have a sound inform me in case I'm busy daydreaming (sosumi seems like the appropriate sound to play here).

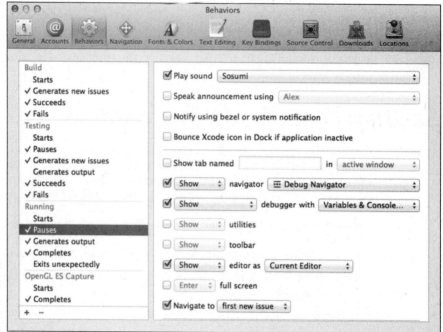

Figure 3-7:
Setting
behaviors.

Figure 3-8 shows the behaviors I have chosen if a build fails. I like to use a sound for this occurrence as well. I also want to have the Issue navigator display. (See Chapter 8 for more about the value and use of the Issue navigator.) I also want it to navigate to the first new issue.

5. **Click the Downloads tab at the top of the Preferences window.**

6. **Select the Check for and Install Updates Automatically check box, and then click the Check and Install Now button.**

   This step ensures that the documentation remains up-to-date and allows you to load and access other documentation.

7. **(Optional) Click the Fonts & Colors tab at the top of the Preferences window and use the options to change your workspace theme.**

   As you click the various theme options, you see a preview in the center of the window.

Figure 3-8:
Choosing
a behavior
for when a
build fails.

8. **(Optional) Click the Text Editing tab at the top of the Preferences window and set your text editing preferences.**

    I set the Indent width to 2 in the Indentation settings to get as much code on a line as possible.

9. **Click the red Close button in the top-left corner of the window to close the Xcode Preferences window.**

Building and Running Your Application

The Xcode toolbar (see Figure 3-9) is where you do things like run your application. I spell out the process a bit more here.

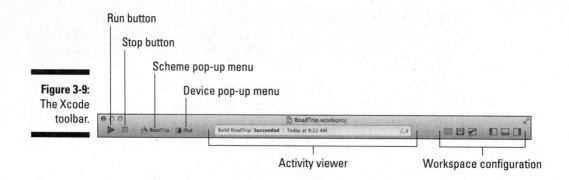

Run button

Stop button

Scheme pop-up menu

Device pop-up menu

Figure 3-9:
The Xcode
toolbar.

Activity viewer

Workspace configuration

The Flow controls are for defining, choosing, running, and stopping projects. They consist of the following:

- ✔ **Run button:** Clicking the Run button builds and runs the *targets* — a target is a product to build and the instructions for building the product from a set of files in a project or workspace for the currently selected scheme. Pressing and holding the mouse button opens a menu — also available in the Product menu — that allows you to run, test, profile, or analyze your application.

  Holding various modifier keys while clicking and holding the Run button allows you to select these other run options:

  > *Control key:* Run, test, or profile without building

  > *Shift key:* Build for running, testing, or profiling

  > *Option key:* Run, test, or profile

  Regardless of the modifier key, Analyze is an option in each case.

- ✔ **Stop button:** Terminates your (executing) application in the Simulator or the device.

- ✔ **Scheme menu:** A *scheme* defines characteristics such as build targets, build configurations, and the executable environment for the product to be built. The *scheme menu* lets you select which scheme and which build destination you want to use. (I describe schemes in greater detail in the next section of this chapter.)

The *Activity viewer* shows the progress of tasks currently executing by displaying status messages, build progress, and other information about your project. For example, when you're building your project, Xcode updates the Activity viewer to show where you are in the process — and whether the process completed successfully. If an Issues icon appears in the Activity viewer, click it to open the Issues navigator and look there for messages about your project. (None exist yet in Figure 3-9, so you won't see an Issues icon there.)

The *Workspace configuration* includes the Editor and View controls (which I explain in Chapter 2).

Building an app

Building an app in Xcode means compiling all the source code files in the project. It's really exciting (well, I exaggerate a bit) to see what you get when you build and run a project that you created from a template. Building and running an app is relatively simple; just follow these steps:

1. **In the toolbar, choose a scheme from the Scheme pop-up menu located to the right of the Run and Stop buttons.**

   A *scheme* tells Xcode the purpose of the built product. The schemes in the Scheme pop-up menu specify which targets (actual products) to build, what build configuration to use when building them, which debugger to use when testing them, and which executable to launch when running them on the device or Simulator. You can use the default RoadTrip scheme for now.

2. **From the selected scheme, hold down the mouse button and slide to the right to choose your device or the simulator.**

   Choose one of the installed simulators. Do not choose iOS Device because that will run on a connected iPhone or iPad, and you need further preparation to do that.

3. **Choose Product⇨Run from the main menu to build and run the application.**

   You can also click the Run button in the top-left corner of the Workspace window. The Activity viewer (shown in Figure 3-9) tells you all about the build progress, flags any build errors (such as compiler errors) or warnings, and (oh, yeah) tells you whether the build was successful.

Figure 3-10 shows you what you'll see in the Simulator (in the Portrait mode) when you tap the Master button. (The Master button is located in the view that's underneath the master view controller at the left of Figure 3-10. Its purpose is to show the master view controller you see in Figure 3-10.) I know it's not much to look at, but it's a start — and it *is* a functioning iPad app.

Carrier 🗢			2:45 PM	100% ▬
Edit	**Master**	+	**Detail**	

l view content goes here

Figure 3-10:
Not much of
an app, but
it *is* yours.

If you rotate the Simulator by choosing Hardware⇨Rotate Left, in the Simulator
menu, you see a nice Split view (as shown in Figure 3-11). (I talk more about
the mechanics behind this — the use of a Split view controller — in the next
section, and in even more detail in Chapter 13.)

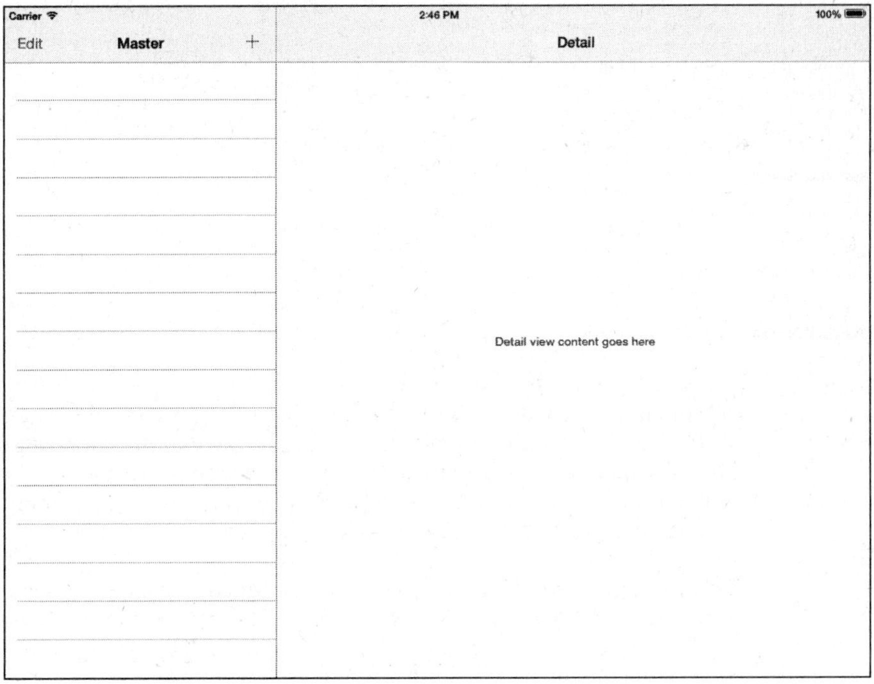

Figure 3-11:
Your app in landscape mode.

The iPad's Split views

Although it's true that on the iPhone, you often see only one view at a time, on the iPad you get to see two views, courtesy of the Master-Detail Application template (and something called a Split view controller, which I explain in detail in Chapter 13). If you take another look at Figure 3-11, you can see what I'm talking about. The view on the left displays what is called the Master view. Although technically it could be any type of view you'd like, in the case of the Master-Detail Application template, you get something called a Table view, which displays a list of what are referred to as cells, entries, or rows. On the left side of Figure 3-12, I tapped the + button and you see a timestamp (in Coordinated Universal Time [UTC], the primary time standard and the successor to Greenwich Mean Time [GMT]) in the first cell in the master view. When I tap that cell, as I have on the right side of Figure 3-12, the same timestamp is displayed in the detail view and the cell is highlighted in the master view.

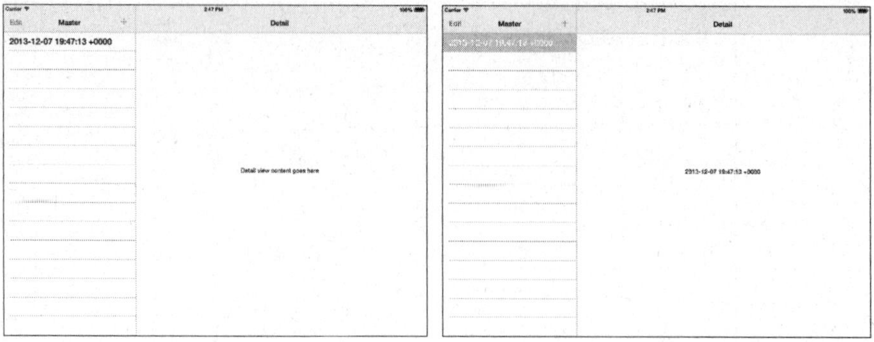

Figure 3-12:
Splits aren't
just for
bananas.

All the detail view does right now is display "Detail view content goes here." Well, that's not all it does. When you rotate the iPad into portrait mode, it's also responsible for both displaying a nice Master button as well as for displaying the Master view in the popover that you see when you tap the nice Master button. (Refer to Figure 3-10.)

In landscape view, the master view on the left side also includes a toolbar with Edit and + *bar button items* that allow the user to modify content in this particular example program.

Again, it probably doesn't seem like much, but (as you'll see when I explain the RoadTrip app in Chapter 4), this is pretty much all the "infrastructure" you'll need to put together a really cool app.

The Log navigator

If you want to look at how the build works, now is as good a time as any to explain how the Log navigator works.

Xcode generates a series of logs during the build process, which meticulously record the actions performed. You can view these logs by selecting the Log navigator, either by using the Navigator selector or by choosing View⇨Navigators⇨Show Log Navigator from Xcode's main menu. In Figure 3-13, you can see a log of all my recent builds.

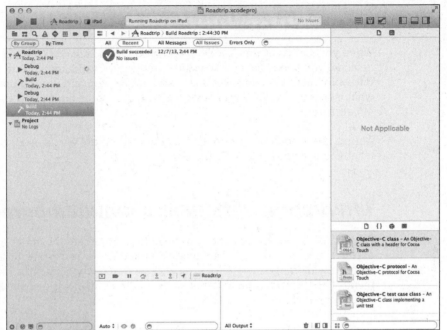

Figure 3-13:
Build
results.

The Log navigator lists these two types of actions:

- ✔ **Tasks:** The Task log lists all the operations Xcode performed to carry out the task, such as building operations, archiving operations, and source control operations.

- ✔ **Sessions:** A Session log is the transcript of the events that occurred during a session (a period during which an activity is performed). Running or debugging an application, for example, generates a session log that would include all debugger output.

The Log navigator contains the Task and Session list. When you select an item in this list, the corresponding log appears in the Log viewer. You can filter this list with the Filter bar.

It turns out you won't need to use the Log navigator for the sample app in this book, simply because I have you examine all debug activity in the Debug area instead and any task-related issues in the Issue navigator.

The ultimate success (or failure) of your build is also displayed in the Activity viewer.

Running in the Simulator

When you run your app, Xcode installs it on the Simulator (or on a real device if you specified a device as the active SDK) and launches it. Using the Hardware menu and your keyboard and mouse, the Simulator mimics most of what a user can do on a real device, albeit with some limitations that I point out shortly.

At first, the iPad Simulator looks like any iPad model would — kind of like what you can see back in Figure 3-11.

Interacting with your simulated hardware

Any simulator worth its salt has to be able to duplicate the actions you'd expect from a real device. The Xcode Simulator — no surprise here — can mimic a wide range of activities, all accessed from the Simulator Hardware menu. The Hardware menu items allow you to control various simulator behaviors, including

- ✔ **Choose a device.** Switch the simulated device to an iPad, any model iPhone, or the Retina display found on iPhone 4, iPhone 4S, and fourth-generation iPod touch models.

- ✔ **Choose a version.** Switch to a different version of iOS.

- ✔ **Rotate left.** Choosing Hardware⇨Rotate Left rotates the Simulator to the left. If the Simulator is in Portrait view, it changes to Landscape view; if the Simulator is already in Landscape view, it changes to Portrait view.

- ✔ **Rotate right.** Choosing Hardware⇨Rotate Right rotates the Simulator to the right. Again, if the Simulator is in Portrait view, it changes to Landscape view; if the Simulator is already in Landscape view, it changes to Portrait view.

- ✔ **Use a shake gesture.** Choosing Hardware⇨Shake Gesture simulates shaking the device.

- ✔ **Go to the Home screen.** Choosing Hardware⇨Home does the expected — you go to the Home screen.

- ✔ **Lock the Simulator (device).** Choosing Hardware⇨Lock locks the Simulator, which then displays the Lock screen.

✔ **Send the running app low-memory warnings.** Choosing Hardware➪Simulate Memory Warning fakes out your app by sending it a (fake) low-memory warning.

✔ **Simulate the hardware keyboard.** Choose Hardware➪Simulate Hardware Keyboard to check out how your app functions when the device is connected to an optional physical keyboard dock or paired with a Bluetooth keyboard.

✔ **Choose an external display.** To bring up another window that acts like an external display attached to the device, choose Hardware➪TV Out and then choose 640 x 480, 1024 x 768, 1280 x 720 (720p), or 1920 x 1080 (1080p) for the window's display resolution. Choose Hardware➪TV Out➪Disabled to close the external display window.

Making gestures

On the real device, a gesture is something you do with your fingers to make something happen in the device — a tap, a drag, a swipe, and so on. Table 3-1 shows you how to simulate gestures using your mouse and keyboard.

Table 3-1	Gestures in the Simulator
Gesture	*iPad Action*
Tap	Click the mouse.
Touch and hold	Hold down the mouse button.
Double tap	Double-click the mouse button.
Two-finger tap	1. Move the mouse pointer over the place where you want to start.
	2. Hold down the Option key, which makes two circles appear that stand in for your fingers.
	3. Click the mouse button.
Swipe	1. Click where you want to start and hold down the mouse button.
	2. Move the mouse slowly in the direction of the swipe and then release the mouse button.
Flick	1. Click where you want to start and hold the mouse button down.
	2. Move the mouse quickly in the direction of the flick and then release the mouse button.

(continued)

Table 3-1 *(continued)*

Gesture	iPad Action
Drag	1. Click where you want to start and hold down the mouse button.
	2. Move the mouse slowly in the drag direction.
Pinch	1. Move the mouse pointer over the place where you want to start.
	2. Hold down the Option key, which makes two circles appear that stand in for your fingers.
	3. Hold down the mouse button and move the circles in (to pinch) or out (to unpinch).

Uninstalling apps and resetting your device

You uninstall applications on the Simulator the same way you do on the iPad, except you use your mouse instead of your finger. Follow these steps:

1. **On the Home screen, place the pointer over the icon of the app you want to uninstall and hold down the mouse button until all the app icons start to wiggle.**

2. **Click the app icon's Remove button — the little *x* that appears in the upper-left corner of the icon — to make the app disappear.**

3. **Click the Home button (use Hardware⇨Home) to stop the other app icons from wiggling and finish the uninstall.**

On a separate note, you can always reposition an app's icon on the Home screen by clicking and dragging it around with the mouse.

You can remove an application from the background the same way you'd do on the iPad, except that you use your mouse instead of your finger. Follow these steps:

1. **Simulate double-tapping the Home buttons with the keyboard equivalent Shift-Command-H twice.**

2. **Scroll left and right with the mouse to locate the app you want to stop.**

3. **Drag the view of the app up and out of the horizontal scrolling list of apps.**

To reset the Simulator to the original factory settings — which also removes all the apps you've installed — choose iOS Simulator⇨Reset Content and Settings, and then click Reset in the warning dialog that appears.

You have some of the basic apps installed on the Simulator — these include Settings. You can use Settings just as you do on an iOS device. This is particularly useful if you want to set an Apple ID for the Simulator to use. One reason for doing this would be to use the Simulator to test iCloud code in an app you have written. The app on the Simulator will use the Apple ID you have specified in Settings rather than the Apple ID under which you may be running on your app. iCloud on the Simulator is a new feature in iOS 7. This book doesn't go into iCloud, but rest assured that when you're ready to go there, the Simulator will be ahead of you.

Living with the Simulator's limitations

Keep in mind that, despite the Simulator's many virtues, running apps in the Simulator is still not the same thing as running them on an iOS device. Here's why:

- **Different frameworks:** The Simulator uses OS X versions of the low-level system frameworks, instead of the actual frameworks that run on the device. That means that occasionally some code may run fine in the Simulator but not on actual iOS devices. Although the Simulator is useful for testing functionality, there's no substitute for debugging the app on the device itself if you want to find out how it will really run.

- **Different hardware and memory:** The Simulator uses the Mac hardware and memory. To accurately determine how your app will perform on an honest-to-goodness iOS device, you have to run it on a real iOS device.

- **Different installation procedure:** Xcode installs *your* app in the Simulator automatically when you build the app using the iOS SDK. It's a different kettle of fish to install your app on the device for testing. And, by the way, you don't have a way to get Xcode to install apps from the App Store in the Simulator.

- **Lack of GPS:** You can't fake the Simulator into thinking that it's lying on the beach at Waikiki.

  You can, however, choose to simulate a location in the Debug area.

- **Two-finger limit:** You can simulate a maximum of two fingers. If your application's user interface can respond to touch events involving more than two fingers, you need to test that on an actual device.

- **Accelerometer differences:** You can access your computer's accelerometer (if it has one) through the UIKit framework. Its reading, however, will differ from the accelerometer readings on an actual iPad (for some technical reasons that I don't have the space to go into).

- **Differences in rendering:** OpenGL ES (Open Graphics Library for Embedded Systems, in other words) is one of the many 3D graphics libraries that works with the iOS SDK. It turns out that the renderers it uses on devices are slightly different from the ones it uses in the iOS Simulator. As a result, a scene on the Simulator and the same scene on a device may not be identical at the pixel level.

✔ **Telephony:** You can't make a phone call on the iPhone simulator.

Using Asset Catalogs

Now that there are several screen sizes for iPhones and (currently) two resolutions, your images need to be managed in a more sophisticated way than in the past. Initially, images had specific names that indicated if they were icons, launch images, or other images. With Xcode 5, things are much simpler because instead of relying on naming conventions, you use *asset catalogs*.

Images inside an asset catalog are divided into *sets*. Each set contains one or more image *representations*. You create an asset catalog by creating a new file (File➪New➪File) and choosing Asset Catalog from the Resource section at the left of the window.

Figure 3-14 shows an asset catalog with three image sets in it — AppIcon, Launch Image, and MyImage. The navigation at the left of the workspace window and the Utility area at the right are hidden. Inside the Editor area are two columns. At the left of the Editor area, a list of the sets is shown.

1. **Select the image set you want to work with in the set list.**

   In Figure 3-14, the App Icon set is selected. To follow along, select it now.

2. **Notice that the set viewer (the right-hand column in the asset catalog) now reflects the images of the selected set (AppIcon in this case).**

   There may be several *representations* of a single image reflecting the appropriate *idioms* (iPhone or iPad).

3. **If you want, you can change the name of the set either in the Status area or by double-clicking and editing the name in the set list.**

   You can also specify which representations (iPad, iPhone, Mac) you want to use at the top of the Status area and the appropriate *scales* for each (1x for non-Retina and 2x for Retina displays).

4. **Select the representation you want to work with in the Editing area.**

   The Status area at the right of the workspace window reflects the details for the selected representation below the set information.

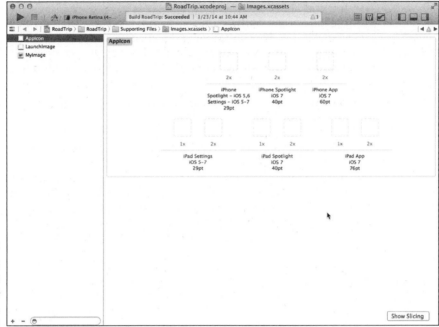

Figure 3-14:
Look inside
an asset
catalog.

An asset catalog can contain four types of images:

- ✔ **App icons:** You may think you have a single app icon, but you would be wrong. You actually have an app icon image set with a multitude of idioms and scales. Each representation has its size shown both in the Editor area and in the Status area so that you know what you should be working with. (Remember that app icons are square, so only one dimension is provided.) It is best not to rename this set.

- ✔ **Launch images:** These are images that are shown as early as possible in the app's launch. They should provide the background of the first screen the user sees. When the launch is completed, the actual screen and its data appear. The effect is that the background is drawn and relevant text and graphics are drawn on top of it. There's a launch image set in the Master-Detail template so you can explore it. Note that in the Status area, you can specify the details of the launch images, including not only the idiom but also the orientation. These are check boxes: You only have to provide the ones you choose. It is best not to rename this set.

✔ **Images:** These are all the other images in your app. Using the button at the lower right of the Editor area, you can show the overview that lets you edit the representations for a specific image set (by defaults, there are two idioms and two scales, but this may well change over time). You can also look at image slicing, but that is an advanced topic that I don't cover in this book. Each image will have its own image set.

✔ **OS X icons:** For completeness, these are mentioned, but in this book, I focus on iOS.

You can see the representations for launch images in Figure 3-15.

You drag your images from your disk into the appropriate representation of the appropriate set. For app icons and launch images, if the image you try to drag is the wrong size, you will get an error. Note that for both app icons and launch images, there are different images for the different devices. Also note that there are separate versions for Retina (2X) and non-Retina (1X) displays.

If you are using one of the Xcode templates, you will have an asset catalog (usually called `Images.xcassets`) with an icon and launch images. You can add your own image sets to it. Figure 3-16 shows an image set called `MyImage` added to `Images.xcassets`. It has Retina and non-Retina display representations for Universal, iPhone, iPad, and Mac. (There is also a Retina display for the iPhone 4.)

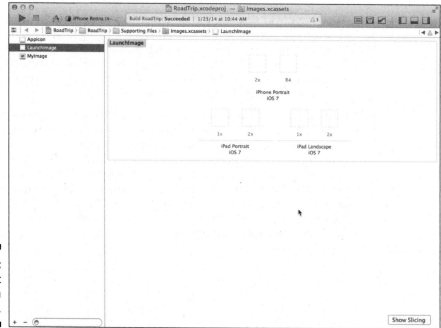

Figure 3-15:
Look at launch images.

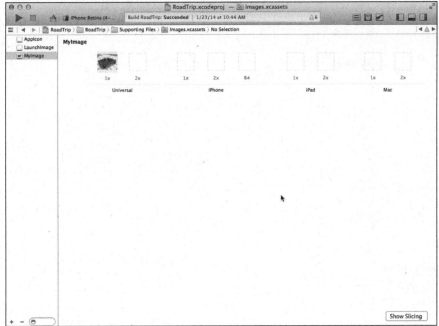

Figure 3-16:
Add your
own image
set.

You can choose the representations you want for your image set using the
Editor⇨Device Image Reps submenu, as shown in Figure 3-17.

Many developers don't modify the template's asset catalog which contains
the launch images and app icons. Instead, they create a separate asset catalog for their own image sets. Here's how to do that:

1. **Choose File⇨New⇨File.**
2. **In the dialog that appears, select Resource under iOS at the left.**
3. **Select Asset Catalog.**
4. **Name and save the file in your project.**

   If you want, you can place the file in the Supporting Files group in your
   project (or anywhere else you choose).

Pre-Xcode 5 code for manipulating images was not pretty. Today, after you
have set up your image catalog(s), you simply select the image set name that
you want (often from a pop-up menu in the Utility area of a storyboard). At
runtime, the appropriate image is chosen for you depending on the device
in use. You don't have to do anything but use the image set name: iOS will
choose the correct file.

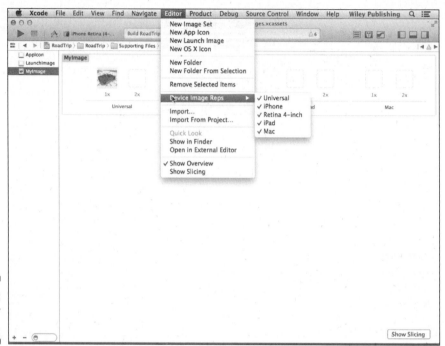

Figure 3-17:
Choose your
image reps.

Adding the Image and Sound Resources and an App Icon

As a starter, you can download image and sound resources as well as an app icon. Here are the steps:

1. Download the iOS 7 RoadTrip Resources folder from this book's companion website.

To find out how to access this book's companion website, please see the Introduction. Store the folder somewhere handy where you'll be sure to find it again.

This folder includes not only the application icon, but also a number of other resource files (images and sound) you'll be using in your application.

You'll start by adding the resources you'll need.

2. **Control-click RoadTrip project in the Project Navigator, choose Add Files to "RoadTrip" from the contextual menu, use the dialog that appears to navigate to the RoadTrip Resources folder you downloaded, and then select non-image resources to add, such as sound files (.aif files). Choose File⇨Add Files to RoadTrip and pick the sound files.**

   Xcode asks you (via a check box in the aforementioned dialog) whether you want to make a copy of the file. If you don't select the check box, Xcode creates a pointer (alias) to the file. The advantage of using an alias is that if you modify the file later, Xcode will use that modified version. The disadvantage is that Xcode won't be able to find the file if you move it.

3. **Select the Copy Items into Destination Group's Folder (If Needed) check box, make sure the check box in front of Road Trip in the Add to Targets section is selected, and then click Add to copy the files.**

   This adds the sound files you need.

   You can also drag sound files into the Project navigator.

4. **Create an image set for each named image and drag the appropriate representations (iPhone and iPad, for example) to that image set.**

   Note that these are a starter set of images. You will not have all the representations. For your own app, it's important to have all relevant representations.

Part II
Building RoadTrip

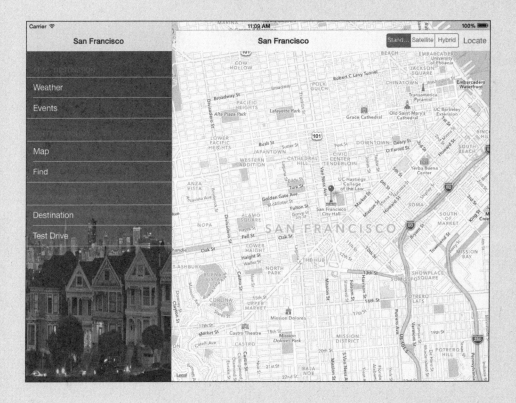

In this part . . .

- ✔ Getting to know storyboards
- ✔ Developing a user interface
- ✔ Managing memory and using properties
- ✔ Working with the source editor

Chapter 4

Storyboards and the User Experience

*A*s I mention in the Introduction, my goal for this book is for you to understand the *right way* to develop apps for the iPhone and iPad. Because you'll be using the knowledge I impart to you to develop my RoadTrip app, now is probably a good time to explain the app — what it actually does, how it is organized, and what the program architecture looks like.

One thing that makes iOS software development so appealing is the richness of the tools and frameworks provided in the iOS Software Development Kit (SDK). In this regard, the frameworks are especially important. Each one is a distinct body of code that actually implements your app's generic functionality — in other words, frameworks give the app its basic way of working. This is especially true of one framework in particular: the UIKit framework, which is the heart of the user interface.

In this chapter, you get an overview of the iOS user interface architecture, meaning you'll find out what the various pieces are, what each does, and how they interact with each other. The idea here is for this chapter to lay the groundwork for developing the RoadTrip app's user interface, while succeeding chapters take you to the next level(s).

I also go through what classes and frameworks are available in the SDK — well, at least the main ones you'll need to know about in order to build the RoadTrip app, as well as a number of other classes and frameworks any self-respecting app developer would need to know in order for her to build her own apps. For added measure, I also talk about something Apple calls *design patterns,* or programming paradigms that the frameworks are based on.

But the place I want to start is a feature that is typical of Apple in its development process: a way to visually lay out your app's interface and the sequencing of screens. The technology is called *storyboarding* or *storyboards,* depending on whether you want to focus on the process or the tool.

Apple didn't invent storyboards. According to Wikipedia, storyboards were used by Constantin Stanislavski in preparing his production of Anton Chekhov's *The Seagull* in 1898 and were popularized by Walt Disney in the 1930s. Storyboards moved from live theater to animated films and on to *Gone with the Wind* in 1939. The engineers and designers at Apple recognize an efficient tool when they find it. True to form, they adopted storyboards and improved on the basic concept.

Introducing the Storyboard

I really like Xcode's Storyboard feature. When I saw a storyboard for the first time, it was like a dream come true. (Well, okay, not quite.) To me, the Storyboard feature represented exactly what I needed — not only for building my own apps, but also for teaching other people how to build their own apps.

Using a storyboard is analogous to sketching the user interface and app flow on a white board, and then having that sketch turn into something your app can use. This last part is what's really important to you. Your sketch is not a free-form drawing. Rather, you assemble graphical elements such as buttons and views using the library of such objects in the Utility area. At build time, these graphical elements turn into their corresponding functional elements on the screen. As you proceed through this chapter, you'll see how you make the connection between the graphical element and the code-based element. That's where the magic of storyboards happens.

Working with a storyboard can save you lots of time and effort by reducing the code you have to write. Moreover, it can really help when it comes to fully understanding the app flow. If you haven't developed before, you'll find that using a storyboard makes it easier to get a more complex app up and running.

The idea behind a storyboard is that you'd use it to lay out the entire flow of your app. Figure 4-1 shows you what the iPad storyboard for a finished app would look like. You'll find that when you lay out an app in a storyboard, you can actually run your program before you even add any content, so you can get a sense of how the user experience will unfold.

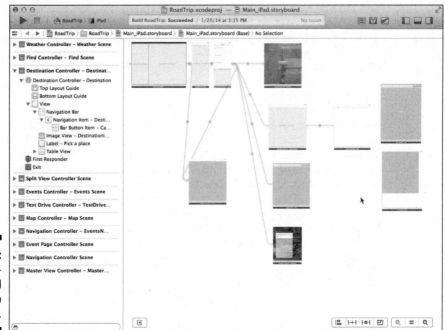

Figure 4-1:
The com-
pleted
RoadTrip
storyboard.

To get to the storyboard so you can actually edit it, you use the Project navigator and select the storyboard file you're interested in. Doing so brings up the
Interface Builder editor. You'll use the Utility area as well to add user interface
elements, use the inspectors to set attributes, and so on.

Telling your story

As you develop your app, you use Interface Builder to graphically add user
interface elements to each one of your *views* in the storyboard. (I tell you more
about views in the "Working with Windows and Views" section, later in this
chapter; for now just think of views as containers for displaying what you see
on the device screen.) In this context, user interface elements include things
like controls, images, and placeholders for content you'll display. After you've
added the elements you need, all you have to do is fill in code where it's needed.
If you've used Xcode to program in the past, you'll find that you have to write
a lot less *plumbing code* — code that is specifically designed to do things like
launch view controllers — and, in some cases, no plumbing code at all.

Typically, I try to lay out the entire flow of my app early on in the development
process, but for the example app developed for this book, I decided not to
do that because I wanted to first show you all the basics of developing an
app with Xcode. That means you'll see some of the storyboard stuff now, but

will have to wait until Chapter 14 to storyboard the rest of the RoadTrip app. This actually is not far from the way most apps are developed. If you have an experienced team and a large budget, you can work out everything in advance and then code from beginning to end. In many cases, though, the app evolves as you work on it. Xcode and particularly storyboards make it easy to handle these evolutions as you change the sequence of screens and the ways in which the transitions occur.

Ready for a storyboard tour? To follow along with me, go back to Xcode and select the `Main_iPad.storyboard` file for your sample project in the Project navigator. This is the iPad storyboard, one of the storyboards that Xcode created for you when you used the Master-Detail Application template and selected the Universal Device Family. (See Chapter 3 for more on the specifics of the Master-Detail Application template.) The name *Main* in the `Main_iPad.storyboard` file implies that, of course, there can be *other* storyboards. (In this case, you'll notice there are two `MainStoryboards` — one for iPad and one for iPhone.)

Selecting the `Main_iPad.storyboard` file in the Project navigator opens that file in the Interface Builder editor, as shown in Figure 4-2. Although all this may look a bit daunting at first, I promise you that by the time you're finished with this book, it will seem like old hat. (For a detailed explanation of what's going on in Figure 4-2, see Chapter 13.)

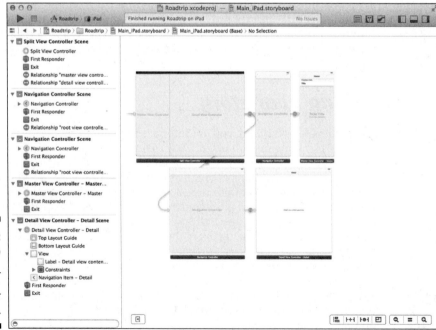

Figure 4-2: RoadTrip `Main_iPad.storyboard`.

In the olden days (pre-storyboards), you used *nib* files to define your user interface one view controller at a time. The term *nib* (with its corresponding file extension .xib) is an acronym for NeXT Interface Builder, a bit of software originally developed at NeXT Computer, whose OPENSTEP operating system was used as the basis for creating OS X and iOS. A nib file is a special type of resource file that you use to store the user interface you create with the Interface Builder editor. Storyboards are actually just a series of connected nib files.

View controllers manage what you see on the iPad or iPhone screen — the views themselves. Views are visible objects (images, buttons, and the like), while view controllers are just what the name suggests: controllers of the visible objects. If this terminology reminds you of the Model-View-Controller design pattern previously mentioned, you're right. The model is the data, and we'll get to that in Part IV. For more specifically on view controllers, check out the section "View Controllers — the Main Storyboard Players," later in this chapter.

Working with object graphs

Continuing with the storyboard tour, note that as you create your storyboard, you create an *object graph* that is then archived when you save the file. When you load the file, the object graph is unarchived.

So, what's an *object graph?* Here's the short answer: Object-oriented programs are made up of complex webs of interrelated objects. They are linked to one another in a variety of ways. One object can contain another object, for example, or it can own it, or it can reference it. All the items that you see in your storyboard (and some items that you don't see) are all objects and are part of that web of objects. The Interface Builder editor allows you to create this network graphically and then, at runtime, it makes the connections for you.

A storyboard file can capture your entire user interface in one place and lets you define both the individual view controllers and the transitions between those view controllers. As a result, storyboards capture the flow of your overall user interface in addition to the content you present.

In the app you build in this book, you use just one storyboard file to store all the view controllers and views for each device. Behind the curtain, however, Interface Builder takes the contents of this one storyboard file and divides it into discrete pieces that can be loaded individually for better performance.

That's the 100-yard-dash tour of the storyboard and its purpose. For you to truly get a feel for the essence of the storyboard, however, you need to see how the storyboard replicates the way an iOS app is structured — in other words, you need an in-depth look at the iOS app architecture. The best way to do that is within the context of a real app. So, before I get into even more detail about working in the storyboard, I want to give you a sense of the basic functions and purpose of the app developed throughout this book — the app I've affectionately named RoadTrip.

Defining What You Want an App to Do: The RoadTrip App

A year ago, my friend Skippy got a new job which necessitated him moving from California to New York. He decided to drive his car across the country and see what some people refer to as "flyover country"— the land between the two coasts. He started surfing the web and soon had a whole collection of web pages bookmarked on his iPad. Sorting through them was starting to take more time than the trip was going to take. He asked me if I couldn't do something on the iPad that would organize the information and even collect it for him so that he didn't have to spend time using a search engine over and over. That's how RoadTrip started.

To make RoadTrip a useful app, I had to move from Skippy's problem — all those searches and web bookmarks — to the app's solution, which is to present information that's relevant to the following questions:

- Where are you?
- Where do you plan to be?
- What do want to do, or where do you want to go when you get there?

By concentrating on what is truly relevant, you reduce the app to the amount of information you need to deal with at any one time.

Guided by the app's purpose — as well as by what the iPad or iPhone does best — I developed a clearer picture of what Skippy would want the app to do. That clearer picture comes into focus in Figure 4-3, where — there on the left side — you can see the app functionality in what Xcode calls the Master view. The pane on the right — displaying the appropriately named Detail view — gives Skippy the chance to watch his car go back and forth onscreen (with sound effects, no less). That animation is included in the app and this book as a demonstration of what's possible to do on the iOS devices. It's also there to get you started with animation techniques that are frequently used in games. (For more on Master and Detail views, check out Chapter 13.)

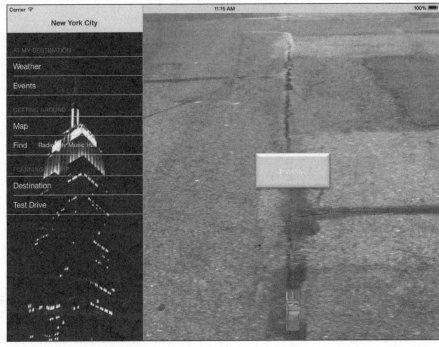

Figure 4-3:
A real-live
example of
the Master
view/
Detail view
combination.

The iPad's split-view interface allows the user to sometimes see a Master view and a Detail view at the same time. The iPhone's smaller screen requires that you design your user interface to only show one or the other at a given time. I use the iPad storyboard file as the example in this chapter, but the storyboard for the iPhone is basically similar — it just differs in some of the details. You'll see how to manage both iPad and iPhone user interfaces in later chapters.

This division into Master view and Detail view is an elegant way of allowing the user to pick a task from the navigation list on the left and see the content associated with that task on the right. The tasks I came up with for my RoadTrip app are as follows:

 ✔ **Get real-time weather access.** Snow in New York in August? Not likely, but these days you never can tell. You can see real-time weather access at work in Figure 4-4.

 ✔ **Find out what's going on wherever you are.** Figure 4-5 shows an event that Skippy might be interested in.

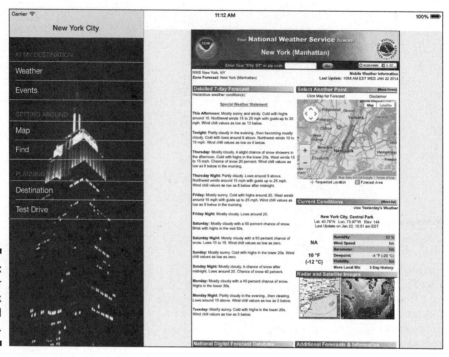

Figure 4-4:
The weather
in New York
on the iPad
screen.

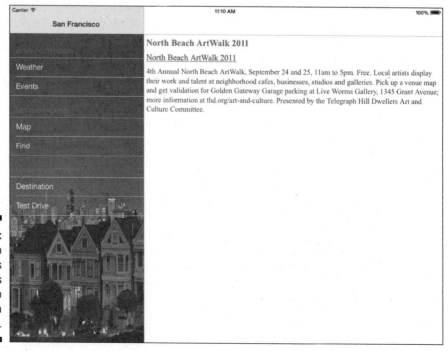

Figure 4-5:
RoadTrip
describes
some things
for you to do
while in a
city.

✔ **Bring up a map based on the destination.** The map shows Skippy's destination and points of interest, and even allows him to zero in on his current location. (See Figure 4-6.)

✔ **Find some place on a map.** If Skippy has an address that he wants to find on the map, he should be able to do that *and* get its GPS coordinates as well. Figure 4-7 gives an example of finding a point of interest on a map.

There are of course a lot of other features you'd want to add to this app to make it worth the $.99 you'll be charging, and I talk about some of those in Chapter 21. When you start thinking of pricing and features, browse the App Store to see what other apps are doing. You may wind up creating several versions of your app such as a low-priced (or free) "Lite" version along with the full-featured version. In addition, the *freemium* model has become popular in certain categories of apps (most particularly games). The app itself is typically free in these cases. It may generate a revenue stream from ads inside the app, but it also generates revenue from in-app purchases of advanced game levels, new content, and the like. In the case of RoadTrip, new destinations might be in-app purchases, but the overall structure of the app should be independent of which destinations are included, and that is how it is built in this book.

Given the user interface described in this section, the big questions are a) how do you create an app from your knowledge of the problem, and b) how do you want the app to help solve it?

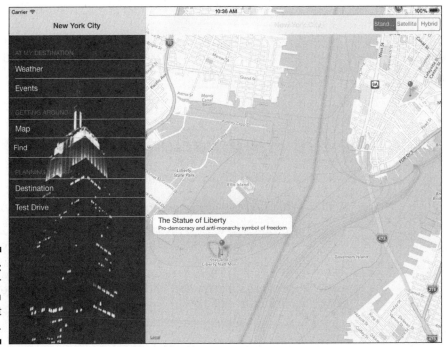

Figure 4-6:
Finding your
way with
pinpoint
accuracy.

Carrier 📶   10:22 AM   📶 🔋

〈 Back **Radio City Music Hall**   Locate

Figure 4-7:
Where is
Radio City
Music Hall,
anyway?

The answers to those questions can be found in the application architecture.

In the Apple Human Interface Guidelines, Apple suggests the current selection in the Master view (left pane) should be indicated. In Chapter 13, I give you the option of having the current Master View selection remain highlighted, but until then, I won't bother with that.

Creating the Application Architecture

At a basic level, the RoadTrip app is made up of the following:

- **Models:** Model objects encapsulate the logic and content (data) of the app.

- **Views:** Data content is useless if your user never sees it. *Views* are the windows to your content — the pathway to the user experience — and it's up to you to decide what information to display and how to display it. Part of the decision will involve what *kind* of view best serves your content. (Xcode offers you a number of different ways to display both information and navigation choices.)

> ✔ **View controllers:** View controllers manage the user experience. They connect the views that present the user experience with the models that provide the necessary content. View controllers also manage the way the user navigates the app.

The MVC (Model-View-Controller) model is pretty much the basis for all iOS app development projects. I explain MVC in more detail in the "The Model-View-Controller (MVC) design pattern" section, later in this chapter. The trick here is to come up with just the right views, view controllers, and model objects to get your project off the ground.

What You Add Where

Table 4-1 summarizes the chapters in which you will add new Objective-C classes and new view controller scenes to your project. The Chapter 3 classes and storyboard scenes are built with Apple's Master-Detail template, but the rest are up to you as you work through this book.

Table 4-1	Classes and Scenes by Chapter	
Chapter	*Create Objective-C Class*	*Add Storyboard Scene*
3	AppDelegate	Master View controller
	MasterViewController	Detail View controller
	DetailViewController	
5		Test Drive controller
9	TestDriveController	
11	Trip	
	Destination	
14		Weather controller
		Map controller
		Find controller
		Destination Controller
15	WeatherController	
16	EventsController	
	EventPageController	
	Events	
19	FindController	
20	DestinationController	

But before you decide what you need to build your app, you'll need to understand what's available. *Frameworks* supply the classes you have to work with in your app — classes like `UIView`, `UIViewController`, `UIControl`, and a whole lot more.

Using Frameworks

A *framework* offers common code that provides generic functionality. The iOS SDK provides a set of frameworks for incorporating technologies, services, and features into your apps. For example, the `UIKit` framework gives you event-handling support, drawing support, windows, views, and controls that you can use in your app.

A framework is designed to easily integrate the code that runs, say, an app or game or that delivers the information your user wants. A framework is similar to a software library, but with an added twist: It can also implement a program's *flow of control* (in contrast to a software library, whose components are arranged by the programmer into a flow of control). So, when working within a framework, the programmer may not have to decide the order in which things should happen — such as which messages are sent to which objects and in what order when an app launches, or when a user touches a button on the screen. Instead, the order of those events, or flow of control, may be a part of the framework.

When you use a framework, it provides your app with a ready-made set of basic functions; essentially you've told it "Here's how to act," and it's in a position to take the ball and run with it. With the framework in place, all you need to do is add the specific functionality that you want in the app — the content as well as the controls and views that enable the user to access and use that content.

The frameworks and iOS provide pretty complex functionality, such as

- Launching the app and displaying a window on the screen
- Displaying controls on the screen and responding to a user action — changing a toggle switch, for example, or scrolling a view, such as the list of your contacts
- Accessing sites on the Internet, not just through a browser but also from within your own program
- Managing user preferences
- Playing sounds and movies

Some developers talk in terms of "using a framework" — but in reality, your code doesn't use the framework so much as the framework uses your code. Your code provides the functions that the framework accesses; the framework needs your code to become an app that does something other than start up, display a blank window, and then end. This perspective makes figuring out how to work with a framework much easier.

If this seems too good to be true, well, okay, it is — all that complexity (and convenience) comes at a cost. It can be really difficult to get your head around the whole thing and know exactly where (and how) to add your app's functionality to the functionality that the framework supplies. That's where design patterns, which I discuss next, come in. Understanding the design patterns behind the frameworks gives you a way of thinking about a framework — especially UIKit because it's based on the MVC design pattern — that doesn't make your head explode.

Using Design Patterns

When it comes to iOS app development, the UIKit framework does a lot of the heavy lifting for you. That's all well and good, but working with that framework is a little more complicated than just letting it do its work on its own. The framework is designed around certain programming paradigms, also known as *design patterns.* The design pattern is a model that your own code must be consistent with.

To understand how to take best advantage of the power of frameworks — or (better put), figuring out how the framework objects want to best use your code — you need to understand design patterns. If you don't understand them or if you try to work around them because you're sure that you have a "better" way of doing things, your job will actually end up being much more difficult. (Developing apps can be hard enough, so making your job more difficult is definitely something you want to avoid.) Getting a handle on the basic design patterns that the framework uses (and expects) will help you develop an app that makes the best use of the framework. This means doing the least amount of work in the shortest amount of time.

The design patterns can help you to understand not only how to structure your code but also how the framework itself is structured. They describe relationships and interactions between classes or objects, as well as how responsibilities should be distributed among classes, so that the iOS device does what you want it to do. In programming terms, a design pattern is a commonly used template that gives you a consistent way to get a particular task done.

The iOS design patterns

To develop an iOS app, you need to be comfortable with the following basic design patterns:

- ✔ Model-View-Controller (MVC)
- ✔ Delegation
- ✔ Block Objects
- ✔ Target-Action
- ✔ Managed Memory Model

Of these, the Model-View-Controller design pattern is the key to understanding how an iPad or iPhone app works and is the focus of the following section. I explain the remainder of the patterns as they're put to use in this book.

Another basic design pattern exists as well: Threads and Concurrency. This pattern enables you to execute tasks concurrently (including the use of Grand Central Dispatch, that aiding-and-abetting feature introduced in OS X Snow Leopard for taking full advantage of all that processing power available, even on the smaller iPad and much smaller iPhone). Particularly with the advent of 64-bit multi-core processors in some of the iOS devices, the ability to use that power with tools such as Grand Central Dispatch is increasingly important. Unfortunately, the Threads and Concurrency design pattern — as well as Grand Central Dispatch — is beyond the scope of this book.

The Model-View-Controller (MVC) design pattern

The iOS frameworks are *object oriented.* An easy way to understand what that really means is to think about a team working in an office. The work that needs to get done is divided up and assigned to individual team members (in this case, objects). Each team member has a job and works with other team members to get things done. What's more, a good team member doesn't care how other members do their work, just that they do it according to the agreed upon division of labor. Likewise, an object in object-oriented programming takes care of its own business and doesn't care what the object in the virtual cubicle next door is doing, as long as it will do what it's supposed to do when asked to do it.

Object-oriented programming was originally developed to make code more maintainable, reusable, extensible, and understandable by encapsulating all the functionality behind well-defined interfaces. The actual details of how something works (as well as its data it uses to do that work) are hidden, which makes modifying and extending an app much easier.

Great — so far — but a pesky question still plagues programmers:

Exactly how do you decide on the objects and what each one does?

Sometimes the answer to that question is pretty easy — just use the real world as a model. (Eureka!) In the RoadTrip app, for example, some of the classes of model objects are `Trip`, `Events`, `Destination`, and so on. But when it comes to a generic program structure, how *do* you decide what the objects should be? That may not be so obvious.

The MVC pattern is a well-established way to group app functions into objects. Variations of it have been around at least since the early days of Smalltalk, one of the very first object-oriented languages. MVC is a high-level pattern — it addresses the architecture of an app and classifies objects according to the general roles they play in an app, rather than drilling down into specifics.

The MVC pattern creates, in effect, a miniature universe for the app, populated with three distinct kinds of objects. It also specifies roles and responsibilities for all three types of objects and specifies the way they're supposed to interact with each other. To make things more concrete (that is, to keep your head from exploding), imagine a big, beautiful, 60-inch, flat-screen TV. Here's the gist:

- ✔ **Model objects:** These objects together comprise the content "engine" of your app. They contain the app's data and logic — making your app more than just a pretty face. In the RoadTrip app, for example, the model maintains a list of events and sights, as well as the name and location of the destination and a background image to use.

  You can think of the *model* (which may be one object or several that interact) as a particular television program, one that, quite frankly, doesn't give a hoot about what TV set it's shown on.

  In fact, the model shouldn't give a hoot. Even though it owns its data, it should have no connection to the user interface and should be blissfully ignorant about what's done with its data.

- ✔ **View objects:** These objects display things on the screen and respond to user actions. Pretty much anything you can see is a kind of view object — the window and all the controls, for example. Your views know how to display information they receive from the model object and how to get any input from the user the model may need. But the view itself should know nothing about the model. It may handle a request to display some events, but it doesn't bother itself with what that request means.

You can think of the *view* as a television screen that doesn't care about what program it's showing or what channel you just selected.

The UIKit framework provides many different kinds of views, as you find out in the next section.

If the view knows nothing about the model, and the model knows nothing about the view, how do you get data and other notifications to pass from one to the other? To get that conversation started (Model: "I've just updated my data." View: "Hey, give me something to display," for example), you need the third element in the MVC triumvirate, the controller.

✔ **Controller objects:** These objects connect the app's view objects to its model objects. They supply the view objects with what they need to display (getting it from the model) and also provide the model with user input from the view.

You can think of the *controller* as the circuitry that pulls the show off of the cable and then sends it to the screen or requests a particular pay-per-view show.

With Xcode, both the model and view objects are often built with graphical user interfaces such as Interface Builder for views and view controllers and the Data Model Editor for Core Data objects. Controllers are almost always built with code. Building a controller object is the part of MVC that, for many developers, "feels" like traditional coding.

The basic application architecture looks like Figure 4-8.

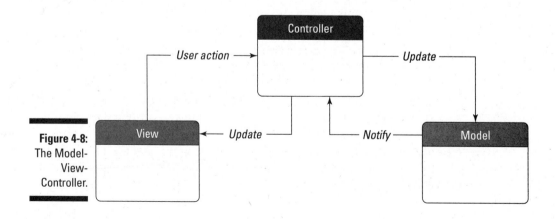

Figure 4-8:
The Model-
View-
Controller.

When you think about your app in terms of model, view, and controller objects, the UIKit framework starts to make sense. Understanding the framework this way also begins to lift the fog hanging over where to make at least part of your app-specific behavior go. Before you delve into that topic, however, you need to know a little more about the classes that the UIKit provides, because these are the guys you will task with implementing the MVC design pattern — window classes, view classes, and view controller classes.

Throughout this book, I'll be talking about both classes and objects, and now is as good a time as any to remind you of the difference between the two.

In Objective-C, classes include instance variables, properties, and methods (that can access the instance variables of a class). Classes are about files in your project that contain code. Classes are *types* in your program.

Objects, on the other hand, exist at runtime and are *instances* of a class. You can think of a class as a blueprint to build an object of that type.

Working with Windows and Views

iOS apps have a single window, so you won't find additional document windows for displaying content as you do an a Mac. When your app is running — even though other apps may be hibernating or running in the background — your app's interface takes over the entire screen.

Looking out the window

The single window that you see displayed on an iPad or iPhone is an instance of the UIWindow class. This window is created at launch time, either programmatically by you or automatically by UIKit when you use a storyboard. In general, after you create the Window object (that is, if you create it instead of having it done for you by the framework, which is the most common case), you never really have to think about it again.

A user can't directly close or manipulate an iOS window. It's your app that programmatically manages the window.

Although your app never creates more than one window at a time, iOS can support additional windows on top of your window. The system status bar is one example. You can also display alerts on top of your window by using the supplied Alert views.

Admiring the view

In an iOS app world, view objects are responsible for the view functionality in the Model-View-Controller architecture. A *view* is a rectangular area on the screen (it appears to be on top or within a window).

In the `UIKit` framework, windows are really a special kind of view, but for the purpose of this discussion, I'm referring to views that sit on top of the window.

What views do

Views are the main way for your app to interact with a user. This interaction happens in two ways:

- **Views display content.** This happens, for example, by making drawing and animation happen onscreen. The view object displays the data from the model object.

- **Views handle touch events.** Views respond when the user touches a button, for example. Handling touch events is part of a responder chain (which I explain in Chapter 6).

The view hierarchy

Views and subviews create a view hierarchy. You have two ways of looking at it (no pun intended this time): visually (how the user perceives it) and programmatically (how you create it). You must be clear about the differences or you'll find yourself in a state of confusion that resembles the subway at rush hour.

Looking at it visually, the window is at the base of this hierarchy with a *Content view* on top of it (a transparent view that fills the window's Content rectangle). The Content view displays information as well as allowing the user to interact with the app, using (preferably standard) user interface items such as text fields, buttons, toolbars, and tables.

In your program, that relationship is different. The Content view is added to the window view as a *subview.* But the Content view can also have its own subviews, and so on. Possible relationships include

- Views added to the Content view become *subviews* of it.

- Views added to the Content view become the *superviews* of any views added to them.

- A view can have one (and only one) superview and zero or more subviews.

It seems counterintuitive, but a subview is displayed *on top of* its parent view (that is, on top of its superview). Think about this relationship as containment: A superview *contains* its subviews. Figure 4-9 shows an example of a view hierarchy.

The visual hierarchy ... translates to a structural one.

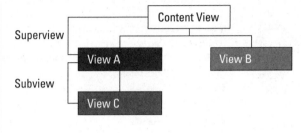

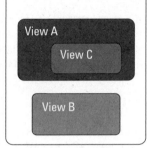

Figure 4-9:
The view
hierarchy
is both
visual and
structural.

Controls — such as buttons, text fields, and so on — are actually view sub-classes that become subviews. So are any other display areas that you may specify. The view must manage its subviews, as well as resize itself with respect to its superviews. Fortunately, much of what the view must do is already coded for you. The `UIKit` framework supplies the code that defines view behavior.

The view hierarchy also plays a key role in both drawing and event handling. I explain event handling in Chapter 6.

You create or modify a view hierarchy whenever you add a view to another view, either programmatically or with the help of the Interface Builder. The `UIKit` framework automatically handles the relationships associated with the view hierarchy.

Developers typically gloss over this visual-versus-programmatic-view-hierarchy stuff when starting out — and without understanding these concepts, it's really difficult to get a handle on what's going on.

The kinds of views you use

The `UIView` class defines the basic properties of a view, and you may be able to use it "as is" — as you'll do in the Test Drive screen of the RoadTrip app — by simply adding an image view and some controls.

In the Detail view shown back in Figure 4-3, the user can take a test drive by tapping the Test Drive button. (Later in the book, in Chapter 10, I show you how to animate the car so that it leisurely drives to the other side of the screen, turns around, drives back, and then turns around one more time so that it's back to where it started on the screen.)

The UIKit framework also provides you with a number of other views that are subclassed from UIView. These views implement the kinds of things that you as a developer need to do in the user interface.

It's important to think about the view objects that are part of the UIKit framework. When you use an object such as a UISlider or UIButton, your slider or button behaves just like a slider or button in any other iOS app. This enables the consistency in appearance and behavior across apps that users expect.

Container views

Container views are a technical (Apple) term for content views that do more than just lie there on the screen and display your controls and other content. The UIScrollView class, for example, adds scrolling without you having to do any work. Most of the time, Container views just do their thing in the background (as part of other views you use — Table views, for example), and I don't explain any more about them in this book because you won't need to use or manage them explicitly.

UITableView inherits this scrolling capability from UIScrollView and adds the ability to display lists and respond to the selections of an item in that list. Think of the Contacts app on your iPad (and a host of others, come to think of it). UITableView is one of the primary navigation views on the iPad.

Table views are used a lot in iOS apps to do these two things:

- ✔ **Display hierarchal data:** For an example, think of the Music app, which gives you a list of albums and, if you select one, a list of its songs.

- ✔ **Act as a table of contents:** Now, think of the Settings app, which gives you a list of apps that you can set preferences for. When you select one of those apps from the list, it takes you to a view that lists what preferences you're able to set as well as a way to set them.

In the RoadTrip app, the *List* views — such as the ones in the Master view shown earlier in Figure 4-3 — are Table views. The List view shown in the figure acts as an introduction to the app; it provides the user with a way to decide where he wants to go, for example, by selecting Destination in the Table view.

Another Container view, the UIToolbar class, contains button-like controls, which you find everywhere on an iOS device. In the Mail app, for example, you tap an icon on the bottom toolbar to respond to an e-mail. In RoadTrip, you find such controls at the top of the Map view (refer to Figure 4-6) to allow you to decide on how you want the map to be displayed.

Controls

Controls are the fingertip-friendly graphics that are used extensively in a typical app's user interface. Controls are actually subclasses of the `UIControl` superclass, a subclass of the `UIView` class. They include touchable items such as buttons, sliders, and switches, as well as text fields in which you enter data. You use them in your views, including, as you just saw, in a toolbar.

Controls make heavy use of the Target-Action design pattern, which is used when you touch the Test Drive button, as shown in Figure 4-10.

I explain the Target-Action pattern in detail in Chapter 9.

Display views

Think of *Display views* as controls that look good but don't really do anything except, well, look good. These include the following: `UIImageView` (check out the background to the Master view shown earlier in Figure 4-3 for an example); `UILabel` (for adding labels to buttons and other controls); `UIProgressView`; and `UIActivityIndicatorView`. I like to add an activity indicator to those views where I download data so folks have something to watch while waiting.

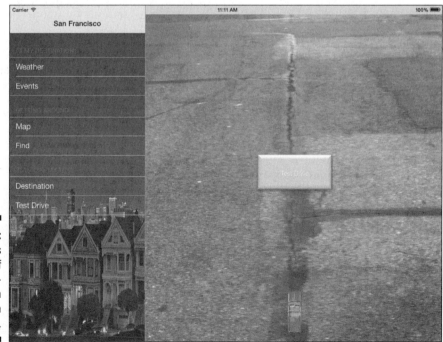

Figure 4-10: A button is the tip of the Target-Action design pattern.

Text and Web views

Text and *Web views* provide a way to display formatted text in your app. The `UITextView` class supports the display and editing of multiple lines of text in a scrollable area. The `UIWebView` class provides a way to display HTML content. These views can be used as the Main view, or as a subview of a another view. (You encounter `UIWebView` in the RoadTrip app as Weather views.) `UIWebView` is also the primary way to include graphics and format-ted text in Text Display views.

The views that display content — such as the Detail views shown previously in Figures 4-4 and 4-5 — are *Web* views, for some very good, practical reasons:

✓ **Some views must be updated regularly.** *Web views,* in that context, are the perfect solution; they make it easy to access data from a central repository on the Internet. (Client/server is alive and well!)

✓ **Web views can easily display formatted data that's locally stored.** Real-time access isn't always necessary — sometimes it's perfectly fine to store some data on the iPad or iPhone. Web views have no problem with locally stored data, which is very handy.

✓ **Web views can access websites!** Don't overlook the obvious: Web views open the door to websites, which means you have the whole Internet at your beck and call. If users want more detailed weather information, for example, they can get to the ten-day forecast by simply touching a link.

Alert views and Action sheets

Alert views and *Action sheets* present a message to the user, along with but-tons that allow the user to respond to the message. In the case of an alert, the response may be yes or no or a simple OK to indicate that the user has read the alert. An action sheet can present multiple buttons. I have you add an Alert view to the RoadTrip app in Chapter 8 to inform the user when the Internet isn't available. Figure 4-11 shows what the user would see if no Internet connection is available.

Navigation views

Tab bars and Navigation bars work in conjunction with view controllers to provide tools for navigating in your app. (For more on navigation bars, see Chapter 5.) Normally, you don't need to create a `UITabBar` or `UINavigationBar` directly — it's easier to let Interface Builder do the job for you or configure these views through a Tab bar or Navigation controller, respectively.

The window

You'll remember this one: The *window* provides the surface for drawing content and is the root container for all other views.

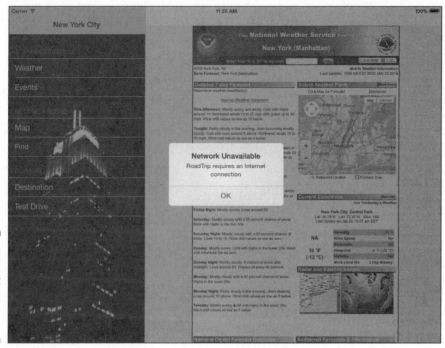

Figure 4-11:
Users need
the Internet
alert, so
be sure to
include it.

View Controllers — the Main Storyboard Players

Early in this chapter, I provide an overview of the *storyboard* — the whiteboard, so to speak, on which you lay out the flow of the elements, or *design pattern,* of your app. In this book, the example app developed throughout — Road Trip — uses the Model-View-Controller (MVC) design pattern, and in this particular design pattern, it's the *view controllers* that implement the pattern's controller component. These controller objects contain the code that connects the app's view objects to its model objects. Whenever the view needs to display something, the view controller goes out and gets what the view needs from the model. Similarly, view controllers respond to controls in your Content view and may do things like tell the model to update its data (when the user adds or changes text in a text field, for example), compute something (the current value of, say, your U.S. dollars in British pounds), or change the view being displayed (like when the user presses the Detail Disclosure button on the Music app to find out more about a song).

View controllers, as you can see in Figure 4-12, are the objects that control what is displayed and that respond to user actions. They are the heart and soul of the storyboard.

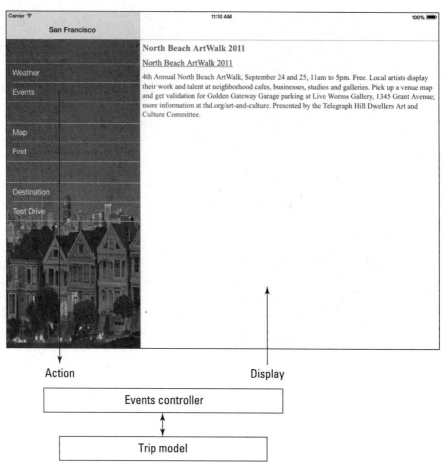

Figure 4-12:
It's all about
the view
controller.

As I explain in more detail in Chapter 9, a view controller is often the (target) object that responds to the onscreen controls. The Target-Action mechanism is what enables the view controller to be aware of any changes in the view, which can then be transmitted to the model.

Imagine that an iPad user launches the RoadTrip app. On the left side (or in a popover), she sees a Table view and on the right side a Detail view (the Weather, for example). (Refer to Figure 4-4.) The user may tap an entry (cell) in the Table view to display events. The Events controller is then launched and sends a message to the appropriate method in the model to get the events. The model object returns a list of URLs, and so on. The controller then delivers that information to the view, which promptly displays the information to the user.

If your imaginary user now launches the RoadTrip app on the iPhone (or iPod touch), the user will see a full-screen table view. The screen will shift to a detail view when the user taps a cell in the table. The same information is available in the iPhone version as in the iPad version, but the user interface has to be slightly different.

You will be pleased to know that you can build one set of Objective-C classes that works with both the iPhone and iPad storyboard files, so you only need one set of code to build your Universal app.

The sequence of events is as follows:

1. A message is sent to that view's view controller to handle the request.
2. The view controller's method interacts with the `Trip` model object.
3. The model object processes the request from the user for the current events.
4. The model object sends the data back to the view controller.
5. The view controller sends the data to the view to display the information.

View controllers have other vital iOS responsibilities as well, such as the following:

- ✔ **Managing a set of views:** This includes creating the views as well as flushing them from memory during low-memory situations.

- ✔ **Responding to a change in the device's orientation:** If, say, the user causes the iPad to switch from landscape to portrait orientation, the view controller responds by adjusting its views to match the new orientation.

- ✔ **Creating a Modal (not model) view:** A Modal view is a child window that displays a dialog that requires the user to do something (tap the Yes or Cancel button, for example) before returning to the app.

  You use a Modal view to ensure that the user has paid attention to the implications of an action (for example, "Are you *sure* you want to delete all your contacts?").

- ✔ **Display a popover:** A popover is a transient view that is shown when people tap a control or an onscreen area. Popovers are used in a variety of ways, including displaying the Master view when a Split View app (like RoadTrip) is in Portrait orientation, or displaying additional information about a selection. They are only available on the iPad.

✔ **Respond to user input and navigation:** While the view processes a touch using the Target-Action pattern, it is almost always the view that is the target of the action — responding to the touch appropriately (like having the image of a '59 Cadillac Eldorado Biarritz convertible drive right up the center of the screen — sound effects included).

View controllers are also typically the objects that serve as delegates and data sources for Table views (more about those in Chapter 19) as well as for other kinds of framework views.

In addition to the base `UIViewController` class, `UIKit` includes the following:

✔ Subclasses such as `UITabBarController` (to manage the Tab bar)

✔ `UITableViewController` (which you use to manage Table views)

✔ `UINavigationController` (which implements navigation back and forth between view controllers)

✔ `UIPageViewController` (to allow users to navigate between view controllers using the specified transition)

✔ `UIImagePickerController` (to access the camera and Photo library on the iPad)

✔ `UISplitViewController` (which you'll be using on the iPad only to display the side-by-side views you see in Figure 4-3, for example)

What About the Model?

As this chapter shows (and as you'll continue to discover), much of the functionality you need in an app is already in the frameworks.

But when it comes to the *model objects* — the things you build to actually hold the data and carry out the logic for your app — you're on your own, for the most part. In the RoadTrip app, for example, you're going to need to create a `Trip` object that owns the data and logic and uses other objects to perform some of the actions it needs.

I talk about the model and model classes in more detail in Chapter 11. That's where you'll also find much more on implementing model objects.

You may find classes in the framework that help you get the nuts and bolts of the model working. But the actual content and specific functionality are up to you.

Using naming conventions

When creating your own classes, methods, and variables, it's a good idea to follow a couple of standard naming conventions:

✔ **Class names** (such as `View`) should start with a capital letter.

✔ The names of **methods** (such as `viewDidLoad`) should start with a lowercase letter, and additional words within the name should start with an uppercase letter (`viewDidLoad`).

✔ The names of **instance variables** and **properties** (such as `frame`) should start with a lowercase letter.

When you follow these conventions, you can tell from the name what something actually is. A few more such conventions are good to know, and I explain them as they arise in the course of the book.

To implement the structure that enables me to include several destinations in the RoadTrip app, I need to have the data. I use *property lists* (XML files, in other words) to take care of that because they're well suited for the job, and (more importantly) support for them is built into the iOS frameworks. (For more on property lists, see Chapter 11.) Property lists are great for relatively small amounts of data. For larger amounts, the Core Data persistent objects framework is a great choice, but it's not part of this book. You can start with property lists to get a feel for data management on iOS and then move on to Core Data for your next app.

iOS includes a `UIDocument` class for managing the data associated with a user's documents. If you're implementing a document-based app, you can use this class to reduce the amount of work you must do to manage your document data. If you're implementing an app that supports iCloud storage, the use of document objects makes the job of storing files in iCloud much easier. I don't cover the `UIDocument` class in this book.

It's Not That Neat

It would be nice (not to mention amazing) if everything fit neatly into model, view, or controller, but it doesn't work that way.

You really need to know about one other kind of class. The `UIApplication` class handles routing of incoming user events, dispatches action messages from controls, and deals with numerous other basic plumbing functions that aren't the responsibilities of a model, view, or controller. It typically works with an *application delegate,* a set of methods that allows you to customize how your app responds to events such as app launch, low-memory warnings, and app termination. The app delegate (as it's often referred to) is also the place where you'll create your model. I explain the mysteries of the `UIApplication` class as well as the role of the app delegate in Chapter 6.

Taking a Look at Other Frameworks

So far, almost all the things that I've talked about can be found in the `UIKit` framework, whose sole purpose in life is to provide a developer with all the classes an app needs in order to construct and manage its user interface. The `UIKit` framework does a majority of the heavy lifting for you, but developers don't live by the `UIKit` framework alone; quite a few other frameworks get put into play as well. The next few sections give you a rundown of some of the other frameworks you may encounter.

The Foundation framework

The `Foundation` framework is similar to the `UIKit` framework in that it defines general-purpose classes. The difference is that whereas `UIKit` limits itself to classes that implement the user interface, the `Foundation` framework stakes a claim on all the other stuff — the non–user-interface stuff — you need in your app. In practical terms, this means that the `Foundation` framework defines basic object behavior, memory management, notifications, internationalization, and localization.

The `Foundation` framework also provides *object wrappers* or *equivalents* (for numeric values, strings, and collections) and *utility classes* (for accessing underlying system entities and services, such as ports, threads, and file systems as well as networking, and date and time management).

The CoreGraphics framework

The `CoreGraphics` framework contains the interfaces for the Quartz 2D drawing API and is the same advanced, vector-based drawing engine that's used in OS X. It provides support for path-based drawing, anti-aliased rendering, gradients, images, colors, coordinate-space transformations, and PDF document creation, display, and parsing. Although the API is C based, it uses object-based abstractions to make things easier for you. Although it is the basis for many things you see on the screen, you won't be using it directly in this book.

Even more frameworks

Besides the UIKit, Foundation, and CoreGraphics frameworks, you use a handful of others in this book's example app, as well as (I'm sure) in your own apps down the road. They are as follows:

- ✔ MapKit: Lets you embed a fully functional map interface into your app. The map support provided by this framework includes many of the features normally found in the Maps app.

- ✔ AVFoundation: Provides an Objective-C interface for managing and playing audio-visual media in your iOS app.

- ✔ AudioToolbox: Contains the APIs that provide application-level services — for playing sounds, for example.

- ✔ MediaPlayer: Provides basic functionality for playing movie, music, audio podcast, and audiobook files, as well as access to the iPod Library.

- ✔ SystemConfiguration: Contains interfaces for determining the network configuration of a device.

- ✔ CoreLocation: Provides location data to support functionality such as social networking. It also includes classes to do both forward and reverse geocoding (which I explain in Chapter 18).

You can find many, many more frameworks for your apps in iOS Technology Overview Appendix B: iOS Frameworks, which you can find in the iOS Developer Library, at http://developer.apple.com/library/ios/navigation/index.html; then enter iOS Technology Overview. Be advised that if you want to be able to do something, there's probably a framework to support it.

Understanding the MVC in the Project

As one might expect, when you create an Xcode project, any and all classes added to the project by the template correspond to the Model-View-Controller design pattern. No surprises there.

If you look carefully, you can actually see how the features of the MVC model end up getting translated into a real, live project. Start by checking out the Project navigator, where you see MasterViewController .h and .m files, DetailViewController .h and .m files, and AppDelegate .h and .m files.

(Remember that, because everything in the iPad version is built using a split view, you're going to see two controllers — one for the Master view and one for the Detail view. I explain that in detail in Chapter 13.)

The interface (`.h` file) contains the class declaration and the methods and properties associated with the class. But although the interface file has traditionally also included the instance variables, you're actually going to include all instance variables in the implementation file instead, so you can keep them away from prying eyes. (You can find more on hiding the instance variables in Chapter 6.)

The implementation (`.m` file) contains the actual code for the methods of the class and — as just mentioned — also includes your instance variables.

The `MasterViewController` and `DetailViewController` correspond to the controllers I explain in the "View Controllers — the Main Storyboard Players" section, earlier in this chapter. But where are the classes that correspond to the views?

To find out, select the `Main_iPad.storyboard` file in the Project navigator and you see two view controllers in the Document Outline. Each view controller in a storyboard file manages a single scene. Select the disclosure triangle to expand the Master View controller and you see its view, shown in Figure 4-13.

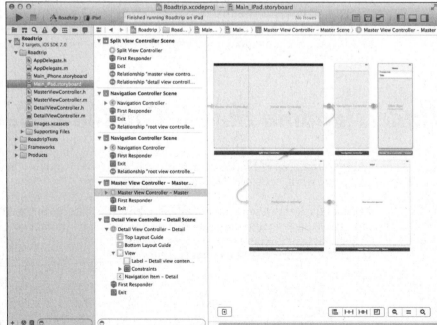

Figure 4-13:
The view controller highlighted on the Canvas.

When you click the view controller in the Document Outline, you see a (blue) line around the window to represent the view controller.

If you can't see the Document Outline, you can use the Hide/Show Document Outline control, shown in Figure 4-14. You can also zoom in and out of a storyboard by double-clicking in the Interface Builder editor or using the zoom control shown in Figure 4-14.

Now click the view in the Document Outline, and you'll see a display of the view itself — waiting for you to add all sorts of interesting images and controls (which you do in the next chapter). You can see that in Figure 4-14.

You see, of course, that the window changes — the view has been highlighted on the Canvas — but I explain more about that when I have you actually add the user interface elements in Interface Builder.

So now that you have controllers and views, what about models? (The design pattern is called Model-View-Controller, after all.) Well, the models aren't there . . . at least not yet. For that other shoe to drop, you'll have to go to Chapter 11, where I explain in great detail all about model classes and how to add them.

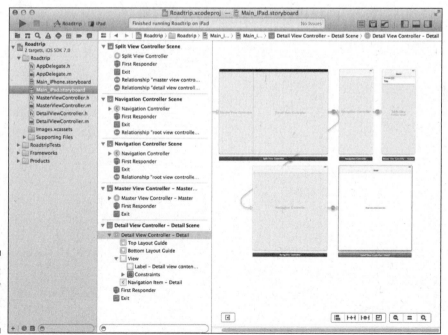

Figure 4-14:
The view in the storyboard.

You can also see some of the other parts of the application infrastructure I mention earlier in the *Project navigator.* The AppDelegate .h and .m files in the Project navigation area correspond to the app delegate.

You'll see one other element in the Document Outline — the first responder: This object is the first entry in an app's dynamically constructed responder chain (a term I explain along with more about the application infrastructure at runtime in Chapter 6) and is the object designated to be the first handler of events other than touch events, such as motion events and a few other events you won't be working with in this book.

But because the responder chain of an app can't be determined at design time, the first responder proxy acts as a stand-in target for any action messages that need to be directed at the app's responder chain.

Although you might use the first responder mechanism quite a bit in your apps, you don't have to do anything to manage it. It's automatically set and maintained by the UIKit framework.

Chapter 5

Creating the RoadTrip
User Interface

● ●

In This Chapter

▶ Seeing how storyboards work

▶ Working in the Utility area

▶ Understanding and adding navigation controllers

▶ Using Interface Builder to add objects to your storyboard

● ●

*I*f you've read the preceding chapters, you have the foundation for understanding the tools you need to build an app, with particular focus on the
example app developed in this book. Now you're ready to find out how to add
a user interface to your app via the storyboard.

In this chapter, I show you how to add items to the `TestDriveController`'s
view using both Interface Builder and the user interface objects available to
you in the Library pane in the Utility area. You first add these items to your
iPad storyboard and then add similar items to your iPhone storyboard.

Creating Your User Interface in the iPad Storyboard

In the Project navigator, select the `Main_iPad.storyboard` file and you'll see
several view controllers in the Document Outline (Split View Controller, Master
View Controller, and Detail View Controller). Each view controller in a storyboard file manages a single *scene* (a scene, in this sense, is really just a view
controller). On the iPad, courtesy of the Split View Controller (which I explain
in more detail in Chapter 13) or a popover controller, you can have multiple
scenes on a screen. (On the iPhone, you can generally see only one scene on a
screen at a time.) In the Document Outline, select the disclosure triangle next
to the Master View Controller in the Master View Controller – Master Scene to
expand the view controller and you'll see its view.

If you can't see the Document Outline, you can use the Hide/Show Document Outline control shown in the lower-middle of Figure 5-1. You can also zoom in and out of a storyboard by double-clicking in the storyboard's Canvas, or by using the zoom control shown in the lower-right in Figure 5-1. The = sign returns the storyboard to full size, which is the only way views are editable.

To add user interface elements, select the view you want to work with under the view controller heading listed in the Document Outline.

It's about the view controller

Selecting a storyboard file in the Project navigator launches Interface Builder, which is the editor you use to edit the storyboard files for your application. Most applications need only one storyboard file, but because you're creating a *universal* app, you'll have two storyboards, one for the iPad user interface (`Main_iPad.storyboard`) and one for the iPhone user interface (`Main_iPhone.storyboard`). Each storyboard file you create has its own *initial view controller,* which serves as the entry point into the storyboard. In your application's main storyboard file, the initial view controller would be the first view controller presented by your application.

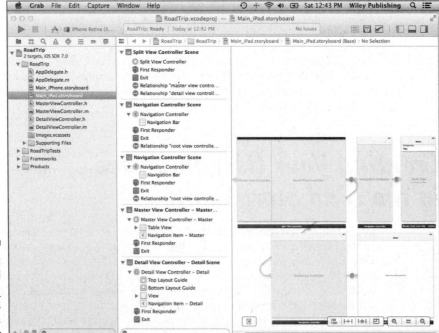

Figure 5-1:
The initial
`Main_
iPad`
storyboard.

The view controller is the big kahuna here, and each view controller in a story-board file, as I said, manages a single scene. For iPhone applications, a scene manages one screen's worth of content, but for iPad applications, the content from multiple scenes can be onscreen simultaneously. To add new scenes to your storyboard file, all you have to do is drag a view controller from the Library to the storyboard canvas. You can then add controls and other views (such as Image, Web, or even Table views) to the view controller's view.

Besides the ability to lay out your application as a whole, storyboards also reduce the amount of code you have to write. Say you want to create a transition from one view controller to another; all you would need to do is Control-click a button or Table View cell in one view controller and drag to the other. Dragging between view controllers creates a *segue,* which appears in Interface Builder as a configurable object. Segues support all the same types of transitions available in UIKit, such as navigation and modal transitions. A segue also enables you to define custom transitions.

I explain more about segues and view controller transitions in Chapter 14, when you add more scenes and segues to the RoadTrip app.

Using Interface Builder to add the user elements

Xcode's Interface Builder enables you to create a storyboard by letting you lay out your user interface graphically in each view controller. You use Interface Builder to design your app's user interface and then save what you've done as a resource file, which is included in your app and loaded into your app at runtime. This resource file is then used to automatically create the window and your app's view controllers, as well as all your views and controls.

If you don't want to use Interface Builder, you can also create your objects pro-grammatically — creating views and view controllers and even things like buttons and labels using your very own application code. I show you an example of creating a button programmatically in Chapter 15.

So how do you actually get those little controls into the view that lives in the view controller scene? For that, you use another area of the workspace — the Utility area.

You use the View selector on the toolbar to display or hide the Utility area. The Utility area is an optional area on the right side of the Workspace window. To hide or show the Utility area, click the Utility button on the View selector on the right on the Workspace toolbar. (In Figure 5-2, I'm using the View selector to open the Utility area.)

When you hover your mouse pointer over a toolbar button, a tooltip describes its function.

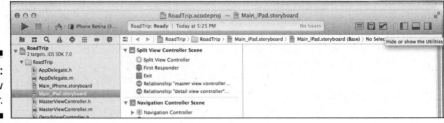

Figure 5-2:
The View
selector.

Figure 5-2:
The View
selector.

Figure 5-3 shows the Utility area in all its glory. I have resized the Library pane.

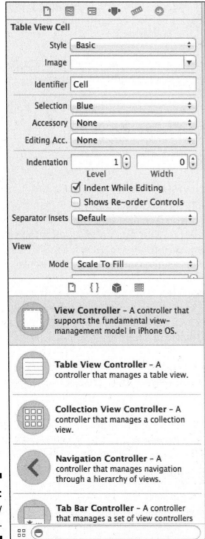

Figure 5-3:
The Utility
area.

As you can see, this area includes two panes, the top one for Quick Help and other inspectors (the Attributes inspector is selected here), and the bottom one for libraries of resources.

Working within the Utility Area

The Utility area consists of the Inspector and Library panes and their corresponding Inspector and Library selector bars. The idea is to use the Inspector pane to view and access Quick Help and other inspectors, and to scour the Library pane for ready-made resources you want to use in your project. You'll be using both the Inspector and Library panes in this chapter.

Inspector and Quick Help pane

You use the Inspector selector (shown in Figure 5-4) to toggle on the particular inspector you want to use. (Xcode makes the decision-making process a bit easier by having your choice of Navigator or Content editor predetermine which inspectors in fact show up in the Inspector selector.)

Figure 5-4:
The
Inspector
selector.

Utility area inspectors perform a variety of tasks. Following is a list of important inspectors and what you use them for:

✔ **File inspector (first button):** Lets you view and manage file metadata such as its name, type, and path.

✔ **Quick Help (second button):** Lets you view applicable details about what has been selected in an editor. Details include an abstract or concise description, where and how the selected element is declared, its scope, the parameters it takes, its platform and architecture availability, references, sample code, and so on. Different editors support different elements for selection, as follows:

   • *Symbols,* available for selection in the Source editor

   • *Interface objects,* available for selection in Interface Builder

   • *Build settings,* available for selection in the Project editor

Additional inspectors are available in some editors; for example, Interface Builder offers the following:

 ✔ **Identity inspector:** Lets you view and manage object metadata such as its class, runtime attributes, label, and so forth.

 ✔ **Attributes inspector:** Lets you configure the attributes specific to the selected interface object. For example, some text field attributes include text alignment and color, border type, and editability.

 ✔ **Size inspector:** Lets you specify characteristics such as the initial size and position, minimum and maximum sizes, and autosizing rules for an interface object.

 ✔ **Connections inspector:** Lets you view the outlets and actions for an interface object, make new connections, and delete existing connections. The Connections inspector is where you'll find things like outlets and targets that I explain in Chapter 9.

Library pane

A selection in the Library selector in the Library pane does the obvious: It selects a particular library of resources that you can then use in your project. Figure 5-5 shows the choices offered by the Library selector; the following list gives the details:

Figure 5-5:
The Library
selector.

 ✔ **File templates:** Click here to find templates for the common types of files you create using the New File menu. To add a file of that type to your project, simply drag it from the File Templates library to the Project navigator.

 ✔ **Code snippets:** Need just a smidgeon of code? Click here to find short pieces of source code you can then use in your application. Just drag the bit you found directly into your source code file.

 ✔ **Objects:** This library consists of interface objects you can use as part of your user interface. To add one to a particular view, drag it directly into your storyboard or nib file in Interface Builder.

 ✔ **Media files:** Here's where you'll find graphics, icons, and sound files. To use one, drag it directly to your storyboard or nib file in Interface Builder.

You can filter out what gets displayed in a selected library by entering your Search text into the text field in the Filter bar at the bottom of the Library pane.

Understanding iPad Navigation

Although the iPhone and iPad are very similar, one area in which they often differ is in how a user can navigate through an application.

For example, in iPhone apps that use a master-detail architecture, a Back button is prominently displayed in a detail view to go back to the Master view. (Figure 5-6 shows what I mean.) An iPad app that uses Split view functionality for the master-detail architecture will not need that Back button. But there are many other user interface designs on the iPad where a Back button is often used.

Apple has built this ability into the iOS architecture and has made it an integral part of the view controller architecture, as personified in the Navigation controller. (Okay, I know it isn't a "person," but you get the idea.)

Figure 5-6:
An iPhone application sequence.

A Navigation controller is a Container view controller that enables the user to navigate back and forth between view controllers. A Navigation controller is an instance of the `UINavigationController` class, which is a class you use "as is" and don't subclass. The methods of this class provide support for managing a stack-based collection of custom view controllers. This stack represents the path taken by the user through the application, with the bottom of the stack reflecting the starting point and the top of the stack reflecting the user's current position in the application.

Apple's `UIKit` framework (one of the Cocoa Touch frameworks) generally uses class names that begin with *UI,* such as `UIView`, `UIViewController`, `UIImageView`, `UIButton`, and many more. To avoid confusion, you should not use the UI prefix for your own class names. Apple also has special prefixes for many other frameworks. For example, the Core Image framework includes classes such as `CIColor`, `CIContext`, `CIFaceFeature`, and so on. These naming conventions provide hints so that when you come across an Apple class named `CIImage`, you can expect to find it in the Core Image framework.

Some developers adopt their own special prefixes for all their custom classes, including simple schemes such as using the RT prefix, so that class names could be `RTMasterViewController`, `RTMapController`, `RTWeatherController`, and so on. It's not necessary to use a unique prefix for every custom class name, but you should avoid using Apple's class names for your own classes.

A *stack* is a commonly used data structure that works on the principle of "last in, first out." Imagine an ideal boarding scenario for an airplane: Passengers would start being seated in the last seat in the last row, and they'd board the plane in back-to-front order until they got to the first seat in the first row, which would contain the seat for the last person to board. When the plane reached its destination, everyone would deplane (is that really a word?) in the reverse order. That last person on — the person in row one, seat one — would be the first person off.

A computer stack works on the same concept. Adding an object is called a *push* — in this case, when you tap the Travel button, for example, the view controller for that view is pushed onto the stack. Removing an object is called a *pop* — touching the Back button pops the view controller for the view being displayed. When you pop an object off the stack, it's always the last one you pushed onto it. The controller that was there before the push is still there and now becomes the active one.

Although the Navigation controller's primary job is to act as a manager of other view controllers, it also manages a few views. Specifically, it manages a *Navigation bar* that displays information about the user's current location in the data hierarchy, a Back button for navigating to previous screens, and any custom controls the current view controller needs.

Take another look at Figure 5-6 and notice that, when the user taps Events in the iPhone version of RoadTrip, the Navigation controller (courtesy of the storyboard) pushes the next view controller onto the stack. The new view controller's view slides into place and the Navigation bar items are updated appropriately. When the user taps the Back button on the Navigation bar, the current view controller pops off the stack, that view slides off the screen, and the user finds himself back in the previous view.

The Navigation controller maintains the stack of view controllers, one for each of the views displayed. The very first view controller that the Navigation controller pushes onto its stack when a Navigation controller is created is called the *Root view controller*. It remains active until the user selects the next view to look at.

Navigation bars enable a user to navigate the hierarchy. Here's what you need to know in order to make that work:

- ✔ The view beneath the Navigation bar presents the current level of the application.
- ✔ A Navigation bar includes a title for the current view.
- ✔ If the current view is lower in the hierarchy than the top level, a Back button appears on the left side of the bar; the user can tap it to return to the previous level. (Back in Figure 5-6, these buttons are named Road Trip and New York City and are shaped like a left-pointing arrow; the text in the Back button tells the user what the previous level was.)
- ✔ A Navigation bar may also have an Edit button on the right side — used to enter Editing mode for the current view — or even custom buttons.

On the iPad, the Master-Detail Application template has not one, but *two* Navigation controllers already included in the storyboard — one for the Master View controller and the other for the Detail View controller, as you can see in Figure 5-7.

The only "problem" right now is that each Navigation controller has only one view controller to manage, which means you won't be able to select anything and see a new view, with its accompanying Back button.

In this chapter, you get to fix that for the Detail View controller, at least.

What you're working toward right now is shown in Figure 5-8. When you tap the first cell in the Master View controller (you'll add the Test Drive label shortly), a new view controller will slide its view into place. If you select the Back button, you will slide back to the previous Detail view.

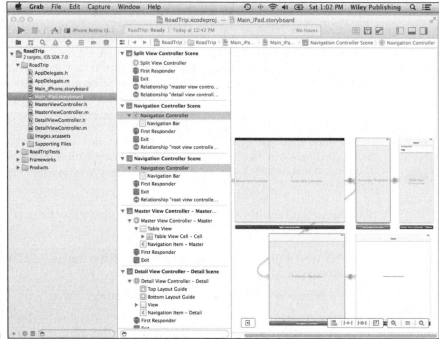

Figure 5-7:
The
Navigation
controllers
are already
in.

Figure 5-8:
Navigating
in RoadTrip
on the iPad.

You have other (even slicker) iPad navigation options at your disposal, and I get to them in Chapter 13, where you get a chance to change from navigation that uses the Navigation controller to something a bit more appropriate for the RoadTrip application. For now, though, you'll go with the Navigation controller approach, just to get you off and running.

So, on your mark, get set, and go. Time to add a new view controller.

Adding a New View Controller

Your first step in adding a new view controller is to select the iPad storyboard file in the Project navigator. With the storyboard displayed, you then make sure that the Utility area is visible by clicking its icon in the Xcode toolbar's View selector. With that done, you can now hide the Project navigator by clicking *its* icon in the Xcode toolbar's View selector. (See Figure 5-9; remember, the button is a toggle, as I explain in Chapter 2.) Doing so gives you a little more real estate onscreen. (If you are blessed with a large monitor, though, you can keep the Project navigator open.)

Because I have limited space on a book page, I'm hiding the Navigator area, as you can see in Figure 5-10. (When I work on my large-screen monitor, I usually keep the Navigator area shown.)

As the last step in getting your canvas ready, click the Attributes inspector button in the Inspector selector in the Utility area.

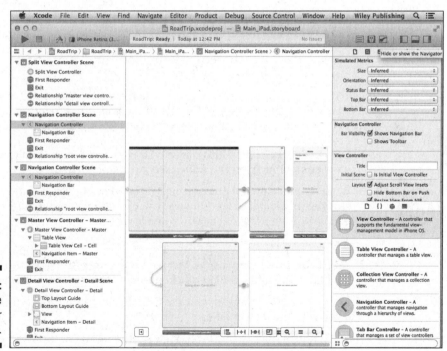

Figure 5-9: Hiding the Navigator area.

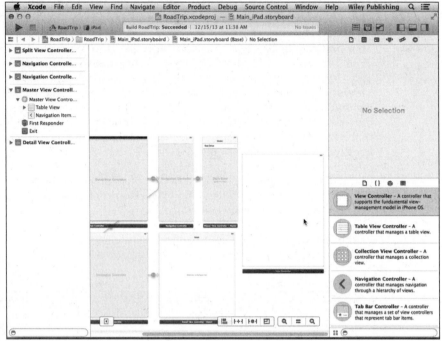

Figure 5-10:
Drag in
a view
controller.

To add the `Test Drive controller` (which manages the view that will allow you to have RoadTrip's little car drive up the screen, turn around, and then go back to its original position, all with sound effects), you need to do the following:

1. **Select Objects in the Utility area's Library pane, and then drag a new view controller from the pane into your storyboard.**

   Whereas you can add controls and other views to views only when the storyboard elements are full size, you can add view controllers (and, as you'll soon see, segues) at any zoom level.

   A new scene is created, as shown in Figure 5-10.

2. **Select the Table view in the Master View Controller – Master Scene (as I have in Figure 5-11) and then select the Attributes inspector.**

   If you look at the Canvas, you see a Table view with Prototype Cells, and a cell with the text of Title.

   You'll notice that, in the Table View section of the Attributes inspector, the Dynamic Prototypes option is selected.

   Right now, if you select a cell, nothing happens. That's because with Dynamic Prototype cells, you have to implement a method in your view controller to do something when a cell is selected (as you will in Chapter 20, where you create cells based on the information for each destination in the `Destinations plist`).

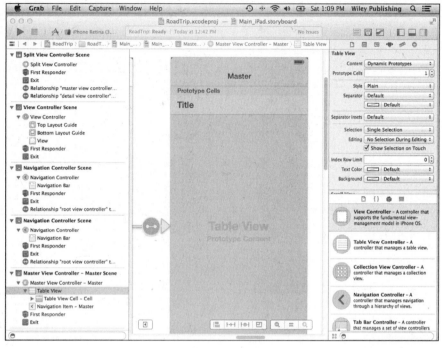

Figure 5-11:
The Table
view.

For now, all I want to do is to be able to launch a Test Drive controller when the first cell is selected (and I really don't care about the time stamp). To do that in the most expeditious way possible, I'll have you use the Attributes inspector to change the Master view from Dynamic Prototypes to Static Cells.

Static cells are used when you know in advance what needs to be displayed in a cell. Instead of having to implement a method in your view controller to return the cell with the text you want, you can format the cells in the storyboard. But more importantly, you can create a segue from a static cell that will launch the Test Drive Controller for you when the cell is tapped.

That's all I am going to say about static cells for now — I really want to get on with explaining how to create the user interface in the storyboard using Interface Builder, but I promise I'll return to static cells in detail in Chapter 12, because they are a feature that you'll probably be using often.

3. **In the Attributes inspector, select Static Cells from the Content drop-down menu, as I have in Figure 5-12.**

   You'll notice a change in the Table view. The heading Prototype Cells will disappear and you'll see three cells each with the text Title.

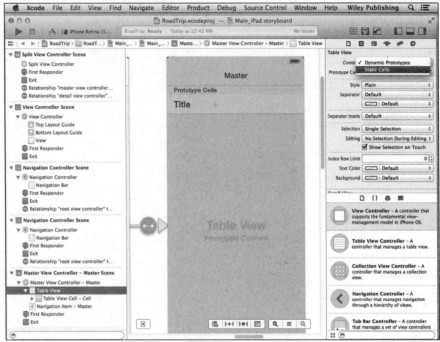

Figure 5-12:
Make them
static cells.

4. In the Outline view, expand the disclosure triangle next to the table view and you'll see a Table View section.

Expand the Table View section and you'll see three Table View cells. Expand the first Table View cell and you'll find a content view and then a label. Select the label, and in the Attributes inspector Title field, enter **Test Drive** as I have in Figure 5-13.

5. Select the first Table View cell (the cell, not the Test Drive label) in the Document Outline, and Control-drag from the cell in the Master View controller to the view controller you just added, as shown in Figure 5-14. Then release the mouse button.

Control-clicking from a button or Table View cell and dragging to the view controller you want displayed creates a selection segue or an accessory action. When you release the mouse button, you'll see the Storyboard Segues contextual menu, which pops up onscreen. You'll learn more about segues in this section and in Chapter 14. We won't be using an accessory action, but it's a way to trigger a segue — from an accessory button in a table view cell rather than from a tap anywhere in the cell (a selection segue).

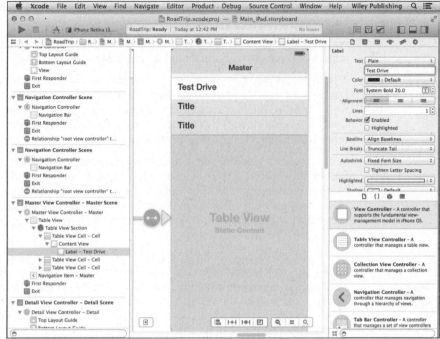

Figure 5-13:
Your Test
Drive cell.

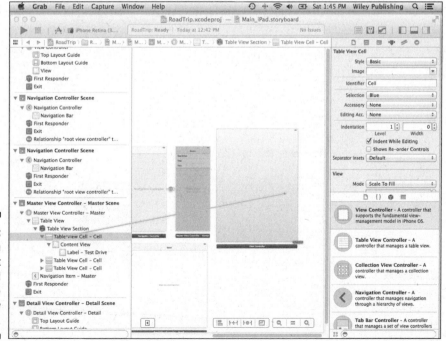

Figure 5-14:
Drag from
the Test
Drive cell
to the
Table view
controller.

6. **Select Push from the Selection Segue pop-up menu, as shown in Figure 5-15.**

   A *segue* performs the visual transition between two view controllers and supports push (navigation), modal, and custom transitions.

   A *push* segue changes the scene — and the user sees the new view controller's view (with its Back button) slide into place when the user taps a button; the Navigation bar items are updated appropriately. (See the "Understanding iPad Navigation" section, earlier in this chapter, for more on adding a Navigation controller.)

   In contrast to a push segue, a *modal* segue presents the view controller modally, with the transition style you specify, and requires the user to do something (tap Save or Cancel, for example) to get back to the previous view controller. As for custom transitions, segues support the standard visual transition styles such as Cover Vertical, Flip Horizontal, Cross Dissolve, and Partial Curl.

   Segue objects are used to prepare for the transition from one view controller to another, which means segue objects contain information about both view controllers involved in a transition. When a segue is triggered — but before the visual transition occurs — the storyboard runtime calls the current view controller's `prepareForSegue:sender:` method so that it can pass any needed data to the view controller that's about to be displayed.

Figure 5-15: Creating a push segue.

You'll notice that selecting Push from the Storyboard Segue's pop-up menu causes the Navigation bar to appear but also shrinks the view. I explain that in Chapter 13.

7. **Select the Push segue in the Master View Controller scene. After making sure that *Push* appears on the Style menu in the Attributes inspector, enter** TestDrive **in the inspector's Identifier field, as I have in Figure 5-16; then press return (or enter).**

   You won't always use the identifier, but it's good practice to name it so that you can identify the segue.

   The field in the storyboard isn't updated until you press return, or sometimes until you click in another field *in that inspector*.

8. **Choose Detail Split from the Attributes inspector's Destination drop-down menu, as I have in Figure 5-16.**

   The size of the view in the Test Drive controller changes.

9. **Finally, select the two unused Table View cells in the Document Outline and delete them by pressing Delete. (You won't be using them.)**

   The default destination was set to Current, which meant that it was set to the Master view, because that's where you were dragging from. With that default, the view controller had been resized for the Master view, which is 320 points wide in the standard Split View Controller. But you want the destination to be in the Detail view; choosing Detail Split in this step takes care of that for you.

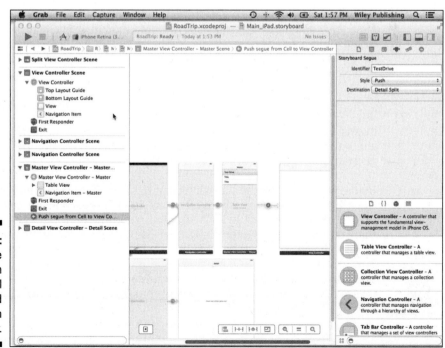

Figure 5-16: Make the destination a Detail view and add an identifier.

If you look closely at Figure 5-16, you can see that the view has now been sized down and that a Navigation bar has been added to the top of the view. If you expand the view controller in the View Controller Scene in the Document Outline, you can see that a Navigation bar was added there as one would expect.

You'll also notice that a Disclosure Indicator (the *chevron* — a right-arrowhead-like shape on the right side of the Test Drive cell) has also been added. For now we'll leave it there, but in Chapter 13, I explain how to remove or change it if you'd like.

When you select the Detail cell and create the Push segue with the Detail view as the destination, the new Test Drive controller becomes *embedded* in the Detail view's Navigation controller. This Navigation controller manages the view controller stack for everything in the Detail view of the Split View Controller.

Danger Will Robinson

If you were to build and run RoadTrip for iPad at this point, the app would crash because Apple's Master-Detail template has added code for dynamic table cells that can't be used for our static table cell. You will soon delete that unwanted code, so the app will work properly by the end of this chapter.

After the unwanted code is deleted, there will be two ways to test the app for iPad.

First, you could choose Landscape orientation, and select Test Drive, which would allow a new view controller's view to slide into place, Back button and all. If you then selected the Back button, the old Detail view would slide back into place.

However, in Portrait orientation, if you selected the Master button and then selected Detail, you'd see the new controller with a Back button as well. The Master button, however, will only appear again after you have selected Back and returned to the Detail View controller (the Root View controller). You'll find out how to fix that annoying bit of business in Chapter 13.

Before you go any further, take a look at the View Controller you just added in the Attributes inspector, which I have selected in the Inspector selector bar in the Utility area in Figure 5-17. As you can see, the controller has properties that you can set using Interface Builder (including a title and identifier which I explain next).

The Attributes inspector is the place where you'll set properties of the view controllers, controls, and other view objects you add to the view.

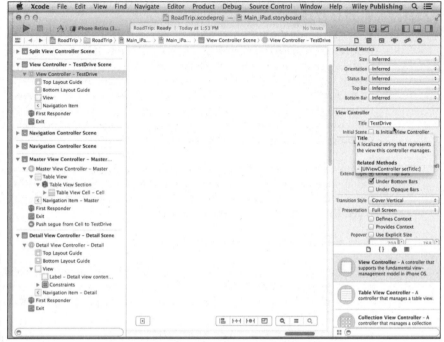

Figure 5-17:
Adding a
title and
identifier.

Adding an identifier to the view controller

If you take another look at Figure 5-17, you can see that I've set Interface Builder's zoom to full size, clicked on the view controller I just created, selected the Attributes inspector in the Inspector selector bar, and then entered **TestDrive** in the Title field in the View Controller section. I then selected the Identity Inspector tab, and set the Storyboard ID to **TestDriveID.** The Title string is used in the Outline view, whereas the Storyboard ID string is used from code in the app.

I did all that for one simple reason: If you want to do *anything* special with a view controller in a storyboard, you need to be able to find it, and the easiest way to keep tabs on a view controller is by giving it a name using the identifier. Although you may not need an identifier for every view controller, it's a good idea to get in the habit of adding it just in case you do. As for the name you enter in the Title field, it enables you to distinguish which view controller is which in the storyboard. You'll notice that in the Document Outline, the selected view controller is now named View Controller – TestDrive and the scene now is named View Controller – TestDrive Scene.

Whatever you type in a field isn't added until you press Return or click in another field.

View Layout

Before you start to add another view — which will be a subview of the view that's already there — it's necessary to talk about view layout options. View layout is particularly important on mobile devices because the pesky user might rotate her device. So why is that an issue? Look at the specific case of the original iPad. When held in Portrait orientation, the screen is 768 pixels wide by 1,024 pixels tall. But when rotated to Landscape position, the screen becomes 1,024 pixels wide, but only 768 pixels tall.

If your app handles rotation properly, components such as buttons, text fields, images, and so on usually need to move and resize. In other words, you need a layout strategy, so that subviews are moved and resized correctly when their containing superview is resized.

Here are three strategies for view layout:

- ✔ **Hard-code the layout.** Here, you set the location, width, and height of each view yourself, and change those properties when the device is rotated. This is a really bad idea for most apps. It's difficult, error-prone, and inflexible.

- ✔ **Use iOS autosizing.** Autosizing has existed since early versions of the iOS SDK and provides a mechanism for automatically moving and resizing a view in response to changes in its superview's position or size. You can set the default autosizing behavior for your views from the Size pane of the inspector. The Size inspector contains an autosizing section with springs and struts that let you specify which edges of an object (if any) are pinned to the edge of its container (which is often the screen itself) and which edges can move. Although currently supported and used in much older code, it is not the first choice for many developers today.

- ✔ **Use Auto Layout.** You use the Auto Layout system to define layout constraints for user interface elements. Constraints represent relationships between user interface elements. Auto layout improves upon Autosizing's "springs and struts" model in many ways. It was introduced in iOS 6 and is the preferred method of handling autosizing today.

Autosizing isn't just about rotation. Yes, the screen image must adjust as you rotate a device, but when Apple releases a new device with a new screen size, ideally, you want your app to adjust automatically to the new screen size. Using Auto Layout for autosizing can give you a big leg up here.

And there's even more. If your app will be localized, you need to prepare separate storyboards for each language. Depending on which languages you use, you may have to accommodate scripts that run from right to left as well as from left to right (not to mention languages that can run vertically). On top of that, some languages require more space to express the same thought, although this varies somewhat based on the subject matter of the thought

Points, pixels, and Retina displays

With the introduction of Retina displays, we have to be careful about how we talk about screen dimensions. In the past, many people used *points* and *pixels* interchangeably. *Point* is a term that was used mostly in typesetting (particularly for print). It is defined as 1/72 of an inch. *Pixel* is a single element of the screen.

For a long time, most displays supported 72 pixels per inch (PPI). Thus, on those screens, pixels and points were identical. With the Retina display, the pixel count doubled to 144 per inch. This means that every pre-Retina display pixel now was displayed by four pixels (two across and two down). As a result, we can no longer use the two terms interchangeably. The original iPad was 768 x 1,024 pixels and points. An iPad with Retina display is 768 x 1,024 points, but in pixels, it's 1536 x 2,048. As a very rough guide, if you're using an app such as Photoshop to do your work and you're worried about resolution, you're probably worried about pixels. If you're using Xcode and you want to specify the size and location of objects on the screen, you're probably using points.

and the language. When you put these localization issues together, you can see that the objects on your storyboard that contain localized text may need to be able to change size to reflect their content. Auto Layout helps to do this. These are advanced issues, but I bring them up here so that if they apply to you and your app, you'll be aware of Auto Layout and some of its advanced capabilities.

Adding the User Interface Objects

At this point, I could continue building out my storyboard by adding more elements such as views and segues, just like I did in the previous section. But by now I'm itching to really *do* something, which would require me getting some actual objects into the storyboard. When an itch comes, I scratch, so get ready to start editing and adding some objects.

To edit an object in the TestDrive view in the storyboard, select `Main_iPad.storyboard` in the Project editor to open Interface Builder. Expand the View Controller – TestDrive in the View Controller – TestDrive Scene in the Document Outline. Select the View, and then select the Attributes inspector in the Inspector selector.

The Attributes inspector enables you to set various object properties. For example, to change the color of the view's background, you'd choose the background color from the Background pop-up menu.

If you select Default from the pop-up menu or just click in the current color displayed in the Background field, you see the various default colors (shown on the right side in Figure 5-18). You can also click Other to open the Colors palette.

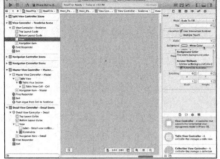

Figure 5-18:
Pick a color,
any color.

The toolbar at the top of the Colors palette gives you a number of options for selecting a color. These are the standard options available for choosing a color on the Mac, and I'll leave you to explore them on your own.

Changing the background color for a view is kind of neat, but the real fun comes from your ability to add your own view object as a background image. That's what you're going to do next. (Feel the excitement!)

Any view object you end up using has *properties* such as color (sometimes), a background image, or the ability to interact with the user — respond to touches, in other words. You generally set these properties using either the Attributes inspector in Interface Builder or programmatically.

To see those properties, you need to zoom to full size or select it in the Document Outline (which zooms it to full size). Full size is the only time view objects are editable.

To add a background image, follow these steps:

1. **Scroll down in the Library window and drag an Image view (the one selected in the Library in Figure 5-19) from the Library onto the view.**

   An Image view is a view that's used to display an image. (See Chapter 4 for more on views.)

   If you click an object in the Library, up pops a dialog telling you what it is. The dialog even tells you what class it is, as you can see in Figure 5-19. Click Done to dismiss it.

   What you just did is add an Image view as a *subview* of the RoadTrip controller's view, the one created for you by the template.

   Except for the view controllers up top and a few gesture recognizers scattered around the middle of the gallery, most of the "objects" you see in the Library are derived from the `View` class.

   You can add horizontal and vertical guides to help you line things up by choosing Editor⇨Add Horizontal Guide or Editor⇨Add Vertical Guide, respectively.

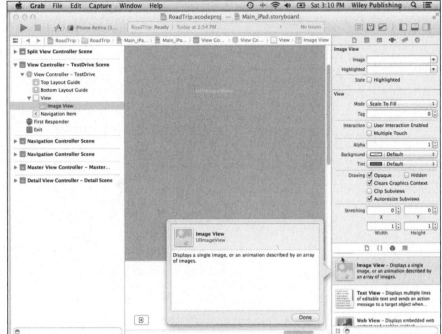

Figure 5-19:
Adding an
Image view.

2. **Select the Image view you just added, either in the Document Outline or on the Canvas.**

   Doing so changes what you see in the Attributes inspector. It now displays the attributes for the Image view.

3. **Using the Attributes inspector's Image drop-down menu, scroll down to select SeeTheUSA, as shown in Figure 5-20.**

   Doing so adds the image you want to use to the Image view, as shown in Figure 5-21. (You should have added this image in Chapter 3 — it was in the RoadTrip Resources file you downloaded and added to an asset catalog — either the template's default asset catalog or a separate one for your own images, which I usually call `Media.xcassets`.)

   The preferred format for the image is `.png`. Although most common image formats display correctly, Xcode automatically optimizes `.png` images at build time to make them the fastest and most efficient image type for use in iPad applications.

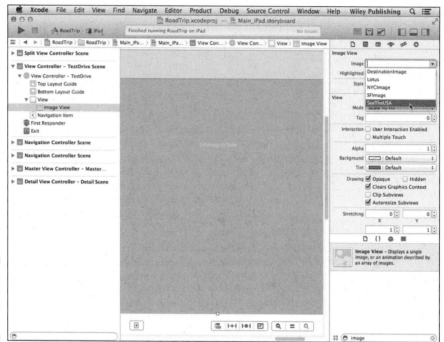

Figure 5-20:
Selecting a
background
image.

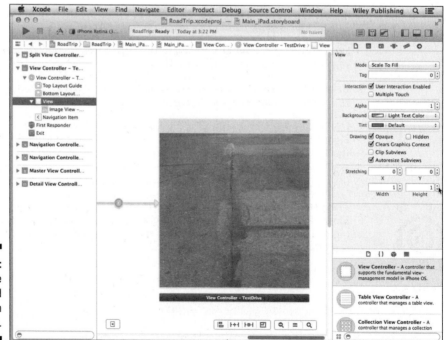

Figure 5-21:
The image
selected
and in
place.

4. **Drag in another Image view and place it at the bottom-center of the Image view you just added, as shown in Figure 5-22.**

5. **Return to the Attributes inspector's Image drop-down menu, but this time select CarImage.**

   The image you selected is added to the new Image view.

6. **Select the Image view you just added and choose Editor⇨Size to Fit Content from the main menu.**

   If the command is not enabled, you may need to select it in the Document Outline. The Image view is resized so that it better fits the enclosed content. (See Figure 5-23.) If you look closely, you'll recognize a vintage pink 1959 Cadillac Eldorado Biarritz convertible.

7. **With the car Image view still selected, choose Editor⇨Add Horizontal Guide and Editor⇨Add Vertical Guide.**

   I'll take any help I can get when it comes to positioning objects, and these guides can help me keep track of a particular location on the larger scene.

In Chapter 10, I show you how to animate the Eldorado Biarritz so it leisurely drives to the top of the screen, turns around, drives back, and then turns around one more time so that it's back where it started.

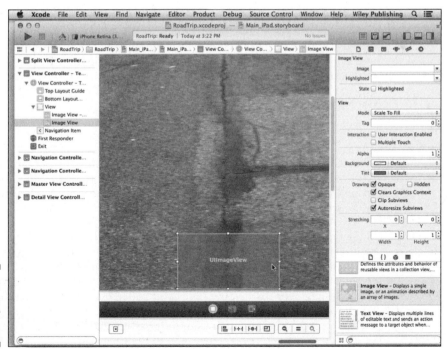

Figure 5-22:
Adding another image view.

Figure 5-23:
The family
car.

Autosizing with Auto Layout

Because you're sure to decide — as all good app developers have decided and will continue to decide in perpetuity — that the RoadTrip app needs to function well in both Portrait and Landscape orientations, you'll need to make sure that, when you rotate the view, the car (subview) remains positioned at the bottom of the screen.

Luckily for you, most of that work gets done for you in `UIView-Controller` — the class from which we've derived `TestDriveController`. (The technical term for this bit of work is *autosizing*.) The only thing you have to do is tell the view controller exactly how you want it to move things around when the view changes orientation. You can make such wishes known in the storyboard using the Size inspector.

You'll need to select some of the views to manage their autosizing. For this process, make certain that the Document Outline is shown at the left of the storyboard. The reason for this becomes clear if you look at the Document Outline in Figure 5-24. Inside the View Controller – TestDrive, you have a view (I'm skipping over the layout guides you added just now). Within that view, you have an image view containing SeeTheUSA image from the asset catalog. The image view is now the same size as its containing view. You need to be able to select each one separately, so the easiest way to do that is in the Document Outline. Figure 5-24 shows the settings you want to set for the Size inspector of the main view.

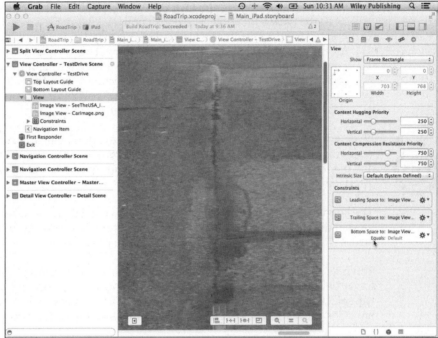

Figure 5-24:
Understand
the
Document
Outline view
structure.

There are four sections of the Size settings. From top to bottom, they are

- **Metrics:** Here at the top of the Size inspector, you set the location coordinates and the view size. Most of the time, I use the Interface Builder tools described in this and the following section, but when I want specific and accurate sizes, I type them in here. (That's what you'll do when you add a button soon.)

- **Content Hugging Priority and Content Compression Resistance Priority:** These sections are used mostly for adjusting the view's size based on its contents. As you see in Figure 5-24, each of these has a slider where you can adjust the horizontal and vertical values. This is not an on/off situation: at runtime, the values are weighed and the highest values win out where there's a conflict. You may set constraints (coming up soon) that are contradictory. For example, you may want a view to be positioned in a certain location based on another view (next to it by 10 points, say). In order to do that, the view may need to be resized. In such a case, a higher hugging priority will mean that view will resist resizing at the expense of not fulfilling the request to position it 10 points away from another view. Compression is the other side of the coin. If the compression resistance has a higher value, resizing that might truncate the view's content will be resisted.

- **Intrinsic Size:** This is set to default, which is where you'll leave it for basic layouts. This is the natural size of the view that may be resized or reshaped.

✔ **Constraints:** These are the heart of Auto Layout. You provide constraints as to the view's location. The ones shown in Figure 5-24, which you'll create shortly, specify the view's location relative to its container that, for the top-level view, is the screen window. These constraints may be contradictory in some cases, but you can assign a weight to each one to indicate which constraints are more important than others. At runtime, Auto Layout quickly figures out the optimal collection of constraints that does as much as possible of what you want.

If you don't see the Constraints section, Auto Layout may be turned off for your storyboard. To turn it on, select the storyboard in the Project navigator and open the File inspector. The Use Auto Layout option is a check box in the Interface Builder Document section.

The simplest way to set the constraints is shown in Figure 5-25. Select the view in the Document Outline, and choose Editor ➪ Resolve Auto Layout Issues ➪ Reset to Suggested Constraints in View Controller.

You now should have the three constraints shown in Figure 5-24. All three have the same basic structure. The first one specifies the trailing space from the selected view (the top-most View object) to the image view. The second specifies the leading space, and the third specifies the bottom space.

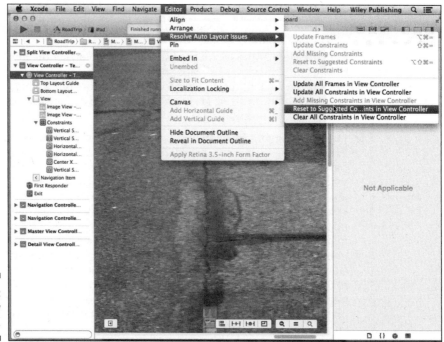

Figure 5-25:
Set View
constraints.

You may wonder what *leading* and *trailing* are in this context. Remember the comment about localization and the directions in which various languages write? In a left-to-right script such as English, Spanish, French, and the like, the leading space is the space between the left edge of the two views, and trailing is the space between the right edges.

For a right-to-left language such as Hebrew or Arabic, the leading space is the space on the right and the trailing space is the space on the left. Spaces for top and bottom are independent of language direction.

If you select the first one, you'll see that you can click the gear wheel at the right of each constraint to open more details, as shown in Figure 5-26. The default is quite simple: The spacing between right edges of the top-most View and the image view is zero points. If you explore further, you'll see that the bottom spacing is the default, which is also zero.

You're not yet done with managing Auto Layout. Select the image view and pin it to the bottom of its superview. Use Editor ⇨Pin ⇨Bottom Space to Superview. This means that it will be the right size when the device is rotated.

Repeat the process for the car image. The defaults show you another aspect of constraints. You'll have the default bottom space to superview again, but you'll have a new constraint that aligns the center of the car image to the center of the image view for the X (horizontal) coordinate.

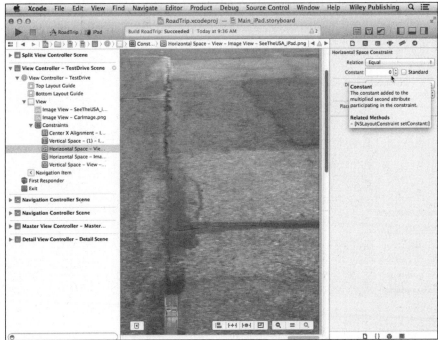

Figure 5-26:
View and edit constraints.

Although the app won't run until you enter the code in the following section, trust me that when you do enter that code, you'll be able to rotate the app in the simulator, as shown in Figure 5-27.

Figure 5-27:
Try rotating the simulator.

This process is typical of using Auto Layout. Draw your layout in the storyboard scene. Some constraints will be created for you automatically, and you can test to see what happens. You may need to tweak the constraints (such as by pinning an object to a superview). You also may choose to clear all the constraints and reset to the defaults. Another tweak may be necessary. But consider that, in this section, you've used two menu commands to make the interface handle rotation as well as new screen sizes and shapes.

Adding the Test Drive button

I say the more objects, the merrier. I want to add a nice Test Drive button which, when clicked, will send our 1959 Cadillac Eldorado Biarritz convertible on its merry way. Here's how it's done:

1. **Select the Button in the Library and drag it onto the view.**

2. **Click the Attributes Inspector button on the Inspector selector bar.**

   The button attributes you're going to set using the Attributes inspector are all Objective-C properties. Note that you can also set these properties programmatically; I show you how to do that in Chapter 8.

   As you can see in Figure 5-28, the Type pop-up menu in the Attributes inspector is set to System. The button is shown in its default State configuration — in this case, unselected and unhighlighted. If you were to click the State Config pop-up menu and choose another configuration, such as Highlighted or Selected, you'd be able to change the font, text color, shadow, background, and other attributes in the Attributes inspector for the selected state.

   This particular button, being distinctly generic, is remarkably unexciting. To liven things up just a tad, I'm going to have you add a background image I created. (You'll find that image in the RoadTrip Resources folder that you should have downloaded and added to your asset catalog in Chapter 3.)

3. **In the Attributes inspector, choose Custom from the Type pop-up menu, as shown in Figure 5-29.**

4. **Choose Button from the Background drop-down menu, as shown in Figure 5-30.**

   So why are you using the Background drop-down menu rather than the Image drop-down menu to place an image as your button? When you choose an image from the Background drop-down menu, you're simply doing that — setting the image for the button. You'll still add the title and so on using the Attributes inspector. If you were to choose from the Image drop-down menu, you would have included the title as part of the image and you wouldn't have been able to add it in the Inspector.

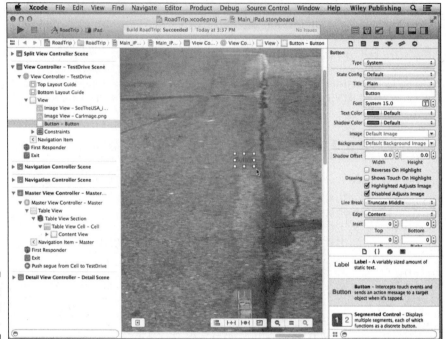

Figure 5-28:
Adding a
button.

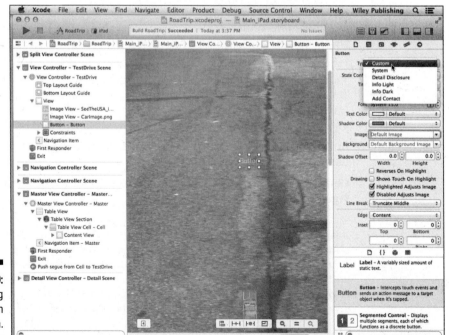

Figure 5-29:
Creating
a custom
button.

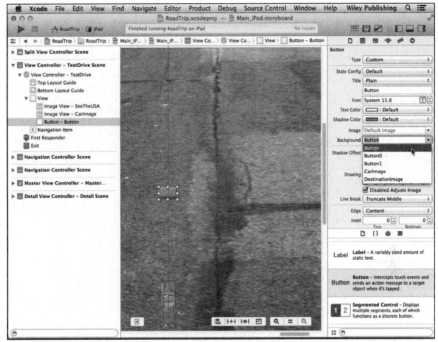

Figure 5-30:
Choose
a custom
image for
the button.

5. **Using Size inspector (as shown in Figure 5-31), resize the button to 96 points by 37 points using the width and height in the fields provided.**

   You can also use the resize handles.

6. **To center the button, select it and choose Editor➪Align➪Horizontal Center in Container.**

   Another constraint will automatically be added.

7. **To center it vertically, select it and choose Editor➪Align➪Vertical Center in Container.**

   The vertical constraint will be added.

8. **Give this button a title (buttons don't have text; they have titles) by going back to the Attributes inspector, entering** Test Drive **in the Title field, and pressing Return.**

   You could double-click the button and enter the Title there and press Return as well. In my experience, though, doing so may cause the button to resize itself.

TIP

You could select a different Background image and title for each button state by cycling through the State Config choices and repeating Steps 2 through 5. I'll leave that for you to explore on your own.

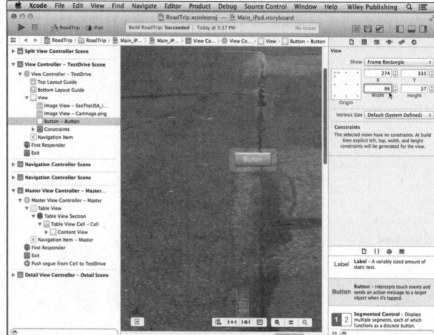

Figure 5-31:
Using
the Size
inspector.

Whenever you enter text, be sure to press Return. Anything you enter won't change the current setting unless you press Return or click in another field.

Massaging the Template Code

If you have been playing around with the code generated for you by the Master-Detail Application template, you've probably discovered that not only can you select the + (plus sign) button to create a timestamp displayed both in the Master and Detail views, but you can also select the Edit button and delete the timestamp entry in the Master (and consequently) Detail views.

All this functionality is built into the template courtesy of the `UITableViewController`. I explain how Table views work in Chapter 20, but because you are using a segue and static cells in the Master view, you won't need that functionality in the Master view. But not only don't you need it, it also actually interferes with the functioning of the segue, which you'll also understand when I explain Table view (and its `UITableViewDelegate` and `UITableViewDataSource` protocols) in detail in Chapter 20.

To deal with this issue, I want you to delete the code in Listing 5-1. Here I'm talking about the code in `MasterViewController.m` starting with the `#pragma mark - Table View` statement and up to — but not including — the @end statement. This is the code that implements the Table View functionality, and also another method, prepareForSegue, that lets you pass data to the view controller you are transitioning to — unused here, but explained in detail in Chapter 13.

Listing 5-1:   Delete This Code from MasterViewController.m

```
#pragma mark - Table View

- (NSInteger)numberOfSectionsInTableView:(UITableView *)
        tableView
{
  return 1;
}

- (NSInteger)tableView:(UITableView *)tableView
        numberOfRowsInSection:(NSInteger)section
{
  return _objects.count;
}

- (UITableViewCell *)tableView:(UITableView *)tableView
        cellForRowAtIndexPath:(NSIndexPath *)indexPath
{

    UITableViewCell *cell = [tableView
        dequeueReusableCellWithIdentifier:@"Cell"];

  NSDate *object = [_objects objectAtIndex:indexPath.row];
  cell.textLabel.text = [object description];
    return cell;
}

- (BOOL)tableView:(UITableView *)tableView
        canEditRowAtIndexPath:(NSIndexPath *)indexPath
{
    // Return NO if you do not want the specified item to
        be editable.
    return YES;
}

- (void)tableView:(UITableView *)tableView commitEditingS
        tyle:(UITableViewCellEditingStyle)editingStyle
        forRowAtIndexPath:(NSIndexPath *)indexPath
{
    if (editingStyle == UITableViewCellEditingStyleDelete)
        {
        [_objects removeObjectAtIndex:indexPath.row];
        [tableView deleteRowsAtIndexPaths:[NSArray
        arrayWithObject:indexPath]
        withRowAnimation:UITableViewRowAnimationFade];
    } else if (editingStyle ==
        UITableViewCellEditingStyleInsert) {
```

(continued)

Listing 5-1 *(continued)*

```
            // Create a new instance of the appropriate class,
            insert it into the array, and add a new row to
            the table view.
    }
}

/*
// Override to support rearranging the table view.
- (void)tableView:(UITableView *)tableView
          moveRowAtIndexPath:(NSIndexPath *)fromIndexPath
          toIndexPath:(NSIndexPath *)toIndexPath
{
}
*/

/*
// Override to support conditional rearranging of the
            table view.
- (BOOL)tableView:(UITableView *)tableView canMoveRowAtInd
          exPath:(NSIndexPath *)indexPath
{
    // Return NO if you do not want the item to be
            re-orderable.
    return YES;
}
*/

- (void)tableView:(UITableView *)tableView didSelectRowAtI
          ndexPath:(NSIndexPath *)indexPath
{
    if ([[UIDevice currentDevice] userInterfaceIdiom] ==
            UIUserInterfaceIdiomPad) {
        NSDate *object = [_objects
            objectAtIndex:indexPath.row];
        self.detailViewController.detailItem = object;
    }
}

- (void)prepareForSegue:(UIStoryboardSegue *)segue
          sender:(id)sender
{
    if ([[segue identifier]
          isEqualToString:@"showDetail"]) {
        NSIndexPath *indexPath = [self.tableView
          indexPathForSelectedRow];
        NSDate *object = [_objects
          objectAtIndex:indexPath.row];
        [[segue destinationViewController]
          setDetailItem:object];
    }
}
```

You'll also need to delete some code in the `viewDidLoad` method. This code adds the edit and + (plus) buttons to the Navigation bar. Delete the code in Listing 5-2 that I've commented out in bold, underline, and italic in `viewDidLoad` in `MasterViewController.m`.

Listing 5-2:   Delete the Code in viewDidLoad

```
- (void)viewDidLoad
{
  [super viewDidLoad];
// Do any additional setup after loading the view,
         typically from a nib.
//self.navigationItem.leftBarButtonItem =
                                  self.editButtonItem;
//UIBarButtonItem *addButton = [[UIBarButtonItem alloc]
    initWithBarButtonSystemItem:UIBarButtonSystemItemAdd
         target:self action:@selector(insertNewObject:)];
//self.navigationItem.rightBarButtonItem = addButton;
  self.detailViewController = (RTDetailViewController *)
    [[self.splitViewController.viewControllers lastObject]
                                     topViewController];
}
```

Finally, in Listing 5-3, delete the `insertNewObject:` method in `MasterViewController.m` (the action method specified in the + button created in `viewDidLoad`, which was the selector used).

Listing 5-3:   Delete insertNewObject:

```
- (void)insertNewObject:(id)sender
{
    if (!_objects) {
        _objects = [[NSMutableArray alloc] init];
    }
    [_objects insertObject:[NSDate date] atIndex:0];
    NSIndexPath *indexPath =
              [NSIndexPath indexPathForRow:0 inSection:0];
    [self.tableView insertRowsAtIndexPaths:
        [NSArray arrayWithObject:indexPath]
      withRowAnimation:UITableViewRowAnimationAutomatic];
}
```

Occasionally you might make a change to your app (usually having to do with a resource) and then, when you run your app, nothing seems to have changed. When you click Run, Xcode does only what it needs to do to the parts of your app that have changed, and if it gets "confused" (yes, there are bugs in Xcode), your change won't be linked into the app. If you think that has happened, choose Product➪Clean, and Xcode will recompile all the pieces of your app. And if that doesn't work, go to the Projects tab in the Organizer and delete Derived Data for your project.

Getting Rid of Warnings

Earlier, I warned you the app would not run until you cleaned up the unneeded code. You should have done that now with the code you just deleted, and the app should run.

You may have some warnings. If you do, it's a good idea to clean them up. If they are related to misplaced views on a storyboard, you have a good deal of help waiting for you. Here's what you can do:

1. **Select the warning for the misplaced view in the Issue navigator.**

   You'll see details of the warning.

2. **You can adjust the values yourself, but look for another yellow warning icon at the right of the warning and click it.**

3. **You'll be given a choice of automatic corrections. Choose the one you want to try, as shown in Figure 5-32.**

   The solutions are presented in less- to more-extreme order from top to bottom.

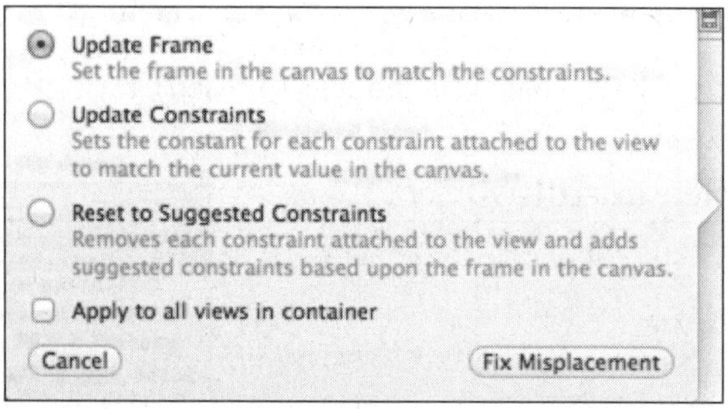

Figure 5-32:
Automatically fix misplaced views.

○ **Update Frame**
   Set the frame in the canvas to match the constraints.

○ **Update Constraints**
   Sets the constant for each constraint attached to the view to match the current value in the canvas.

○ **Reset to Suggested Constraints**
   Removes each constraint attached to the view and adds suggested constraints based upon the frame in the canvas.

☐ Apply to all views in container

(Cancel)   (Fix Misplacement)

Creating the iPhone User Interface

All the code that you write in Chapters 1 through 5 for the iPad will work fine for the iPhone. That will also be true for later chapters in this book. All you need to do is add the following items to your iPhone storyboard file, in a very similar manner to what you just did for the iPad storyboard:

- Drag a `UIViewController` into the iPhone storyboard. Change its class name to `TestDriveController` and its Storyboard ID to TestDrive.

- Add a `UIImageView`, using the `SeeTheUSA_iPhone.png` image.

- Add a `UIImageView`, using the `CarImage.png` image.

✔ Add a Test Drive button.

✔ Select the Master View Controller scene in the iPhone storyboard.

✔ Select the Table view in the Master View Controller.

✔ Use the Attributes inspector to change the Master view from Dynamic Prototypes to Static Cells.

✔ Select the Label in the first Table View cell, and change its text to Test Drive.

✔ Control-drag from the Table View cell to the `TestDriveController`; choose a Push segue from the pop-up menu.

✔ Select the unused Table View cells from the Table view and delete them.

Now the iPhone app should work in a similar manner to the iPad app.

Chapter 6

The Runtime, Managing Memory, and Using Properties

. . . .

In This Chapter

▶ Understanding the application life cycle

▶ Handling interruptions

▶ Using Automatic Reference Counting to manage memory

▶ Understanding the five rules of memory management

▶ Customizing framework behaviors

▶ Taking advantage of the power of declared properties

. . . .

*P*revious chapters provide you with at least a basic understanding of how to graphically build your user interface. Now it's time to add some code to have your app actually do something. But before you do that, I want to explain three things about writing iOS apps.

First, a lot of what you'll be doing is customizing and extending the behavior of framework classes. You customize and extend the behavior of these classes through *subclassing, delegation,* and using a powerful Objective-C feature called *declared properties.*

Second, on iPhone or iPad, like any other device, you create objects to do your bidding — which means that you allocate memory, which happens to be a scarce resource, particularly on relatively small mobile devices. Running out of memory is the main cause of apps crashing (not to mention being rejected from the App Store), so you need to understand *memory management.*

And finally, to know what message to send to what objects at what time, as well as what messages will be sent to your app at runtime, you need to understand the *application life cycle.*

Dealing with these three aspects of writing iOS apps is your pass to the Successful iOS Programmers' Society, and in this chapter, you start your initiation. And because you'll find all this stuff easier to understand if you understand the overall context, I begin with the application life cycle.

This chapter is enough to get you started and also keep you going as you develop your own iOS apps. It provides a frame of reference on which you can hang the concepts I throw around with abandon in upcoming chapters — as well as the groundwork for a deep enough understanding of the application life cycle to give you a handle on the detailed documentation. However, the full and definitive documentation is on `https://developer.apple.com/`.

So relax. Get yourself a cup of coffee (or something stronger if you want) and be prepared to be entertained.

Stepping Through the App Life Cycle

Although simple for the eventual user, the birth, life, and death of an app is a pretty complex process. In this section, I explain what happens throughout the time that the user launches the app from the Home screen, uses the app, and then stops using the app, either because she is done or decides to respond to an interruption such as an SMS message or phone call.

The life of an iOS app begins when a user launches it by tapping its icon on the Home screen. The system launches your app by calling its `main` function — which Xcode kindly lets you peek at if you go to the Project navigator, open the disclosure triangle next to the Supporting Files group, and select `main.m`.

The details of the implementation shown here may change, but the overall architecture will stay the same from one iOS version to another.

```
#import <UIKit/UIKit.h>
#import "AppDelegate.h"

int main(int argc, char *argv[])
{
  @autoreleasepool {
      return UIApplicationMain(argc, argv, nil, NSString
          FromClass([RTAppDelegate class]));
  }
}
```

The `main` function is where a program starts execution. This function is responsible for the high-level organization of the program's functionality and typically has access to the arguments given to the program when it gets executed.

The `main` function does only these two things:

1. Sets up an autorelease pool:

   ```
   @autoreleasepool {
   ```

   This is a piece of memory-management plumbing that you don't need to use in this book (other than here), or perhaps ever, but feel free to investigate on your own if you are interested.

2. Calls the `UIApplicationMain` function to create the application object and delegate and set up the event loop:

   ```
   return UIApplicationMain(argc, argv, nil,
               NSStringFromClass([AppDelegate class]));
   ```

   This is your entrance into the entire app startup process and its underlying architecture.

You may notice that with the exception of the `@autoreleasepool` directive, what you're looking at in `main` is C code. This is the bootstrap code that gets you into the world of Objective-C.

UIApplicationMain

The `UIApplicationMain` function creates the *application object* (a singleton — the only — `UIApplication` object) and the *application delegate* (a class created for you by the Xcode template). It also sets up the *main event loop,* including the app's *run loop* (which is responsible for polling input sources) and begins processing events.

In the following section, I explain the role of each of these elements in the application life cycle.

UIApplication provides application-wide control

The `UIApplication` object provides the application-wide control and coordination for an iOS app. It's responsible for handling the initial routing of incoming user events (touches, for example) as well as for dispatching action messages from control objects (such as buttons) to the appropriate target objects. The application object sends messages to its application delegate to allow you to respond in an application-unique way to occurrences such as application launch, low-memory warnings, and state transitions such as moving into background and back into foreground.

Delegation is a mechanism used to avoid subclassing complex UIKit objects, such as the UIApplication object. Instead of subclassing and overriding methods in a framework or other object, you go ahead and use that object unmodified and opt for putting your custom code inside a delegate object instead. As interesting events occur, the framework or other object sends messages to your delegate object. You use these methods to execute your custom code and implement the behavior you need. I explain the delegation pattern more in "The Delegation pattern" section, later in this chapter.

The Application Delegate object (the AppDelegate you see in the template) is responsible for handling several critical system messages and must be present in every iOS app. The object can be an instance of any class you like, as long as it adopts the UIApplicationDelegate protocol. In the template, you'll find that it's a subclass of UIResponder, which enables it to respond to and handle events. (UIApplication is also derived from UIResponder.)

The methods of this protocol correspond to behaviors that are needed during the application life cycle and are your way of implementing this custom behavior. Although you aren't required to implement all the methods of the UIApplicationDelegate protocol, you'll often find yourself writing code to handle the following:

- Initialization in your application delegate's application:didFinish LaunchingWithOptions: method.

- State transitions such as moving in and out of background and foreground. I explain these in more detail in the section "Knowing what to do when the normal processing of your application is interrupted," later in this chapter.

- Low-memory warnings, which I cover in the section "Observing Low-Memory Warnings," later in this chapter.

The UIApplication is a singleton object (there is just the one in an app). To get a reference to it, you send the sharedApplication message to the UIApplication class. (In Objective-C, you can send messages to classes, which are really objects on their own.) Sending the sharedApplication object the delegate message gives you a pointer to the delegate object:

```
AppDelegate *appDelegate =
            [[UIApplication sharedApplication] delegate];
```

You'll be doing that a lot, so much so, in fact, that it should become second nature to you.

UIApplicationMain loads the storyboard

If the application's `Info.plist` file specifies a storyboard file (or a main nib file), as RoadTrip's `Info.plist` file does, the `UIApplicationMain` function loads it. The app's `Info.plist` file provides a map to the high-level structure of the app.

To see the `RoadTrip-Info.plist` file, select RoadTrip-Info.plist under the Supporting Files heading in the Project navigator, as shown in Figure 6-1. The file dutifully appears in the Editor area.

A *nib* file is a resource file that contains the specifications for one or more objects and is used to graphically create your user interface using Interface Builder in apps when you've opted not to use a storyboard. (A storyboard consists of a series of linked nib files created for you; for more on storyboards, see Chapters 4 and 5.)

If you're using a storyboard, the initial view controller is instantiated for you. As you can see in the Attributes inspector in Figure 6-2, the Initial View Controller setting is a View Controller property. It is set for you by most of the Xcode templates. Note the check box in the View Controller attributes in the Utility area at the right of Figure 6-2. (You usually don't even have to think about it.) In the iPad storyboard file, the initial view controller is a Split view controller that was included by the template. The nib-loader will also instantiate both Navigation controllers as well as their Root view controllers. (I explain Navigation controllers and Root view controllers in Chapter 5.)

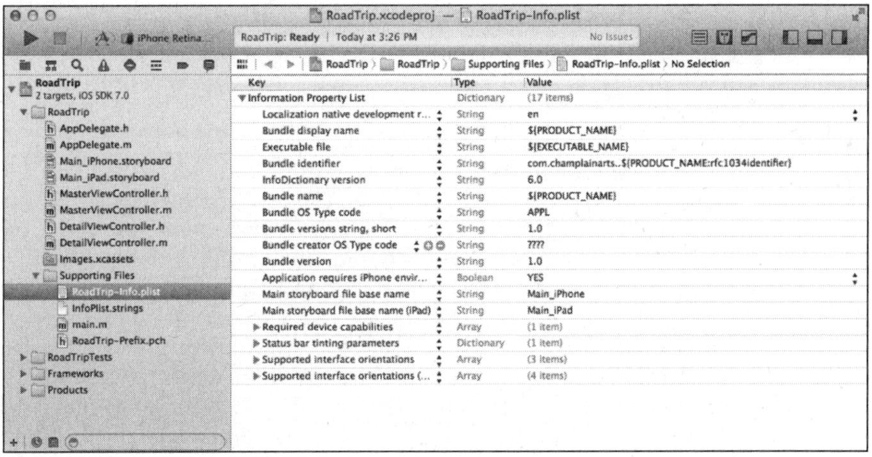

Figure 6-1:
The Road
Trip-
Info.
plist file.

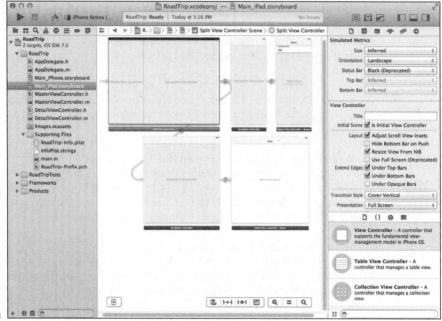

Figure 6-2:
The initial
view con-
troller is
specified
for the iPad
storyboard.

In the iPhone storyboard file, the initial view controller is a Navigation controller that uses a Table View controller as its root view controller.

UIApplication sends the application:didFinishLaunchingWithOptions: message to its delegate

If the method is implemented in the application delegate, the `application: didFinishLaunchingWithOptions:` message is sent to the application delegate.

Launch time is a particularly important point in an application's life cycle. In addition to the user launching an app by tapping its icon, an app can be launched to respond to a specific type of event. For example, it could be launched in response to an incoming push notification, it could be launched to open a file, or it could be launched to handle some background event that it had specified it wanted to handle (a location update, for example). In all these cases, an Options dictionary passed to the `application:didFinish LaunchingWithOptions:` method provides information about the reason for the launch. (An app launched by the system for a specific reason — other than the user tapping its icon — is beyond the scope of this book.)

The `application:didFinishLaunchingWithOptions:` message is sent to the delegate when the app has launched and its storyboard has been loaded. In this step, as you will see, you initialize and set up your app. At the time this message is sent, your app is in the inactive state. At some point after this method returns (completes) — unless your app does some kind of background processing — your app will become active and will receive the `applicationDidBecomeActive:` message when it *enters the foreground* (becomes the app that the user sees on the screen).

If you're thinking that somewhere in this startup process you should display your app's splash screen with a welcome message (and maybe some copyright mumbo-jumbo), forget about it. Ideally, you get your users directly into the app as quickly as possible without those outdated welcome screens. In fact, the way in which you do this is to provide one or more *launch images* that you typically place in your app's asset catalog. A launch image is the background of the first screen the user sees. An easy way to create them is to set a breakpoint in a viewDidLoad method for the first view the user will see. Stop the action just before you add any data to the view. At runtime, the launch image for the appropriate device and orientation will be presented immediately, and, if you look very carefully, you'll be able to see the content appear to be quickly placed on the background. In fact, as long as your launch image is the same size, shape, and general color of the live view, the illusion of putting content onto the background will succeed. In reality, you're simply presenting another view instead of the launch image.

The class interface (usually declared in the `.h` file) lists the messages to which an object of that class can respond. The actual code for implementing a message is called a method and will be found in the associated .m file. When you want to have an object execute a method, you send it a message. In other words, the message is *what* you want done, while the method is *how* to do it.

Your goal during startup is to present your app's user interface as quickly as possible — and quick initialization equals happy users. Don't load large data structures that your app won't use right away. If your app requires time to load data from the network (or perform other tasks that take noticeable time), get your interface up and running first and then launch the task that takes a longer time on a background thread. Then you can display a progress indicator or other feedback to the user to indicate that your app is loading the necessary data or doing something important.

In the templates that don't use a storyboard, the `application:didFinish LaunchingWithOptions:` method allocates and initializes the window and the Split view controller (as well as its initial view controllers), adds it all to the window, and makes the window visible.

In a storyboard-based app, this is all done by the storyboard for you, and the `application:didFinishLaunchingWithOptions:` method does nothing other than return `YES` (the usual return).

You would return `NO` only if your app was launched because another app opened a URL that's owned by your app and your app can't handle the URL.

You will be adding some code to this method in Chapter 8.

Handling events while your application is executing

Most events sent to an app are encapsulated in an event object — an instance of the `UIEvent` class. In the case of touch-related events, the event object contains one or more touch objects (`UITouch`) representing the fingers that are touching the screen. As the user places fingers on the screen, moves them around, and finally removes them from the screen, the system reports the changes for each finger in the corresponding touch object.

Distributing and handling events is the job of responder objects, which are instances of the `UIResponder` class. The `UIApplication`, `UIViewController`, `UIWindow`, and `UIView` classes (and your own `AppDelegate`) all inherit from `UIResponder`. After pulling an event off the event queue, the app dispatches that event to the `UIWindow` object where it occurred. The window object, in turn, forwards the event to its first responder, designated to be the first recipient of events other than touch events. In the case of touch events, the first responder is typically the view object (`UIView`) in which the touch took place. For example, a touch event occurring in a button is delivered to the corresponding button object.

If the first responder is unable to handle an event, it forwards the event to its next responder, which is typically a Parent view or view controller. If that object is unable to handle the event, it forwards it to its next responder, and so on until the event is handled. This series of linked responder objects is known as the *responder chain.* Messages continue traveling up the responder chain — toward higher-level responder objects, such as the window, the app, and the app's delegate — until the event is either handled or discarded.

The responder object that handles an event often sets in motion a series of programmatic actions by the app. The following list provides the chronology of what actually happens when the user taps something:

1. A touch event object is created in response to the user's tap.

   The touch of a finger (actually the lifting of a finger from the screen) adds a touch event to the app's event queue, where that event is *encapsulated* in — placed into, in other words — a UIEvent object. A UITouch object exists for each finger touching the screen, so that you can track individual touches. As the user manipulates the screen with her fingers, the system reports the changes for each finger in the corresponding UITouch object.

2. The run loop monitor dispatches the event.

   When something occurs that needs to be processed, the event-handling code of the UIApplication processes touch events by dispatching them to the appropriate *responder* object — the object that has signed up to take responsibility for doing something when a specific type of event happens (when the user touches the screen, for example). As mentioned previously, responder objects can include instances of UIApplication, UIWindow, and UIView (and any of its subclasses), as well as UIViewController (and any of *its* subclasses). All these classes inherit from UIResponder.

3. A responder object decides how to handle the event.

   For example, a touch event occurring with a button in a view is delivered to the button object. The button object handles the event by sending an action message to another object — in this case, the UIViewController object. This enables you to use standard button objects without having to muck about in their internals — you just tell the button what method you want to have invoked in your target (usually the view controller, as I explain in Chapter 9), and you're basically set.

   Processing the message may result in changes to a view, a new view altogether, or some other kind of change in the user interface. When one of these results occurs, the view and graphics infrastructure takes over and processes the required drawing events.

4. Your app then returns to the run loop.

   After an event is handled or discarded, app control passes back to the run loop. The run loop then processes the next event or puts the thread to sleep if it has nothing more to do.

But because your app isn't alone on the device, it can be interrupted by an SMS message, or the user touching the Home button. When your app is interrupted, you'll have to take care of some things before control is switched to another app.

Knowing what to do when the normal processing of your application is interrupted

On an iOS device, various events besides termination can interrupt your app to allow the user to respond — for example, calendar notifications or the user pressing the Sleep/Wake button — and your app moves into the *inactive state.* If the user chooses to ignore an interruption, your app moves back into the *active state* and continues running as before. If the user decides to tap the alert to deal with it (or if the interruption was from the user touching the Home button to switch out of your app), your app then moves into its *background state,* where it's suspended but remains in memory.

iOS sends you a number of messages to let you know exactly what's happening as well as to give you the opportunity to take actions such as save user data and *state information,* which means saving the point where the user was in the app. (If an app needs to continue running, it can request execution time from the system.) Because the app is in the background (running or suspended) and still in memory, relaunching is nearly instantaneous. An app's objects (including its windows and views) remain in memory, so they don't need to be re-created when the app relaunches. If memory becomes constrained, iOS may purge background apps to make more room for the foreground app.

Because these interruptions cause a temporary loss of control by your app, touch events are no longer sent to your app. When developing your app, you need to take this fact into account. For example, if your app is a game, you should pause the game when your game is interrupted. In general, your app should store information about its current state when it moves to the inactive state and be able to restore itself to the current state upon a subsequent relaunch.

In all cases, the sequence of events starts the same way — with the `applicationWillResignActive:` message sent to your app delegate when the app is about to move from active to inactive state. In this method, you should pause ongoing tasks, disable timers, throttle down OpenGL ES frame rates (that is, you should use this method to pause the game), and generally put things on hold.

What happens after this depends on a) the nature of the interruption, and b) how the user responds to the interruption. Your app may be either moved to the background or reactivated. I explain these occurrences next.

Before I do that, however, check out Figure 6-3, which shows the application life cycle and how interruptions are handled.

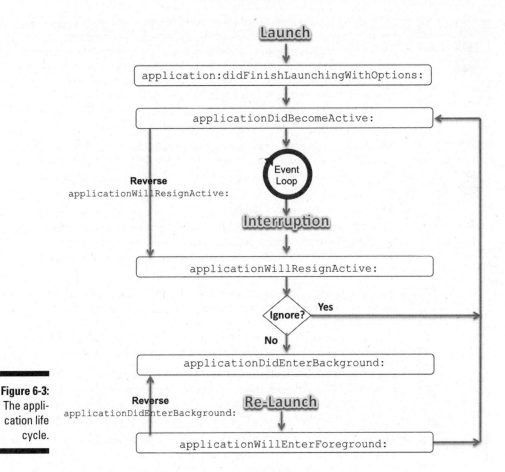

Figure 6-3:
The application life cycle.

If the user responds to the interruption (the SMS message, for example) or has launched another app, your app is moved to the background.

The next two bullets explain the messages your app can respond to after it's been moved into the background:

✔ **The** applicationDidEnterBackground: **message:** When your app first enters the background state, it's sent the applicationDidEnter Background: message. In this method, you should save any unsaved data or *state* (where the user is in the app — the current view, options selected, and stuff like that) to a temporary cache file or to the preferences database on disk. (Apple calls the iOS storage system a *disk* even though it is a solid-state drive.)

Even though your app enters the background state, you have no guarantee that it will remain there indefinitely. If memory becomes constrained, iOS will purge background apps to make more room for the foreground app. You need to do everything necessary to be able to restore your app in case it's subsequently purged from memory so that the next time the user launches your app, your app can use that information to restore your app to its previous state. You also have to do additional cleanup operations, such as deleting temporary files.

If your app is purged when it's in this suspended state, *it receives no notice that it's removed from memory.* That's why you need to save any data when you receive the `applicationDidEnterBackground:` message.

When your delegate is sent the `applicationDidEnterBackground:` method, your app has an undocumented amount of time to finish things up. If the method doesn't return before time runs out (or if your app doesn't request more execution time from iOS), your app is terminated and purged from memory.

If your app requests more execution time or it has declared that it does background execution, it's allowed to continue running after the `applic ationDidEnterBackground:` method returns. If not, your (now) background application is moved to the *suspended* state shortly after returning from the `applicationDidEnterBackground:` method.

If the app is in the background, it then may be relaunched. This can happen if the user selects the app from the Home screen or the multitasking bar, or it's launched by the system if the app processes events in the background or monitors a significant location change, for example.

✔ **The** `applicationWillEnterForeground:` **message:** When your app is relaunched from the background, it's sent the `applicationWillEn terForeground:` message. In this method, you need to undo what you did in the `applicationDidEnterBackground:` method.

If the user ignores the SMS message, or the app is relaunched from the background, your app is reactivated and starts getting touch and other events.

When your app is reactivated, it's sent the `applicationDidBecomeActive:` message.

You can use the `applicationDidBecomeActive:` method to restore the app to the state it was in before the interruption. Here you undo what you did in the `applicationWillResignActive` method, such as restart any tasks that were paused (or not yet started) while the app was inactive. If the app was previously in the background, you might need to refresh the user interface.

While an app is in the suspended state, the system tracks and coalesces (really *nets out*) events that might have an impact on that app when it relaunches. As soon as your app is up and running again, the system delivers those events to it. For most of these events, your app's existing infrastructure should just respond appropriately. For example, if the device orientation changed, your app's view controllers would automatically update the interface orientation in an appropriate way.

Apps are generally moved to the background when interrupted or when the user quits. But if the app was compiled with a very early version of the SDK, or is running on an early version of the operating system that doesn't sup- port multitasking — or if you decide that you don't want your app to run in the background and you set the `UIApplicationExitsOnSuspend` key in its `Info.plist` file — iOS terminates your app.

Even if your app supports multitasking (almost all do at this point), you must still be prepared for your app to be killed without any notification. The user can kill apps explicitly using the multitasking bar. In addition, if memory becomes constrained, the system might remove apps from memory to make more room. If it does remove your *suspended* app, *it doesn't give you any warning, much less notice after the fact!* However, if your app is currently running in the background state, the system does call the `applicationWillTerminate:` method of the app delegate.

When your application delegate is sent the `applicationWillTerminate:` message in nonmultitasking applications, or those running in the back- ground, you need to do the same kinds of things you do in `applicationDi dEnterBackground:`, except this time you do them knowing that your app won't be returning from the background.

Your `applicationWillTerminate:` method implementation has a limited (albeit undocumented) amount of time to do what it needs to do and return. Any longer than that and your app is terminated and purged from memory. (The Terminator doesn't kid around.)

An overview of the view controller life cycle

View controllers have a life cycle just as apps do, but I don't need to go into much detail about it here. The important part to know is certain messages that are sent as views are displayed and hidden.

The two methods you need to know about in order to work with views are the following:

- ✔ `viewDidLoad`
- ✔ `viewWillAppear:`

The `viewDidLoad` message is sent to your view controller. This message is sent after the view controller has loaded its associated views into memory. This method is used to perform additional view initialization on views loaded from the storyboard or nib file, and the message isn't *necessarily* sent every time the view appears. If, for example, the user makes a selection in the view that causes a new view controller to load and slide its view into place, and the user then taps the Back button, this message isn't sent when the originating view reappears. That's the job of `viewWillAppear:`.

The `viewWillAppear:` message is sent when the view is about to become visible. The first time it's sent is after the `viewDidLoad` message, and then whenever the view reappears, such as when you tap the Back button, for example. You use this method to do the things that are necessary to present the view. For example, if you are displaying the location of the nearest book store that carries *iOS App Development For Dummies*, update that information in this method.

Numerous other methods are also placed in the view controller for you as stubs. I leave you to explore them on your own.

Of course, aside from all this system stuff that happens, your app will be chugging along doing what the user wants it to do. And in responding to user requests, you'll create objects to do the user's bidding — which means that you allocate memory. And because memory is a scarce resource on iOS devices (and, indeed, on even the largest computers), you need to understand *memory management,* discussed in the next section.

Working within the Managed Memory Model Design Pattern

As powerful as it is, the iPhone — and even the iPad — are limited in resources, and the most critical of these resources is memory. To truly understand how to manage memory correctly in your app, you need to understand how the iOS memory works.

Understanding memory management

Whenever you (or a framework object) create an object using Objective-C, you allocate memory for the object. Although iOS devices and the Mac all use what's known as *virtual memory,* unlike the Mac, virtual memory in iOS is limited to the actual amount of physical memory. So when it begins to run low on memory, the Memory Manager frees memory pages that contain read-only content (such as code); this way, all it has to do is load the "originals" back into memory when they're needed. In contrast to what the Mac does, iOS doesn't temporarily store "changeable" memory (such as object data) to the disk to free space and then read the data back later when it's needed. This state of affairs limits the amount of available memory.

So as you can see, when one object is done using memory, it's critical that the memory be released for use by other objects.

If memory continues to be limited, the system may also send notifications to the running app, asking it to free additional memory. This is one of the critical events that all apps must respond to, and I explain this process in the section "Observing Low-Memory Warnings," later in this chapter.

In Objective-C, memory is managed in iOS apps by *reference counting* — keeping the system up-to-date on whether an object is currently being used. Read on for all the details.

Using reference counting

In fact, memory management is simply an exercise in counting. Every object has its own reference count, or *retain count,* which is the number of other objects that are currently using the object. As long as the retain count is greater than zero, the memory manager assumes that someone cares about that object and leaves it alone. When an object's retain count goes to zero, the memory manager knows that no one needs it anymore and sends the object a `dealloc` message, and after that, its memory is returned to the system to be reused.

That process sounds pretty straightforward, but how does the retain count get incremented and decremented? Until Xcode 4.2 and iOS 5.0, you had to manage the retain count in your app. When an object is created via `alloc` or `new` or through a `copy` or `mutableCopy` message (which creates a copy of an object but has subtleties beyond the scope of this book), the object's retain count is set to 1. When your app uses one of those methods, ownership is transferred to the object that sent the message — that is, the object has been retained and that object that sent the message becomes a nonexclusive *owner* of the object. *Ownership* here means that the object will be there to use until it's explicitly released by sending it a `release` message when it's no longer needed (although if other active owners exist, it wouldn't be deallocated until all of them have released it).

Before Xcode 4.2 and iOS 5.0, if you didn't create an object by one of those methods but you wanted to become an owner, thereby making sure that the object stayed around for you to use until you were done with it, it was up to you to send a `retain` message to increase the retain count, and when you were done, to send a `release` message. This was because the creator of the object (which caused the retain count to be set to 1) may have autoreleased it — sent an object a release message that will cause it to be released later (usually the next time the run loop is entered). This is useful in situations in which you want to relinquish ownership of an object but avoid the possibility of its being deallocated immediately (such as when you return an object from a method). In either instance, you were maintaining a pointer to the object so that it could be used.

Although this approach was simple in theory, it was a real headache for programmers. The vast majority of system crashes occurred because apps ran out of memory and were shut down by the system. In some of these cases, the app *didn't* respond to the memory warning methods and manage the low-memory warnings I explain in the section "Observing Low-Memory Warnings," later in this chapter.

Most of the time, however, even if the app responded to the low-memory warnings, it was limited to what it could do because the memory was *leaked*. Memory was actually available because some objects were not being used, but those objects' memory had not been released back to the system. In fact, there were no longer pointers to these objects (for a variety of reasons), so they *couldn't* be released and then deallocated and the memory reused.

Developers have had a number of ways to manage memory automatically. One is *garbage collection,* which scans through memory and releases objects that have no pointers to them. Garbage collection for Objective-C was available on the Mac (and for many other languages on other platforms), but garbage collection has a few problems. It can start up and pause your apps at the most inopportune time, and it affects performance and the user experience because you have no control, or any idea, when it will occur. It was never implemented on iOS and is deprecated beginning with OS X 10.8 (Mountain Lion).

Having to do all this memory management in your app has changed with the latest versions of the Objective-C compiler, which now comes with *automatic reference counting (ARC),* which is enabled by default whenever you create a project. (For more on options when creating a project, see Chapter 3.) ARC does for you in the compiler what you used to have to do on your own.

It handles all those `releases`, `autoreleases`, and `retains` for you. I tell you much more about ARC in the next section, but in a nutshell it's still about counting. The only difference is that Xcode and the compiler do the counting for you.

Automatic Reference Counting (ARC)

Automatic reference counting (ARC) is a compiler-level feature that simplifies the process of managing the lifetimes of Objective-C objects. Instead of you having to remember when to retain or release an object, ARC evaluates the lifetime requirements of your objects and automatically synthesizes the appropriate method calls at compile time. It isn't a new runtime memory model — and it isn't a garbage collector. All the action takes place in the compiler.

ARC takes care of the process of retaining and releasing objects by taking advantage of (and having the compiler enforce) naming conventions. It also relies on new object pointer ownership qualifiers (more on that later).

Lest you worry, ARC is actually much faster (has better performance) than doing memory management on your own.

ARC doesn't automate `malloc()` and `free()` (C functions I won't get into here) and doesn't automate `CoreFoundation` (CF) or `CoreGraphics` (CG). You'll be using some of those kinds of functions, and I talk about them in Chapter 10.

To be able to manage memory for you, ARC imposes some restrictions — primarily enforcing some best practices and disallowing some other practices. You won't have to worry about most of this in an app that was created to use ARC. You may see some things in non-ARC samples, but hopefully my discussion here will help you figure out how to work within the ARC restrictions.

In the following, I explain the rules that you have to follow to use ARC in your app.

> ✔ **Rule 1: Don't call the** `retain`, `release`, **or** `autorelease` **methods.** In addition, you can't implement custom `retain` or `release` methods.
>
> If you're new to Objective-C programming, this rule won't mean anything to you because it isn't something you'll have been doing in your existing apps. The only reason you'll need to know about this rule is to understand what non-ARC code is doing to manage memory. If you're an old hand, you'll have been using these methods, and you'll be happy to be told *not* to use them.

You can provide a custom implementation of `dealloc` if you need to manage other resources — but I don't have you do that for the example app developed in this book.

✔ **Rule 2: Don't store object pointers in C structures.** Because the compiler must know when references come and go, you can't store object pointers in `struct`s. For most readers, that won't be a problem because you'll be using objects rather than C structures.

✔ **Rule 3: Inform the compiler about ownership when using Core Foundation–style objects.** In iOS apps, you often use the `CoreFoundation` framework. An example is in Chapter 10, when you add sound to your app.

`CoreFoundation` objects are anything beginning with a `CF` — things like the address book functions, for example. A `CoreFoundation` object would look like this:

```
AudioServicesCreateSystemSoundID(
    (__bridge CFURLRef)burnRubberURL, burnRubberSoundID);
```

ARC doesn't automatically manage the lifetimes of `CoreFoundation` types, and there are `CoreFoundation` memory management rules and functions you can use, such as `CFRetain` and `CFRelease` (or the corresponding type-specific variants).

In this book, and most of the time, you don't have to worry about memory management because you usually will be casting an Objective-C object to a `CoreFoundation` type object, or vice versa — with the result that you end up with no `CoreFoundation` memory management in your code. You still have to let the compiler know about any memory management implications, though.

Again, in this book, and much of the time elsewhere, you simply tell ARC not to worry by using a `__bridge` cast. (You'll use a `__bridge` cast in Chapter 10.)

If you do have `CoreFoundation` memory management, macros such as `CFBridgingRetain` or `CFBridgingRelease` will transfer ownership between ARC and `CoreFoundation`. (This topic is beyond the scope of this book, however.)

✔ **Rule 4: Use the `@autoreleasepool` keyword to mark the start of an autorelease block.** This isn't something you'll be concerned about — or will ever do, for that matter. But it's a rule nonetheless.

✔ **Rule 5: Follow the naming conventions.** The compiler knows whether to retain an object based on what gets returned. Sometimes the object being returned by a method is retained, and sometimes it's autoreleased later. If the object is going to be autoreleased, the object needs to be retained. If it's already retained, you don't want the compiler to do anything.

The only way the compiler knows whether an object has been retained when it's returned is through certain naming conventions. Under ARC, these naming conventions are now part of the language, and you must follow them.

The compiler knows that a retained object has been returned when the first word in the first part of the *selector* (the method name) is `alloc`, `new`, `copy`, `mutableCopy`, or `init`. These methods transfer ownership — where *transferred ownership* means that the object has been retained for you. An example is the `NSString initWithFormat:` method. (Remember that "ownership" is not exclusive ownership: Several object may simultaneously own a single object.)

In addition, you can't give a property a name that begins with `new`.

✔ **Rule 6: Just follow the rules.** That's it — no retaining releasing or autoreleasing. Just follow the rules and code to your heart's content without worrying about memory management.

Except, of course, in some situations, you'll need to explicitly tell the compiler about what you want to do. In those cases, you'll have to tell the compiler explicitly about an object's lifetime. I explain how to do that in the next section.

Working with variable types according to ARC

Because the reference to an object lives in a variable, object pointers can be qualified using ownership type or lifetime qualifiers. These qualifiers determine when the compiler can deallocate an object to which a pointer points. These qualifiers are as follows:

```
__strong
__weak
__unsafe_unretained
__autoreleasing
```

The following sections describe the function of each of these qualifiers.

✔ `__strong` **variables retain their values.** `__strong` is the default. You almost never have to specify it, and all stack local variables, including parameters, are `__strong`. A `__strong` pointer to an object will cause that object to be retained while it's in scope (or not set to `nil`). No more *dangling references* (objects that have been deallocated that you expect to be there)!

✔ __weak **variables don't retain values.** _ weak variables don't cause an object to be retained (that is, you don't use them in the reference count) and are, in fact, set to nil (zeroed) as soon as the referenced object starts deallocating. You need to be concerned with these only to prevent retain cycles, which I explain shortly.

✔ __unsafe_unretained **variables don't retain values and aren't zeroed.** Some Apple-provided classes (only on the Mac and some third-party libraries) don't work with zeroing weak references. These have to be cleared in a dealloc method elsewhere.

TIP

Using ARC, __strong, __weak, and __autoreleasing stack variables are now implicitly initialized with nil.

✔ __autoreleasing **for indirect pointers.** These variables aren't for general use. They're used for out parameters that pass values back to the calling routine. They're retained and then autoreleased when they're read into, and are beyond the scope of this book.

Understanding the deadly retain cycle

ARC works very well to manage memory except in one circumstance. In this section, I explain how that circumstance can arise, and what you'll need to do to keep it from happening.

When you create an object, the compiler makes sure that ownership is transferred and all is well. The compiler will release that object when it goes out of scope, so if it's an instance variable, it will stay in scope until the object itself is deallocated.

I take you through this process using a little program called RetainCycle that I wrote to illustrate the retain cycle.

I create a new RetainIt object in the viewDidLoad method of my RetainCycleViewController object. It will be released only when the retainIt variable goes out of scope (it's __strong by default). In this case, it will be released and then deallocated (assuming that no other object takes ownership) at the end of viewDidLoad because the retainIt variable will go out of scope:

```
- (void) viewDidLoad
{
  [super viewDidLoad];
  RetainIt* retainIt = [[RetainIt new] init];
}
```

But when I create the `RetainIt` object, in the `RetainIt` class's initialization method, `init` (see the following), I create a `Cycle` object and assign it to the `cycle` instance variable I declared. As you might expect, the `Cycle` object will be retained until the `RetainIt` object is deallocated because it's referenced by an instance variable, which stays in scope until the object is deallocated:

```
- (id)init
{
  self = [super init];
  if (self) {
    self.cycle = [[Cycle new] init];
    cycle.retainIt = self;
  }
  return self;
}
```

I als   property a reference
bac   e this:

@

@   etainIt;

A

                                                    ocated until the Cycle
                                                    eallocated only when the

                                                    t actually can occur in real
                                                    the object that creates it
                                                    each with a strong refer-

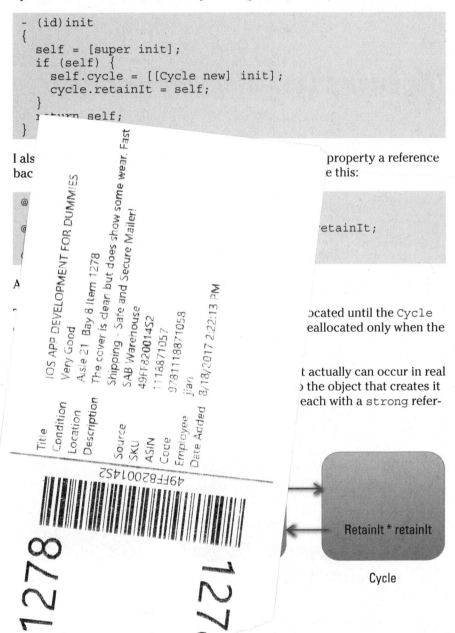

Figure
The re
c

RetainIt * retainIt

Cycle

The __weak lifetime qualifiers for objects take care of this. Although I haven't explained properties yet, the solution is to make the lifetime qualifier back pointer __weak.

```
@property (weak, nonatomic) RetainIt* retainIt;
```

I explain this more when I explain property attributes later in this chapter.

Observing Low-Memory Warnings

Even if you've done everything correctly, in a large app, you may simply run out of memory. When that situation occurs, the system dispatches a low-memory notification to your app — and it's something you must pay attention to. If you don't, it's a reliable recipe for disaster. (Think of your low-fuel light going on as you approach a sign on the highway that says, "Next services 100 miles.") UIKit provides several ways for you to set up your app so that you receive timely low-memory notifications:

- Override the didReceiveMemoryWarning methods in your custom UIViewController subclass.
- Implement the applicationDidReceiveMemoryWarning: method of your application delegate.
- Register to receive the UIApplicationDidReceiveMemoryWarningNotification: notification.

The didReceiveMemoryWarning method

The didReceiveMemoryWarning method is sent to the view controller when the app receives a memory warning. Your implementation of this method should do anything it can to reduce its use of memory. This may involve drastic steps such as actually closing views, but there are many other steps you can take that depend on your specific view controller and its views. For example, if you have stored data and objects, they may be able to be removed and set to nil if you can recreate them as needed.

The applicationDidReceive MemoryWarning: method

Your application delegate should set any references to objects it can safely free to nil.

The UIApplicationDidReceiveMemory WarningNotification: notification

Low-memory notifications are sent to the Notification Center, where all notifications are centralized. An object that wants to get informed about any notifications registers itself to the Notification Center by telling which notification it wants to be informed about, and a *block* (to be explained in Chapter 10) to be called when the notification is raised. Instead of a block, you can supply a target method to be called. A model object, for example, could then release data structures or objects it owns that it doesn't need immediately and can re-create later by setting references to nil. However, this approach is beyond the scope of this book.

For those of you who are curious, in your model object (which you create in Chapter 11), you could add the following:

```
[[NSNotificationCenter defaultCenter] addObserverForName:
   UIApplicationDidReceiveMemoryWarningNotification
   object:[UIApplication sharedApplication] queue:nil
   usingBlock:^(NSNotification *notif) {

       //your code here
       }];
```

You can test `applicationDidReceiveMemoryWarning:` and `UIApplicationDidReceiveMemoryWarningNotification:` in the Simulator by choosing Hardware⇨Simulate Memory Warning.

Picking the right memory-management strategy for your application

Each of these strategies gives a different part of your app a chance to free the memory it no longer needs (or doesn't need right now). How you actually get these strategies working for you depends on your app's architecture, so you'll have to explore that on your own.

Not freeing enough memory will result in iOS sending your app the `application WillTerminate:` message and shutting the app down. For many apps, though, the best defense is a good offense, which means you need to manage your memory effectively and eliminate any memory leaks in your code by following the ARC rules.

For testing, implement all of these methods and place NSLog statements in them along with breakpoints so that you can see the memory issues as they happen. It's easy to pinpoint places where you can free up memory, but it's most efficient to address the ones that provide the biggest bang for your programming buck.

Customizing the Behavior of Framework Classes

Although you'll be creating classes of your own (especially model classes), often you're going to want to customize the behavior of a particular framework class. You have three ways to go about it:

- ✔ Subclassing
- ✔ Delegating
- ✔ Declared properties

In this section, I'll cover the first two, and the third in the following section.

Subclassing

Objective-C, like other object-oriented programming languages, permits you to base a new class on a class that's already declared. The base class is called a *superclass;* the new class is its *subclass.* Each subclass that you define *inherits* methods and instance variables of its superclass.

Some framework classes are expected to be subclassed. Among them are view controllers, which you'll be subclassing quite a bit. In fact, there are some classes that are never instantiated directly: These are called *abstract* classes. Their subclasses can be instantiated directly: These are called *concrete* instances.

Almost all object-oriented programming languages support subclassing. However, there's a bit of a problem sometimes. It's called the *multiple inheritance* problem: it's when you want a class to be a subclass of two classes. There's no problem if both subclasses are in the class hierarchy. You could have a class called structure, a subclass called residential structure, and a subclass of both called house.

But what do you do if you want house to be a subclass both of structure and of investment? Read on.

The Delegation pattern

Delegation is a pattern used extensively in the iOS frameworks, so much so that, if you want to do any serious app development work, you're going to have to get your head around it. In fact, when you *do* understand it, your life will instantly become much easier to manage.

Delegation is a way of customizing the behavior of an object without sub-classing it. Instead, one object (a framework or any other object) delegates the task of implementing one of its responsibilities to another object. You're using a behavior-rich object supplied by the framework *as is* and putting the code for program-specific behavior in a separate (delegate) object. When a request is made of the framework object, the method of the delegate that implements the program-specific behavior is automatically called.

iOS frameworks rely heavily on the delegation pattern.

For example, the `UIApplication` object handles most of the actual work needed to run the app. But, as you saw, it sends your application delegate the `application:didFinishLaunchingWithOptions:` message to give you an opportunity to create model objects that are unique to your app.

When a framework object has been designed to use delegates to implement certain behaviors, the behaviors it requires (or gives you the option to implement) are defined in a *protocol*.

Protocols define an interface that the delegate object implements. In iOS, protocols can be formal or informal, although I concentrate solely on the former because formal protocols include support for things like type checking and runtime checking to see whether an object conforms to the protocol.

In a formal protocol, you usually don't have to implement all the methods; many are declared optional, meaning that you have to implement only the ones relevant to your app. Before a formal protocol attempts to send a message to its delegate, the host object determines whether the delegate implements the method (via a `respondsToSelector:` message) to avoid the embarrassment of branching into nowhere if the method isn't implemented.

A protocol can be adopted by any class as long as it implements the required methods of the protocol. Thus, by adopting one or more protocols and becoming a delegate, a single class can implement functionality from two other classes — it provides an approximation of multiple inheritance.

Understanding Declared Properties

Although properties and instance variable access and accessors are often mashed together in the minds of programmers, I want to make sure that you understand the unique nature of properties and how they really work.

Whereas *methods* are concerned with sending messages to objects to get things done, *properties* are concerned with the state of the objects. Frameworks and other objects behave based on what they find in their properties (hence you can modify object behavior by changing a property); for example, a button's background image is a property you set (indirectly, in Interface Builder) in Chapter 5.

You also may want to know something about the state of the object, such as its color, or about a window's Root view controller.

In Chapter 12, I discuss creating a model object — `Trip`. Your app's view controllers, which act as a bridge between the views and the model, need to be able to find the `Trip` object to get data and send it updates. All of this is done using properties. A property looks like the following:

```
@property (strong, nonatomic) IBOutlet UIImageView *car;
```

But not all properties are outlets. If you select the `RTAppDelegate.h` file in the Project inspector, you can see that it includes a `window` property:

```
@property (strong, nonatomic) UIWindow *window;
```

And in Chapter 11, you add a `trip` property to `RTAppDelegate`:

```
@property (nonatomic, strong) Trip *trip;
```

 As you can see, the order of the attributes (`strong, nonatomic` versus `nonatomic, strong`, which I explain in the later section "Setting attributes for a declared property") doesn't matter.

What comprises a declared property

A declared property has two parts: its declaration and its implementation.

The declaration uses the `@property` keyword, followed by an optional parenthesized set of attributes, the type information, and the name of the property.

Access to properties is implemented by accessor methods (although within the class that declares the property, the property can be accessed directly, just as instance variables are). You can write your own accessor methods or you can let the compiler do it for you. To do it yourself, you use the attributes in the upcoming "Setting attributes for a declared property" section.

The default names for the getter and setter methods associated with a property are *whateverThePropertyNameIs* for the getter and *setWhateverTheProperty NameIs:* for the setter. In the case of `trip`, the getter method is `trip`, and the setter method is `setTrip:`.

To access the `trip` property in the `appDelegate`, you would use

```
AppDelegate* appDelegate =
            [[UIApplication sharedApplication] delegate];
Trip* thisTrip = [appDelegate trip];
```

or to set that property, use

```
AppDelegate* appDelegate =
            [[UIApplication sharedApplication] delegate];
 [appDelegate setTrip:newTrip];
```

`delegate`, by the way is a `UIApplication` property.

Using dot syntax

Objective-C provides a dot (`.`) operator that offers an alternative to square bracket notation (`[ ]`) to invoke accessor methods. You use dot syntax in the same way you would when accessing a C structure element:

```
Trip* thisTrip = appDelegate.trip;
```

or to set that property, use

```
appDelegate.trip = newTrip;
```

When used with objects, however, dot syntax acts as "syntactic sugar" — it's transformed by the compiler into an accessor message. Dot syntax doesn't directly get or set an instance variable. The code examples using it are the exact equivalent to using the bracket notation.

Many programmers like the dot syntax because it may be more readable; just think of those bracket notation situations where you're accessing a property that is a property of another object (that itself is a property of another object, and so on). The real advantage of dot syntax, though, is that the compiler will generate an *error* when it detects an attempt to write to a read-only declared property. This is so much better than having to settle for an undeclared method *warning* because you invoked a nonexistent setter method, with the app subsequently failing at runtime.

When you use the compiler to create accessor methods for you, the compiler creates an instance variable of the type you have declared that it will then use to store and retrieve the property value with the name of the property. For example for the following property:

```
@property (weak, nonatomic) IBOutlet UIImageView *car;
```

the statement

```
@synthesize car;
```

generates an instance variable with the name of `car` of type `UIImage`.

However, if you let the compiler automatically generate an `@synthesize` statement for you, it actually uses an instance variable name beginning with an underscore character, so you would get the following code generated for you behind the scenes:

```
@synthesize car = _car;
```

This allows you to distinguish between the property name (accessed by `self.car`) and the instance variable name (accessed simply as `_car`).

Apple recommends that you use the property reference (`self.car`) in normal methods, but use the `_car` variable in `init` methods. This applies only to the code within a `.m` file. Code elsewhere in your app accesses the property as it is declared in the `@interface` section of the .h. There is no way that code anywhere in the app except in the .m file of a class can access the instance variable directly when you let the compiler do the work. And that's a good thing to ensure that encapsulation is properly provided.

Setting attributes for a declared property

I mention earlier in this chapter that you can set certain property attributes when you declare a property. I cover some of those attributes in this section.

Setter semantics/ownership

These properties specify how instance variable storage should be managed (see the earlier section "Working with variable types according to ARC" for more):

- ✔ `strong` (similar to `retain`, which was used previous to ARC) creates an accessor method that means that the object this property points to will be retained while it is in scope (or until it's set to `nil`). This is the default value.

- ✔ `weak` (similar to `assign`, which was used previous to ARC) creates an accessor that uses simple assignment. You typically use this attribute for scalar types such as `NSInteger` and `CGRect`, or (in a reference-counted environment) for objects you don't own — delegates, for example — and to avoid retain cycle problems, as I explain in "Understanding the deadly retain cycle," earlier in this chapter.

- ✔ `copy` specifies that a copy of the object should be used for assignment. The previous value is sent a `release` message.

  The copy is made by invoking the `copy` method. This attribute is valid only for object types, which must implement the `NSCopying` protocol (and is beyond the scope of this book).

For object properties, you must explicitly specify one of the types listed previously; otherwise, you get a compiler warning. So you need to think about what memory management behavior you want, and type the behavior explicitly.

Writability

The following attributes specify whether a property has an associated set accessor. They are mutually exclusive.

- ✔ `readwrite` indicates that the property should be treated as read/write. This attribute is the default. The getter and setter methods are synthesized automatically.

- ✔ `readonly` indicates that the property is read-only. Only a getter method is synthesized. If you implement your own accessors, only a getter method is required. If you attempt to assign a value using the dot syntax, you get a compiler error.

Accessor method names

You'll remember that the default names for the getter and setter methods associated with a property are `propertyName` and `setPropertyName:`, respectively. For example, for the property `trip`, the accessors are `trip` and `setTrip:`. You can, however, specify custom names instead. They're both optional and can appear with any other attribute (except for `readonly` in the case of `setter =`):

- `getter = getterName` specifies the name of the `get` accessor for the property. The getter must return a type matching the property's type and take no parameters.

- `setter = setterName` specifies the name of the `set` accessor for the property. The setter method must take a single parameter of a type matching the property's type and must return `void`.

Typically, you should specify accessor method names that are key-value coding compliant (which is beyond the scope of this book). A common reason for using the getter decorator is to adhere to the `isPropertyName` convention for Boolean values. If you have a Boolean property called `alphabetized` that you use to keep track of how an array of names is sorted, the default getter would be `alphabetized`. Using the naming convention, you would create an accessor method called `isAlphabetized`, which is a bit clearer.

Atomicity

You can use this attribute to specify that accessor methods aren't `atomic`. (No keyword denotes `atomic`.) This has to do with concurrency issues that are way beyond the scope of this book. If you specify `nonatomic`, a synthesized accessor for an object property simply returns the value directly. Otherwise, a synthesized `get` accessor for an object property uses a lock and retains and autoreleases the returned value. You use `nonatamic` throughout this book.

Writing your own accessors

You don't have to use the accessors generated by the compiler; and, sometimes, it even makes sense to implement them yourself (although such times don't arise in this book). If you implement the accessor methods yourself, you should make sure that your approach matches the attributes you've declared. (For example, if you specify `copy`, you must make sure that you do copy the input value in the setter method.)

For example, if you have a lot of overhead to create an object that might not be used, you can create your own getter accessor that creates the object the first time it's accessed. In addition, writing your own accessor means you don't have to have an instance variable associated with the property. You could, for example, have an `area` property on a object representing a rectangle. The getter for `area` might perform `length x width` and never bother with an instance variable.

Accessing instance variables with accessors

If you don't use `self`, you access the instance variable directly. In the following example, the `set` accessor method for `_currentDestinationIndex` isn't invoked:

```
_currentDestinationIndex = [[NSUserDefaults
  standardUserDefaults]objectForKey:CurrentDestinationKey];
```

The preceding isn't the same as

```
self.currentDestinationIndex = [[NSUserDefaults
  standardUserDefaults]objectForKey:CurrentDestinationKey];
```

To use an accessor, you must use `self`.

Hiding Instance Variables

When properties were first developed, they were looked at as a way to avoid the tedium of writing accessors for instance variable-based properties.

People used to think about properties as a way to access instance variables. In fact, instance variables shouldn't be equated to properties, and more important, instance variables shouldn't be made public. (Doing so violates the object-oriented principle of encapsulation, but that's a conversation for a different time.) In fact, Apple's new approach is to put instance variable declarations in the implementation file of the class.

Xcode 4.2 came about, we declared instance variables in the header file in the `@interface` class declaration. In the old times, you would've added the following bolded code to the `TestDriveController.h` file:

```
@interface TestDriveController : UIViewController
                    <DestinationControllerDelegate> {

    AVAudioPlayer *backgroundAudioPlayer;
    SystemSoundID burnRubberSoundID;
    BOOL touchInCar;
}
```

This approach made instance variables (`ivars`) visible to everyone and everything and was, as I mentioned, at odds with the principle of encapsulation (even if the variables couldn't be accessed).

Starting with Xcode 4.2, you can now hide instance variables by declaring them in the implementation file in one of two ways. The first is as a *class extension,* which you create by adding a second interface section in the implementation file followed by open and close parentheses:

```
@interface TestDriveController () {

  AVAudioPlayer *backgroundAudioPlayer;
  SystemSoundID burnRubberSoundID;
  BOOL touchInCar;
}
@end
```

The second way is by declaring the instance variable in the @ implementation block of the class:

```
@implementation TestDriveController

AVAudioPlayer *backgroundAudioPlayer;
SystemSoundID burnRubberSoundID;
BOOL touchInCar;
```

A class extension is a variation of an Objective-C category, which is beyond the scope of this book.

The approach you use is your choice; I prefer the class extension because I think it makes the variables easier to distinguish.

You can also use class extensions to have a publicly declared set of methods and then declare additional methods for use solely by the class:

```
@interface TestDriveController () {

  AVAudioPlayer *backgroundAudioPlayer;
  SystemSoundID burnRubberSoundID;
  BOOL touchInCar;
}
- (void) privateMethod;
        @end
```

These methods are not really private, but are not visible in the header file. They are "private APIs."

Chapter 7

Working with the Source Editor

. . . .

In This Chapter

▶ Using the Standard source editor to add code

▶ Fixing syntax errors as you code

▶ Getting the help you need from the documentation and other forms of help

▶ Searching and finding symbols

. . . .

You may be chomping at the bit to write code, but that's exactly what you've been doing ever since Chapter 2. (Chapter 1 was an introductory overview, as you may recall.) You've started building a storyboard for your app's interface — that was writing code just as much as typing `print "Hello World"` is. You've configured your project's settings with the graphical user interface tools of Xcode — that, too, is writing code.

But typing code into an editor is still a major part of the developer's work, and in this chapter, you'll look at the source code editing features of Xcode.

In this chapter, I tell you how to navigate the files in your project using the Jump bar and the navigators, as well as how to work with the source editor to enter code. And for when you are confused, or simply just curious, I explain how to access the documentation and Xcode's Help system. This chapter finishes the explanation on how to use Xcode.

Navigating in the Xcode Source Editors

In previous chapters, I give you quite a bit of information about the Xcode Workspace, albeit primarily focusing on storyboards. I mention the Assistant as well, and in this chapter, I want to extend that knowledge and describe most of the rest of the tasks you need to be able to do in Xcode.

As you've seen, most development work in Xcode is done in the Editor area, the main area that's always visible within the Workspace window. The Editor area can also be further configured, with the Standard editor pane always shown, as well as one or more optional Assistant panes that show related content. (If you select an interface [.h] header file, the Assistant pane can automatically show the corresponding implementation [.m] code file, and vice versa; I don't talk about the Version pane, but showing that area is also an option.) I use the term *pane* (Standard editor *pane* and Assistant *pane*) to refer to certain configurations. I do this to distinguish between the *Editor area* configuration (the Standard editor isn't actually an editor at all, but simply a single pane configuration in the editor area) and the built-in *editors* — an editor operates in an *Editor area.* The main editors are the following:

- ✔ **Source editor:** You use this editor to write and edit your source code, as well as to set and enable (or disable, for that matter) breakpoints as well as to control program execution.

- ✔ **Project editor:** With this editor, you view and edit project and target settings, such as build options, target architectures, and code signing characteristics.

- ✔ **Core Data Model editor:** If you use Core Data, you can design your data model for tables and relationships graphically. The Core Data Model editor also can convert your graphical representation of your data model to Objective-C code. Core Data is outside the scope of this book, but the Core Data model editor is definitely worth exploring.

- ✔ **Interface Builder:** Here, you graphically create and edit user interface files in storyboards and .xib files.

The editor you use is determined by what you have selected in the Project navigator. An editor pane appears for that (selected) item in the Editor area.

So far, you've worked primarily in the Interface Builder editor, but when you code, you do the bulk of your work in the source editor in the Standard editor pane, with some forays, as needed, in the Assistant editor pane and an occasional excursion into the Utility area as well.

As described earlier in the book, you use the View selector in the Workspace toolbar to hide or show the Navigator, Debug, and Utility areas. (To review the Xcode workspace landscape, see Chapter 2.) If you like, you can hide the other areas and see just the source editor (and perhaps the Assistant).

Figure 7-1 shows the Project navigator. Because I selected MasterView Controller.m, you see the *source editor* displaying that file in the Standard editor pane. (If you were to select one of the storyboard files in the Project navigator, you'd see Interface Builder as your editor of choice; that's the editor I highlight in Chapter 5.) In Figure 7-1, I also selected the Assistant in the Editor selector and split the panes using the split controls ("+" icon at the far right in the Jump bar).

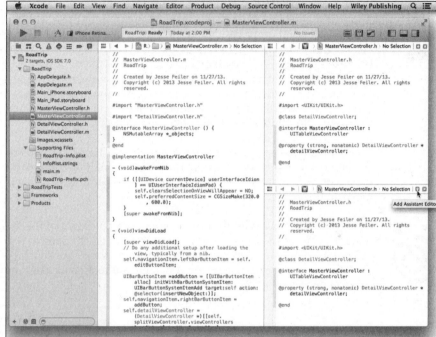

Figure 7-1:
The source
editor with
Standard
and
Assistant
editor
panes.

Notice that when I selected the Assistant, the `MasterViewController.h`
file opened. That's because the Assistant editor pane automatically (depending how you have set it — see the next section) shows the related content for
whatever I select in the Project navigator so that you can edit both easily. You
then see `MasterViewController.m` (the implementation code file) in the
Standard source editor pane and `MasterViewController.h` (the header
file) in the Assistant editor pane. Clicking the split control (the + at the right
of the jump bar) opens a second pane in the Assistant editor pane as well,
giving you a total of three panes.

The Standard editor pane (the left editor pane, or the top one if you have a
horizontal split) is the one that's affected by changing your selection in the
Project navigator.

The interface (`.h`) header file defines the class's interface by specifying the
following:

✔ **The class declaration (and what it inherits from)**

✔ **Methods**

✔ **Any *instance variables* (that is, variables defined in a class)**

✔ **Declared properties**

In recent updates to Xcode and the sample code on developer.apple.com, Apple has rejiggered the world of variables and properties with regard to classes. Declared properties are preferred to instance variables because they can contain more information than just the type and name of a variable and because their accessors can further encapsulate the data. However, instance variables rather than properties are often more appropriate for scalars such as `ints` and `floats`. In addition, declaring instance variables as well as properties in a class extension in the implementation file further keeps them out of the way so that they are not visible to other classes.

The implementation (`.m`) code file, on the other hand, contains the code for the class, which includes each method definition. It also can contain a class extension with instance variable and property declarations. See Chapter 6 for more on this topic.

By default, the Assistant editor pane appears to the right of the source editor pane. To change the orientation of the Assistant editor pane to the source editor pane, choose View⇨Assistant Editor and then choose a layout. If the header file doesn't appear for you, navigate to it using the Jump bar, as explained in the next section.

Using the Jump bar

A Jump bar appears at the top of each Editor area pane to provide an alternative way to navigate through the files and symbols in your project. You can use the Jump bar to go directly to items at any level in the Workspace.

A *Jump bar* is an interactive, hierarchical mechanism for browsing items in your workspace. Each editor area includes a Jump bar, as do Interface Builder and the documentation organizer. The configuration and behavior of each Jump bar is customized for the context in which it appears.

The active pane is indicated by slightly darker arrows in the Jump bar. Experiment for yourself and you'll soon notice the difference. It's subtle enough that it's not easy to distinguish on the screenshots in this book.

The Standard editor Jump bar

The Standard editor Jump bar has the *basic configuration,* which includes the following:

- ✔ **Context-related items:** Click the Related Items menu (represented by an icon showing a cluster of tiny rectangles on the far left side) to see additional selections relevant to the current context, such as recently opened files or the interface (`.h`) header file for an implementation (`.m`) code file you're editing.

✔ **Previous and Next buttons:** These are the left- and right-arrow buttons on the left side of the Jump bar. You use these to step back and forth through your navigation history just as you would with a web browser.

✔ **A hierarchical path menu:** This menu shows the same structure that you see in the Project navigator, down to individual files and the symbols inside the files. The path you would see in the source editor in the Standard editor pane is shown in Figure 7-2.

The hierarchical path menu lets you quickly choose a file. For example, in Figure 7-3, I get an overview of all the RoadTrip files when I select the RoadTrip project in the hierarchical path menu.

Selecting the last item in the hierarchical path menu provides a list of all the symbols in that file, as shown in Figure 7-4.

Hierarchical path menu

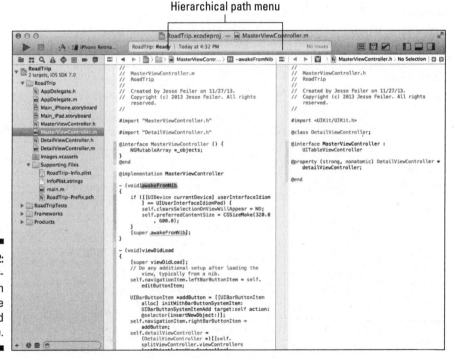

Figure 7-2:
The hierarchical path menu in the Standard editor pane.

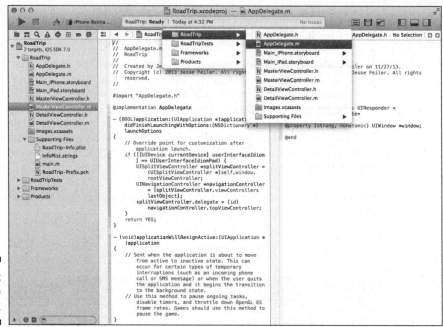

Figure 7-3:
A file
hierarchy.

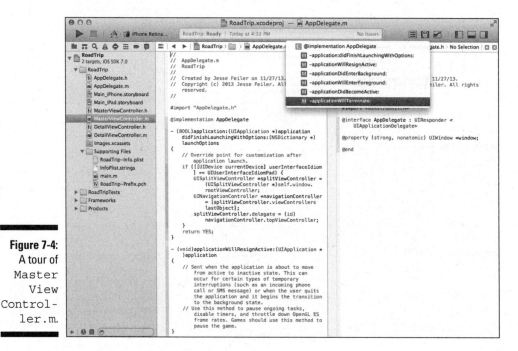

Figure 7-4:
A tour of
Master
View
Control-
ler.m.

The Assistant modes and the Jump bar

When you use the Assistant, you'll find that the Jump bar differs somewhat from the Jump bar of the Standard editor. The Assistant's Jump bar has two modes: Tracking (or Automatic) mode and Manual mode:

✔ **Manual mode:** You select the file to display in the Assistant pane on your own, rather than have the Assistant choose for you. (As mentioned previously, you can also split the Assistant editor pane to create multiple assistant editors.)

✔ **Tracking mode:** As you can see in Figure 7-5, you can automatically see the counterpart files (.h files for .m files and vice versa), the interface files, and other related files. This can be a great time-saver because most of the files you are probably looking for are only a click away.

Hold down the Option key when selecting an item in the Project navigator to open the Assistant and display that item in the Assistant editor pane.

If you have any questions about what something does, just position the mouse pointer above the icon; a tooltip appears to explain it.

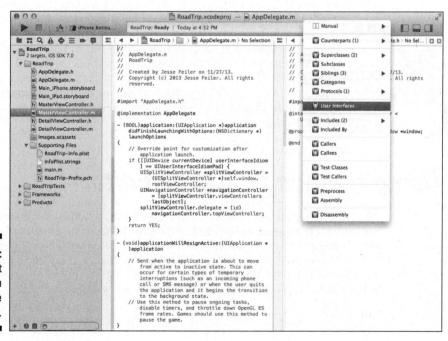

Figure 7-5: Assistant options in the source editor.

Organizing your code using the #pragma mark statement

While you're here, this is a good time to introduce the `#pragma mark` statement. If you look in `DetailViewController.m`, you can see how this statement can be used to group things in your file; such statements are also displayed in the list of symbols.

You use the `# pragma mark` statement with a label (such as `View life cycle` or `Animation`) to add a category header in the Methods list so that you can identify and keep separate the methods that fit logically in the list.

For example, in the `DetailViewController` template, I added

```
#pragma mark - Managing the detail item
```

The first part of the statement (with a space and a dash) places a horizontal line in the Methods list. The second one places the text "Managing the detail item" in the Methods list.

This is a useful trick for finding code sections, organizing your code, and adding new code in the proper sections.

Some sections for your code are easy to identify, but, as you'll see in some of the sample code on `http://developer.apple.com`, developers differ as to how they organize their code. Should `viewDidLoad` go in a section called User Interface or Initialization? Do whatever makes the most sense to you. It's probably a good idea to stick with the code sections in the templates and sample code at least to start.

Using the Xcode Source Editor

The main tool you use to write code for an iOS app is the Xcode source editor, which appears as the Standard editor pane in the editor area on the right side of the Xcode Workspace window after you select a source code file in the Project navigator. It also appears as the Assistant editor in a second pane if you click the Assistant Editor button — the middle Editor selector button in the top-right corner of the Workspace window.

Apple has gone out of its way to make the source editor as useful as possible by including the following:

- ✔ **Code completion:** Code completion is a feature of the editor that shows symbols — arguments, placeholders, and suggested code — as you type statements. Code completion can be really useful, especially if you're like me and forget exactly what the arguments are for a function. When code completion is active (as it is by default), Xcode uses the text you typed — as well as the context within which you typed it — to provide inline suggestions for completing what it thinks you're going to type. You can accept inline suggestions by pressing Tab or Return. You can also see a pop-up list of suggestions while typing; move up and down the list with the up and down arrows. Press Return to use the selected completion. Press the Esc key, or Control+spacebar, to cancel a code completion operation. You can turn off code completion, or set options for code completion, by choosing Xcode⇨Preferences and clicking the Text Editing tab.

- ✔ **Automatic indenting, formatting, and closing braces:** As I explain in Chapter 3 in the section on preferences, the source editor indents the text you type according to rules you can set in the Text Editing preferences pane. It also uses fonts and colors for the various syntax elements (variables, constants, comments, and so on) according to the settings in the Fonts & Colors pane of Xcode preferences. As for closing braces, anytime you type an opening brace ({) and then press Return, Xcode automatically adds a closing brace (}) — unless you've deactivated the Automatically Insert Closing "}" option in the Text Editing preferences.

- ✔ **Code folding in the Focus ribbon:** With code folding, you can collapse code that you're not working on and display only the code that requires your attention. You do this by clicking in the Focus ribbon column (see Figure 7-6) to the left of the code you want to hide (between the gutter, which can display line numbers and breakpoints, and the editor). A disclosure triangle appears, and clicking it hides or shows blocks of code. Notice that in Figure 7-6, the code inside `awakeFromNib` has been folded up.

- ✔ **Opening a file in a separate window:** Double-click the file in the Project navigator to open the file in its own window.

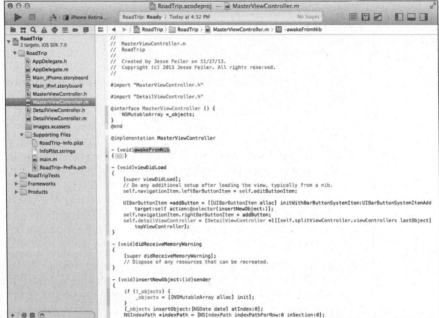

Figure 7-6:
The Gutter
and Focus
ribbon.

Using Live Issues and Fix-it

The Apple LLVM compiler engine wants to be your best friend, so *Live Issues* continuously evaluates your code in the background and alerts you to coding mistakes. Before this feature came along, you had to build your app first, and trust me, this new way saves lots of time and effort.

But not only is Live Issues happy to point out your mistakes (like someone else I know, but I won't go there), *Fix-it* will also offer (when it can) to fix the problem for you. Clicking the error displays the available Fix-its, such as correcting an assignment to a comparison, repairing a misspelled symbol, or appending a missing semicolon. With a single keyboard shortcut, you can instantly have the error repaired, and you can continue coding. Fix-it marks syntax errors with a red underline or a caret at the position of the error and with a symbol in the gutter.

For example, in Figure 7-7, the semicolon is missing after the [super viewDidLoad] statement. (Notice the error indicator — the red stop sign with exclamation point — in the Activity viewer along with the red circle in the gutter at the left of the offending line of code.) Clicking the red circle in the gutter at the left will automatically fix this problem. This is a very useful feature and will cut down your debugging time significantly (especially if you actually use it).

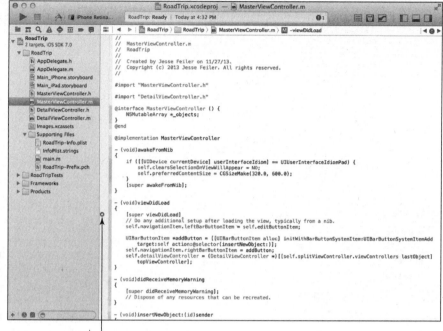

Figure 7-7:
Live Issues
and Fix-it.

The Fix-it error indicator

Compiler warnings

Although Xcode and the compiler working together are very good at giving you warnings and errors, sometimes they're a little slow on the uptake when you actually get around to fixing the problem. So don't be surprised by random warnings and errors, especially if the compiler for some reason can't find the header file.

If you see a warning or error that you're just sure you've fixed, you can click the Run button. Xcode and the compiler will reset, and the warning will go away. (Unless, of course, it was right all along and you hadn't fixed the problem.)

The Issue navigator

The Issue navigator is one of the navigators provided by Xcode. The error displayed in Figure 7-7, shown previously, also appears in the Issue navigator, as shown in Figure 7-8.

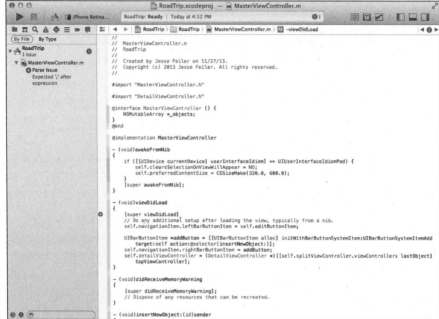

Figure 7-8:
An error
message
displayed
by the Issue
navigator.

 To get to the Issue navigator, you select it in the Navigator selector bar.

If, in spite of Live Issues and Fix-it (or any other) warnings, you decide to compile the program, the Issue navigator will automatically launch for you.

The Issue navigator displays the error and warning messages generated in a Project or Workspace and is similar to the other navigators you've used so far.

When you select a warning or error in the Issue navigator, an editor displays the item with the issue, and if the error occurs in a source file, the issue message is placed on the line of code with the issue.

 Place the pointer over an issue message that ends with an ellipsis (which appears if the pane is too narrow to display the entire message) to get a complete description of the issue.

You can display issues by file or by type using the buttons on the Scope bar at the bottom of the navigator pane (refer to Figure 7-7), filter the issue list with the Filter bar, and even step through issues using the Issue stepper in the Jump bar. Use the Next and Previous buttons in the Jump bar to jump to the previous and next issues.

As you may recall from Chapter 3, I changed Xcode preferences to have the Issue navigator displayed and a sound played when a build fails.

Accessing Documentation

The ability to quickly access documentation is a major feature of Xcode, and one you'll want to use regularly. If you have no idea how to do something, or how something works, you can often find the answer in the documentation.

Being able to figure out what's going on will make your life easier. You saw that Xcode will complete your code for you, which is useful when you can't quite remember the method signature and parameters, but what if you don't even have a clue?

Or like many developers, you may find yourself wanting to dig deeper when it comes to a particular bit of code. That's when you'll really appreciate things like Xcode's Quick Help, the Documentation and API Reference pane in the Help menu, and the Find tools. With these tools, you can quickly access the documentation for a particular class, method, or property.

Getting Xcode help

To see how easy it is to access the documentation, say that you've selected `MasterViewController.m`. What if you wanted to find out more about `UITableViewController`, the super class of `MasterViewController`?

 The Quick Help section of the Utility area provides documentation for a single symbol. (To see the Utility area, click the rightmost View selector button in the top-right corner of the Workspace window and select the second button in the Inspector selector bar.) In an editor, click anywhere in the symbol or select the entire symbol, as shown in Figure 7-9.

The Quick Help section of the Utility area shows a description of the symbol and provides links to more information. For example, you can click the `UITableViewController` Class Reference link near the bottom of the Quick Help section (refer to Figure 7-9) to bring up the class reference definition in a Documentation window, as shown in Figure 7-10. I use class references a lot!

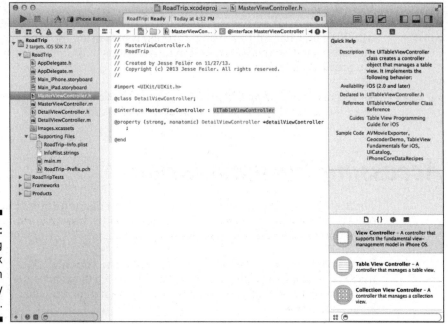

Figure 7-9:
Accessing
the Quick
Help section
of the Utility
area.

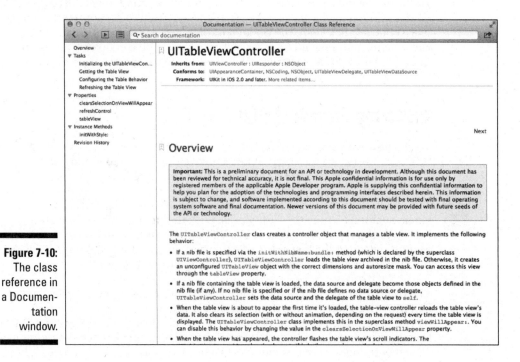

Figure 7-10:
The class
reference in
a Documen-
tation
window.

With the Quick Help section open, information is available for three types of elements in your project, depending on your selection in the open editor:

- ✔ **Symbols,** in the source editor
- ✔ **Interface objects,** in Interface Builder
- ✔ **Build settings,** in the Project editor

It may be more convenient to use a Quick Help window if, for example, you prefer to work with the Utility area hidden. To do so, press Option and click Symbols in the source editor.

As you can see in Figure 7-11, a Quick Help window appears with the pointer indicating the item you selected (in this case, the symbol `UITableViewController`):

If you're like me and want to go directly to the class reference, press Option and double-click the symbol instead.

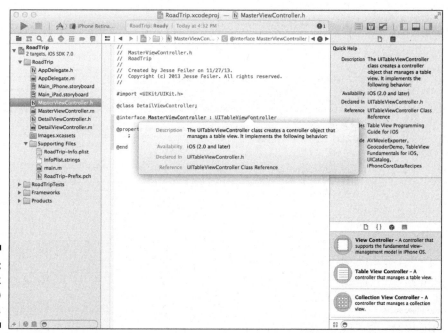

Figure 7-11:
The Quick Help window.

The Organizer window

You can have only one Organizer window (shown in Figure 7-12). You use the organizers in this window to manage the development resources such as devices (for testing), projects, and archives.

To display the Organizer window, choose Organizer from the Window menu. The window includes three individual organizers, whose tasks I describe in the following list:

- ✔ **Devices organizer:** Lets you provision a device, manage your developer profile, install iOS on the device, and work with your app and its data. This organizer is present only if the iOS SDK is installed.

- ✔ **Projects organizer:** Lets you find, view, and manage an open project or Workspace, its derived data, and its snapshots. Note that a project organizer lets you managed derived data — that consists of data that doesn't have to be recompiled each time. The Delete button lets you delete a set of derived data. It's a bit like a "Super Clean" button to force everything to be recompiled.

- ✔ **Archives organizer:** Lets you view and manage build product archives resulting from your distribution scheme.

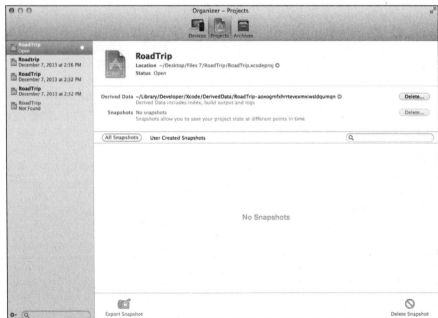

Figure 7-12:
The
Organizer
window.

Each of these organizers includes task-oriented contextual help articles that you can view by choosing the Organizer and clicking in its content pane while pressing Control.

I explain a bit more about some of the other organizers as you use them in upcoming chapters.

The Help menu

The Help menu's search field (in the Xcode menu bar) also lets you search Xcode Help, the Xcode User Guide, and Documentation and API Reference. You can also choose Quick Help for *Selected Item,* which displays a Quick Help panel above the selected symbol in the editor.

Finding and Searching in Your Project

You'll find that, as your classes get bigger, sometimes you'll want to find a symbol or some other text in your project. Xcode provides a number of ways to do that.

Using the Find command to locate an item in a file

Need to track down a single symbol or all occurrences of a symbol in a file or class? You can easily locate what you're looking for by using the Find menu or pressing ⌘+F, which opens a Find toolbar above the Editor pane to help you search the file in the editor.

The Find menu has 15 find-and-replace submenus. The keyboard equivalent ⌘+F opens a find-and-replace bar above the Editor pane. They are not the same.

For example, as shown in Figure 7-13, I entered **viewDidLoad** in the Find toolbar. Xcode found two instances of viewDidLoad in the source editor and highlighted them. (Admittedly, the first highlight is a tad darker.)

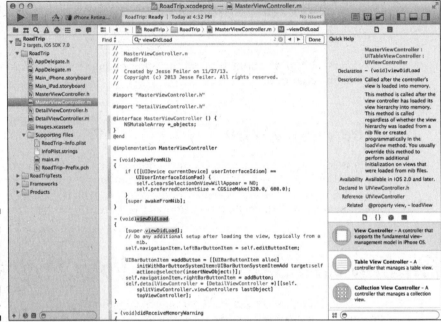

 You can jump from one instance to the next by pressing ⌘+G. Or you can use the Previous and Next buttons (left and right arrows) on the Find bar.

Click the Find pop-up menu on Find toolbar and choose Replace to do a file-level replace.

Click the magnifying glass in the Search field in the Find toolbar to display a menu that allows you to show or hide the Find options. For example, you can choose to ignore or match the case of the text in the Search field. Changes you make to this set of options remain persistent for future searches.

Using the Search navigator to search your project or framework

 Whereas the Find command works for locating an item in a file or class, you use the Find navigator (the third button from the left in the Navigator selector) to find items in your project or even frameworks. You can use Shift+Command+F as a handy keyboard shortcut for the Find command in the Workspace menu item, which also opens the Find navigator pane.

In Figure 7-14, I entered **viewDidLoad** in the Find field. I also clicked the magnifying glass in the Find field to display search options. (Clicking in the Find pop-up menu will also let you choose Replace to perform a global replace.)

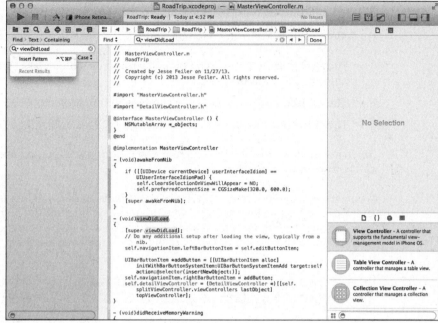

Figure 7-14:
The Search
navigator
shows a
specific
use of the
search term
in the file.

Note how the initial results of my search are displayed in the Find navigator; if I wanted to filter the Results list still further, I could enter text into the field at the bottom of the pane. Any items that don't match the text are removed from the Results list.

To go directly to where the search term appears in a file, click an entry under the file's name in the Find navigator, as shown in Figure 7-14. The file appears in the editor pane on the right, open to the location where the search term appears.

Using the Symbol navigator

 The Symbol navigator allows you to browse through the symbols in your project — just click the Symbol button on the Navigator selector bar. Note that you need to wait until Xcode finishes indexing your project before you can use this feature.

You can display symbols in a hierarchical or flat list using the buttons at the top of the Symbol navigator.

You can specify which symbols are displayed by using the buttons at the bottom of the navigator. Buttons are blue when on and black when off. Use the following buttons in any combination:

- ✔ **The first button** on the Symbol navigator shows only class symbols and hides global symbol types.
- ✔ **The middle button** shows only symbols in this project.
- ✔ **The third button** shows only containers (classes and categories).

You can refine the Results list still more by entering text in the Filter field at the bottom of the navigator.

If you select a symbol to display, its header file definition will be displayed in the source editor. In Figure 7-15, I've hidden everything but the member symbols. In the resulting list, I then filtered on the viewDidLoad method, and its declaration in the header file was highlighted in the source editor.

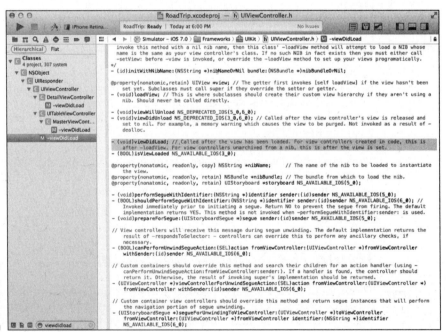

Figure 7-15:
The Symbol
navigator.

You're Finally Ready to Write Code!

Yes, it's finally time to write code, and from here on, it's full-steam ahead.

Part III
Getting Your Feet Wet: Basic Functionality

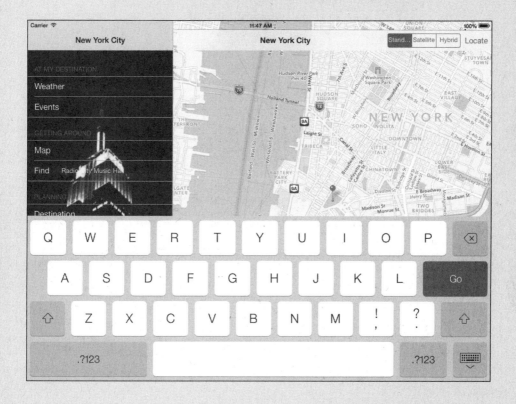

Visit www.dummies.com/extras/iosapplicationdevelopment for more on how to develop your iOS app with storyboarding.

In this part . . .

- ✔ Getting started with coding
- ✔ Adding outlets and actions to your code
- ✔ Adding animation and sound to your app

Chapter 8

It's (Finally) Time to Code

*Y*es, it's finally time to start coding, although this chapter doesn't get you going on the RoadTrip app functionality itself yet (the example app developed in this book). In this chapter, I show you some code you have to include to make sure that your app isn't rejected out of hand by Apple.

Next, I give you an introduction to your new friend, the debugger. While some of you out there (but not me) may code perfectly, most developers make some mistakes as they develop an app. Fortunately, the debugger in Xcode starts helping you right from the start — so you want to understand how to use it as soon as you start coding.

Checking for Network Availability

One of the easiest ways to get your app rejected by Apple is to fail to make sure that you have an Internet connection when your app needs it, and therefore fail to notify the user that the functionality that requires the connection will be unavailable (or even worse, have your app just hang there).

Downloading the Reachability sample

Apple provides a sample app called Reachability that shows how to determine whether you have an Internet connection (as well as quite a bit of additional network information I won't be going into), and you'll be using that code in the RoadTrip app developed in this book. Here's how to use code from that valuable sample program:

1. **Download the Reachability sample from Apple by clicking Sample Code at** `http://developer.apple.com/devcenter/ios`.

2. **Type** Reachability **in the Search field.**

3. **Click the Reachability project in the search results, and in the iOS Developer Library window that appears, click the Download Sample Code button.**

4. **In your Downloads folder, double-click the Reachability folder to open it.**

   You set your Safari Downloads folder in Safari⇨Preferences using the General tab.

5. **Open the inner Reachability folder and drag the** `Reachability.m` **and** `Reachability.h` **files into your project.**

   (I put them in my Supporting Files group just to keep them out of the way.)

6. **Select the check box in front of Road Trip in the Add to Targets section.**

   Be sure to select the Copy Items into destination group's folder option (if it isn't already selected).

In order for you to be able to use this code, you need to add the `SystemConfiguration` framework. To do so, follow these steps:

1. **In the Project navigator, select the project icon (in this case, RoadTrip) at the top of the Project navigator content area to display the Project editor.**

2. **In the targets pop-up menu just below the jump bar for the project, select RoadTrip.**

3. **On the Build Phases tab, scroll down to the Link Binary with Libraries section.**

4. **Expand the Link Binary with Libraries section if it isn't already expanded (see Figure 8-1) by clicking the disclosure triangle.**

5. **Click the + (plus sign) button underneath the list of current project frameworks.**

   A list of frameworks appears.

6. **Scroll down and select SystemConfiguration.framework, as shown in Figure 8-2.**

7. **Click the Add button.**

   You'll see the framework added to the Linked Frameworks and Libraries section.

8. **Close the Linked Frameworks and Libraries section.**

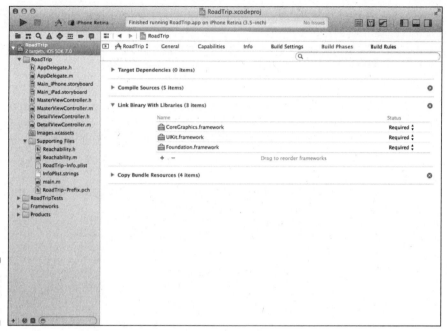

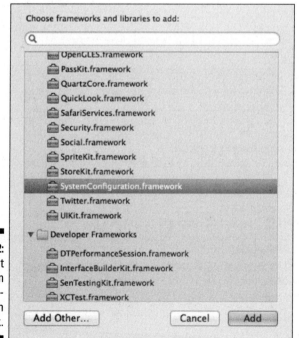

Adding the code to check for reachability

The place to check for whether you have access to the Internet is right when you start up. The method for doing that is the app delegate protocol method `application:didFinishLaunchingWithOptions:`.

You also need to include the `Reachability.h` file to be able to use Reachability, so add the bolded code in Listing 8-1 to the beginning of both the `AppDelegate.m` file and the `application:didFinishLaunchingWith Options:` method.

Listing 8-1:   Updating the RTAppDelegate Implementation and application:didFinishLaunchingWithOptions:

```
#import "AppDelegate.h"
#import "Reachability.h"

@implementation AppDelegate


- (BOOL)application:(UIApplication *)application
        didFinishLaunchingWithOptions:
                            (NSDictionary *)launchOptions
{
  if ([[UIDevice currentDevice] userInterfaceIdiom] ==
                                UIUserInterfaceIdiomPad) {
    UISplitViewController *splitViewController =
        (UISplitViewController *)
                        self.window.rootViewController;
    UINavigationController *navigationController =
        [splitViewController.viewControllers lastObject];
    splitViewController.delegate =
                (id)navigationController.topViewController;
  }
NetworkStatus networkStatus =
  [[Reachability reachabilityForInternetConnection]
                            currentReachabilityStatus];
  if (networkStatus == NotReachable) {
    UIAlertView *alert = [[UIAlertView alloc]
      initWithTitle:@"Network Unavailable"
      message:@"RoadTrip requires an Internet connection"
      delegate:nil
      cancelButtonTitle:@"OK"
      otherButtonTitles:nil];
    [alert show];
  }
  return YES;
}
```

Ignore the code not in bold for the time being. I explain it in detail in Chapter 13.

In the main bolded section of Listing 8-1, you start by creating a `Reachability` object and then send it the `currentReachabilityStatus` message:

```
NetworkStatus networkStatus =
   [[Reachability reachabilityForInternetConnection]
                              currentReachabilityStatus];
```

`reachabilityForInternetConnection` is an initializer that creates a `Reachability` object that checks for the availability of an Internet connection. As I said, Reachability has a lot of functionality, but all you really care about right now is whether you can reach the Internet.

Next, check to see whether you have network access:

```
if (networkStatus == NotReachable) {
```

If you don't have network access, you post an alert:

```
UIAlertView *alert = [[UIAlertView alloc]
      initWithTitle:@"Network Unavailable"
      message:@"RoadTrip requires an Internet connection"
      delegate:nil
      cancelButtonTitle:@"OK"
      otherButtonTitles:nil];
[alert show];
```

This is the standard way to configure and then show an alert. You have filled in the various (self-explanatory) parameters required by the initialization method. Configured this way, the alert will have a single button.

The `show` message to the `alert` object causes the alert to be displayed in the window, and when the user taps OK, the alert is dismissed.

If you had added other buttons to give the user a choice of responses, you would have had to make the object posting the alert (the `AppDelegate`, in this case) a `UIAlertViewDelegate`, assigned the delegate parameter to `self`, and added the title of the other buttons using a `nil` terminated list. You would then have needed to implement the `alertView:clickedButtonAtIndex:` method in the delegate.

Explaining how Reachability works is beyond the scope of this book, but by examining the code, you can easily figure out how to get any other network status information you want.

If you run the app now, and either turn off your Internet connection on the computer (if you're running the Simulator) or turn on Airplane mode or turn off your Wi-Fi connection on the device, you see the message shown in Figure 8-3. (If this doesn't seem to work, read on. What matters isn't the behavior on the simulator but, later on, the behavior on a device.)

You can also temporarily change the

```
if (networkStatus == NotReachable) {
```

to

```
if (networkStatus != NotReachable) {
```

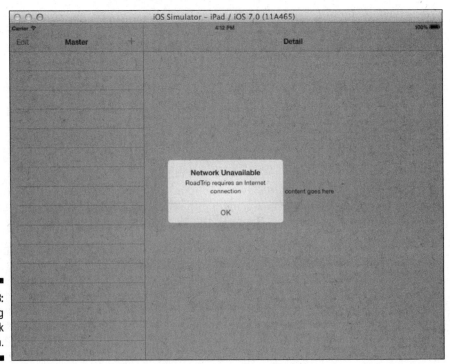

Figure 8-3:
Checking
the network
connection.

so that the test works in reverse. Just be sure to change it back!

Of course, in a real app, you would want to do something further here, such as give the user options and so on. I'll leave that up to you.

Congratulations! You've had your first adventure in coding land.

Exploring the Changes in iOS 7

iOS 7 introduces a major revision to the user interface of iOS. It addresses two main issues: the dated look of the interface and the fact that content was getting lost on the app screen.

The dated interface

Change for the sake of change may or may not be a good idea — it depends on the context and the cost. In the case of a new user interface, users and developers have to learn new skills.

With iOS 7, the functionality of the interface changes very little. Apple was able to make relatively small changes in the interface appearance, and for most users, not much changed. Developers have a few extra items to think about.

The "datedness" of the interface wasn't so much the fact that it had been around for a while, but that it was designed originally for the iPhone with a small screen and a much less powerful processor than we have today. The screen on the iPhone is larger today, and its resolution is much higher with the Retina display. The iPad, of course, is the same size (although the iPad Mini came along a little while ago), but both are now sporting Retina displays.

This means that not only is there more screen real estate to use, but the details can be much smaller and subtler. In demonstrations of the Retina display, we usually see beautiful photos. However, the fact that very small elements on the screen can now be visible does have an effect on the user interface.

This has all happened before. If you look at screenshots of the original Mac (or a PC), you'll see interfaces that look very old and clunky. We just don't use those enormous interface elements any more the way we had to a couple of decades ago. It's also important to note that Apple has significant tools in the accessibility area so that, even with small interface elements, people with limited vision can still use the devices.

Losing the content

The second issue that the interface revision addressed was the fact that content was sometimes getting lost on the screen. At the Worldwide Developers Conference in June 2013 where iOS 7 was first demonstrated, speaker after speaker stressed that part of the design goal was to make the content stand out and the interface disappear as much as possible.

Part of the strategy to make the content stand out was to simplify the user interface. One important simplification is to introduce the idea of a *tint color* (really a highlight color). If you set a tint color for your app, the interface is drawn basically in gray on a white background with the exception of items that are highlighted: All highlighted items use the tint color. You can set it for your app or for an individual window. Users may not even notice the fact that all highlights appear in the same color unless you point it out to them, but it makes learning how to use the app and — most importantly — distinguishing between content and interface much easier.

If your app uses color in its content, a good tint color is one that is unlikely to show up in the content, if that's possible. Remember, the point of the tint color is to distinguish the interface from the content. A secondary point is to remind users what app they're in. Apple, for example, uses blue as the tint color in many of the built-in apps. You're welcome to use it, but if you choose a different color (a significantly different color) you can help people know where they are.

Furthermore, if the tint color picks up a color from your app icon, you also may establish your own palette identity. You can set a tint color for an individual window, but many apps set it globally. To do so, select a storyboard file from in the Project navigator and use the File inspector to set the tint color, as shown in Figure 8-4. This method makes it easy to use different tint colors for each storyboard. So that means you can set the tint color dynamically in code for a window regardless of device, for a storyboard and all of its views and view controllers, or for a specific view (that, too, would require code).

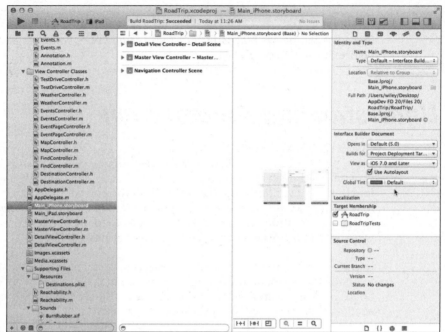

Figure 8-4:
Set the tint
color.

Setting the Master View Controller Title

You'll also want to be able to set the title in the Navigation bar for the view. You could have done that in Interface Builder, but I'm showing you how to do it programmatically because you want to be able to set the title of the view based on where the user is going.

To set the MasterViewController title, add the bolded code in Listing 8-2 to viewDidLoad in MasterViewController.m.

Listing 8-2: Updating viewDidLoad

```
- (void)viewDidLoad
{
  [super viewDidLoad];
  // Do any additional setup after loading the view,
    typically from a nib.
  self.detailViewController =
    (DetailViewController *)
    [[self.splitViewController.viewControllers
      lastObject] topViewController];
  self.title = @"Road Trip";
}
```

How did I know to put this code here, rather than in some other section of the code? `viewDidLoad` is the message sent when the view is loaded for the first time, but before it's displayed. If you want a title, you want to set it here, before the view is displayed.

Understanding Autorotation

One of the responsibilities of the `UIViewController` class is to work with the app's window to handle device rotation (also known as *device orientation changes*). Although the `UIViewController` class itself already includes the functionality to animate the transition from the current orientation to the new one (which you can override if you need to lay out the view again for the new orientation), it must also communicate to the application window whether it in fact wants to support a particular orientation.

In earlier versions of iOS, you had to override certain `UIViewController` methods to control autorotation, but you can manage this now by simply choosing your desired Device Orientations in the Target's Deployment Info section of the General tab, as shown in Figure 8-5.

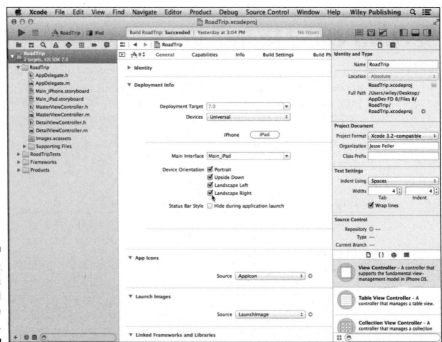

Figure 8-5:
The Target's
Supported
Device
Orientations.

Writing Bug-Free Code

Although some developers think that writing code is where they spend the vast majority of their time when they're developing an app, debugging is actually right up there as a very close second. (And yes, I know that the title of this section is wishful thinking.)

Because debugging plays such a crucial role in writing workable code, I want to use this section to emphasize two points:

- ✔ App developers should strive to write code with as few bugs as possible (duh!).
- ✔ App developers need to know how to use the debugger so they can track down the inevitable bugs they do introduce into their code as efficiently as possible.

With the release of Xcode 5, Apple has made it easier to write code with fewer bugs, as well as use the debugger to track down bugs you do have.

Because the best defense is a good offense, I want to start with the tools that Xcode provides that help you to write less buggy code. Xcode has figured out that the best way to make sure your code has as few bugs as possible is by giving you the opportunity to fix the code as you write it. Such opportunities come in the form of Xcode's various compiler warnings. More specifically, by taking advantage of the Live Issues and Fix-it features, which I explain in Chapter 7, you'll catch many of your errors before you even run your app, and fixing them will be easy. (Well, some of them, at least.) Live Issues continuously evaluates your code in the background and alerts you to coding mistakes, and Fix-it will also offer to fix the problem for you. I suggest that unless you are crystal clear about what you're doing, don't run your app without first resolving any outstanding compiler warnings.

Although Live Issues and Fix-it can catch many problems and help you resolve them, they can't identify and fix everything. (I can tell you that they have made my life more difficult. When I want to demonstrate how to fix a coding error in a book or class, it's much harder to set it up because Live Issues and Fix-it tend to catch the error before I can finish typing it.)

Working in the Debug area and Debug navigator

The Debug area consists of the Debug bar, partnered with the Variables pane and the Console pane, each of which has a Scope bar fitted out with a pop-up menu. You usually use the Debug area in conjunction with the Debug navigator.

You access the Debug area by selecting it in the Xcode toolbar's View selector (as shown in Figure 8-6). You select the Debug navigator by showing the Navigator area and then selecting the Debug navigator in the Navigator selector bar. The default behavior is to show the Debug navigator and the relevant debugging gauges (you can change this in Debug preferences).

If you get a runtime error (or if you click the Pause button or a breakpoint is triggered), the Debug area and the Debug navigator open automatically.

Figure 8-7 show what happens when you hit a breakpoint (which I explain shortly) in your program.

What you see in the Debug area is controlled by using the Debug area Scope buttons, shown in Figure 8-8 at the bottom right of the Debug area. You use this bar to toggle between the Variables pane only (left button), both Variables and Console panes (both buttons), and Console pane only (right button).

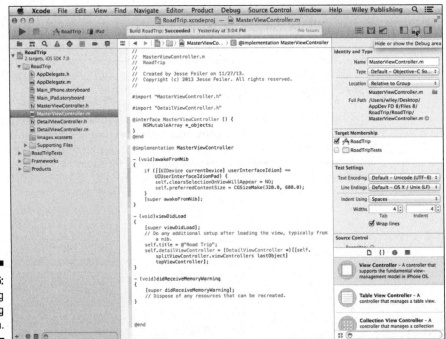

Figure 8-6:
Accessing
the Debug
area.

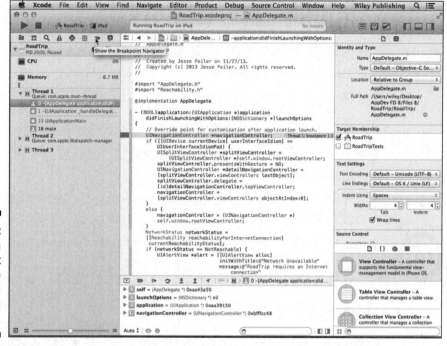

Figure 8-7: Hitting a breakpoint displays the Debug area and Debug navigator.

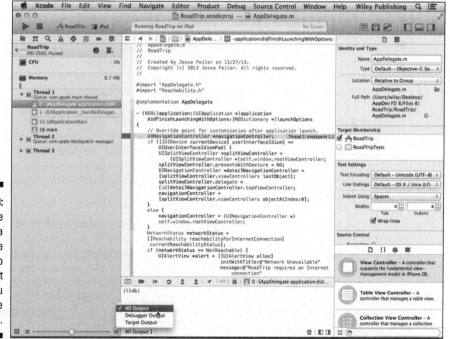

Figure 8-8: Use the Debug area Scope buttons to control what panes you see in the Debug area.

The Variables pane and the Console pane have their very own Scope bars as well. The pop-up menu in the Variables pane Scope bar lets you display

- ✔ **Auto:** Recently accessed variables
- ✔ **Local:** Local variables
- ✔ **All:** All variables and registers

The pop-up menu in the Console pane Scope bar lets you display

- ✔ **All Output:** Target and debugger output
- ✔ **Debugger Output:** Debugger output only
- ✔ **Target Output:** Target output (program logging to the debugger, for example) only

Xcode offers other controls and filters for what gets displayed that I encourage you to explore on your own.

Managing breakpoints

You can use the debugger to pause execution of your program at any time and view the state of the running code.

As mentioned previously, you won't find much to see in the Debug area and Debug navigator unless your program is stopped at a breakpoint or paused (and not much at those points, either). The debugger is more useful to you if you set breakpoints to stop at known points and then view the values of the variables in your source code. Given that fact, it's probably time to show you how to set a breakpoint and explain what a breakpoint is.

A *breakpoint* is an instruction to the debugger to stop execution at a particular program instruction. By setting breakpoints at various methods in your program, you can step through its execution — at the instruction level — to see exactly what it's doing. You can also examine the variables that the program is setting and using. If you're stymied by a logic error, setting breakpoints is a great way to break that logjam.

To set breakpoints, open a file in the Source editor and click in the Gutter — the column between the Navigator area and the Focus ribbon that is adjacent to the Editor area in Figure 8-8 — next to the spot where you want execution to stop. You can toggle the state (on or off) of all the breakpoints in your program at any time by clicking the Breakpoints button at the left of the Debug bar: it's the colored button that's the second from the left. In Figure 8-8, note that the button looks like the breakpoint that's set in the gutter next to UINavigationController.

To disable an individual breakpoint, click its icon in the gutter. To get rid of a breakpoint completely, simply drag it off to the side. You can also right-click (or Control-click) the breakpoint and choose Delete Breakpoint from the pop-up menu that appears.

In Figure 8-9, I've added a breakpoint to the statement just before I check to see if the device is an iPad. You'll also notice that I've displayed the Breakpoint navigator by selecting the appropriate icon in the Navigator selector bar. The Breakpoint navigator lets you see all breakpoints at once; if you select a given breakpoint in the Breakpoint navigator, it displays in the Source editor (where you can also edit it).

You can set several options for each breakpoint by Control-clicking the breakpoint and choosing Edit Breakpoint from the shortcut menu that appears, as shown in Figure 8-10.

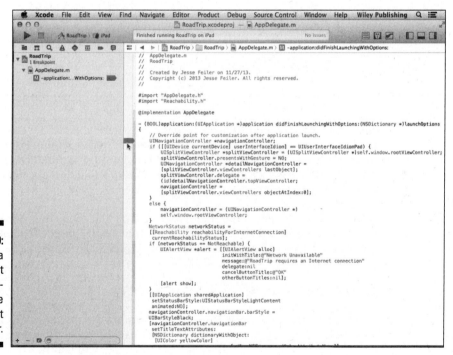

Figure 8-9:
Setting a breakpoint and displaying the Breakpoint navigator.

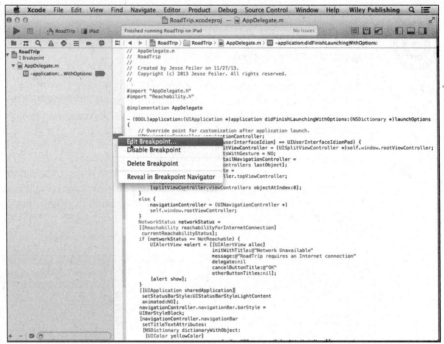

Figure 8-10:
Editing a
breakpoint.

Doing so opens the Edit Breakpoint window, where you can set the actions and options you want for breakpoints added in the Breakpoint editor. As shown in Figure 8-11, you can set a condition for a breakpoint, ignore it a set number of times before stopping, add an action, and automatically continue after evaluating actions.

In Figure 8-11, I selected the Add Action button and then chose to add a sound in Figure 8-12. I also set a condition that I want the breakpoint to be triggered only if the networkStatus isn't equal to notReachable. In this case, as you can see in Figure 8-12, I had to specify

```
networkStatus != 0
```

This is because networkStatus is not a symbol the debugger has access to, but rather an enumerated type (a set of named values that behave as constants). If you examine the Reachability.h file, you'll find

```
typedef enum {
        NotReachable = 0,
        ReachableViaWiFi,
        ReachableViaWWAN
} NetworkStatus;
```

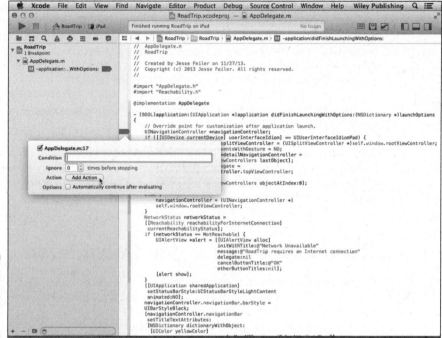

Figure 8-11:
Some
breakpoint
options.

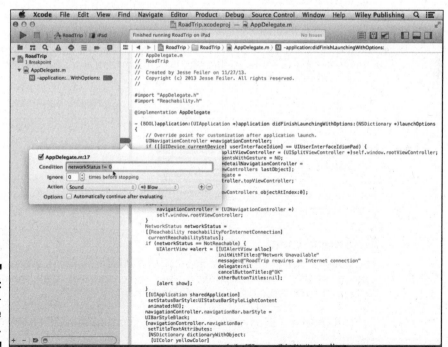

Figure 8-12:
Fine-
tuning the
breakpoint.

The "normal" condition, of course, would be to set the breakpoint to stop when the condition is something you don't expect, like the networkStatus *equal to* NotReachable. But I want to keep my Mac connected to my network (which connects the Simulator as well), so I set the breakpoint condition to be equal to Not Reachable so it would stop at the breakpoint every time (unless of course my network unexpectedly goes down).

Set this breakpoint and run your program in Xcode. As you saw previously in Figure 8-7, you'll be stopped at the breakpoint.

As you can see in the figure, when the breakpoint is reached, the Debug area is displayed and the Debug navigator opened automatically. (You can change that response in the Behaviors tab of Xcode Preferences.) It stopped because the condition I set (networkStatus != 0) evaluated YES.

What you'll find in the Debug area

On one side of the Debug area you have the Variables pane (which displays the values of variables), and on the other side, you have the Console pane. You select one or both with the Debug area Scope buttons at the lower right of the Debug area. In Figure 8-7, for example, you saw only the Variables pane.

The Variables pane

The Variables pane displays the variables you're interested in. Click the disclosure triangle next to self to see the instance variables in the object. You'll see the local variables to a method as well. As mentioned earlier, you can specify which items to display by using the pop-up menu in the top-left corner of the Variables pane:

✔ **Auto:** Displays only the variables you're most likely to be interested in, given the current context

✔ **Local:** Displays local variables

✔ **All:** Displays all variables and registers

You can also use the Search field on the toolbar to filter the items displayed in the Variables pane.

The Console pane

The Console pane displays program output. Again, as mentioned earlier, you can specify the type of output you see in the console by using the pop-up menu in the top-left corner of the Console pane:

✔ **All Output:** Displays target and debugger output

✔ **Debugger Output:** Displays debugger output only

✔ **Target Output:** Displays target output only

When you are stopped at the breakpoint you set earlier, what you see is a lot of boilerplate and then this:

```
2012-02-19 12:02:12.486 RoadTrip[26123:f803] Reachability
          Flag Status: -R -----1- networkStatusForFlags
(lldb)
```

Not much of interest here, but in Chapter 11, you'll find out how to *print* (really *display*) the contents of a variable to the Console pane — and in Chapter 15, you'll have the opportunity to examine some runtime error messages.

The (rather boring) stuff you see here is the result of an NSLog statement in Reachability:

```
2012-02-19 12:02:12.486 RoadTrip[26123:f803] Reachability
          Flag Status: -R -----1- networkStatusForFlags
```

NSLog allows you to display information in the Console pane during execution. For example, if you wanted to know how many points of interest your app had to display (the number of elements in the poiData array — you find out about poiData in Chapter 17), instead of using a breakpoint and displaying a variable, you could add the following NSLog statement:

```
NSLog(@"Number of points of interest %i",
                                    [poiData count]);
```

which would display

```
2012-02-19 12:06:52.688 RoadTrip[26145:f803]
                        Number of points of interest 1
```

in the Console pane.

NSLog is pretty useful and uses the same formatting as NSString's stringWithFormat and other formatting methods.

What you'll find in the Debug navigator

Selecting an item in the Debug navigator causes information about the item to be displayed in the Source editor. For example, selecting a method displays the source code for that function in the Source editor.

Each app within iOS is made up of one or more *threads,* each of which represents a single path of execution through the app's code. Every app starts with a single thread, which runs the app's main function. The main thread encompasses the app's `main` run loop, and it's where the `NSApplication` object receives events. Apps can add (spawn) additional threads, each of which executes the code of a specific method.

Threads per se are way beyond the scope of this book, but that's okay: Here you'll be concerned with only the `main` thread.

Every time you send a message (or make a function call), the debugger stores information about it in a *stack frame* and then it stores all such frames in the *call stack.* When you're thrown into the debugger because of an error (or if you pause the application by clicking the Pause button on the toolbar), Xcode displays the thread list, and within each thread the call stack for that thread, putting the most recent call at the top. The call stack shows a trace of the objects and methods that got you to where you are now.

You can do a lot more as far as threads are concerned, but again, that's outside of the scope of this book. (If you don't know whether to be disappointed or relieved, hold that thought.)

Although the trace isn't really all that useful in this particular context, it can be *very* useful in a more complex application — it can help you to understand the path that you took to get where you are. Seeing how one object sent a message to another object — which sent a message to a third object — can be really helpful, especially if you didn't expect the program flow to work that way.

Getting a look at the call stack can also be useful if you're trying to understand how the framework does its job, and in what order messages are sent. As you'll soon see, you can stop the execution of your program at a breakpoint and trace the messages sent up to that point.

Displaying variables in the Source editor

In the Debugger window, you can move your pointer over an object or variable in the Source editor to show its contents and move your pointer over disclosure triangles to see even more information when the app is stopped at a breakpoint.

In Figure 8-13, for example, I moved the pointer over `navigationController` to see its value (information about the current status of the Internet connection).

When you move your pointer over a variable, its contents are revealed — and if more disclosure triangles appear, you can move your pointer over them to see even more information (which I explain in more detail in Chapter 11).

You see the value of the variable in the Variables pane as well.

In the next section, I show you how to step through your program after it's stopped at a breakpoint.

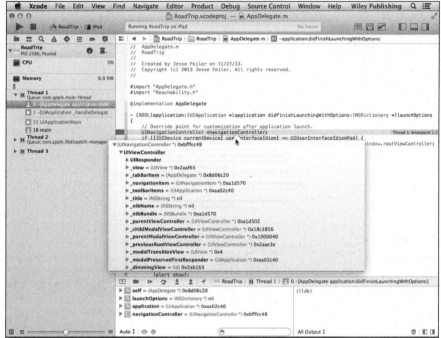

Figure 8-13:
Showing the
navigation
controller.

Tiptoeing through your program

When you build and run the program with breakpoints, the Debug bar appears in the Workspace window as the program runs in the Simulator. The program stops executing at the first breakpoint (if you have set a condition, it stops executing if that condition is met).

To control the execution, you use the Debug bar (located at the top of the Debug area that you see in Figure 8-14). The Debug bar includes buttons to

- ✔ **Open or close the Debug area.** As mentioned previously, you can hide the Debug area if you don't need it for what you're doing right now.

- ✔ **Turn all breakpoints on or off.** This will let you keep them in place for whenever you need to debug them again.

- ✔ **Pause or resume execution of your code.** Click this button to stop your program from executing or continue execution after it stopped when it entered the debugger.

- ✔ **Step over.** Click this button to make the *process counter (PC)*, which is identified by the green arrow in the gutter, move to the next line of code to be executed. If that line of code sends a message, it will send the message (and run the method) — but then, from your perspective, it just moves to the next line of code.

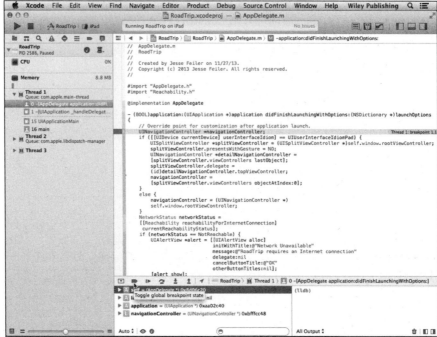

Figure 8-14:
The Debug
area and
Debug bar.

✔ **Step in.** Click this button to move the process counter to the next line of code to be executed. If the line of code sends a message to a method in your source code, the debugger will step to the method and then return to the next line of code after the line that sends the message.

✔ **Step out.** Click this button to step out of the current function or method. The Source editor then displays either the method that sent the message or the function's caller.

✔ **Simulate location.** You can have the debugger simulate the location of the iPad for you. I explain this in Chapter 17.

When I build and run RoadTrip in Figure 8-14, you can see that the program has stopped executing at the breakpoint. If I then want to watch what happens as RoadTrip executes step-by-step, I would select Step In and proceed line by line. At each line, I can view the values of the variables as they change (changed values are shown in blue). When I have seen what I want to see, I can resume execution or stop the app and make my repairs.

This concludes your introduction to the debugger and Debug navigator. I do want to show you a couple more things, but I need to have you add more code to have them make sense. In Chapter 11, I show you how to print (display) the contents of a variable in the Console pane, and then in Chapter 15, I show you a couple of my favorite runtime errors.

Chapter 9

Adding Outlets and Actions to Your RoadTrip Code

In This Chapter

▶ Connecting your user interface to your code

▶ Using the Assistant

▶ Taking advantage of the Connections inspector

▶ How connections are made at runtime

*O*ne of the things that the RoadTrip app will be able to do is send the image of a car to the top of the screen, have it move back down the screen, and then have it turn around so it's back where it started, all from a simple tap of the Test Drive button. This isn't an essential for an app like RoadTrip, but it's an interesting add-on that lets me show you how to add animation and sound to an app in the next chapter. So if you're more interested in developing games than a data-based travel guide, you'll be on your way.

To get ready to add sound and animation to your app, you're going to need to add some logic to your code. You do that in a custom view controller, which gets detailed coverage in this very chapter — especially the bits about adding custom view controllers and connecting them to the view controllers you create in your storyboard. But that's only one part of the story. For all the pieces to fit, you'll need to be able to access the elements stipulated in your storyboard — elements like the car image — and then connect those elements to the code in your custom view controller.

The way you add the logic to connect the view to the model via the view controller in this chapter is going to be the model for how you deal with the rest of the view controllers in the storyboard. Keep in mind that, although you can add all the view controllers you'll ever need to the storyboard graphically, you still need to add some code on your own if you ever want the controller to actually *do* anything, such as get data from the model and send it to the view.

Using Custom View Controllers

The view controller provided by the storyboard is a `UIViewController` (or `UITableViewController`, which is a type of view controller) and is blissfully unaware of what you want to display in a view, or how to respond to view actions (such as the user tapping the Test Drive button). In this section, you create a custom controller that *does* know about its view. (In Chapter 10, you get to add the logic you need to the custom view controller to make the car move and make noise.)

Adding the custom view controller

You start the process of adding a custom view controller to your project by adding the custom view controller class, as follows:

1. **To create a new group to keep your view controller classes in, select the RoadTrip group in the Project navigator and either right-click and choose New Group from the menu that appears or choose File⇨ New⇨New Group from the main menu.**

   Note that you need to select the RoadTrip *group,* right there under RoadTrip Resources, and not the RoadTrip *project,* which is at the top of the Project navigator.

   To change a file's group, select the file and drag it to the group you want it to occupy. The same goes for groups as well (after all, they can go into other groups).

2. **The New Group should be selected so you can name your new group** View Controller Classes **by typing it.**

   If it is not already selected, or you want to change the name, select the name and name it (this is the same way you would name a folder on the Mac).

3. **In the Project navigator, select the (newly created) View Controller Classes group and either right-click and then choose New File from the menu that appears or choose File⇨New⇨New File from the main menu (or press ⌘+N) to bring up the New File dialog.**

4. **In the left column of the dialog, select Cocoa Touch under the iOS heading, select Objective-C class template in the top-right pane, and then click Next.**

5. **In the Class field, enter** TestDriveController, **choose UIViewController from the Subclass Of drop-down menu, make sure that the Target for iPad option is selected and that the With XIB for User Interface option is deselected, and then click Next.**

You could also name this `TestDriveViewController`. It *is* a view controller but it generally controls the test drive feature. It's up to you. Apple engineers have gradually been moving to longer and more descriptive names for things. Even the most typing-challenged engineers can live with longer names thanks to Xcode's Fix-it and code completion logic. I'm opting for the shortest name in part because it makes the code listings in this book a little easier for the layout (and reading!) process.

6. **In the Save sheet that appears, select a location, and then click Create.**

If you examine the (generated) code added in `TestDriveController`, you'll notice two methods.

The first one I'll draw your attention to is `viewDidLoad` — you'll be adding code to it to do any view controller or view initialization after the view controller and its view have been loaded from the storyboard:

```
- (void)viewDidLoad
{
    [super viewDidLoad];
    // Do any additional setup after loading the view,
        typically from a nib.
}
```

Setting up the TestDriveController in the MainStoryboard for iPad

Now that you have a custom view controller (it doesn't do anything yet, but it will), you need to let the storyboard know that you want to load your custom view controller rather than a `UIViewController`.

In the Project navigator, select the `Main_iPad.storyboard` file, and in the Document Outline, select View Controller – TestDrive in the View Controller – TestDrive Scene. (I had you enter **TestDrive** in the Title field way back when, and now you're actually using it.)

Using the Inspector selector bar, open the Identity inspector in the Utility area and then choose `TestDriveController` (replacing `UIViewController`) from the Class drop-down menu in the Custom Class section, as I have in Figure 9-1). This means that when the Detail cell in the Master Controller is tapped, your custom controller — the `TestDriveController` — will be instantiated and initialized, meaning it will now receive events from the user and connect the view to the `Trip` model you'll create in Chapter 11.

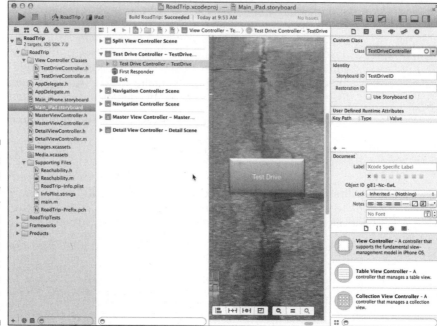

Figure 9-1:
Connecting
the view
controller
object in
the iPad
storyboard
to the Test
Drive
Control-
ler class.

When you write your own code, it's pretty obvious how an app works: You create an object, initialize it, and then send it messages. When you work with storyboards, however, how your app works may not be so obvious. How do you go from the objects you added to your user interface in Interface Builder to code that enables you to access these objects? How do you get an Image view to change its image or receive a message that the user has tapped a button, for example?

The objects in your user interface must communicate with each other and with your source code if your app is to allow the user to interact with it. In order to access a user interface object and specify which messages are sent and received, you use Interface Builder to create connections. There are two basic types of connections you can create:

- **Outlet connections,** which connect your code to Interface Builder objects that enable you to get and set *properties* (change the image in an Image view, for example)

- **Action connections,** which specify the message to be sent to your code when the control is *interacted with* (the user taps a button, for example)

In this chapter, I explain how to create both outlets and actions in your code.

Understanding Outlets

An *outlet* is a way to connect your code to an object you added to a view in your storyboard that you've decided will become part of your user interface at runtime. The connections between your code and its outlets are automatically reestablished every time the object referenced by the outlet is loaded.

The object containing an outlet is often a custom controller object such as the view controller generated for you by the template. In the class declaration of that custom controller, you declare an outlet as a property with the type qualifier of IBOutlet.

Listing 9-1 shows you what the TestDriveController class extension (in the .m file) will look like after you're done mucking about with it at the end of this chapter.

Listing 9-1: Outlets (and Actions) Declared

```
@interface TestDriveController () {
   AVAudioPlayer *backgroundAudioPlayer;
   SystemSoundID burnRubberSoundID;
   BOOL touchInCar;


}
@property (weak, nonatomic) IBOutlet UIImageView *car;
@property (weak, nonatomic)
                       IBOutlet UIButton *testDriveButton;
- (IBAction)testDrive:(id)sender;
@end
```

An *outlet* is a property that points to another object, enabling an object in an app to communicate with another object at runtime. Using an outlet, you have a reference to an object defined in the storyboard (or a nib file) that is then loaded from that storyboard file at runtime. You can make outlet connections between any objects that you add to your storyboard in Interface Builder.

For example, in Figure 9-2, you use an outlet to get the text the user typed in the Find text field.

But before you go setting up outlets for anything and everything, make sure that you really need one. You don't have to use outlets to be able to access all Interface Builder objects.

Figure 9-2:
Using an outlet to get the text entered by the user.

Adding Outlets

To recap from the previous section, outlets are the way your code can *access* — either by sending messages or setting properties — the Interface Builder objects in your storyboard. You can do all this graphically in Interface Builder, and the required code is generated for you. Read on to find out more about how this works.

Opening the Assistant editor

To create an outlet, you need to connect the interface object in Interface Builder with your code. Although you have a couple of ways to make this connection, the easiest and most clear-cut way is to use the Assistant editor to automatically display the code file that's most relevant to the interface element you're working with. To make the Assistant editor automatically display a likely code file, follow these steps:

1. **Select the Main_iPad.storyboard file in the Project navigator.**

2. **Close the Utility area if it's open (and you need the space) by deselecting it in the View selector in the Xcode toolbar.**

3. **In Interface Builder, select the View Controller – TestDrive in the View Controller – TestDrive Scene (see, it is handy to actually label things) in the Document Outline; then click the Assistant Editor button in the Editor selector on the toolbar (see Figure 9-3).**

   The Assistant editor pane opens. If Automatic is chosen in the toolbar, you will have a choice of views in `TestDriveController.h` and Test `DriveController.m`. That's because both files are relevant to the selected view in the Document Outline. You want to work with `TestDriveController.m` so, if necessary, choose it as shown in Figure 9-4.

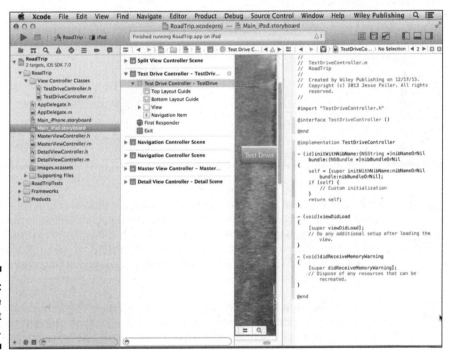

Figure 9-3:
Select the Assistant editor.

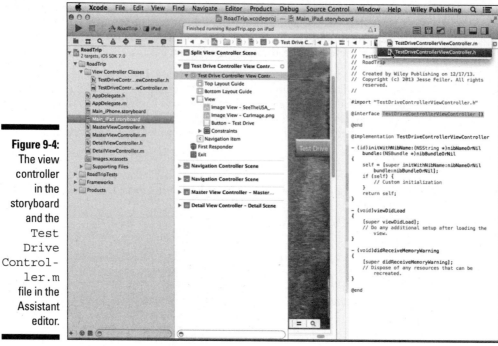

Figure 9-4:
The view
controller
in the
storyboard
and the
`Test
Drive
Control-
ler.m`
file in the
Assistant
editor.

A *Jump bar* (a handy thing to know about) appears at the top of each Editor area pane and gives you a way to navigate through the files and symbols in your project. The configuration and behavior of each Jump bar is customized for the context in which it appears. In addition to a hierarchical path that enables you to navigate to a file or symbol in your project, the basic configuration of a Jump bar includes the following:

- ✔ The **Related Items menu** (accessed by clicking the icon shown in the left margin) grants you access to additional selections relevant to the current context, such as recently opened files or the interface (`.h`) header file for an implementation (`.m`) code file you're editing.

- ✔ **Previous and Next buttons** enable you to step back and forth through your navigation history.

I explain the Jump bar in detail when discussing the Standard editor in Chapter 7.

Creating the outlet

After you have the `TestDriveController` implementation displayed (as I do in Figure 9-4), either by having the Assistant editor display it automatically or by navigating to it using the Jump bar, the actual creating-an-outlet business using the Interface Builder editor is very straightforward and pretty easy. You do it by Control-dragging from the element you're interested in to the `TestDriveController` interface, as detailed in the following steps:

1. **Control-click and drag from the element in the view (the car image, in this example) to the** `TestDriveController.h` **file between the** `@interface` **and** `@end` **statements, as shown in Figure 9-5.**

2. **In the dialog that appears, name this outlet car (see Figure 9-6) and then click the Connect button.**

   The outlet is added as a property. (I explain properties in Chapter 6.)

   Figure 9-7 shows your new outlet in all its glory.

A connection between an object and its outlets is actually stored in a nib file. (Come to think of it, a storyboard is really just a series of nib files.) When the nib file is loaded, each connection is reconstituted and reestablished, thus enabling you to send messages to the object. `IBOutlet` is the keyword that tags an instance-variable declaration so that the Interface Builder app knows that a particular instance variable is an outlet — and can then enable the connection to it.

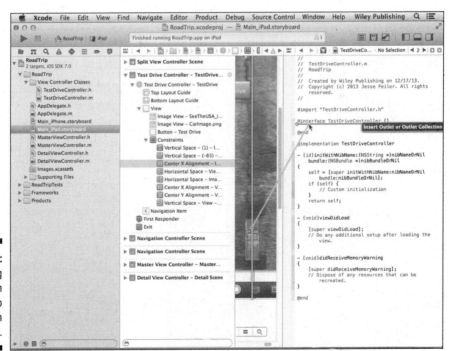

Figure 9-5: Control-drag from an object to create an outlet.

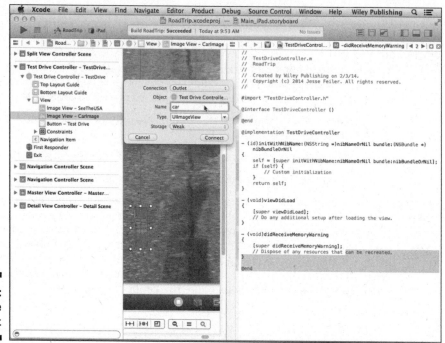

Figure 9-6:
Name the
outlet *car*.

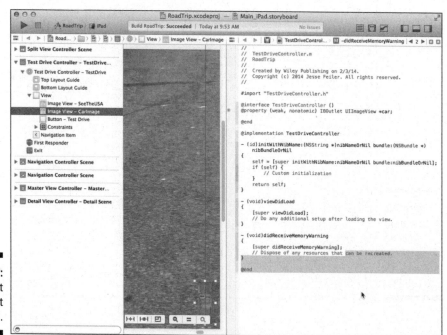

Figure 9-7:
The outlet
you just
created.

3. **Go back to the Interface file and create an outlet for the Test Drive button (name it** `testDriveButton`**).**

   Control-drag from the button to the `TestDriveController` interface in the same way as you do the car image (between the `@interface` and `@end` statements).

The only reason you need to create an outlet for a button (normally you'll attach an action to the button, which you'll do in the later section "Working with the Target-Action Design Pattern") is to change a Button property. You'll be using this outlet in Chapter 10 to make the button blink on and off.

The Connections inspector

While clicking and dragging is the easy way to go, you should know that you can make the same outlet connections using the Connections inspector in the Utility area, with a bit more work. But the real value of the Connections inspector is that it shows you what the outlets and received actions — covered next — and the segues actually are. To use the Connections inspector, follow these steps:

1. **Select Standard editor on the View selector in the toolbar.**

   The Assistant editor closes.

2. **Show the Utility area by selecting it in the View selector.**

3. **Select the Connections inspector by clicking its icon in the Inspector selector bar. (The icon is shown here in the left margin.)**

4. **In the Document Outline, select the View Controller in the Test Drive Controller – Test Drive Scene.**

Freedom of outlet reference choice

You actually have a choice — you can add the outlet reference to the public class interface declared in the .h file, or you can add the outlet reference to the private class interface declared in the .m file. An outlet declared in the .h file will be a public property that can be used by methods in other classes in your app. An outlet declared in your .m file can only be used by methods defined in that .m file. A general programming guideline is to keep things private unless they need to be public, so you might keep your outlet references in the .m file.

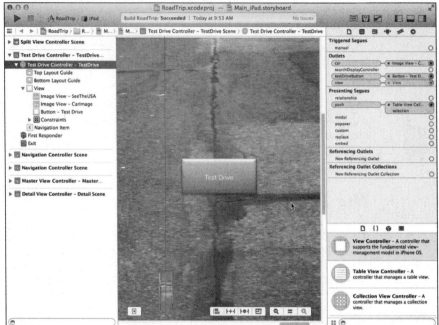

Figure 9-8:
The
Connections
inspector
and window.

In Figure 9-8, you can see that in the Outlets section of the Connections inspector, the view controller contains both `car` and `testDriveButton` outlets (as should yours, if you followed along and created them). You'll also see in the Referencing Storyboard Segues section a Push from Table View Cell – Cell. The view outlet has always been there — it's part of the template.

You can also Control-click the view controller in the Document Outline to get a similar picture in the Connections window.

Besides showing the outlets, if you need to change what an existing outlet points to, the Connections inspector or window is the way to go. Just drag from the circle at the end of the connection in the Outlets section in the Connections inspector or Connections window to the Interface Builder object you want that outlet to point to.

If you wanted to create an outlet without all this dragging, you would simply enter the code that Interface Builder created for you in the view controller's @ `Interface` (the property — don't forget the `IBOutlet`):

```
@property (weak, nonatomic) IBOutlet UIImageView *car;
```

The new outlet will show up in the Connections inspector and window, and then all you need to do is drag from the circle at the end of the connection in the Outlets section to the Interface Builder object you want that outlet to point to.

When you add outlets, you have some memory management considerations, not to mention the entire subject of properties, both of which I explain in Chapter 6. But in this chapter, I'm keeping the focus on what you need to know about interacting with Interface Builder objects in a storyboard. That interaction also includes working with a design pattern called Target-Action, which I explain next.

Working with the Target-Action Design Pattern

The other requirement of a user interface that I mention at the beginning of this chapter is being able to deal with situations where you want to connect a button to your code so that when a user taps the button, something happens. This requirement involves using the *Target-Action pattern,* which is one of the key design patterns in iOS programming.

You use the Target-Action pattern to let your app know that it should do something when prompted. A user might tap a button or enter some text, for example, and the app must respond in some way. The control — a button, say — sends a message (the Action message) that you specify to the target (the receiving object, which is usually a view controller object) that you have selected to handle that particular action.

Using the Target-Action pattern: It's about controls

When a user acts on the control by, say, tapping a button, the iPhone or iPad generates an event. The event triggering a particular action message can be anything, just as the object sending the message can be any object. For example, a gesture-recognizer object might send an action message to another object when it recognizes its gesture. However, the Target-Action pattern is usually found with controls such as buttons and sliders.

The event as such probably doesn't tell you much, but Target-Action provides a way to send an app-specific instruction to the appropriate object.

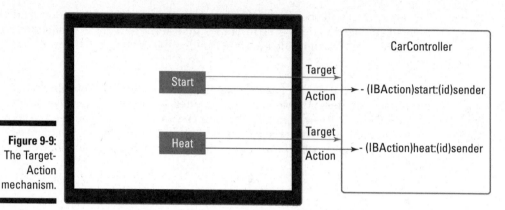

Figure 9-9:
The Target-
Action
mechanism.

If you wanted to develop an app that could start a car from an iOS device (not a bad idea for those who live in a place like Hibbing, Minnesota in winter), you could display two buttons, Start and Heater. You could use Interface Builder to specify that when the user taps Start, the target is the CarController object and the method to invoke is ignition. Figure 9-9 shows the Target-Action mechanism in action.

The Target-Action mechanism enables you to create a control object and tell it not only which object you want handling the event but also the message to send. For example, if the user taps a Ring Bell button onscreen, you want to send a Ring Bell message to the view controller. But if the Wave Flag button on the same screen is touched, you want to be able to send the Wave Flag message to the same view controller. If you couldn't specify the message, all buttons would have to send the same message. It would then make the coding more difficult and more complex because you would have to identify which button sent the message and what to do in response. It would also make changing the user interface more work and more prone to errors.

You set a control's action and target using Interface Builder. You get to specify what method — in which object — should respond to a control without having to write any code.

Action methods have a certain *signature* (format, in other words):

```
- (IBAction)testDrive:(id)sender;
```

The type qualifier IBAction, which is used in place of the void return type, flags the declared method as an action so that Interface Builder is aware of it. (This is similar to the IBOutlet tag, used in the "Creating the outlet" section, earlier in this chapter.) And just as with outlets, you can actually make the connections in the Interface Builder editor, and Xcode will generate the necessary code for you.

The `sender` parameter is the control object sending the action message. When responding to an action message, you may query the sender to get more information about the context of the event triggering the action message.

You can set the action and target of a control object programmatically or in Interface Builder. Setting these properties effectively connects the control and its target via the action. If you connect a control and its target in Interface Builder, the connection is archived in a nib file. When an app later loads the nib file, the connection is restored.

`IBAction` is like `IBOutlet` — it does nothing in the code but rather is a tag used by Interface Builder.

Adding an action

After you have the `TestDriveController` interface displayed, either by having the Assistant editor display it automatically or by navigating to it using the Jump bar, the actual business of creating an action is pretty straightforward. From within the Interface Builder editor, just Control-drag from the element you're interested in (the Test Drive button, in this case) to the `TestDriveController` interface, as detailed in the following steps:

1. **In the Project navigator, select the** `Main_iPad.storyboard` **file.**

2. **Close the Utility area by deselecting it in the View selector.**

   You don't need it to create the action.

3. **Open the Assistant editor by clicking its button in the Editor selector in the toolbar.**

   You should see the `TestDriveController.m` interface file displayed in the Assistant editor. If it doesn't appear, navigate to it using the steps in the earlier section "Creating the outlet."

4. **Control-click and drag from the Test Drive button in the view (the car image, in this example) to the** `TestDriveController.m` **file, right between the** `@interface` **and** `@end` **statements.**

5. **In the dialog that appears, choose Action from the Connection drop-down menu, as shown in Figure 9-10.**

6. **In the same dialog, leave Touch Up Inside as the selection in the Event drop-down menu.**

   To create an Action for a control, you need to specify what event triggers the action. In the case of a button, a Touch Up Inside event is the usual choice because Touch Up Inside is the event that's generated when the very last place the user touched *before* lifting her finger is still inside the button. (This allows a user to change her mind about touching the button by moving her finger off the button before lifting it.)

7. **Still in the same dialog, name this action *testDrive* by entering** testDrive **in the Name field; then click Connect.**

   As shown in Figure 9-11, a new action method

   ```
   - (IBAction)testDrive:(id)sender;
   ```

   gets added to your code.

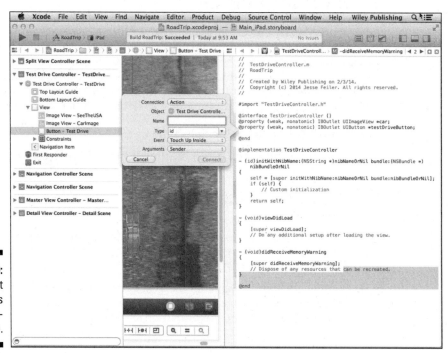

Figure 9-10:
Select
Action as
the connec-
tion type.

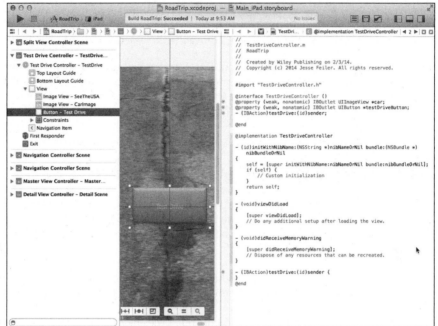

Figure 9-11:
A new
action
message.

Xcode also adds code for you in the .m file to support whatever it is that you're doing. (In this case, the added code supports the action.)

 You can always double-check the status of your Target-Action connections with the help of the Connections inspector, mentioned earlier in this chapter as part of my coverage of outlets. With the Utility area displayed, click the Connections inspector icon in the Inspector selector bar to open the Connections inspector or right-click the view controller in the Document Outline to get a similar picture in the Connections window. In the Received Actions section, you'll see the new action. As I explain earlier, you can change the Interface Builder object you are receiving the action from by dragging from the circle to the new Interface Builder object. You can also add an action by entering the code the Interface Builder would have added for you (the method declaration and definition) in view controller's @interface

```
- (IBAction)testDrive:(id)sender;
```

and @implementation

```
- (IBAction)testDrive:(id)sender {
}
```

and then dragging from the circle in the Received Actions section in the Connections inspector or window to the control and choose an Event type from the contextual menu that appears when you release the mouse button.

I'm sure you've noticed that RoadTrip has a bunch of other buttons that also need connecting. It turns out, though, that you won't be using the Target-Action pattern to connect them. You'll be using a storyboard feature called *segues* to do that for you. I explain using segues in Chapter 14.

How Outlets and Actions Work

You need to be able to connect the objects you added to your user interface in Interface Builder to code that enables you to access these objects (such as to an Image view to change its image) or receive a message that the user has tapped a button.

In the chapter, I show you how to create outlets and actions to do that, but I haven't really explained how all that is connected at runtime.

Storyboards are a collection of (resource) nib files that you use to store the user interface of your app. A *nib file* is an Interface Builder document. When you use Interface Builder in Chapter 4 to create your user interface, you create an *object graph* that is saved (archived) as part of the resource file. When you load the file, the object graph is then used to re-create the relationships between the objects in the file, and your program objects as well.

Every storyboard file has an initial view controller. At runtime, it's loaded along with its view and all the other Interface Builder objects you added in Chapter 5 — and you get an exact replica of the objects that were in your Interface Builder document. The nib-loading code instantiates the objects, configures them, and reestablishes any inter-object connections *including the outlets and actions* that you created in Interface Builder. Not bad for a bunch of 0s and 1s, right?

Update the iPhone storyboard file

As in previous chapters, the code you added in this chapter works for both the iPhone and iPad. But, as in previous chapters, you now should add objects to the iPhone storyboard file to keep it on an equal footing with its iPad sibling. You don't want the iPhone storyboard to think that you love it less than the iPad.

You created the Test Drive scene way back in Chapter 5. Now make sure that the `TestDriveController` in the iPhone storyboard file has the connections shown in Figure 9-12, which are very similar to the iPad storyboard connections shown earlier in Figure 9-8.

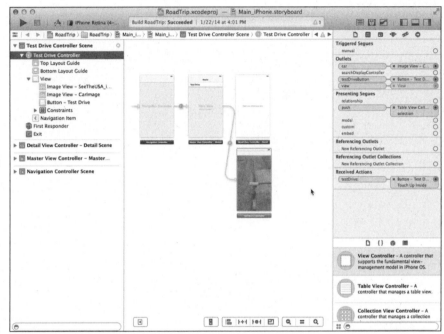

Figure 9-12:
Test-
Drive-
Control-
ler
connec-
tions in
the iPhone
storyboard
file.

Chapter 10

Adding Animation and Sound to Your App

*A*lthough it may take some time before you go on your road trip, as well as complete the building of the app I'm showing you in this book, the least I can do is show you how to take a test drive in your '59 pink Cadillac Eldorado Biarritz convertible.

In this chapter, you find out how to make the car move up the screen, turn around, and move back to its original position — with the appropriate sound effects.

I also show you how to drag the car on the screen to position the ride from wherever you'd like. And to add just a little more pizzazz, I show you how to make the Test Drive button blink.

This chapter provides you with a very good base for understanding animation, sound, and how to manage touches on the screen. They're particularly useful in games, but they also find a very comfortable home in advanced interfaces for all types of apps.

Understanding iOS Animation

Fortunately, most of what you need to do as far as iOS animation is concerned is already built into the framework. Some view properties can be animated (the center point, for example), which means that you just need to tell the view where to start and where to end its move, and a few other optional parameters, and you're done. The view itself (in the UIView base class) has the functionality to animate the move. To give you some context in which to understand how animation on the iPhone and iPad works, however, I need to explain what goes on under the hood when a framework takes care of the animation chores for you. More specifically, I need to delve a bit deeper into views, their properties, and the coordinate systems on the iPad.

View geometry and coordinate systems

The default coordinate system in UIKit places its origin in the top-left corner and has axes that extend down and to the right from the origin point. Coordinate values are represented using floating-point numbers, and you don't have to worry about the screen resolution; the frameworks take care of that automatically. In addition to the screen coordinate system, views define their own local coordinate systems that allow you to specify coordinates relative to the view instead of relative to the screen. In practice, you often do both depending on what you're trying to do.

Because every view and window defines its own local coordinate system, whenever you're drawing or dealing with coordinates, you'll need to pay attention to which coordinate system you're using. I know that sounds ominous, but it's really not that big a deal after you get into the rhythm of working with the coordinate systems.

Points versus pixels

Okay, so where does the high-resolution Retina display come in?

In iOS, all coordinate values and distances are specified using floating-point values in units referred to as *points*. The main thing to understand about points is that they provide a fixed frame of reference for drawing. That fixed frame of reference is derived from the fact that a point is 1/72 of an inch. (This was set for the original Macintosh and LaserWriter and remains a milestone — perhaps the cornerstone — of desktop publishing. In our context, a point is a commonly accepted unit of length.)

The original Macintosh had a screen resolution of 72 pixels per inch (PPI). This meant that points and pixels were identical. However, over time, technology has advanced and now the pixel size and density (PPI) have changed. No longer do most devices actually have 72 PPI, but because pixels and points have been used interchangeably, the arrival of high-density displays such as the Retina display has caused confusion.

When you are talking about size or location, you are probably talking in points. If you are talking about the resolution of the image you will place on an object with a certain size or location, you are probably talking in pixels. On a Retina display, your image will have twice the pixels that you have on a non-Retina display, and you probably use a separate .png file. (Don't worry: The asset manager makes it easy to have two files for a single image.)

Keep this distinction in mind, particularly when you are looking at old (pre-2013) documentation. You have to sort out when "pixel" means pixel and when it means point. Some developers use as a basic rule of thumb, "Xcode=points and Photoshop=pixels." That's a generalization and it's not true in all cases, but as generalizations go, it's generally right.

A view's size and position

A view object's location in a coordinate system is determined using either its frame or its center property:

- ✔ The frame property contains the frame rectangle, which specifies the size and location of the view in its *superview's coordinate system.* (If you're still hazy about the whole superview/subview thing, check out Chapter 4.)
- ✔ The center property contains the known center point of the view *in its superview's coordinate system.*

In your wanderings, you may someday encounter the bounds property. It's tied up with the bounds rectangle, which specifies the size of the view (and its content origin) in the *view's own local coordinate system.* I mention it here for completeness, but I don't use it in this book.

The view coordinates you set for your view's location in Interface Builder are in points. The coordinates start from 0,0 in the top left and increase as you go down and to the right. You usually place your objects below the 20-point status bar, but with iOS 7, views can appear through a navigation or toolbar, so you may place them even lower if you don't want them to show through.

Working with data structures

In addition to knowing what goes where, you'll need to understand how data structures impact how you work with views.

The `frame` is a `CGRect` — a `struct` (a C language type that aggregates conceptually related variables into a single type) with an `origin` and a `size` that are comprised of `CGPoints`. CG here stands for Core Graphics, one of the frameworks included by the Xcode when you selected the Single-View Application template. (See Chapter 4 to remind yourself about frameworks.) The following code shows the `CGRect` `struct`:

```
struct CGRect {
    CGPoint origin;
    CGSize size;
};
```

An `origin` is a `CGPoint` with an x and y value, and a `CGSize` is a `CGPoint` with a `width` and `height` value. The following code shows the `CGPoint` struct:

```
struct CGPoint {
    CGFloat x;
    CGFloat y;
};

struct CGSize {
    CGFloat width;
    CGFloat height;
};
```

Similarly, the `center` property is a `CGPoint`. And that's all you need to know about the data structures you'll be using.

Coordinating Auto Layout, Frames, and Constraints

If you are using Auto Layout (and you should be), you need to know at least the basics of how it interacts with your view's frame. Whereas the Size inspector lets you specify the exact size and location of each point in the frame, the constraints-based Auto Layout system lets you prioritize constraints. This means that at runtime, the constraints are juggled together with their priorities affecting the whole layout. Into the mix, the size of the device, its orientation, and the sizes of views that depend on what their contents happen to be are all taken into account. You cannot know exactly what will happen.

In the Size inspector before Auto Layout came into the picture, you could pin edges of objects to their container view. As a result, there was a certain amount of dynamism, but Auto Layout brings much more to the table, and it lets you deal with changing device and view sizes easily.

In Apple's documentation as well as in this book, most of the discussion of Auto Layout assumes that the things that change at runtime are the orientation of the device as well as the size and position of views that respond to orientation and content changes.

With this chapter, however, another variable comes into play. You are going to be moving the view containing the car image. Unless you are careful, the results may be other than what you expect to see. Here is what you should keep in mind.

If you will be transforming a view (and you will be doing that when you rotate the car image), make certain that is constraints don't undo what you are trying to do. Positional constraints work with the center point of a view. Sizing constraints (pinning to the frame of another view or container view) are working with frames most of the time.

Before moving ahead to animate the car image, check what its constraints are by opening the Constraints section in the Document Outline for the `Main_iPad.storyboard` file. It should be pinned vertically to `Bottom Layout Guide`. It should also be horizontally centered (that uses the center point and not the frame). Any other constraints for the car image view that may have accumulated in your experiments should be removed. Just delete them from the Constraints section of the Document Outline using the Delete key.

If necessary, use Editor⇨Align⇨Horizontal Center in Container to add the centering constraint. Select the car image and control-drag from it to `Bottom Layout Guide` in the Document Outline to add the vertical constraint (choose the vertical spacing option).

Animating a View

Whenever you assign a new value to certain view properties (such as the `frame` and `center` properties, as explained in the previous section), the view is immediately redrawn and the change is immediately visible on the screen.

In addition, changes to several view properties (such as those just mentioned) can be animated. This means that changing the property creates an animation that conveys the change to the user over a short period of time — and it's all handled for you by the `UIView` class. What's more, it takes only one method call to specify the animations to be performed and the options for the animation.

You can animate the following properties of the `UIView` class (the first three are explained previously):

- ✔ `frame`: This property contains the frame rectangle, which specifies the size and location of the view in its *superview's coordinate system.*

- ✔ `bounds`: This property contains the bounds rectangle, which specifies the size of the view (and its content origin) in the *view's own local coordinate system.*

- ✔ `center`: This property contains the known center point of the view in *its superview's coordinate system.*

- ✔ `transform`: I get to this one a bit later in the chapter.

- ✔ `alpha`: This property controls the degree of transparency. If you animate it, you can get views to fade in and fade out.

- ✔ `backgroundColor`: This property allows you to transition from one color to another.

Finally, More Code

In this section, you add the code to animate your '59 pink Cadillac Eldorado Biarritz convertible and have it travel up the screen, turn around, and travel back down the screen.

Implementing the testDrive Method

In Chapter 9, you learned how to create an action for the Test Drive button using Interface Builder, which generated a method stub for you. Now it's time to fill that stub with code.

Add the bolded code in Listing 10-1 to the `testDrive:` method in `TestDrive Controller.m`. I'm also having you add the stubs for code you'll be adding later so that you can run your program before you're completely finished with the back and forth of the animation.

Listing 10-1:   Updating testDrive: to Move the Car up the Screen

```
- (IBAction)testDrive:(id)sender {

  CGPoint center = CGPointMake(self.car.center.x,
      self.view.frame.origin.y +
          self.car.frame.size.height/2);
  [UIView animateWithDuration:3 animations:^ {
      self.car.center = center;
      }
    completion:^(BOOL finished){
      [self rotate];
      }];
}

- (void)rotate {
}

- (void)returnCar {
}

- (void)continueRotation {
}
```

Now, run your program and click or touch the Test Drive button. You'll see your car move up the screen. You're on your way!

Looking more closely at Listing 10-1, you see that you start by creating the coordinate (`CGPoint`) of where you would like the car to end up.

A car is just another view. The following code shows how to move the car on-screen by simply moving the center of the view that holds the image of the car.

```
CGPoint center = CGPointMake(self.car.center.x,
    self.view.frame.origin.y +
        self.car.frame.size.height/2);
```

You use the `center` and `frame` properties primarily for manipulating the view. If you're changing only the position of the view (and not its size), the `center` property is the preferred way to do so.

`CGPointMake` is a function that creates a point for you when you specify the y and x coordinates as parameters. (You'll be setting the car's new `center` point.)

You can leave the x coordinate as is. Doing so makes the car drive right up the center of the screen.

```
self.car.center.x
```

Here's the y coordinate:

```
self.view.frame.origin.y + self.car.frame.size.height/2)
```

`self.view.frame.origin.y` is the top of the view, but if you have the center there, half the car is off the screen. To keep it all on the screen, you add back half the car's height by including `car.frame.size.height/2`.

Notice I'm *adding* to the y coordinate because y increases as you move down the screen from the origin.

So, how do you get the sucker to actually move? Listing 10-1 uses the following code:

```
[UIView animateWithDuration:3 animations:^ {
    self.car.center = center;
    }
    completion:^(BOOL finished) {
      [self rotate];
    }];
```

`animateWithDuration:animations:completion:` is a `UIView` class method that allows you to set an animation duration and specify what you want animated as well as a completion handler that's called when the animation is complete.

First you specify that you want the animation to take three seconds:

```
animateWithDuration:3
```

and then you pass in an animation *block* with what you want animated:

```
animations:^ {
   self.car.center = center;
}
```

This sets the new center you just computed, taking three seconds to move it from start to finish.

If the preceding syntax seems mysterious (what's the ^ doing there and what's up with the code as part of the message?), don't worry: I explain blocks in the next section.

So although that's all there is to get the car to move across the screen, you're not done. You want it to rotate and then drive back across the screen and then rotate again. That's where the completion handler comes in.

Although you can use a completion handler to simply let you know that an animation is finished, you can also use a completion handler to link multiple animations. (In fact, it's the primary way to take care of that task.)

The completion handler that you specify

```
completion:^(BOOL finished){
  [self rotate];
}
```

causes the `rotate` message to be sent when the animation is complete. You do the actual rotation in the `rotate` method.

Of course, right now, the `rotate` method does nothing. I have you add it so that the app will compile and run. I have you add `returnCar` and `continueRotation` to prevent the Incomplete Implementation `TestDriveController.m` compiler warning.

`animateWithDuration:animations:completion:` is only one of a number of block-based methods that offer different levels of configuration for the animation block. Other methods include

```
animateWithDuration:animations:
```

and

```
animateWithDuration:delay:options:animations:completion
```

`animateWithDuration:animations:` has no completion block, as you can see.

Both `animateWithDuration:animations:completion:` and `animateWith Duration:animations:` run only once, using an *ease-in, ease-out animation curve* — the default for most animations, it begins slowly, accelerates through the middle of the animation, and then slows again before completing. If you want to change the default animation parameters, you must use the `animateWith Duration:delay:options:animations:completion:` method, which lets you customize the following:

- ✔ The delay to use before starting the animation
- ✔ The type of timing curve to use during the animation
- ✔ The number of times the animation should repeat

✔ Whether the animation should reverse itself automatically when it reaches the end

✔ Whether touch events are delivered to views while the animations are in progress

✔ Whether the animation should interrupt any in-progress animations or wait until those are complete before starting

As you probably noticed (and I even admitted to), one of the things I tiptoed around was an explanation of the animation syntax:

```
[UIView animateWithDuration:3 animations:^ {
  self.car.center = center;
}
```

Animations use *blocks,* which is a primary design pattern in iOS and is becoming increasingly more important. So before I get to the `rotate` completion handler, I want to explain blocks.

Understanding Block Objects

Objective-C blocks are like traditional C functions in that blocks are small, self-contained units of code. They can be passed in as arguments of methods and functions and then used when they're needed to do some work. (Like many programming topics, understanding block objects is easier when you use them, as you do in the previous section.)

With iOS 4 and newer versions, a number of methods and functions of the system frameworks are starting to take blocks as parameters, including the following:

✔ Completion handlers

✔ Notification handlers

✔ Error handlers

✔ Enumeration

✔ View animation and transitions

✔ Sorting

In the code listings in this chapter, you get to use a block-based method to animate the car, but block objects also have a number of other uses, especially in Grand Central Dispatch and the `NSOperationQueue` class, the two recommended technologies for concurrent processing. But because concurrent processing is beyond the scope of this book (*way* beyond the scope, in fact), I leave you to explore that use on your own.

One of the values of using blocks is that you can access local variables (as well as instance variables), which you can't do in a function or a callback. You also don't have to pass data around — a block can modify variables to pass data back. In addition, if you need to change something, there's no API to change, with its concomitant ripple effect.

In the animation explained in the previous section, you passed a block as the argument to a method. You created the block *inline* (it's there in the message you are sending to the `UIView` to do the animation) because there wasn't that much code, and that's often the way it's done. But sometimes it's easier to follow what's happening by declaring a block variable and passing that as the argument to the method. The declaration syntax, however, is similar to the standard syntax for function pointers, except that you use a caret (^) instead of an asterisk pointer (*).

If you look at `animateWithDuration:animations:completion:` in the `UIView` class reference, you'll see

```
+ (void)animateWithDuration:(NSTimeInterval)duration
    animations:(void (^)(void))animations
    completion:(void (^)(BOOL finished))completion;
```

I know this looks a bit advanced for a *For Dummies* book, but I cover it here because Apple is now treating blocks as a primary design pattern, up there with inheritance and delegation — so don't be surprised to find blocks being used more and more.

Nevertheless, because it's a tad advanced, I'll go through the code slowly, and by the end — I promise — you'll be comfortable with blocks, despite the really weird syntax.

To start, this is the syntax that defines `animations` as a block that has no parameters and no return value:

```
void (^)(void))animations
```

`completion` is defined as a block that has no return value and takes a single Boolean argument parameter:

```
(void (^)(BOOL finished))completion
```

When you create a block inline, you just use the caret (^) operator to indicate the beginning of a block and then follow with the code enclosed within the normal braces. That's what was going on in Listing 10-1, with

```
animations:^ {
  self.car.center = center;
}
```

and

```
completion:^(BOOL finished){
   [self rotate];
}
```

Although in this example you use blocks inline, you could also declare them like any other local variable, as you can see in Listing 10-2. Add the code in bold in Listing 10-2 to your `testDrive` method replacing what you already have in that spot.

Listing 10-2: Using Declared Blocks

```
- (IBAction)testDrive:(id)sender {

   CGPoint center = CGPointMake(car.center.x,
      self.view.frame.origin.y + car.frame.size.height/2);

   void (^animation)() = ^() {

      self.car.center = center;
   };

   void (^completion)(BOOL) = ^(BOOL finished){
      [self rotate];
   };

      [UIView animateWithDuration:3 animations:animation
                                    completion:completion];
}
```

When you declare a block, you use the caret (^) operator to indicate the beginning of a block with the code enclosed within the normal braces, and a semicolon to indicate the end of a block expression.

The declaration in Listing 10-2 is pretty much the same as you see in the following `animateWithDuration:animations:completion:` method declaration, except that the identifiers have been moved around a little. I have bolded both to make that a little easier to see:

```
+ (void)animateWithDuration:(NSTimeInterval)duration
      animations:(void (^)(void))animations
      completion:(void (^)(BOOL finished))completion;
```

Here, you're declaring two block variables by using the ^ operator: one with the name of `animations` that has no return value, and one with the name of `completion` that has no return value and takes `BOOL` as its single argument:

```
void (^animation)()
void (^completion)(BOOL)
```

This is like any other variable declaration (`int i = 1`, for example), in which you follow the equal sign with its definition.

You use the `^` operator again to indicate the beginning of the *block literal* — the definition assigned to the block variable. The block literal includes argument names (`finished`) as well as the body (code) of the block and is terminated with a semicolon:

```
void (^animation)() = ^() {
  self.car.center = center;
};

void (^completion)(BOOL) = ^(BOOL finished){
  [self rotate];
};
```

You'll be using blocks a few more times in this book, so at some point (despite the weird syntax), you'll become comfortable with them. (Frankly it took me a while to get used to them myself.) After you do get the hang of them, though, you'll find all sorts of opportunities to use them to simplify your code, as you discover in Chapter 19.

Rotating the Object

In this section, I show you how to rotate a view (in this case, turn the car around). To do so, you update the `rotate` code stub you started out with back in Listing 10-1 with the bolded code in Listing 10-3.

Listing 10-3: Updating rotate

```
- (void) rotate {

  CGAffineTransform transform =
          CGAffineTransformMakeRotation(M_PI);

  void (^animation)() =  ^() {
    self.car.transform = transform;
  };

  void (^completion)(BOOL) = ^(BOOL finished){
    [self returnCar];
  };

  [UIView animateWithDuration:3 animations:animation
          completion:completion];
}
```

This method uses the block declarations I explain in the previous section.

The CGAffineTransform data structure represents a matrix used for *affine transformations* — a blueprint for how points in one coordinate system map to points in another coordinate system. Although CGAffineTransform has a number of uses (such as scaling and translating a coordinate system), the only one covered here is the rotation method you use in Listing 10-3:

```
CGAffineTransformMakeRotation(M_PI)
```

To rotate a view, you specify the angle (in radians) to rotate the coordinate system axes. Whereas degrees are numbers between 0 and 360, radians, though similar, range from 0 to 2∏. So when you create a rotation that turns an object around one half-circle, that rotation in radians is pi. (M_PI is a system constant that represents pi.)

Just to make your life interesting, you should note that in iOS, positive is counterclockwise, but on Mac OS X, positive is clockwise.

The end result of Listing 10-3 is that the car will rotate 180 degrees in three seconds, and when it's done, you send the returnCar message in the completion handler.

To return the car to its original position, add the bolded code in Listing 10-4 to the returnCar method stub in TestDriveController.m.

Listing 10-4:   Updating returnCar

```
- (void)returnCar {

    CGPoint center = CGPointMake(self.view.center.x,
            self.view.frame.size.height -
            self.car.frame.size height);


    void (^animation)() =  ^() {
      self.car.center = center;
    };

    void (^completion)(BOOL) = ^(BOOL finished){
      [self continueRotation];
    };

    [UIView animateWithDuration:3 animations:animation
                                  completion:completion];
}
```

This approach is pretty much the same as that of the `testDrive` method. You put the `center` back by computing the bottom of the view

```
        self.view.frame.size.height
            - self.car.frame.size.height);
```

You can experiment with these formulas to see how to move the car around the view.

But you're not done yet. You need to rotate the car back to its original position (unless you want to drive in reverse from California to New York). Add the bolded code in Listing 10-5 to the `continueRotation` method stub in `TestDriveController.m`.

Listing 10-5:   Updating continueRotation

```
- (void)continueRotation {

  CGAffineTransform transform =
                        CGAffineTransformMakeRotation(0);

  void (^animation)() = ^() {
    self.car.transform = transform;
  };

[UIView animateWithDuration:3 animations:animation
                                    completion:NULL];
}
```

You need to understand that the transform (in this case, a view rotation) is still there; that is, you created a transform to rotate the car 180 degrees. If you want to get the car back to the original position, you need to return the transform to 0.

You could extend this action by having the car drive around the perimeter of the screen — but I'll leave that up to you.

Working with Audio

Cars make noise, and a '59 Cadillac certainly doesn't disappoint in that respect. So in this section, I show you how to add some sound to the RoadTrip app so that everyone can hear your car coming down the road.

More specifically, I discuss using two different ways iOS has for implementing audio. One is an instance of the `AVAudioPlayer` class — called, appropriately enough, an *audio player* — which provides playback of audio data from a file or memory. You use this class unless you're playing audio captured from a network stream or in need of very low I/O latency (lag time). The `AVAudioPlayer` class offers quite a lot of functionality, including playing sounds of any duration, looping sounds, playing multiple sounds simultaneously, and having one sound per audio player with precise synchronization among all the players in use. It also controls relative playback level, stereo positioning, and playback rate for each sound you're playing.

The `AVAudioPlayer` class lets you play sound in any audio format available in iOS. You implement a delegate to handle interruptions (such as an incoming SMS message) and to update the user interface when a sound has finished playing. The delegate methods to use are described in the `AVAudioPlayerDelegate` Protocol Reference (which you can access in the Organizer window as I explain in Chapter 7).

The second way to play sound is by using System Sound Services, which provides a way to play short sounds and make the device vibrate. You can use System Sound Services to play short (30 seconds or shorter) sounds. The interface doesn't provide level, positioning, looping, or timing control and doesn't support simultaneous playback: You can play only one sound at a time. You can use System Sound Services to provide audible alerts; on some iOS devices, alerts can even include vibration.

You have seen how to add frameworks to your app. You now need to add both AVFoundation.framework and AudioToolbox.framework. You see how to do this in Chapter 8 in the section on network availability. Just as a reminder, you add them to Linked Frameworks and Libraries in the project's General tab.

I showed you how to do that because I wanted you to understand that you often need to add new frameworks to support your code. Starting with Xcode 5, the process is easier (that is to say, it's automated), so I won't be asking you to add the new frameworks.

Later in this chapter, you will import the two framework header files using this code:

```
#import AudioToolbox;
#import AVFoundation;
```

The libraries will be linked automatically for you.

The sound files you need for RoadTrip (the aptly named `BurnRubber.aif` and `CarRunning.aif`) are already in the Resources folder that you added to your project. (See Chapter 3 if you haven't already done this.)

You can use Audacity, a free, open source software for recording and editing sounds, to create your own sound files. It's available for Mac OS X, Microsoft Windows, GNU/Linux, and other operating systems.

With the added frameworks in place, you now need to import the necessary audio player and system sound services headers and then add the instance variables you'll be using. To accomplish all this, add the bolded code in Listing 10-6 to `TestDriveController.m`.

Listing 10-6:   Updating the TestDriveController Class Extension

```
#import "TestDriveController.h"
#import <AVFoundation/AVFoundation.h>
#import <AudioToolbox/AudioToolbox.h>

@interface TestDriveController () {
  AVAudioPlayer *backgroundAudioPlayer;
  SystemSoundID burnRubberSoundID;
}
@property (weak, nonatomic) IBOutlet UIButton
  *testDriveButton;
@property (strong, nonatomic) IBOutlet UIImageView *car;
@property (weak, nonatomic) IBOutlet UIToolbar *toolbar;
- (IBAction)testDrive:(id)sender;
- (void)rotate;
- (void)returnCar;


@end


@implementation TestDriveController
```

As you can see, I'm having you take advantage of being able to put instance variables in the implementation file to keep them hidden. In fact, the file template already had added the class extension for you, and you have already placed two properties and an action in it.

```
@interface TestDriveController ()

@end
```

Next, you need to set up the audio player and system sound services. Add the bolded code in Listing 10-7 to `viewDidLoad` in `TestDriveController.m`.

Listing 10-7:   Updating viewDidLoad

```
- (void)viewDidLoad
{
  [super viewDidLoad];

  NSURL* backgroundURL = [NSURL fileURLWithPath:
    [[NSBundle mainBundle]pathForResource:
                        @"CarRunning" ofType:@"aif"]];
  backgroundAudioPlayer = [[AVAudioPlayer alloc]
          initWithContentsOfURL:backgroundURL error:nil];
  backgroundAudioPlayer.numberOfLoops = -1;
  [backgroundAudioPlayer prepareToPlay];

  NSURL* burnRubberURL = [NSURL fileURLWithPath:
    [[NSBundle mainBundle] pathForResource:
                        @"BurnRubber" ofType:@"aif"]];
  AudioServicesCreateSystemSoundID(
    (__bridge CFURLRef)burnRubberURL, &burnRubberSoundID);
}
```

In Listing 10-7, the first thing you do is load the sound file from the resources in your bundle:

```
NSURL* backgroundURL = [NSURL fileURLWithPath:
  [[NSBundle mainBundle]pathForResource:
                      @"CarRunning" ofType:@"aif"]];
```

"What bundle?" you say? Well, when you build your iOS application, Xcode packages it as a bundle — one containing the following:

- ✔ The application's executable code

- ✔ Any resources that the app has to use (for instance, the application icon, other images, and localized content — in this case, the plist, .html files, and .png files)

- ✔ The RoadTrip-Info.plist file, also known as the *information property list,* which defines key values for the application, such as bundle ID, version number, and display name

Pretty easy, huh?

Coming back to Listing 10-7, fileURLWithPath is an NSURL class method that initializes and returns an NSURL object as a file URL with a specified path. The NSURL class includes the utilities necessary for downloading files or other resources from web and FTP servers and from the file system.

The sound file you'll be using is a resource, and `pathForResource:` is an `NSBundle` method that creates the path needed by the `fileURLWithPath:` method to construct the `NSURL`. Just give `pathForResource:` the name and the file type, and it returns the path that gets packed in to the `NSURL` and loaded.

Be sure that you provide the correct file type; otherwise, this technique won't work.

Next, you create an instance of the audio player

```
backgroundAudioPlayer = [[AVAudioPlayer alloc]
         initWithContentsOfURL:backgroundURL error:nil];
```

and initialize it with the audio file location (`NSURL`). You'll ignore any errors.

Set the number of loops to `-1` (which will cause the audio file to continue to play until you stop it) and tell the player to get ready to play:

```
backgroundAudioPlayer.numberOfLoops = -1;
[backgroundAudioPlayer prepareToPlay];
```

`prepareToPlay` prepares the audio player for playback by preloading its buffers; it also acquires the audio hardware needed for playback. This preloading minimizes the lag between calling the `play` method and the start of sound output. Without this preloading, although the player would still play when you send the `play` message (later) in `viewDidLoad`, you'll likely notice a lag as it sets up its buffers.

Similarly, you set up the `NSURL` for the `BurnRubber` sound:

```
NSURL* burnRubberURL = [NSURL fileURLWithPath:
  [[NSBundle mainBundle] pathForResource:
                  @"BurnRubber" ofType:@"aif"]];
```

You then call a core foundation method to create a system sound object that you later use to play the sound:

```
AudioServicesCreateSystemSoundID((__bridge
         CFURLRef)burnRubberURL, &burnRubberSoundID);
```

`CFURLRef` is a `CoreFoundation` object, and ARC doesn't automatically manage the lifetimes of `CoreFoundation` types. And although you can use certain `CoreFoundation` memory management rules and functions, you don't need to do that here. That's because all you're doing is casting an Objective-C object to a `CoreFoundation` type object, and you won't need to use any `CoreFoundation` memory management in your code. You have to let the compiler know about any memory management implications, however, so you need to use the `__bridge` cast.

In `testDrive`, you'll play both the `BurnRubber` and `CarRunning` sounds. To do so, add the bolded code in Listing 10-8 to `testDrive:` in `TestDriveController.m`.

Listing 10-8:   Updating testDrive

```
- (IBAction)testDrive:(id)sender {


    AudioServicesPlaySystemSound(burnRubberSoundID);
    [self performSelector:@selector(playCarSound)
                            withObject:self afterDelay:.2];

    CGPoint center = CGPointMake(_car.center.x,
                            self.view.frame.origin.y +
            self.car.frame.size.height/2 );

    void (^animation)() = ^() {

        self.car.center = center;
    };

    void (^completion)(BOOL) = ^(BOOL finished){
        [self rotate];
    };

    [UIView animateWithDuration:3 animations:animation
            completion:completion];
}
```

You also need to add the code in Listing 10-9 to play the `CarRunning` sound.

Listing 10-9:   Adding playCarSound

```
- (void)playCarSound {

    [backgroundAudioPlayer play];
}
```

I'm having you play the `BurnRubber` sound first, followed by the `CarRunning` sound. If you don't wait until the `BurnRubber` sound is complete before you play the `CarRunning` sound, the `BurnRubber` sound is drowned out by the `CarRunning` sound.

To play the `BurnRubber` sound, you use a function call to System Sound Services:

```
AudioServicesPlaySystemSound(burnRubberSoundID);
```

After this sound is done, you start the `CarRunning` sound by using a very useful method that will enable you to send the message to start the audio player after a delay. That method is `performSelector:withObject:afterDelay:`, and it looks like this:

```
[self performSelector:@selector(playCarSound)
                          withObject:self afterDelay:.2];
```

`performSelector:withObject:afterDelay:` sends a message that you specify to an object after a delay. The method you want invoked should have no return value, and should have zero or one argument.

In Listing 10-9, this method meets these rules:

```
- (void)playCarSound {

    [backgroundAudioPlayer play];
}
```

`@selector(playCarSound)` is a compiler directive that returns a selector for a method name. A *selector* is the name used to select a method to execute for an object; it becomes a unique identifier when the source code is compiled.

Selectors really don't do anything. What makes the selector method name different from a plain string is that the compiler makes sure that selectors are unique. Selectors are useful because at runtime they act like a dynamic function pointer that, for a given name, automatically points to the implementation of a method appropriate for whichever class they're used with.

`withObject:` is the argument to pass to the method when it's invoked. `afterDelay:` is the minimum time before which the message is sent. Specifying a delay of 0 doesn't necessarily cause the selector to be performed immediately. When you send the `performSelector:withObject:` message, you specify 0.2 seconds because that's the duration of the `BurnRubber` sound.

Sometimes you may need to cancel a selector. `cancelPerformSelectorsWithTarget:` cancels all outstanding selectors scheduled to be performed with a given target.

Several other variations exist on the `performSelector:withObject:` `afterDelay:` method. Those variations are part of the `NSObject` class, which is the root class of most Objective-C class hierarchies. It provides the basic interface to the runtime system as well as the capability to behave as Objective-C objects.

Finally, to play the sound in the `playCarSound` method, you send the audio player the `play` message:

```
[backgroundAudioPlayer play];
```

The `play` message plays a sound asynchronously. If you haven't already sent the `prepareToPlay` message, `play` will send that for you as well (although you should expect a lag before the sound is played).

Next, you need to stop playing the sound in the `continueRotation` animation's completion block (or it gets really annoying). To stop playing the sound, add the bolded code in Listing 10-10 to `continueRotation` in `TestDriveController.m`. (`completion` replaces the previous value that was `NULL`.)

Listing 10-10:   Updating continueRotation to Stop the Sound

```
- (void)continueRotation {

  CGAffineTransform transform =
                    CGAffineTransformMakeRotation(-0);

  void (^animation)() = ^() {
    _car.transform = transform;
  };

  void (^completion)(BOOL) = ^(BOOL finished){
    [backgroundAudioPlayer stop];
    [backgroundAudioPlayer prepareToPlay];
  };

  [UIView animateWithDuration:3 animations:animation
                    completion:completion];
}
```

In the code in Listing 10-10, you also set up the audio player to play again.

And there you have it. Run your project and you'll notice some very realistic sound effects when you tap the Test Drive button.

Tracking Touches

It would be nice to be able to drag the car and place it anywhere on the screen. In this section, I explain how to code for dragging an object, as well as how touches work on an iOS device.

The touch of a finger (or lifting it from the screen) adds a touch event to the application's event queue, where it's *encapsulated* (contained) in a UIEvent object. A UITouch object exists for each finger touching the screen, which enables you to track individual touches.

The touchesBegan:withEvent: message is sent when one or more fingers touch down in a view. This message is a method of the TestDriveController's superclass, UIResponder, from which the view controller is derived.

As the user continues to touch the screen with his or her fingers, the system reports the changes for each finger in the corresponding UITouch object, thereby sending the touchesMoved:withEvent: message. The touchesEnded:withEvent: message is sent when one or more fingers lift from the associated view. The touchesCancelled:withEvent: message, on the other hand, is sent when a system event (such as a low-memory warning) cancels a touch event.

In this app, you need be concerned only with the first two methods just described.

To begin the process of responding to a touch event, add a new instance variable (bolded in Listing 10-11) to the TestDriveController.m implementation file.

Listing 10-11: Updating the TestDriveController Implementation

```
@interface TestDriveController () {

  AVAudioPlayer *backgroundAudioPlayer;
  SystemSoundID burnRubberSoundID;
  BOOL touchInCar;
}
@end
```

Next, add the touchesBegan: method in Listing 10-12 to TestDrive Controller.m to start tracking touches. (You're actually overriding this method because UIViewController inherited it from the UIResponder base class.)

Listing 10-12:   Overriding touchesBegan:

```
- (void)touchesBegan:(NSSet *)touches withEvent:
                                    (UIEvent *)event
{
  UITouch *touch = [touches anyObject];
  if (CGRectContainsPoint(self.car.frame,
                    [touch locationInView:self.view]))
    touchInCar = YES;
  else {
    touchInCar = NO;
    [super touchesBegan:touches withEvent:event];
  }
}
```

As mentioned previously, the `touchesBegan:withEvent:` message is sent when one or more fingers touch down in a view. The touches themselves are passed to the method in an `NSSet` object — an unordered collection of distinct elements.

To access an object in `NSSet`, use the `anyObject` method — it returns one of the objects in the set. For our purposes here, you're assuming just one object — but you might want to explore this issue further on your own so that you can understand how to handle additional possibilities.

The following code shows how to set up the `anyObject` method:

```
UITouch *touch = [touches anyObject];
```

Next, have the code determine whether the user's touch event is in the `Car` (`UIImage`) view:

```
if (CGRectContainsPoint(self.car.frame,
                    [touch locationInView:self.view]))
```

`CGRectContainsPoint` is a function that returns `YES` when a rectangle (view coordinates) contains a point. You specify the car's `frame` as the rectangle:

```
self.car.frame
```

and you specify the point by sending the `locationInView:` message to the touch:

```
locationInView:self.view
```

`locationInView:` returns the current location of the receiver in the coordinate system of the given view. In this case, you're using the Main view, but you might want to change the view if you're trying to determine the location within another view, for example. Maybe the user is touching an itty-bitty gas pedal. (Just to be clear, in our RoadTrip app, the car does *not* have an itty-bitty gas pedal.)

If it's determined that the touch is in the car, you assign YES to the touchInCar instance variable; if it's not, you assign NO and forward the message up the responder chain. You use touchInCar later to determine whether the user is dragging the car around or just running his finger over the screen.

The default implementation of touchesBegan: does nothing. However, sub-classes derived directly from UIResponder, particularly UIView, forward the message up the responder chain. To forward the message to the next responder, send the message to super (the superclass implementation).

If you override touchesBegan:withEvent: without calling super (a common use pattern), you must also override the other methods for handling touch events, if only as stub (empty) implementations.

Multiple touches are disabled by default. To allow your app to receive multiple touch events, you must set the multipleTouchEnabled property of the corresponding view instance to YES.

As users merrily move the car around the screen (perhaps saying *zoom zoom* to themselves), your app is constantly being sent the touchesMoved: message. Add the code in Listing 10-13 to TestDriveController.m to override that method, which will enable you to move the car to where the user's finger is.

Listing 10-13: Overriding touchesMoved:withEvent:

```
- (void)touchesMoved:(NSSet *)touches withEvent:
                                    (UIEvent *)event {

  if (touchInCar) {
    UITouch* touch = [touches anyObject];
    self.car.center = [touch locationInView:self.view];
  }
  else
    [super touchesMoved:touches withEvent:event];
}
```

If the first touch was in the Car view (touchInCar is YES), you assign car's center property to the touch coordinate. As I explain in the "Animating a View" section, earlier in this chapter, when you assign a new value to the center property, the view's location is immediately changed. Otherwise, you ignore the touch and forward the message up the responder chain.

It's interesting to observe that when you position the car next to a button, it will travel under that button when you touch the Test Drive button. This feature illustrates the subview structure that I explain in Chapter 4 in the section about the view hierarchy. Because I had you add the buttons *last* (they're subviews of the Main view), they're displayed *on top* of the subviews (car) that you added earlier.

Experiment with moving the car around and then using the Test Drive button. If there's anything wrong with your formulas for positioning the car during the Test Drive, you'll see it when the car starts from a different place.

Animating a Series of Images "In Place"

Although I explain animation using the UIView methods earlier in this chapter, this section shows you a way to animate a series of images "in place" — you are not moving the image around as you did earlier with the car; instead you are changing the image where it is to make it appear as if it were animated.

To make the Test Drive button blink, for example, add the bolded code in Listing 10-14 to TestDriveController.m. As you can see in the listing, only a single line of code is needed to animate the button.

Listing 10-14:   Creating a Blinking Button

```
- (void)viewDidLoad
{
  [super viewDidLoad];

  NSURL* backgroundURL = [NSURL
         fileURLWithPath:[[NSBundle mainBundle]
         pathForResource:@"CarRunning" ofType:@"aif"]];
  backgroundAudioPlayer = [[AVAudioPlayer alloc]
         initWithContentsOfURL:backgroundURL error:nil];
  backgroundAudioPlayer.numberOfLoops = -1;
  [backgroundAudioPlayer prepareToPlay];

  NSURL* burnRubberURL = [NSURL
         fileURLWithPath:[[NSBundle mainBundle]
         pathForResource:@"BurnRubber" ofType:@"aif"]];
  AudioServicesCreateSystemSoundID((__bridge
         CFURLRef)burnRubberURL, &burnRubberSoundID);
  [self.testDriveButton setBackgroundImage:[UIImage
         animatedImageNamed:@"Button" duration:1.0 ]
         forState:UIControlStateNormal];
}
```

This blinking button is designed to show you how to animate changing images. Blinking objects on the screen are generally avoided in good interfaces. Remember the famous saying, "Less is more."

In Chapter 5, I show you how to add a custom button with a Button background image. You could have also programmatically added the background image by sending the button the setBackgroundImage:forState: message. (Chapter 5 explains the control state as well.) Normally, you might think of making the background image a single image. However, animatedImageNamed:duration: and some similar methods use instead a series of files, each displayed for a duration you specify. This type of method enables you to animate (this time, in place) not only a button but also any image by simply supplying a series of images:

```
[testDriveButton setBackgroundImage:
   [UIImage animatedImageNamed:@"Button" duration:1.0]
                     forState:UIControlStateNormal];
```

In the animatedImageNamed: method, you supply a *base* name of an image to animate. The method appends a 0 to the base name and loads that image (in this case, Button0). After the time that you specify in duration has elapsed, the animatedImageNamed: method appends the next number (in this case, 1) to the base image name and attempts to load it and the remainder of images (up to 1,024 images) until it runs out of images, and then it starts over.

In the Project navigator, open the disclosure triangle for the RoadTrip Resources group that you created in Chapter 3. If you look in the RoadTrip Resources group, you see two images, Button0 and Button1 — with Button being the base name you specified. This is an "in place" animation, so all images included in the animated image should share the same size and scale.

If you select each image in the Project navigator, you can see that they're slightly different colors, and each will display for 1.0 second (duration:1.0). This makes the button blink and certainly adds some life to the Main view.

iPhone versus iPad

The iOS 7 animation and sound libraries and frameworks are the same for the iPhone and iPad, so the code shown in this chapter works properly on both the iPhone and iPad apps. The differences are confined mostly to the separate storyboards and the support for a navigation view interface as opposed to a split view controller interface.

Part IV
The Model and the App Structure

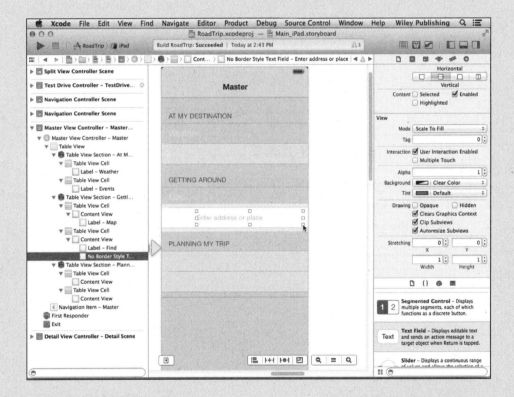

Visit www.dummies.com/extras/iosapplicationdevelopment for more on how to use frameworks in iOS app development.

In this part . . .

- ✔ Implementing the Master View Controller
- ✔ Working with split view controllers and the master view
- ✔ Finishing the basic app structure

Chapter 11

The Trip Model

In This Chapter

▶ Recognizing the importance of models

▶ Working with property lists

▶ Starting the `Trip` class implementation

▶ Displaying variable content in the debugger

I t's time to add some content to RoadTrip. The owner of RoadTrip's data is the model, so I start this chapter with a look at the data you'll need and how the model will manage it. Then I show you how to add a `Trip` class that will serve as the interface to the model. Finally, you see how to add the `Destination` class — which is one of the objects that will be used by the model but is hidden behind the `Trip` interface.

What the Model Contains

In the Model-View-Controller (MVC) design pattern that is the basis for all iOS apps, the model owns the app content logic and data. Therefore, to design your model, the best place to start is with the app design I present in Chapter 4 and consider what will be displayed in the views.

In this first version of RoadTrip, the model needs to provide, for each destination, the following:

✔ The destination name

✔ A background image for the destination

✔ The destination latitude and longitude, along with a title and subtitle to be displayed in the annotation on a map

✔ Events that the user might be interested in

✔ Titles and subtitles of sights or places of interest to be displayed in the annotation on a map

✔ Weather information

I've made the point (several times) that the model is about the data, so where does the data come from? The easy answer is . . . any place you'd like. Given the iOS model, however, you can take several approaches:

✔ **Option 1:** Download the data from a web service (or FTP site) and have the model control it in a file or have Core Data (an iOS object persistence mechanism outside the scope of this book) manage it.

✔ **Option 2:** Have a web service manage your data and get what you need as you need it.

✔ **Option 3:** Include the data as an app resource.

✔ **Option 4:** Access the data on the web as an HTML page.

Although I really like Option 1 (and explain that in my book *Sams Teach Yourself Core Data for Mac and iOS in 24 Hours*), it's beyond the scope of this book, so the `Trip` model uses both Options 3 and 4.

Although the preceding answers most of the model's "Show me the data" responsibility, yet another question still has to be answered: How does the model know where the data is? The answer to that question lies in a very useful structure that's used extensively by not only iOS but also Cocoa apps: property lists (more commonly known as *plists*). The RoadTrip plist that you are about to create will have both data used by the `Trip` model object (Option 3) as well as the URLs for the data you download as HTML pages (Option 4).

Adding the Model Data

For situations in which you need to store relatively small amounts of persistent data — say, less than a megabyte — a property list offers a uniform and convenient means of organizing, storing, and accessing the data.

Using property lists

A property list (or *plist*) is perfect for storing small amounts of data that consist primarily of strings and numbers. What adds to its appeal is the capability to easily read it into your program, use the data, and (although you won't be doing it in the RoadTrip app) modify the data and then write the property list back out again (see the "Using plists to store data" sidebar, later in this chapter). That's because iOS provides a small set of objects that have that behavior built right in.

Apps and other system software in OS X and iOS use property lists extensively. For example, the OS X Finder stores file and directory attributes in a property list, and iOS uses them for user defaults. You also get a Property List editor with Xcode, which makes property list files easy to create and maintain in your own programs.

Figure 11-1 shows a property list that I show you how to build — one that contains the data necessary for the RoadTrip app.

After you figure out how to work with property lists, it's actually easy, but like most things, getting there is half the fun.

Property lists hold serializable objects. A *serializable object* can convert itself into a stream of bits so that it can be stored in a file; it can then reconstitute itself into the object it once was when it's read back in.

These objects, called *property list objects,* that you have to work with are as follows, and you find two types (which I explain in an upcoming paragraph):

Basic Classes:

- ✔ `NSData` and `NSMutableData`
- ✔ `NSDate`
- ✔ `NSNumber`
- ✔ `NSString` and `NSMutableString`

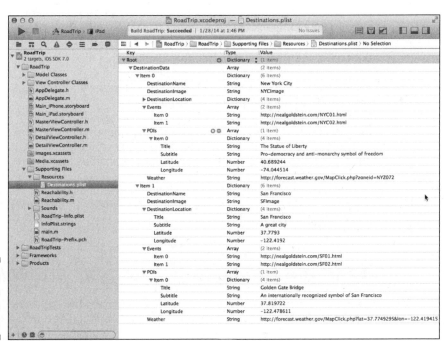

Figure 11-1:
The
RoadTrip
plist.

Containers:

> ✔ `NSArray` and `NSMutableArray`
> ✔ `NSDictionary` and `NSMutableDictionary`

As previously shown in Figure 11-1, the RoadTrip plist is actually an `NSDictionary` named Root (this is true of all property list unless you change it). Root has one entry — `DestinationData`, which is an array of dictionaries — and the data for each one of the destinations is held in a dictionary in that array (`Item 0` and `Item 1`).

Now for that explanation of two kinds of property list objects:

> ✔ **Basic classes:** The term *basic classes* describes the simplest kind of object. They are what they are.
> ✔ **Containers:** *Containers* can hold primitives as well as other containers.

One important feature of property list object containers (such as `NSArray` and `NSDictionary`), besides their ability to hold other objects, is that they both have a `writeToFile:` method that writes the object to a file, and a corresponding `initWithContentsOfFile:`, which initializes the object with the contents of a file. So if I create an array or dictionary and fill it chock-full of objects of the property list type, all I have to do to save that array or dictionary to a file is tell it to go save itself — or create an array or dictionary and then tell it to initialize itself from a file.

Primitives `NSString` and `NSData` and their mutable counterparts also can write and read themselves to and from a file.

`NSData` and `NSMutableData` are wrappers (a *wrapper* is an object whose basic purpose is to turn something into an object) in which you can dump any kind of digital data and then have that data act as an object.

The containers can contain other containers as well as the primitive types. Thus, you might have an array of dictionaries, and each dictionary might contain other arrays and dictionaries as well as the primitive types.

Adding a property list to your project

Given the versatility of property lists, you're sure to turn to them time and time again. Follow these steps to incorporate a plist into your Xcode project:

1. **In the Project navigator, add a RoadTrip Resources group to Supporting Files. Right-click it, and then choose New File from the menu that appears to get the New File dialog.**

Or select the RoadTrip Resources group and choose File➪New➪New File from the main menu (or press ⌘+N).

2. **In the left column of the New File dialog, select Resource under the iOS heading, select the Property List template in the top-right pane, and then click Next.**

A Save sheet appears.

3. **Enter** Destinations **in the Save As field.**

4. **Click Create (and make sure that the Target field has the RoadTrip check box selected).**

A property list will be created with a single element called Root; it is a dictionary, but you can change it to be an array if you want.

5. **Right-click in the Root row to show the context-sensitive menu; then choose Add Row, as shown in Figure 11-2.**

You can also choose Editor➪Add Item to add a row.

A new row appears, as shown in Figure 11-3.

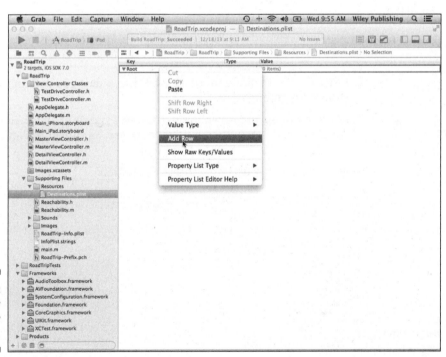

Figure 11-2:
Add a row to the new plist file.

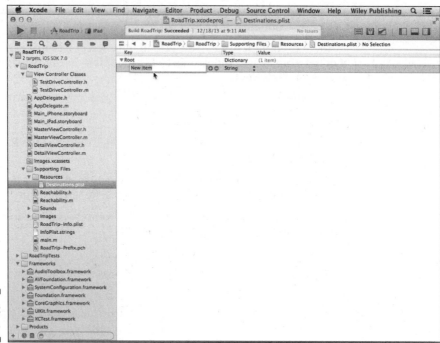

Figure 11-3:
A new row.

6. **Enter** DestinationData **in the Key field, replacing New Item (which should be highlighted).**

7. **Click in the up and down arrows in the Type field and then choose Array from the pop-up menu that appears, as shown in Figure 11-4.**

Change key to DestinationData   Change type to Array

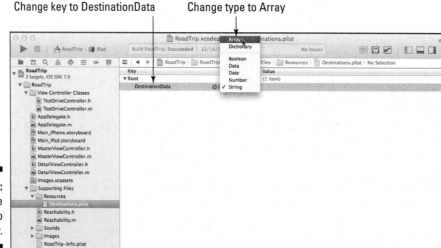

Figure 11-4:
Change the
New Item to
Array.

8. **Click the disclosure triangle in front of the** DestinationData **key so it is pointing down and click the + (plus) button, as shown in Figure 11-5. A new entry appears.**

   DestinationData is an array of dictionaries that will hold all your destination-specific information, with Item 0 being the first one.

   In Figure 11-5, I've added the row, and you can see the + (plus) button in the new row.

Disclosure triangle open   Plus button

Figure 11-5:
Add an
entry.

9. **Make Item 0 a dictionary by selecting Dictionary in the Type pop-up menu (in the same way you select Array in Step 7).**

   Your new entry is made into a dictionary, as shown in Figure 11-6.

10. **Click the disclosure triangle in front of the Item 0 key so that it points down, and click the + (plus) button as you did in Step 7 to add a new entry to the dictionary.**

    You see a new entry under the dictionary like the one in Figure 11-7.

These disclosure triangles work the same way as those in the Finder and the Xcode editor. The Property List editor interprets what you want to add based on the triangle. So if the items are revealed (that is, the triangle is pointing down), the editor assumes that you want to add a sub item or *child.* If the sub items are not revealed (that is, the triangle is pointing sideways), the editor assumes that you want to add an item at that level *(sibling).* In this case, with the arrow pointing down, you add a new entry — a sub item — to the dictionary. If the triangle were pointing sideways, you would be entering a new entry under the root.

Only arrays and dictionaries have children.

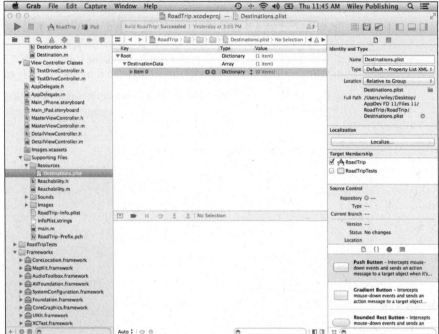

Figure 11-6:
A dictionary
entry.

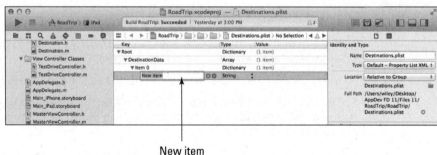

Figure 11-7:
A new
entry in the
dictionary.

New item

11. **In the Key field of your newest entry, enter** DestinationName, **leave the Type as String, and then double-click (or tab to) the Value field and enter** New York City, **as shown in Figure 11-8.**

12. **Click the + button in the row you just entered, and you get a new entry (a sibling of the previous row). In the Key field, enter** DestinationImage, **leave the Type as String, and then double-click (or tab to) the Value field and enter** NYCImage.

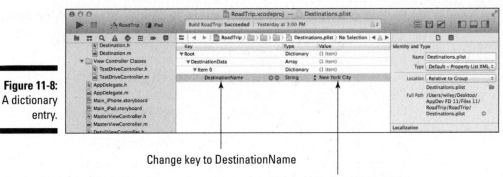

Figure 11-8:
A dictionary entry.

Change key to DestinationName

Change value to New York City

13. **Click the + button in the row you just entered, and you get a new entry (a sibling of the previous row). In the Key field, enter** DestinationLocation **and select Dictionary in the Type pop-up menu.**

14. **Click the disclosure triangle in front of the** DestinationLocation **key so it's facing down, and click the + button.**

    You see a new entry under the dictionary, as you can see in Figure 11-9.

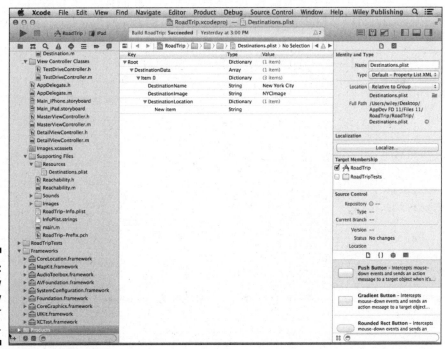

Figure 11-9:
A new dictionary with another entry.

15. **In the Key field, enter** Title, **and enter** New York City **in the Value field.**

16. **Add these three keys with their corresponding type and value:**

Key	Type	Value
Subtitle	String	A great city
Latitude	Number	40.712756
Longitude	Number	–74.006047

When you're done, your plist should look like Figure 11-10.

17. **Click the disclosure triangle to hide the** DestinationLocation **dictionary entries, and add a new array named** *Events* **as a sibling of the** DestinationLocation, **as shown in Figure 11-11.**

As explained previously, when the disclosure triangle is closed, you add a sibling entry.

18. **Continue filling out the plist to make it match Figure 11-12 and Table 11-1.**

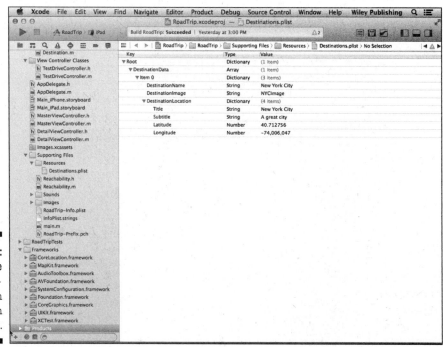

Figure 11-10:
The
Desti-
nation
Location
entries.

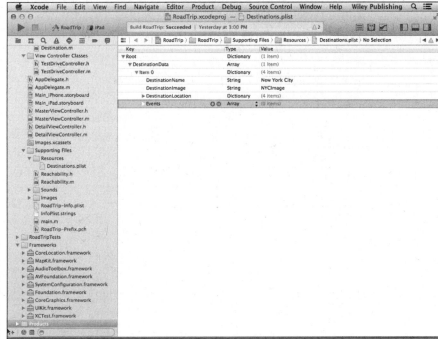

Figure 11-11:
The Events
dictionary
entry is an
array.

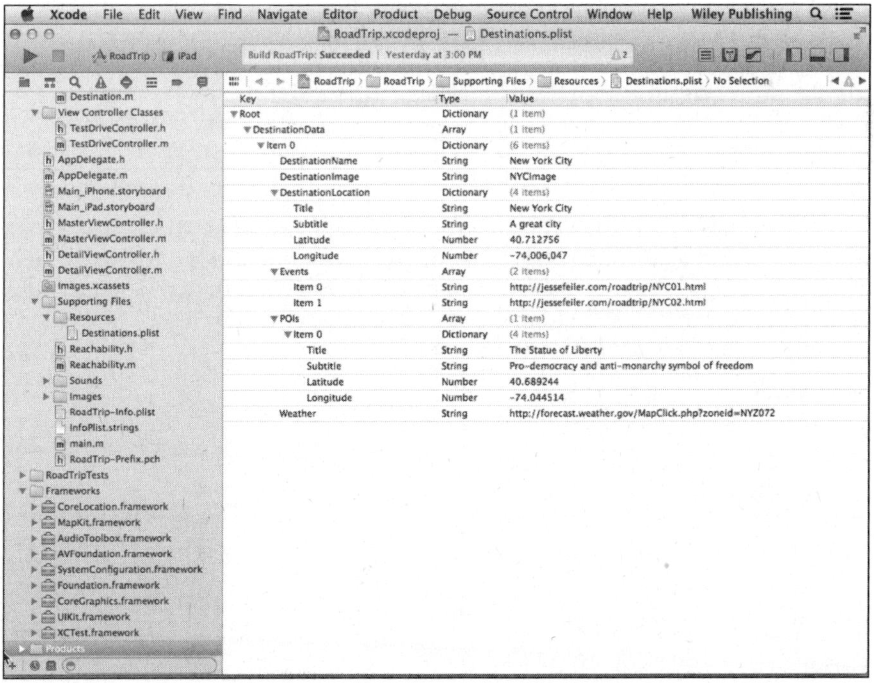

Figure 11-12:
The New
York City
destination
entry.

Table 11-1	New York City plist Keys and Values	
Key	**Type**	**Value**
DestinationName	String	New York City
DestinationImage	String	NYCImage
DestinationLocation	Dictionary	
Title	String	New York City
Subtitle	String	A great city
Latitude	Number	40.712756
Longitude	Number	-74.006047
Events	Array	
Item 0	String	`http://jessefeiler.com/NYC01.html`
Item 1	String	`http://jessefeiler.com/NYC02.html`
POIs	Array	
Item 0	Dictionary	
Title	String	The Statue of Liberty
Subtitle	String	Pro-democracy and anti-monarchy symbol of freedom
Latitude	Number	40.689244
Longitude	Number	-74.044514
Weather	String	`http://forecast.weather.gov/MapClick.php?zoneid=NYZ072`

After you finish entering these items, close Item 0 under `DestinationData` and go through Steps 8 through 18 again to add the San Francisco entry using the keys and values in Table 11-2. If you want to save some typing, you can copy and paste Item 0 and then expand the new Item 1 and simply replace the values. (That's what I did.)

Table 11-2	San Francisco plist Keys and Values	
Key	**Type**	**Value**
DestinationName	String	San Francisco
DestinationImage	String	SFImage
DestinationLocation	Dictionary	
Title	String	San Francisco
Subtitle	String	A great city
Latitude	Number	37.7793
Longitude	Number	–122.4192
Events	Array	
Item 0	String	`http://jessefeiler.com/` `SF01.html`
Item 1	String	`http://jessefeiler.com/` `SF02.html`
POIs	Array	
Item 0	Dictionary	
Title	String	Golden Gate Bridge
Subtitle	String	An internationally recognized symbol of San Francisco
Latitude	Number	37.819722
Longitude	Number	–122.478611

Weather	String	`http://forecast.weather.`
		`gov/MapClick.php?site=`
		`mtr&textField1=37.76&text`
		`Field2=-122.43&smap=1`

Make sure that you spell the entries *exactly as specified* or else you won't be able to access them using the examples in this book. Be especially careful of trailing spaces.

Using plists to store data

Although you won't do it here, you can also modify a plist to store data. The only restriction of note is that you can't modify a plist you've created in your bundle. You need to save it in the file system instead. For example:

```
NSArray *paths = NSSearchPathForDirectoriesInDomains
                      (NSDocumentDirectory, NSUserDomainMask, YES);
NSString *documentsDirectory = [paths objectAtIndex:0];
NSString *filePath = [documentsDirectory
                      stringByAppendingPathComponent:state];
[updatedDestinations writeToFile:filePath atomically:YES];
```

When you're done, refer to Figure 11-1 to see how your plist should look.

You may wonder why you're using this specific data (title and subtitle, for example). You'll understand that when you explore maps in Chapter 17.

Now that you have the information needed by the model to locate the data it's responsible for, it's time to start adding some model classes, which I cover in the following section.

Adding the First Two Model Classes

The first model class I have you add is the `Trip` class. This will become the only model object visible to the view controllers. Although the `Trip` object will use other objects to carry out its responsibilities, hiding them behind the `Trip` object results in the loose coupling I explain in the next section and in "The importance of loose coupling" sidebar, later in this chapter.

Here is how to create your first two model classes:

1. **Create a new group to keep your model classes in by going to the Project navigator, selecting the RoadTrip group (*not* the RoadTrip project, which is at the top), and right-clicking and choosing New Group from the menu that appears.**

   Or you can select the RoadTrip group and choose File⇨New⇨Group from the main menu.

   You'll see a new group. (It looks like a folder.)

2. **Name your new group *Model Classes*.**

   To change a file's group, select the file and drag it to the group you want it to occupy. The same goes for groups as well. (After all, they can go into other groups.)

3. **In the Project navigator, select the Model Classes group, right-click the selection, and then choose New File from the menu that appears to open the New File dialog.**

   Or you can select the Model Classes group and choose File➪New➪File from the main menu (or press ⌘+N).

   You'll see a dialog that enables you to select a file type.

4. **In the left column of the dialog, select Cocoa Touch under the iOS heading. Next, select the Objective-C class template in the top-right pane; then click Next.**

5. **In the Class field, enter** Trip. **In the Subclass Of drop-down menu, select NSObject. Click Next.**

   A Save sheet appears.

6. **In the Save sheet, click Create.**

7. **Repeat Steps 3–6 to create the** Destination **class.**

You'll also be using the MapKit and CoreLocation frameworks, so add them as well:

1. **In the Project navigator, select the RoadTrip Project at the top of the Project navigator area to display the Project editor.**

2. **In the Targets section, select RoadTrip.**

3. **On the General tab, scroll down to the Linked Frameworks and Libraries section.**

4. **Expand the Linked Frameworks and Libraries section, if it isn't already expanded, by clicking the disclosure triangle.**

5. **Click the + button underneath the list of current project frameworks.**

   A list of frameworks appears.

6. **Scroll down and select both MapKit.framework and CoreLocation. framework from the list of frameworks.**

7. **Click the Add button.**

   You'll see the frameworks added to the Linked Frameworks and Libraries section.

8. **Close the Linked Frameworks and Libraries section.**

If you make a mistake and want to delete a file, right-click and choose Delete from the menu that appears or select the file and press Delete. Whichever method you choose, you'll see the dialog in Figure 11-13.

Figure 11-13:
What would
you like
to do?

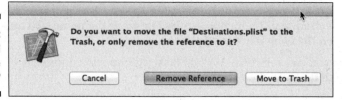

Remove Reference only removes the file from the Project navigator but leaves it on disk. You can't copy a new file with that name to that project until you delete that file from your project on the disk as well.

When you use the template to create a class, it adds the methods it thinks you may need. As a result, there will be some methods you won't need and that appear to sit around doing nothing. You can delete them or just leave them in case you do need them. This is especially true of initialization methods because initialization in this app will be (mostly) taken care of by the storyboard.

Understanding the Trip Interface

Following is what the `Trip` interface will eventually become:

```
#import <Foundation/Foundation.h>
#import <MapKit/MapKit.h>
@class Annotation;

@interface Trip : NSObject

- (UIImage *) destinationImage;
- (NSString *) destinationName;
- (CLLocationCoordinate2D) destinationCoordinate;

- (id)initWithDestinationIndex:(int)destinationIndex;
```

```
-  (NSString *)weather;
-  (int)numberOfEvents;
-  (NSString *)getEvent:(int)index;
-  (NSArray *)createAnnotations;
-  (NSString *)mapTitle;
-  (void)addLocation:(NSString *)findLocation
      completionHandler:(void (^)(Annotation *annotation,
                              NSError* error)) completion;
@end
```

As you can see, this code contains a lot of stuff, and I explain it as you add functionality to the Trip class along the way.

Earlier in the chapter, I mention that Trip is the model interface, and I say this because in many cases more than one class will be involved in delivering the necessary functionality of the model. For example, in this chapter you just added a Destination class that will be responsible for the information about your destination. An Events class that you will add in Chapter 16 will be responsible for managing the list of things going on at your destination, and an Annotation class (coming in Chapter 17) will provide the information you need to plot annotations (places to see) on a map. Hiding additional model objects behind the Trip object is known as *loose coupling* and is an important object-oriented design principle (see the nearby "The importance of loose coupling" sidebar).

You might be tempted to have the view controllers create the model classes they'll use (for example, a WeatherController would create the Weather object, and so on). The problem with that approach is that it makes the coupling between controller objects and the model much tighter.

One advantage of the Model-View-Controller (MVC) design pattern that I explain in Chapter 4 is that it allows you to assign (most) classes into one of three groups in your app and work on them individually. If each group has a well-defined interface, it encapsulates many of the kinds of changes that are often made so that they don't affect the other groups. This little fact is especially true of the model and view controller relationship.

If the view controllers have minimal knowledge about the model, you can change the model objects with minor impact on the view controllers. So although the Trip class will provide this functionality to the various view controllers, as I said, it won't be doing all the work on its own. What makes this possible is a well-defined interface, which I showed you at the start of this section. You create an interface between the model and the controllers by using a technique called *composition,* which is a useful way to create interfaces.

The importance of loose coupling

A loosely coupled system is one in which each of its components has little or no knowledge (or makes no use of the knowledge it may have) of other components. The term *loose coupling* refers to the degree of direct knowledge that one class has of another. This isn't about encapsulation or one class's knowledge of another class's attributes or implementation, but rather knowledge of that other class *itself*.

Applying loose coupling means presenting a minimum interface to other objects. The client deals with the fewest number of objects as possible. So although you may want to break down a function into smaller pieces (for example, by using composition), you never want the client to know that. Clients are happy dealing with one object, even if that object then turns around and redistributes that work to other objects.

There are many ways to implement loose coupling, and Cocoa uses a number of them. Messages can be sent to objects, the identity of which is only known dynamically at run-time. Similarly, notifications can be sent out to any observer that has registered to receive them. In these cases (and more), the tight coupling of a known sender and recipient does not exist.

I'm a big fan of composition because it's another way to hide what's really going on behind the curtain. It keeps the objects that use the composite object (in this case, `Trip` is the composite object) ignorant of the objects that the composite object uses and actually makes the components ignorant of each other, allowing you to switch components in and out at will.

So you'll have `Trip` create the model objects, encapsulating the knowledge of what objects make up the model from the object that uses it. `Trip` hides all implementation knowledge from a view controller; it will know only about the `Trip` object. Again, this setup makes everything *loosely coupled* and makes your app more extensible and easier to change.

Implementing the Trip Class

In this chapter, I show you how to implement the `Trip` model functionality that will enable you to choose between multiple destinations (although you won't be doing the choosing until Chapter 20). You also implement the `Trip` functionality that will be needed by the Master View controller (you add that in Chapter 12) — the name of the destination and its background image.

Start by adding the bolded code in Listing 11-1 to `Trip.h`.

Listing 11-1: Updating the Trip Interface

```
#import <Foundation/Foundation.h>
#import <MapKit/MapKit.h>

@interface Trip : NSObject

-(instancetype)initWithDestinationIndex:(int)destination
Index;
- (UIImage *) destinationImage;
- (NSString *) destinationName;
- (CLLocationCoordinate2D) destinationCoordinate;
@end
```

As you can see, the code in Listing 11-1 contains an initialization method. This method will enable the Trip object to set itself up for the selected destination. Allow me to explain initialization and a few other things.

Initialization is the logical place to start, but first you need to add some instance variables and import the Destination header file if you're going to use it (which you are, in the Trip implementation). Add the bolded code in Listing 11-2 to Trip.m.

Listing 11-2: Updating the Trip Implementation

```
#import "Trip.h"
#import "Destination.h"

@interface Trip ()
  @property (strong, nonatomic) NSDictionary
          *destinationData;
  @property (strong, nonatomic) Destination* destination;
@end

@implementation Trip
```

Now you can add the initWithDestinationIndex: method in Listing 11-3 to Trip.m. Note that until you have completed the code in this chapter, you will have an error related to the not-yet-entered Destination class.

Listing 11-3: Adding initWithDestinationIndex:

```
- (instancetype)initWithDestinationIndex:(int)
          destinationIndex {

  if ((self = [super init])) {

    NSString *filePath = [[NSBundle mainBundle]
        pathForResource:@"Destinations" ofType:@"plist"];
```

(continued)

Listing 11-3 *(continued)*

```
    NSDictionary *destinations =
      [NSDictionary dictionaryWithContentsOfFile:filePath];
    NSArray *destinationsArray =
          destinations[@"DestinationData"];
    _destinationData =
       destinationsArray[destinationIndex];
    _destination = [[Destination alloc]
              initWithDestinationIndex:destinationIndex];
  }
  return self;
}
```

Before I explain the logic in these listings, I want to explain initialization in general. (And yes, you'll see compiler warnings, and you'll be fixing them as you go along.)

Initializing objects

Initialization is the procedure that sets the instance variables of an object (including pointers to other objects) to a known initial state. Essentially, you need to initialize an object in order to assign initial values to these variables. Initialization isn't required in every class in every app; if you can live with all the instance variables initialized to 0 and nil, you need do nothing. Trip, however, will need to create the objects it will be using, and you'll do that during initialization.

Even when you use declared properties, remember that Xcode is automatically creating *backing variables* for them. As a result, you may think you are declaring and then initializing the property, but in reality, Xcode is working with the backing variables.

An initialization method doesn't have to include an argument for every instance variable because some will become relevant only during the course of your object's existence. You must make sure, however, that all the instance variables your object uses, including other objects that it needs to do its work, are in a state that enables your object to respond to the messages it receives.

You may think that the main job in initialization is to, well, initialize the variables in your objects (hence the name), but more is involved when you have a superclass and a subclass chain.

Most of the time you use declared properties to manage your class's data. Xcode automatically creates instance variables (sometimes called backing variables) and creates getters and setters to and from the instance variables that the property uses behind the scenes. However, inside your .m file and, particularly in initialization code, you sometimes work directly with the instance variable.

To see what I mean, start by looking at the initializer I use for the `Trip` class in Listing 11-3 (shown previously). By convention, initialization methods begin with the abbreviation `init`. (This is true, however, only for *instance* — as opposed to *class* — methods.) If the method takes no arguments, the method name is just `init`. If it takes arguments, labels for the arguments follow the `init` prefix. As you can see, the initializer in Listing 11-3 has a return type of `instanceType`. You discover the reason for that in the next section.

Initialization involves these three steps:

1. Invoke the superclass `init` method.

2. Initialize instance variables.

3. Return `self`.

The following sections explain each step.

Invoking the superclass's init method

Here is the type of statement you use to get the `init` method up and running:

```
self = [super init];
if (self) {
```

`[super init]` does nothing more than invoke the superclass `init` method. By convention, all initializers are required to assign `self`. `self` is the "hidden" variable accessible to methods in an object that points its instance variables to whatever object you get back from the superclass initializer, which explains `self = [super init]`.

The `if` statement can be a little confusing to people. You may not get an object returned from the super class `init` method. If that's the case, you don't want to do any further initialization.

Although the scenario just described is possible, it isn't common and won't happen in this book (and in general). You might find it in classes that need certain resources to initialize themselves, and if they aren't present, the object can't be created.

Initializing instance variables

Initializing instance variables, including creating the objects you need, is what you probably thought initialization is about. Notice that you're initializing your instance variable after your superclass's initialization, which you can see in Listing 11-3 (shown previously). Waiting until *after* your superclass does its initialization gives you the opportunity to actually change something your superclass may have done during its initialization, but more importantly, it allows you to perform initialization knowing that what you have inherited is initialized and ready to be used.

In your `initWithDestinationIndex:` method, you start by finding the plist that holds the `Trip` data or location of the data you need:

```
NSString *filePath = [[NSBundle mainBundle]
        pathForResource:@"Destinations" ofType:@"plist"];
```

Next, you create a dictionary to hold the data. You use the method `initWithContentsOfFile:`, which does all the heavy lifting for you. It reads in the `Destinations` plist file and creates a dictionary for you. The plist, as I said previously, is really a dictionary with a single entry with the key `DestinationData`. The `dictionaryWithContentsOfFile:` method creates a dictionary from the plist (and objects and keys for all of its entries) with dictionary keys that are the keys you specified in the plist.

This method also allocates and initializes all the elements in the dictionary (including other dictionaries), so when it's done, you're ready to roll:

```
NSDictionary *destinations =
    [NSDictionary dictionaryWithContentsOfFile:filePath];
```

`NSDictionary`, `NSMutableDictionary`, `NSArray`, and `NSMutableArray` all have the methods `initWithContentsOfFile:` and `writeToFile:atomically:` that read themselves in from a file and write themselves out to a file, respectively. This is one of the capabilities that makes property list objects so useful.

Property list containers — and *only* property list containers (and `NSString` and `NSData`) — can read themselves in from and write themselves out to a file. The other property list objects can only store themselves, without any effort on your part, as part of a file.

Your next step in initializing instance variables is to use the `destinationIndex` to get the right element in the array of dictionaries in the `DestinationData` entry based on the destination chosen by the user. (You'll specify that in the `AppDelegate` in Listing 11-10, later in this chapter, where you'll allocate the `Trip` object.)

```
NSArray *destinationsArray =
          destinations[@"DestinationData"];
_destinationData =
      destinationsArray[destinationIndex];
```

Finally, you allocate and initialize the `Destination` object:

```
_destination = [[Destination alloc]
              initWithDestinationIndex:destinationIndex];
```

Returning self

Earlier in this chapter, I explain that the `self` = statement ensures that `self` is set to whatever object you get back from the superclass initializer. No matter what you get back from invoking the superclass initializer in the initialization method, you need to set `self` to that value and then return it to the invoking method — the method that wants to instantiate the object or a subclass that invoked the superclass's `init` method.

After the code block that initializes the variables, you insert the following:

```
return self;
```

The reason the `return` type is an `instancetype` is that sometimes what you ask for isn't exactly what you get. But don't worry; that becomes transparent to you if you follow the rules for initialization I just explained.

So where do the braces go?

If you look in the code provided by the template, sometimes you see a method implementation that looks like this:

```
- (void)viewDidLoad
{
```

and sometimes you'll see one that looks like this:

```
- (IBAction)testDrive:(id)
  sender {
```

I personally prefer the latter — with the bracket on the same line as the method — and will use it in the methods I have you add.

Quite frankly, it doesn't matter to the compiler, but it can raise itself to a religious issue among programmers. Do what you'd like.

The reason that you may get back a different class than what you asked for is that under certain circumstances when you allocate a framework object, what you may get back may be a class optimized for your use based on the context. The relatively new `instancetype` is used to indicate that the returned value is not any old object but one that is specifically relevant to the initializer. Old code may return an `id` value which, indeed, can be any old object. Using `instancetype` is a safer and preferred style of coding today.

Initializing the Destination Class

Now it's time to turn to the `Destination` class and its initialization. Add the bolded code in Listing 11-4 to `Destination.h` to update its interface to add the header files, the properties you'll be using, and the method declarations.

Listing 11-4: Updating the Destination Interface

```
#import <Foundation/Foundation.h>
#import <MapKit/MapKit.h>

@interface Destination : NSObject

@property (nonatomic, readwrite)
                     CLLocationCoordinate2D coordinate;
@property (nonatomic, readwrite, copy) NSString *title;
@property (nonatomic, readwrite, copy) NSString *subtitle;
@property (nonatomic, strong) NSString *destinationName;
@property (nonatomic, strong) UIImage *destinationImage;

- (instancetype)initWithDestinationIndex:
                     (NSUInteger)destinationIndex;
@end
```

You'll be displaying the destination on a map with an *annotation* (that pop-up window that displays information about the location when you touch the pin on the map). Doing that requires a `coordinate` property of type `CLLocationCoordinate2d` (that's why you need to include the `MapKit` and `CoreLocation` frameworks) and optional `title` and `subtitle` properties. Although you won't be doing anything with this part of `Destination` until Chapter 17, I have you initialize `Destination` with what is described in the plist but defer the explanation until Chapter 17.

When you're done, you can add the `initWithDestinationIndex:` method in Listing 11-5 to `Destination.m`.

Listing 11-5:   Add initWithDestinationIndex:

```
- (instancetype)initWithDestinationIndex:
                             (NSUInteger)destinationIndex {

  self = [super init];
  if (self) {

    NSString *filePath = [[NSBundle mainBundle]
        pathForResource:@"Destinations" ofType:@"plist"];
    NSDictionary *destinations = [NSDictionary
                   dictionaryWithContentsOfFile:filePath];
    NSArray *destinationsArray =
          destinations[@"DestinationData"];
    NSDictionary *data =
       destinationsArray[destinationIndex];


    _destinationImage =
       [UIImage imageNamed:data[@"DestinationImage"]];

    _destinationName =
                  data[@"DestinationName"];
    NSDictionary* destinationLocation =
             data[@"DestinationLocation"];
    CLLocationCoordinate2D destinationCoordinate;
    destinationCoordinate.latitude =
       [destinationLocation[@"Latitude"] doubleValue];
    destinationCoordinate.longitude =
       [destinationLocation
                  [@"Longitude"] doubleValue];
    _coordinate = destinationCoordinate;
    _title =
               destinationLocation[@"Title"];
    _subtitle =
          destinationLocation[@"Subtitle"];
  }
  return self;

}
```

`Destination` initializes itself more or less the same way that `Trip` did.
It starts by loading its data:

```
NSString *filePath = [[NSBundle mainBundle]
        pathForResource:@"Destinations" ofType:@"plist"];
NSDictionary *destinations =
    [NSDictionary dictionaryWithContentsOfFile: filePath];
NSArray *destinationsArray =
          destinations[@"DestinationData"];
NSDictionary *data =
      destinationsArray[destinationIndex];
```

Then it uses the dictionary data to initialize its properties:

```
;
    _destinationImage =
        [UIImageimageNamed:data[@"DestinationImage"]];

;
```

Although there are separate images for the iPad and iPhone, they're in an asset catalog and you just use the basic name for the image set containing the separate images.

```
_destinationName =
                data[@"DestinationName"];
NSDictionary* destinationLocation =
                data[@"DestinationLocation"];
CLLocationCoordinate2D destinationCoordinate;
destinationCoordinate.latitude =
   [destinationLocation[@"Latitude"] doubleValue];
destinationCoordinate.longitude =
   [destinationLocation
                [@"Longitude"] doubleValue];
_coordinate = destinationCoordinate;
_title = destinationLocation[@"Title"];
_subtitle =
         destinationLocation[@"Subtitle"];
```

The initialization of the properties is simply done by using the keys you specified when you created the plist, which turn into dictionary keys when you load the dictionary (and its dictionaries) from the plist file.

Now you can add the `Trip` methods `destinationImage`, `destinationName`, and `destinationCoordinate`, which use the `Destination` object. Add the methods in Listing 11-6 to `Trip.m`.

Listing 11-6:   Adding destinationImage, destinationName, and destinationCoordinate

```
- (UIImage *) destinationImage {

   return  self.destination.destinationImage;
}

- (NSString *) destinationName {

   return  self.destination.destinationName;
}

- (CLLocationCoordinate2D) destinationCoordinate {

   return self.destination.coordinate;
}
```

These `Trip` methods will be used by the Master View controller to request the data it needs for its view.

Interestingly, in this case, all `Trip` does is turn around and send the request to the `Destination` object. This is, of course, an example of loose coupling, which I explain earlier.

In this case, there isn't that much for `Destination` to do, so you could've simply had `Trip` manage the data. But in a more robust app (like one worth 99 cents), it would likely have more to do. In fact, you could start by having `Trip` manage all the data and add a `Destination` object when you felt you needed to. And when you did add the `Destination` object, doing so would have no impact on the objects needing that data — ah, loose coupling in action.

Creating the Trip Object

Finally, you have to create the `Trip` object. You need to make it accessible to the view controllers that need to use it, so you'll make it an `AppDelegate` property. Any object in your app can find the `AppDelegate`, and from it get a pointer to the `Trip` object.

Add the bolded code in Listing 11-7 to `AppDelegate.h`.

Listing 11-7:   Updating the AppDelegate Interface

```
#import <UIKit/UIKit.h>
@class Trip;

@interface RTAppDelegate : UIResponder
          <UIApplicationDelegate>

@property (strong, nonatomic) UIWindow *window;
@property (nonatomic, strong) Trip *trip;

- (void) createDestinationModel:(int)destinationIndex;

@end
```

`createDestinationModel:` is the method that actually creates the `Trip` object.

`@class` is a compiler directive to let the compiler know that `Trip` is a class (or type). You need to import the header to actually use it in your code, however, and you'll do that by adding the bolded code in Listing 11-8 to `AppDelegate.m`.

Listing 11-8: Updating the AppDelegate Implementation

```
#import "AppDelegate.h"
#import "Reachability.h"
#import "Trip.h"

@implementation AppDelegate
```

You also declare a method that will actually create the `Trip` object. Add the bolded code in Listing 11-9 to `application:didFinishLaunchingWith Options:` in `AppDelegate.m` to use that method.

Listing 11-9: Updating application:didFinishLaunchingWithOptions:

```
- (BOOL)application:(UIApplication *)application
        didFinishLaunchingWithOptions:
                          (NSDictionary *)launchOptions
{
  UINavigationController *navigationController;
  if ([[UIDevice currentDevice] userInterfaceIdiom] ==
                          UIUserInterfaceIdiomPad) {
    UISplitViewController *splitViewController =
      (UISplitViewController *)
                        self.window.rootViewController;
    splitViewController.presentsWithGesture = NO;
    UINavigationController *detailNavigationController
        [splitViewController.viewControllers lastObject];
    splitViewController.delegate =
        (id)detailNavigationController.topViewController;
    navigationController =
    [splitViewController.viewControllers objectAtIndex:0];
  }
  else {
    navigationController = (UINavigationController *)
                        self.window.rootViewController;
  }
  NetworkStatus networkStatus = [[Reachability
        reachabilityForInternetConnection]
        currentReachabilityStatus];
  if (networkStatus == NotReachable) {
    UIAlertView *alert = [[UIAlertView alloc]
      initWithTitle:@"Network Unavailable"
      message:@"RoadTrip requires an Internet connection"
      delegate:nil
      cancelButtonTitle:@"OK"
      otherButtonTitles:nil];
    [alert show];
  }

  [self createDestinationModel:0];
  return YES;
}
```

As you can see, you use the `createDestinationModel:` method to actually create the model. I have this as a separate method because you'll need to be able to send the `AppDelegate` a message to create a new `Trip` when the user chooses a new destination in Chapter 20.

Also notice that, for now, you'll be defaulting to the first destination in the plist. You'll fix that in Chapter 20 as well.

Add the `createDestinationModel:` method in Listing 11-10 to `AppDelegate.m`.

Listing 11-10:   Adding createDestinationModel:

```
- (void) createDestinationModel:(int)destinationIndex {

  self.trip = [[Trip alloc]
          initWithDestinationIndex:destinationIndex];
}
```

All you do is allocate and initialize the `Trip` object and assign it to the `trip` property.

More Debugger Stuff

In this section, I give you something more interesting to look at in the Debugger than you've had up to now for this book's example app. As it stands, you can compile RoadTrip with no errors and it runs, albeit the same way that it did before. So you have no idea if all that code you added really works. Does it really find the `Destinations.plist` file and create all the dictionaries with their entries correctly?

One way to find out is to put a breakpoint in your code and see what's there; so go ahead and set a breakpoint in `Trip.m` on the following line (in the `initWithDestinationIndex:` method) by clicking in the gutter next to (in front of) the line:

```
_destination = [[Destination alloc]
              initWithDestinationIndex:destinationIndex];
```

Then set another breakpoint in `Destination.m` (in its `initWith DestinationIndex:` method) on the following line:

```
_subtitle =
          destinationLocation[@"Subtitle"];
```

Run your app.

If your program execution stops at a breakpoint, you can move your pointer over an object or variable in the Source editor to see its contents. In Figure 11-14, I've done that with `destinationData` (and so should you).

`destinationData` is a pointer to the dictionary that contains the data for the first entry in the Destination plist's `DestinationData` array. You'll have six key/value pairs, as you should have, and if you look in the Variables pane in the Debugger, you'll see two objects in the `destinationsArray`, which is also as it should be.

You can explore the display by opening the disclosure triangles to drill down and look at the data as you see in Figure 11-15.

You can use the circled i to reveal the contents of the variable as shown in Figure 11-16.

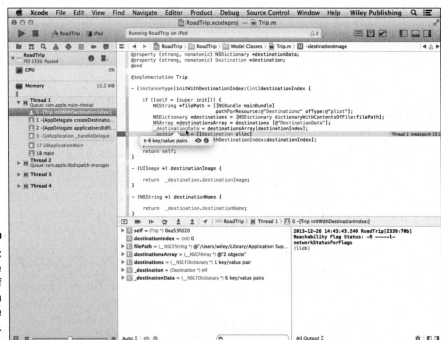

Figure 11-14: Display the contents of a variable in the Source editor.

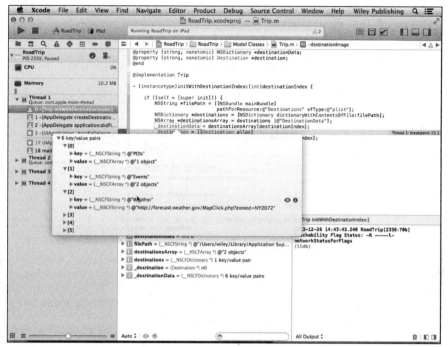

Figure 11-15:
Drill down
into the
data.

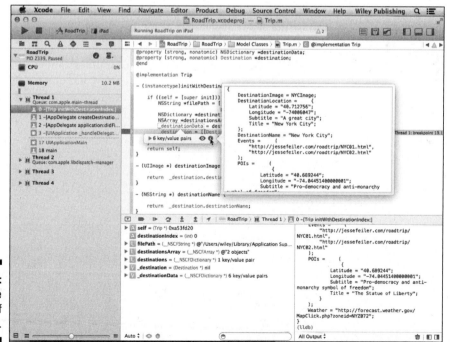

Figure 11-16:
Reveal the
contents of
a variable.

Finally, you can use the Quick Look icon to explore the variable and its memory location, as you see in Figure 11-17.

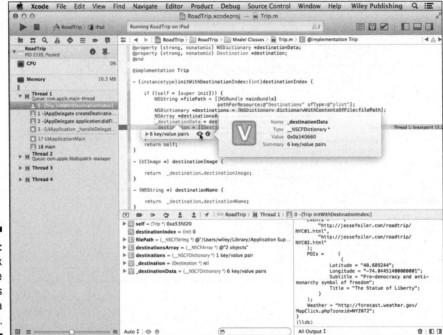

Chapter 12

Implementing the Master View Controller

In This Chapter

▶ Working with custom view controllers

▶ Using the `Trip` model to get data for a view

*W*ith the model in place, you can now return to the Master View controller and transform its view into the user interface you fell in love with way back in Chapter 4. In this chapter, you'll connect the Master View controller for the iPad to the Trip model to create the interface and also to be able to (eventually) respond to user requests. You'll then repeat the process for the iPhone version.

The strategy you adopt in this chapter to add the logic to connect the view to the model via the view controller is the same strategy you'll use for the rest of the view controllers in the storyboard. As always, although you can add the view controllers you'll need to the storyboard graphically, you'll still need to add some code to have the controller actually do anything, such as get data from the model and send it to the view.

Setting Up a Custom View Controller for the iPad

Although `MasterViewController` already actually does something, I want to develop it for use in RoadTrip by customizing its appearance and having it display (through its entries or cells) a table of contents showing the app functionality. Here's how you'd start things off:

1. **In the Project navigator, select `Main_iPad.storyboard`.**

2. **In the Document outline, select Master View Controller – Master in the Master View Controller – Master scene, open the disclosure triangle next to the Master View controller in the scene, and select the Table view.**

3. **Using the Inspector selector bar, open the Attributes inspector in the Utility area.**

You'll notice that, in the Table View section of the Attributes inspector, the Static Cells option is selected in the Content drop-down menu, as shown in Figure 12-1. You changed this Table view to Static cells in Chapter 5.

As I explain in Chapter 5, static cells are used when you know in advance what needs to be displayed in a cell. Instead of having to implement a method in your view controller and return the cell with the text you want, you can format the cells in the storyboard.

4. **In the Document outline, open the disclosure triangle next to the Table view, select Table View Section, and delete it.**

You could've left that cell and added cells to that section and more sections, but I want to show you what it's like to start from a clean slate.

Notice that the segue to the Test Drive controller has been deleted as well. That means you can no longer select Test Drive and have the view slide into place. But you'll fix that in Chapter 13.

You are now ready to add the text you want displayed to the cells, but before you do, I want to give you some background on how Table views work.

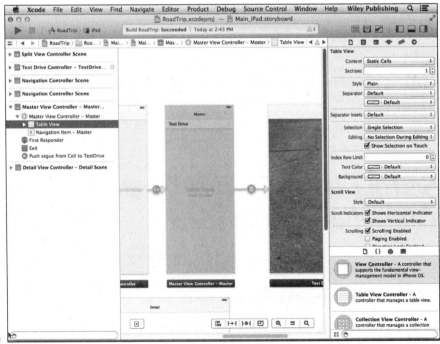

Figure 12-1:
You start with static cells.

Table views require both a *data source* as well as a *delegate.* The data source supplies the content for the Table view and provides the content for each cell (or row). The delegate manages the appearance and behavior of the Table view and determines what to do when the user selects a cell (or row) — it could, for example, push a view controller onto the stack.

In the template (as is the case with many Table views), the table view itself is assigned to both the data source and the delegate properties. This means that all of the Table view functionality is embodied in the Table view class. However, having the ability to assign other classes to the delegate or the data source property opens up the opportunity for you to share the functionality among several objects. You will find a number of cases in the Cocoa frameworks where an object's functionality is provided by itself (as in the Table view) as well as by other objects that may from time to time be the same as the primary object. If you're using the Table view only as a type of table of contents for your app, selecting Static Cells lets you create the cell content in Interface Builder (as I show you how to do next) and use storyboard segues to specify what happens when a user selects a cell — much easier and a lot less work than coding it yourself! I explain more about this in Chapter 20.

The following steps show you how to customize your Table view:

1. **Select Table View in the Document Outline in the Master View Controller – Master Scene.**

2. **Using the Inspector selector, open the Attributes inspector in the Utility area, select Grouped from the inspector's Style drop-down menu, and then enter** 3 in **the Sections field.**

   You see three sections with three rows each, as shown in Figure 12-2.

   Note that Table views come in two basic styles:

   - *Plain:* The default style is called *plain* and looks really unadorned — plain vanilla. It's a list: just one darn thing after another. You can index it, though, just as the Table view in the Contacts app is indexed, so it can be a pretty powerful tool.

     A plain view can also have section titles (as I describe shortly) and footers.

   - *Grouped:* The other style is the *grouped* Table view; unsurprisingly, it allows you to lump entries together into various categories.

     Grouped tables can't have an index.

     When you configure a grouped Table view, you can also have header, footer, and section titles. I show you how to do section titles shortly.

   The details of what you've just done may change as the storyboard defaults are changed, but you get the picture.

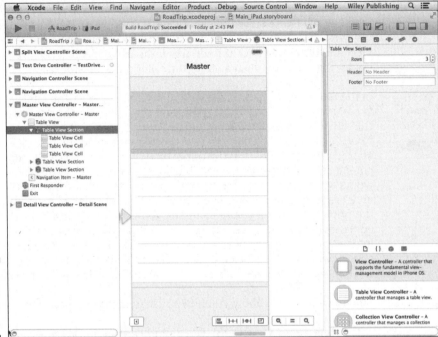

Figure 12-2:
Static cells
and three
sections.

3. **Open the disclosure triangle next to Table View in the Document outline, check out the Table View sections under it, and select the first section.**

   The Attributes inspector refreshes to show the attributes of the first Table View section.

4. **Change the Rows field in the Attributes inspector to 2 (or delete one of the cells) and enter** At My Destination **in the Header field.**

5. **Select the second section and, after the Attributes inspector refreshes, change the Rows field in the Attributes inspector to 2, and enter** Getting Around **in the Header field.**

6. **Select the third section and, after the Attributes inspector refreshes, change the Rows field in the Attributes inspector to 2, and enter** Planning My Trip **in the Header field. (See Figure 12-3.)**

7. **Open the first Table View Section and select the first Table View Cell.**

8. **Still in the Attributes inspector, choose Basic from the Style menu.**

   The Style menu provides a number of options for how the cell is formatted. Each one formats the text in the cell a little differently in the label(s) it adds to the cell to display the text. (Or you can leave it as Custom, drag in a label(s), and format the label any way you want.)

   When you select Basic, a disclosure triangle gets added next to first Table View Cell in the Document Outline in the Master View Controller – Master Scene. If you open it, you see that a single label has been added for you, as shown in Figure 12-4.

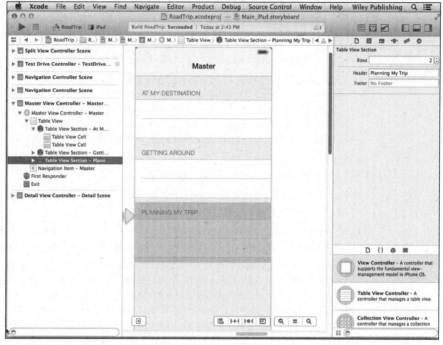

Figure 12-3:
Setting the
number of
rows and
sections
with head-
ers that you
want.

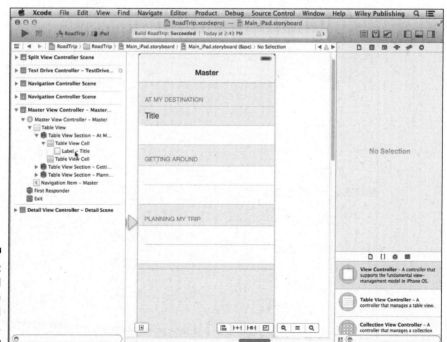

Figure 12-4:
A basic cell
with the
supplied
label.

9. **Select the Label in the Document outline.**

   The Attributes inspector displays the Label properties — including the text, which you can change to your heart's content. (Selecting the Text icon in the Font field allows you to change the font as well.)

   If you want, you can change the font style by selecting the Font icon (the little T inside the Font field). However, remember that the content of your app should be the centerpiece, so using standard fonts and styles for things such as labels (as opposed to content) is usually a good idea. Set the text for the label to Weather as shown in Figure 12-5.

10. **Finally, and this is the pièce de résistance, select White Color from the Label section's Color drop-down menu.**

    Yes, it is in fact the case that you won't be able to see the text very well, as demonstrated by Figure 12-6.

11. **Repeat Steps 7–10 to format the next two cells, this time entering** Events **and** Map, **respectively, in the Text field in the Attributes inspector.**

    Events is the second cell in At My Destination, and Map is the first cell in Getting Around. You have to treat the Find cell in Getting Around a little differently. Rather than just adding a title to the Table View Cell, you're going to add a label and input text field *inside* the table view cell. This is only one example of how you can put almost any view inside a Table View Cell.

    Start by leaving the cell type as Custom in the Style menu. (Because you'll have the user enter the place she wants to find in the cell, you'll have to format it on your own.) Continue with the steps that follow.

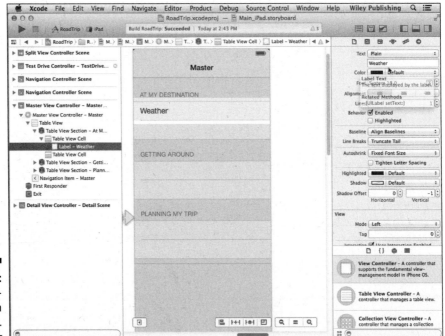

Figure 12-5:
The formatted cell of a table.

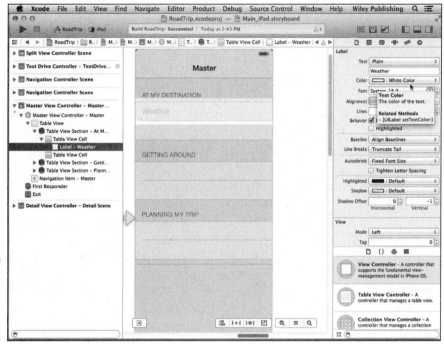

Figure 12-6:
The first cell
and label
are done.

12. **Drag a label from the Library pane onto the cell.**

    As you work, you may notice that Xcode places a Content View object inside the Table View Cell; your new objects such as the label are placed inside the Content View automatically.

13. **With the label selected, go to the Attributes inspector and enter** Find: **in the Text field and set the Label and Table View Cell text to White Color (if it's not already set that way), as you did in Steps 9–11.**

    If you select the label, it should look like Figure 12-7.

14. **Drag a Text Field from the Library pane onto the cell and position it as shown in Figure 12-8.**

15. **At the top of the Text Field section of the Attributes inspector, enter** Enter address or place **in the Placeholder field to help the user understand what this text field is for.**

16. **In the Attributes inspector, select the first Border Style (No Border) in the Text Field section.**

    The text field will seem to disappear, but you can always select it again in the Document outline.

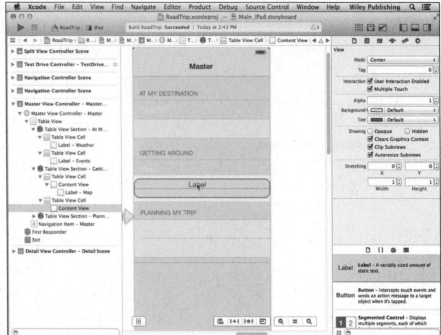

Figure 12-7:
Add a label.

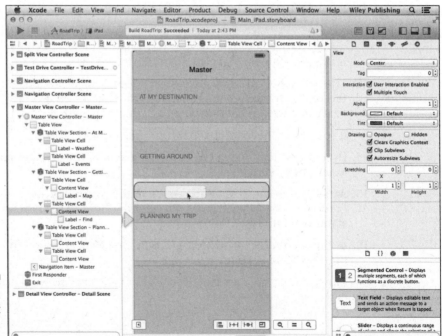

Figure 12-8:
Add a text field.

17. **Using the appropriate drop-down menus, set the background to Clear Color and the text to White Color.**

    Resize and reshape the text field as desired. You can see the results in Figure 12-9.

    Text fields enable the user to enter small amounts of text, which is exactly what you need here.

18. **Repeat Steps 7–10 to format the next two cells, this time entering** Destination **and** Test Drive, **respectively, in the Text field in the Attributes inspector.**

19. **Your Master View controller should look more or less like mine does in Figure 12-10.**

    Pay particular attention to the document outline at the left to make certain that you have all of the pieces in place.

If you were to remove the code breakpoint that you set in Chapter 11, and then click the Run button for the iPad version, you would see the screen shown in Figure 12-11. Clicking or tapping in a cell doesn't get you anything yet, but it soon will.

Of course, this user interface isn't particularly exciting; in fact, it's rather pedestrian. Let's fix that. Doing that requires doing some coding in the Master View controller.

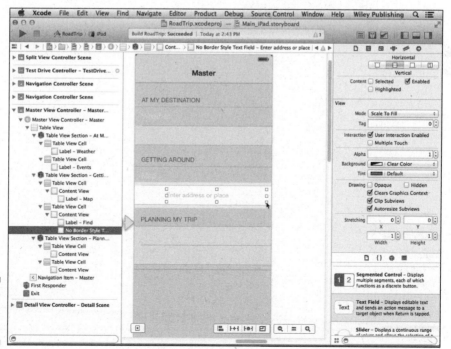

Figure 12-9:
The Find cell complete.

Figure 12-10:
The finished
Content
controller.

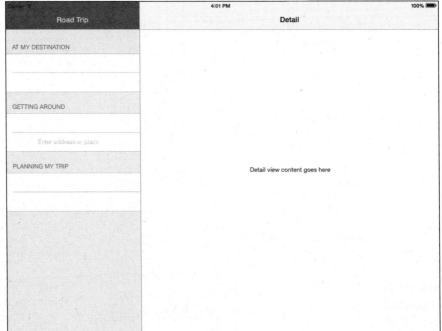

Figure 12-11:
The latest
additions to
the RoadTrip
app for iPad.

Adding a Background Image and Title

The type of Table view highlighted in this chapter has static cells that you set up in Interface Builder, as I mention in the previous section. However, in this view, everything isn't static — including two things based on the destination. Those two things are the background image and the title. You have to set those programmatically.

Start by hiding the Utility area and then show the Project navigator (if you have hidden it) by making the appropriate selections in the toolbar. Then select `MasterViewController.m` in the Project navigator.

You may recall from Chapter 6 that the View Controller method you'd use to customize a view at launch time is `viewDidLoad`, which is the method I'll have you use here as well.

First, import the headers you need by adding the bolded code in Listing 12-1 to `MasterViewController.m`.

Listing 12-1:   Updating the MasterViewController Implementation

```
#import "MasterViewController.h"
#import "DetailViewController.h"
#import "AppDelegate.h"
#import "Trip.h"
```

Now add the bolded code in Listing 12-2 to the `viewDidLoad` method in `MasterViewController.m` and delete the commented out code in bold, underline, and italic.

Listing 12-2:   Updating viewDidLoad

```
-  (void) viewDidLoad
{
    [super viewDidLoad];

//self.title = @"Road Trip";
  AppDelegate* appDelegate = [[UIApplication
                            sharedApplication] delegate];
  self.title = appDelegate.trip.destinationName;
  UIImageView* imageView = [[UIImageView alloc]
        initWithImage:[appDelegate.trip destinationImage]];
  self.tableView.backgroundView = imageView;

_
}
```

You want to add two features to the `MasterViewController`'s view. The first makes the title in the Navigation bar the name of the destination, and the second adds a background image to the view. This data is owned by the `Trip` model, so you're finally getting to use the model.

To get the information the Master View controller needs from the (`Trip`) model, it needs to send a message to the `Trip` object. You may recall that in Chapter 11, when you created and initialized the `Trip` object in `AppDelegate`, you assigned its pointer to the `trip` property to make it accessible to the view controllers.

You find `AppDelegate` just like you previously did: by sending the class message `sharedApplication` to the `UIApplication` class and then sending the `delegate` message to the `UIApplication` object.

You use the following two methods to place your background image and display the destination name:

- ✔ `destinationImage` is a `Trip` method that returns a `UIImage` pointer.
- ✔ `destinationName` is a `Trip` method that returns an `NSString` pointer that contains the destination name.

There's one final step: Beginning with iOS 7, the background color of all table cells is white (although the Interface Builder interface may lead you to think otherwise). You need to set the background color of the table cells to clear so that your background image will show through. Do this by adding the code in Listing 12-3 to `MasterViewController.m`.

Listing 12-3:   Setting a Clear Background for the Table Cells

```
- (void)tableView:(UITableView *)tableView
        willDisplayCell:(UITableViewCell *)cell
        forRowAtIndexPath:(NSIndexPath *)indexPath
{
  cell.backgroundColor = [UIColor clearColor];
}
```

Run the app now and select Travel. Be prepared to be impressed with your work, as evidenced by what you see in Figure 12-12.

As I mention in the preceding section, because you deleted the Test Drive cell, the segue was deleted as well. That means you can no longer select Test Drive and have the view slide into place. But you'll fix that in the next chapter.

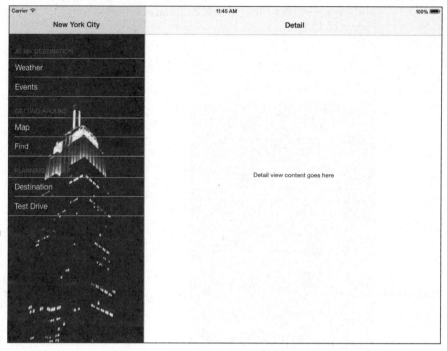

Figure 12-12:
The Master
View con-
troller user
interface for
iPad.

Updating the iPhone Storyboard File

You can reuse the iPad code you just developed for the iPhone version, but you will have to update the iPhone storyboard file with the same kind of changes you just did for the iPad storyboard. Remember, both the iPhone and iPad versions are your children, and you don't want to hurt the iPhone app's feelings by neglecting it.

The simplest way to update the iPhone storyboard is to review all the directions in this chapter that described how to update the iPad storyboard, and repeat those steps for the iPhone storyboard. But you do not need to repeat the code changes — the ones made in this chapter work fine for both iPad and iPhone.

The iPhone Master View controller interface should now look like Figure 12-13.

Figure 12-13:
The Master View controller interface for the iPhone.

Chapter 13

Working with Split View Controllers and the Master View

*T*his chapter is primarily about the iPad user interface because Split View controllers aren't supported on the smaller iPhone. In Chapter 5, I explain a bit about iPad navigation using the example of a Navigation controller within a Split View controller. But the iPad has some even slicker ways to navigate, which I get to in this chapter. You'll be happy to know that you're going to be replacing the Navigation controller style of navigation with something more appropriate to the RoadTrip app.

The Problem with Using a Navigation Controller in Detail View

As I explain in Chapter 5, the Master-Detail Application template you're using sets up the iPad's Split View controller in such a way that, when a cell in the Master view is tapped (Test Drive, for example), the Navigation controller pushes the next view controller onto the stack. The new view controller's view slides into place, and the Navigation bar items are updated appropriately. The result, as you can see on the right side of Figure 13-1, is a Back button (labeled Detail) in the Detail view that enables you to return to the previous Detail view. (I'm using the pre–Chapter 12 version of RoadTrip because it is easier to show you the flow in Figure 13-1.)

Figure 13-1:
On the iPad,
it's back and
forth using a
Navigation
control-
ler and
Navigation
bar.

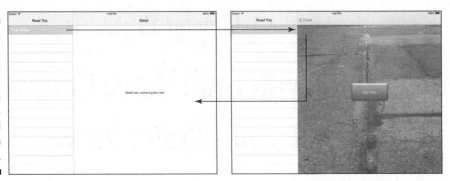

Figure 13-1:
On the iPad,
it's back and
forth using a
Navigation
control-
ler and
Navigation
bar.

Although the user experiences on the iPhone and iPad have similarities, in some ways, the experiences are quite different. And one major and very obvious difference is the screen size — a difference that can have a major impact on the ways you can navigate and display information.

On the iPhone, you go from one view to another using the navigator approach you see in Figure 13-2.

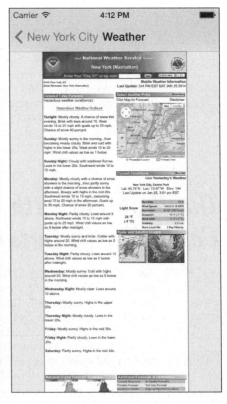

Figure 13-2:
Navigating
with a
Navigation
control-
ler on the
iPhone.

The only difference is that, with the increased real estate on the iPad, you can show both the Table view that you use for navigation as well as the associated content you want to display at the same time, as you see in Figure 13-3.

But while you can take advantage of the larger display using the Navigation controller approach, a problem is lurking in the background that I want to call your attention to.

The process doesn't initially appear to be particularly problematic if you stick to Landscape orientation, but when you switch to Portrait orientation, you soon realize that you're in a bit of a bind. You can see the outlines of that bind in the sequence in Figure 13-4. Again, in the current (unimproved) version of RoadTrip, when you're in Portrait orientation, tapping the Master button displays the Master view in a popover. If you then tap the Test Drive cell, the Test Drive view slides into place. (You also need to tap anywhere in the Test Drive view to dismiss the popover — you'll fix that so it's automatically dismissed when a new view is displayed.)

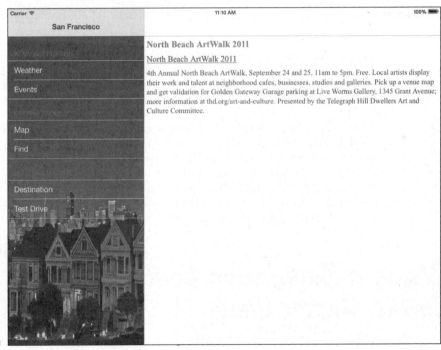

Figure 13-3:
Master view
and Detail
view using a
Split view.

Figure 13-4:
Navigating
in a Split
view using a
Navigation
controller.

At that point, you see a Back button (Detail) that's designed to get you back to the original view. This is the essence of a navigation interface: You move through the sequence of views drilling deeper and deeper into details and then stepping back up until you're at the starting point.

When you are using a Split View controller on the iPad, you can keep the top level of choices visible in the Master view controller at all times. Typically, you leave that view in place and vary the views shown in the detail view in response to choices made in the Master view controller. This gives you two ways to traverse the data. You can use the navigation controller in the Detail view to drill down (and then back up), and you can use the Master View controller to switch from one top-level view to another.

Using a Navigation Controller in the Master View

You might want to use a Navigation controller in the Master view. I'll show you how to do that by creating a *segue* — a storyboard object that creates a transition from one view controller to another — so that when you select Test Drive in the Master view, the Test Drive view will slide into place, Back button and all, in the Master view (as opposed to the Detail view, which had been the case). Then, when you tap the Back button, you'll be back in the Master view.

The technique for replacing a view controller with another is the same whether you're working in the Master or the Detail view, and that's what I'm showing you in this section — replacing the Detail view controller. After I explain it, I'll have you go back to having the Test Drive view display in the Detail view.

Here is how to create a push segue that allows your Test Drive button to display the Test Drive controller in the Master view.

1. **Select `Main_iPad.storyboard` in the Project navigator.**

   The storyboard will appear.

2. **Select the Test Drive cell, control-drag it to the Test Drive controller, as I have done in Figure 13-5, and then release the mouse button.**

   You'll see the pop-up menu that allows you to select the Storyboard Segues type, as shown in Figure 13-6.

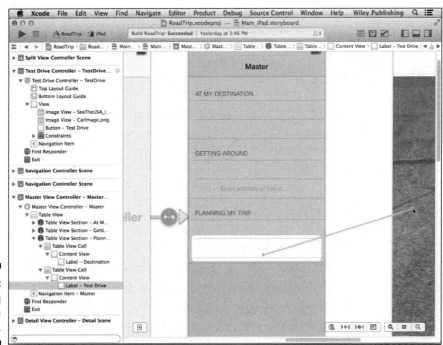

Figure 13-5: Control-drag to create a segue.

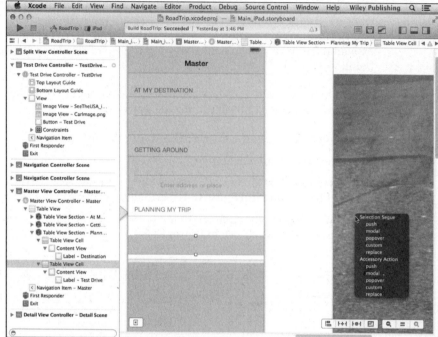

Figure 13-6:
Create a
push segue.

3. Choose Push from the Selection Segue menu items.

Let me remind you that I explained the difference between Selection Segues and Accessory Actions in Chapter 5. You'll notice that the Test Drive view resizes to the same size as the Master view.

Select the segue in the Document Outline, as I have done in Figure 13-7. The Attributes inspector shows you that the Destination is set to Current. (Current is in fact the default.) That means that the Destination view for this segue — the view that is displayed by the Test Drive controller — is the view that the segue is from, or the Master view.

4. Enter TestDrive **in the Identifier field, as I have in Figure 13-7.**

5. Select the Table View cell and, in the Attributes inspector, change the Accessory field from Disclosure Indicator to None.

I'm of the opinion that a disclosure indicator isn't necessary here, but feel free to reject my opinion if you so desire.

If you click the Run button now and then tap Test Drive in the Master view, you get to test drive the 1959 Cadillac Eldorado Biarritz in the Master view; tapping the New York City button (as you recall, what appears in the Back button is the title of the previous view controller, and you made that your destination in Chapter 12) in the Test Drive view takes you back to the Master view. This works even in Portrait orientation, as you can see in Figure 13-8.

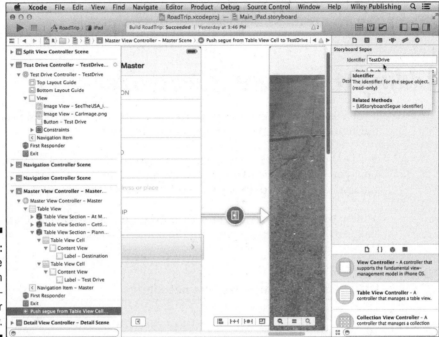

Figure 13-7:
The Destination is Current — the Master View.

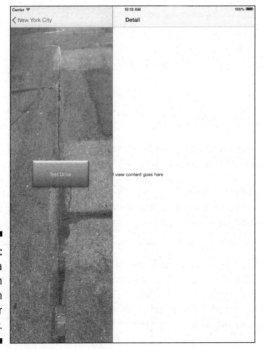

Figure 13-8:
Using a Navigation controller in the Master view.

If you tap Road Trip to return to the Master view, you may notice that the Test Drive cell stays highlighted; not to worry, you'll fix that soon.

Adding a Gesture Recognizer

If you want to truly understand the iOS user experience, you need to understand the importance of gestures, as I explain in Chapter 1.

UIKit includes gesture recognizers that you can use in your app. In this section, you'll use UIKit to add a gesture recognizer to the Main view so that the user can swipe to the left to make the Test Drive view appear.

Adding the gesture recognizer is easy for both the iPhone and iPad. In MasterViewController.m, add the bolded code in Listing 13-1 to viewDidLoad.

Listing 13-1:   Adding a Gesture Recognizer

```
- (void)viewDidLoad
{
  [super viewDidLoad];
  AppDelegate* appDelegate =
            [[UIApplication sharedApplication] delegate];
  self.title = appDelegate.trip.destinationName;
  UIImageView* imageView = [[UIImageView alloc]
      initWithImage:[appDelegate.trip
          destinationImage]];
  self.tableView.backgroundView = imageView;

 detailViewController = (DetailViewController *)
  [[self.splitViewController.viewControllers
  lastObject] topViewController];

  UISwipeGestureRecognizer *swipeGesture =
  [[UISwipeGestureRecognizer alloc] initWithTarget:self
                  action:@selector(handleSwipeGesture:)];
  swipeGesture.direction =
                  UISwipeGestureRecognizerDirectionLeft;
  [self.view addGestureRecognizer:swipeGesture];
}
```

UISwipeGestureRecognizer is a subclass of UIGestureRecognizer — the abstract base class for concrete gesture-recognizer classes. The gesture recognizer does the hard work of recognizing a specific gesture and then sends an action message (that you specify) to the target (that you also specify) to go ahead and do something.

In addition to `UISwipeGesture`, you have gesture recognizers for

- ✔ **Tap:** `UITapGestureRecognizer`
- ✔ **Pinch:** `UIPinchGestureRecognizer`
- ✔ **Rotate:** `UIRotationGestureRecognizer`
- ✔ **Pan:** `UIPanGestureRecognizer`
- ✔ **Touch and hold:** `UILongPressGestureRecognizer`

A window delivers touch events to a gesture recognizer before it delivers them to the *hit-tested view* — the view where it determined the user has touched — attached to the gesture recognizer. (Note that the gesture recognizer is attached to the view and isn't part of the responder chain.) Generally, if a gesture recognizer doesn't recognize its gesture, the touches are passed on to the view. If a gesture recognizer does recognize its gesture, the remaining touches for the view are canceled.

`UISwipeGestureRecognizer` is a concrete subclass of `UIGesture Recognizer` that looks for swiping gestures in one or more directions. Because a swipe is a discrete gesture, the action message is sent only once per gesture.

`UISwipeGestureRecognizer` recognizes a gesture as a swipe when the specified number of touches (`numberOfTouchesRequired`) have moved mostly in an allowable direction (`direction`) far enough to be considered a swipe. You can configure the `UISwipeGestureRecognizer` recognizer for the number of touches (the default is 1) and the direction (the default is right), as follows:

```
UISwipeGestureRecognizer *swipeGesture =
  [[UISwipeGestureRecognizer alloc] initWithTarget:self
                action:@selector(handleSwipeGesture:)];
```

Here, you create a swipe gesture with a target of `self` and an action of `handleSwipeGesture:`. This means that when the gesture recognizer determines it is a swipe, it will send the `handleSwipeGesture:` to the `MasterViewController` (`self` in this case).

Next, because we want the user to swipe to the left to make the Test Drive view appear, you set the direction to `left` from the default `right`, as follows:

```
swipeGesture.direction =

            UISwipeGestureRecognizerDirectionLeft;
```

To handle the swipe — in effect program the response you want to come up with when the swipe occurs — add the code in Listing 13-2 to `MasterViewController.m`.

Listing 13-2: Adding handleSwipeGesture to MasterViewController.m

```objc
- (IBAction)handleSwipeGesture:(id)sender {

UIStoryboard *storyboard =
[UIStoryboard storyboardWithName:@"Main_iPad"

        bundle:nil];
UIViewController *viewController =
  [storyboard instantiateViewControllerWithIdentifier:

        @"TestDrive"];
[[self navigationController]
        pushViewController:viewController
        animated:YES];
}
```

What you do here is first find the storyboard in the *bundle* — in iOS (and OS X), a bundle is a directory that appears to be a single file and contains the executable code, resources such as images and sound, and the nib (storyboard) files.

```objc
UIStoryboard *storyboard =
   [UIStoryboard storyboardWithName:
                        @"Main_iPad"
         bundle:nil];
```

Then the code in Listing 13-2 creates `TestDriveController`. This is the same thing that the storyboard does (in the segue logic) when you tap the Test Drive button:

```objc
UIViewController *viewController =
   [storyboard instantiateViewControllerWithIdentifier:

        @"TestDrive"];
```

Here's where that identifier I told you to enter is needed. It's the only way you can find the view controller that you've configured in the storyboard.

Next, you tell the Navigation controller to push the View controller onto the stack (note that this method also updates the Navigation bar) and have it slide its view into place. (If the `animated` parameter is YES, the view is animated into position; otherwise, the view is simply displayed in place.)

```objc
[[self navigationController] pushViewController:
                        viewController animated:YES];
```

This is what would've been done for you in the segue logic generated by the storyboard.

Oh, and by the way — you've only installed the Swipe gesture in the Master View controller. When you are in the Test Drive view, you can only go back by using the Back (New York City) button. In designing an interface, consistency and symmetry are good features to strive for. If you swipe into a view, maybe you should swipe out of a view. That's how you build powerful, intuitive, and easy-to-learn interfaces. Unfortunately, that's not a great way to write a book. I want to show you as many different ways of working with Cocoa Touch as possible. Sometimes that means swiping into a new view and getting back out of it with a button instead of a matching swipe. Many developers like to show off all of the features and interface elements they've added to their apps. Many others (including the authors of some of the best apps) like to show off how few features and interface elements they've used to build a wide swath of functionality.

So, rather than push view controllers here, there, and everywhere, in the next few sections, you find out how to replace one view controller with another. And the place to start is with the Split View controller.

The Split View Controller

The `UISplitViewController` class is an iPad-only view controller that simply manages the presentation of two side-by-side view controllers in Landscape orientation — it is a container controller. It has no interface — its job is to coordinate the presentation of its two view controllers and to manage the transitions between different orientations.

Using this class, a view controller is created on the left, which is referred to as the *Master view* (and is named that in the template), which presents a list of items, and another view controller on the right, which presents the details, or content, of the selected item and which is referred to as the *Detail view* (and is named that in the template).

After you create and initialize a `UISplitViewController` object, you assign two view controllers to it by using the `viewControllers` property — an array that contains the two (and only the two) controllers. The first view controller (index 0) is displayed on the left side (in the case of RoadTrip, the `MasterViewController`), and the second view controller (index 1) is displayed on the right side (the `RTDetailViewController`).

All of this is set up for you in the storyboard (see Figure 13-9). You'll notice that both of the view controllers managed by the Split View controllers are embedded in Navigation controllers, which is why when you select a cell in the `MasterViewController` view, a Navigation bar appears with a Back button (in either the Master or Detail view).

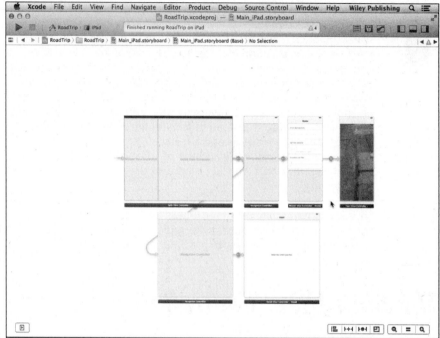

Figure 13-9:
The Master
and Detail
View con-
trollers in the
storyboard.

As you have seen, when the iPad is in Landscape orientation, you can see
both view controllers' views side by side. When you rotate to Portrait orientation, however, the MasterViewController's view is hidden, and
the DetailViewController displays a button *in the Navigation bar* that
enables you to see the MasterViewController's view in a popover. Adding
the button is done in the UISplitViewControllerDelegate protocol
method of the template (you don't have to do anything to implement it).
And if you look at the DetailViewController interface file, you see it has
adopted the protocol — the popover sends its delegate messages at the right
time so that the delegate can add and remove the button.

The user interface I want to show you now uses a toolbar instead of a
Navigation bar, and has the Detail View controller be responsible for managing the toolbar. In fact, I'll show you how to implement the delegate to
use either a toolbar or a Navigation bar when you choose a cell in the
MasterViewController. I'm doing both because some of the features I
want to implement (like the UIPageViewController page transitions in
the EventsController) require a Navigation bar. In addition, at some point
you may want to implement some functionality where a Navigation controller
is the right way to go. Remember my caution about using a limited number
of interface tools. This mixture of Navigation bar and toolbar is designed

primarily to show you different ways of designing the interface; you may well decide to choose one rather than mix them together to possibly befuddle your users. On the other hand, remember that if your user interface makes sense to the user, the fact that behind the scenes you're using two different types of objects doesn't matter.

To start with, you'll add a toolbar to the `TestDriveController` and make `TestDriveController` a `UISplitViewController` delegate. But first I want to explain a little more about how the `UISplitViewController` delegate works.

The UISplitViewController delegate

The `UISplitViewController` does what you'd expect a class doing delegation to do: It sends its delegate messages at the appropriate times to add and remove the button that enables the user to display the Master View controller in the popover you see in Figure 13-10. The Master button is displayed in Portrait view until the user touches it. Then it is covered by the Master view, which slides in from the left.

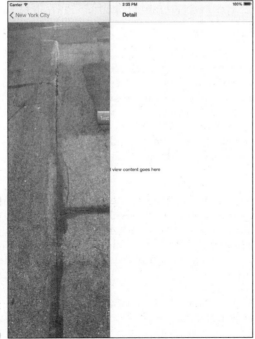

Figure 13-10:
The Road Trip button that displays the Master view in Portrait orientation.

If you look at the `DetailViewController` interface (`DetailViewController.h`) in your project, you can see that this whole delegation business has already been done for you. Listing 13-3 gives the details.

Listing 13-3: The RTDetailViewController Interface

```
#import <UIKit/UIKit.h>

@interface RTDetailViewController : UIViewController

        <UISplitViewControllerDelegate>

@property (strong, nonatomic) id detailItem;
@property (strong, nonatomic)
                IBOutlet UILabel
        *detailDescriptionLabel;

@end
```

You see that `DetailViewController` adopts the `UISplitViewController Delegate` protocol, and as you see in Figure 13-10, it already adds a button to the Navigation bar when the user moves into Portrait orientation. It also removes the button when the iPad is rotated back from Portrait to Landscape orientation.

All you'll need to do is modify what the `UISplitViewControllerDelegate` already does and have it place the button in a toolbar or a Navigation bar, depending on which you're using. You'll do all of that in the `DetailViewController`, and then, if you end up deriving all your view controllers (including the `TestDrive Controller` you've already implemented) from `DetailViewController`, voilà, all your view controllers will be able to add a button to the toolbar or a Navigation bar when the iPad is in Landscape orientation, dutifully display the popover when the user selects the button, and then remove the button when the user rotates the iPad to Portrait orientation.

To prepare for that occurrence, you'll start by getting rid of the "sample" code that was included by the template to display something in the Detail view — you won't use the Detail View controller to actually display anything; that will be done in the individual view controllers you'll create to display the Road Trip content (the weather, for example, or a map) as well as the Test Drive controller you've already created.

Start by pruning two properties used by the Master View controller that you definitely won't need. Delete the commented out bold, underline, and italic lines in Listing 13-4 in `DetailViewController.h`, and add the code in bold. (You'll add some properties that will be used in managing the popover.)

Listing 13-4:   Update DetailViewController.h Interface

```
#import <UIKit/UIKit.h>

@interface DetailViewController : UIViewController

        <UISplitViewControllerDelegate>

//@property (strong, nonatomic) id detailItem;
//@property (strong, nonatomic)
                IBOutlet UILabel
            *detailDescriptionLabel;

@property (weak, nonatomic) IBOutlet UIToolbar *toolbar;
@property (weak, nonatomic)
                        UIBarButtonItem
        * popOverButton;
@property (strong, nonatomic)
            UIPopoverController
        *masterPopoverController;
@end
```

I'll explain these new properties as you use them, but it's worth noting here that you're adding a toolbar as a home for the button the user will use to display the Master View controller in Portrait orientation.

You have more things to prune in the `DetailViewController` implementation file. To do that, delete the commented out code in bold, underline, and italic in Listing 13-5 from the `DetailViewController.m` implementation file.

Listing 13-5:   Update the DetailViewController.m Implementation File

```
#import "DetailViewController.h"

@implementation DetailViewController
```

Here you're mostly getting rid of the class extension and instance variables you no longer need. In Listing 13-4, you also moved the `masterPopoverController` property to the interface file from where it was to the implementation file. As you'll soon see, you had to do that because the Master View controller will need to access the `masterPopoverController` property in order to dismiss the popover after the user makes a selection in the Master View controller in the popover.

Finally you can delete the methods that display "content" in the Detail view — that means the two methods in bold, underline, and italic in Listing 13-6 in `DetailViewController.m`.

Listing 13-6:   Delete the Unnecessary Methods

```
#pragma mark - Managing the detail item

- (void)setDetailItem:(id)newDetailItem
{
    if ( detailItem != newDetailItem) {
        detailItem = newDetailItem;

        // Update the view.
        [self configureView];
    }

    if (self.masterPopoverController != nil) {
        [self.masterPopoverController
                            dismissPopoverAnimated:YES];
    }
}

- (void)configureView
{
    // Update the user interface for the detail item.

    if (self.detailItem) {
        self.detailDescriptionLabel.text =
                            [self.detailItem description];
    }
}
```

You'll need to delete the message sent to configure the view. In `DetailView Controller.m`, delete the commented out code in bold, underline, and italic in `viewDidLoad`, as shown in Listing 13-7.

Listing 13-7:   Delete the Unnecessary Code in viewDidLoad

```
- (void)viewDidLoad
{
    [super viewDidLoad];
// Do any additional setup after loading the view,
        typically from a nib.
//   [self configureView];
}
```

Now, I look at how the delegate mechanism works and how the button is added when the iPad is rotated from Landscape to Portrait orientation and then removed when it is rotated back. In `DetailViewController.m`, the code in this template already does what you need to do to display the kind of popover I just explained. It does so by implementing two `UISplitViewController` delegate methods:

```
splitViewController:willHideViewController:

            withBarButtonItem:forPopoverController:
```

and

```
splitViewController:willShowViewController:

            invalidatingBarButtonItem:
```

The first of these methods is invoked when the Split View controller rotates from a Landscape to Portrait orientation and hides the Master View controller. When that happens, the Split View controller sends a message to add a button to the Navigation bar (or toolbar) of the Detail View controller. If you look in Listing 13-8, this is how it works in `DetailViewController.m`:

Listing 13-8:   Adding the Button

```
- (void)splitViewController:
                (UISplitViewController *)splitController
    willHideViewController:
                      (UIViewController
        *)viewController
    withBarButtonItem:
                        (UIBarButtonItem
        *)barButtonItem
    forPopoverController:
                (UIPopoverController *)popoverController
{
    barButtonItem.title =
                NSLocalizedString(@"Master", @"Master");
    [self.navigationItem setLeftBarButtonItem:
                        barButtonItem animated:YES];
    self.masterPopoverController = popoverController;
}
```

In this method, you are passed a button that you can use to display the popover. This is no ordinary button, however; its target is a selector implemented for you that can display the popover. The way the app works now, only one view controller displays a popover — but in the final version of the RoadTrip app, all the view controllers will be able to display a popover, so you'll need to pass that button to the view controller that's replacing the current one.

You'll notice the presence of `NSLocalizedString` in Listing 13-8. `NSLocalized String` is a macro that can be used to *localize* the text you display. And because I let the term *localize* drop here, I might as well explain about localization.

Localization

When you localize an app, you display the text the user sees on the screen in the user's preferred language (and even a language-specific image).

Localizing an app isn't difficult, just tedious. To localize your app, you create a folder in your application bundle (I'll get to that) for each language you want to support. Each folder has the app's translated resources.

For example, if the user's language is Spanish, available regions range from Spain to Argentina to the United States and lots of places in between. When a localized app needs to load a resource (such as an image, property list, or nib), the app checks the user's language and region and looks for a localization folder that corresponds to the selected language and region. If it finds one, it loads the localized version of the resource instead of the *base* version — the one you're working in.

Looking up such values in the table is handled by the NSLocalizedString macro in your code.

As you can see, the text Master button will change based on the user's preferred language.

```
barButtonItem.title =
              NSLocalizedString(@"Master", @"Master");
```

The macro has two inputs. The first key to an associated string value, and the second is the general comment for the translator. At runtime, NSLocalizedString looks for a strings file named localizable.strings in the language that has been set: Spanish, for example. (A user would've done that by going to Settings and selecting General⇨Internatio nal⇨Language⇨Español.) If NSLocalizedString finds the strings file, it searches the file for a line that matches the first parameter. If the macro doesn't find the file or a specified string, it returns its first parameter — and the string will appear in the base language.

To create the localizable.strings file, you run a command-line program named genstrings, which searches your code files for the macro and places them all in a localizable.strings file (which it creates), ready for the (human) translator. genstrings is beyond the scope of this book, but it's well documented. When you're ready, I leave you to explore it on your own.

Back to the main feature

After absorbing that little localization detour, you then add the longed-for button to the Navigation bar:

```
[self.navigationItem setLeftBarButtonItem:
                     barButtonItem animated:YES];
```

Passing in YES to animated animates the adding of the button. Specifying NO sets the item immediately, without animating the change. In this case, it really makes no difference.

Finally, you save a reference to the popover controller that you'll dismiss when the user makes a selection:

```
self.masterPopoverController = popoverController;
```

As I said, when the user selects a new view in the popover, you'll need to pass this button on to the new view controller so it can display it as well. (You'll do that later in this chapter in a method called prepareForSegue: in Listing 13-15.) In addition, as I explained, you'll also use toolbars in addition to Navigation bars to display the button; adding the button to a toolbar is done differently than adding it to the Navigation bar. To do that, enter the code in bold in Listing 13-9 and delete the bold, underline, and italic code in DetailViewController.m.

Listing 13-9: Extending the splitViewController: willHideViewController: withBarButtonItem:forPopoverController:

```
- (void)splitViewController:
                (UISplitViewController *)splitController
    willHideViewController:
                    (UIViewController
        *)viewController
    withBarButtonItem:
                    (UIBarButtonItem
        *)barButtonItem
    forPopoverController:
                (UIPopoverController
        *)popoverController
{
//  barButtonItem.title = NSLocalizedString(@"Master",
        @"Master");
  barButtonItem.title =
        NSLocalizedString(@"Road Trip", @"Road Trip");
  if ([[self.splitViewController.viewControllers
        lastObject]
        isKindOfClass:[UINavigationController class]])
    [self.navigationItem
        setLeftBarButtonItem:barButtonItem
        animated:YES];
  else {
    NSMutableArray *itemsArray =
                    [self.toolbar.items mutableCopy];
    [itemsArray insertObject:barButtonItem atIndex:0];
    [self.toolbar setItems:itemsArray animated:YES];
  }
  self.masterPopoverController = popoverController;
  self.popOverButton = barButtonItem;
}
```

Listing 13-9 starts off by changing the title of the button from *Master* to *Road Trip* — I think it's less ominous-sounding and more descriptive — indicating the view controller that you'd see if you tap the button:

```
//barButtonItem.title =
              NSLocalizedString(@"Master", @"Master");
  barButtonItem.title =
            NSLocalizedString(@"Road trip", @"Road
        Trip");
```

You then check to see whether you're dealing with a Navigation bar or toolbar.

```
  if ([[[self.splitViewController.viewControllers
        lastObject]
        isKindOfClass:[UINavigationController class]])
```

As I mention earlier, the Split View controller manages two view controllers, with the last one in its list of controllers corresponding to what's displayed in the Detail view. You check if the Detail View controller is embedded in a Navigation controller by sending it the isKindOfClass: message. This method returns a Boolean indicating whether it is, in this case, a UINavigationController.

As you know, classes in Objective-C are first-class objects in and of themselves, so you can use a class method to determine what class something is. This method is defined in the NSObject class, from which all your classes are (ultimately) derived.

If you're dealing with a Navigation controller, you do what you've already been doing and set the left bar button.

```
[self.navigationItem
      setLeftBarButtonItem:barButtonItem
        animated:YES];
```

If you're not dealing with a Navigation controller, you go through some similar logic to add the button to the toolbar.

```
NSMutableArray *itemsArray =
                    [self.toolbar.items mutableCopy];
[itemsArray insertObject:barButtonItem atIndex:0];
[self.toolbar setItems:itemsArray animated:NO];
```

On a toolbar, the buttons are specified in the items property as an array. So you make a copy of the array and add the button you're passed to the top of the array. The items — instances of UIBarButtonItem — are shown on the toolbar in the order they appear in this array. You then take that array and assign it as the items property.

You'll notice that you first make a copy of the toolbar items, insert the button, and then assign the items property. You do it this way because there may be other buttons on the toolbar that you'll want to keep there.

Then you save a reference to the button that you'll use later.

```
self.popOverButton = barButtonItem;
```

The second of the delegate methods is invoked when the view controller rotates from Portrait to Landscape orientation and the "hidden" Master View controller is displayed.

When the iPad is rotated back to Landscape orientation, the `splitViewCon troller:willShowViewController:invalidatingBarButtonItem:` message is sent.

If you added the button to your toolbar to allow the user to display the Master View controller in a popover, you remove the button in the `splitVi ewController:willShowViewController:invalidatingBarButton Item:` method. Listing 13-10 shows how `splitViewController:willSh owViewController:invalidatingBarButtonItem:` is currently imple-mented in `DetailViewController.m:`.

Listing 13-10: splitViewController:willShowViewController: invalidatingBarButtonItem:

```
- (void) splitViewController:
                (UISplitViewController *) splitController
        willShowViewController:
                (UIViewController *) viewController
        invalidatingBarButtonItem:
                (UIBarButtonItem *) barButtonItem
{
// Called when the view is shown again in the split
        view, invalidating the button and popover
        controller.
    [self.navigationItem
            setLeftBarButtonItem:nil animated:YES];
    self.masterPopoverController = nil;
}
```

This method as implemented sets the `leftBarButtonItem` and the `master PopoverController` (the reference to the popover controller) to `nil`.

Here you've simply reversed what you did earlier — you've removed the button from the toolbar and set the `self.popoverController` property to `nil`.

As with the `splitViewController:willHideViewController:withBa rButtonItem: forPopoverController:` method, you'll now have to deal with both a toolbar and a Navigation controller. So add the code in bold in Listing 13-11 to `splitViewController:willShowViewController:inva lidatingBarButtonItem:` in `DetailViewController.m`.

Listing 13-11:   Update splitViewController:willShowViewController: invalidatingBarButtonItem:

```
- (void) splitViewController:
                (UISplitViewController *) splitController
            willShowViewController:
                (UIViewController *) viewController
            invalidatingBarButtonItem:
                (UIBarButtonItem *) barButtonItem
{
  if
    ([[self.splitViewController.viewControllers
        lastObject]
          isKindOfClass: [UINavigationController
        class]])
    [self.navigationItem setLeftBarButtonItem:nil
        animated:YES];
  else {
    NSMutableArray *itemsArray =
                    [self.toolbar.items
        mutableCopy];
    [itemsArray removeObject:barButtonItem];
    [self.toolbar setItems:itemsArray animated:YES];
  }
  self.popOverButton = nil;
  self.masterPopoverController = nil;
}
```

The logic here determines whether it's a Navigation controller or a toolbar, with managing the toolbar identical to what you did in Listing 13-9, when you extended the `splitViewController:willHideViewController: with BarButtonItem:forPopoverController:` method.

While you have the button saved, you still need to transfer the button — and have it displayed — when the user taps the Road Trip button and selects an entry (Weather, for example) that results in a new view controller being instantiated to display its view.

The display part will be done in the `viewDidLoad` method of the new controller.

Currently, the `viewDidLoad` method does nothing but send its superclass the same `viewDidLoad` message (you removed the `configureView` message in Listing 13-7).

```
- (void) viewDidLoad
{
    [super viewDidLoad];
// Do any additional setup after loading the view,
        typically from a nib.
}
```

Add the code in bold in Listing 13-12 to `viewDidLoad` in `DetailView Controller.m`.

Listing 13-12:   Update viewDidLoad

```
- (void)viewDidLoad
{
  [super viewDidLoad];

  if (self.popOverButton) {
   if ([[self.splitViewController.viewControllers
                                    lastObject]
       isKindOfClass:[UINavigationController class]])
         {
     [self.navigationItem
         setLeftBarButtonItem:self.popOverButton
                                     animated:YES];
   }
   else {
     NSMutableArray *itemsArray =
                         [self.toolbar.items
         mutableCopy];
     [itemsArray
             insertObject:self.popOverButton
         atIndex:0];
     [self.toolbar setItems:itemsArray animated:NO];
   }
  }
}
```

When the view is loaded, it's checked to see whether it contains a popover button. If it does, it simply uses the same logic you see in `splitView Controller: willHideViewController:withBarButtonItem:forPo poverController:` (Listing 13-9) using the button that you saved in `split ViewController:willHideViewController: withBarButtonItem:f orPopoverController:` in the `popOverButton` property.

Finally, you can add what you've done to the `TestDriveController`. Update the `TestDriveController.h` interface to make the `TestDrive Controller` a subclass of the `DetailViewController` by deleting the commented out bold, underline, and italic code and adding the bolded code in Listing 13-13.

Listing 13-13:   Update the TestDriveController.h Interface

```
#import <UIKit/UIKit.h>
#import "DetailViewController.h"

//@interface TestDriveController : UIViewController
@interface TestDriveController : DetailViewController

@end
```

Adding the Toolbar

Finally, to eliminate the Navigation controller in the Detail view and set it up so that you always see the button to display the Master view in a popover (Road Trip, in this case), you'll need to add the toolbar to the `Test Drive controller` in the storyboard and create an outlet to the toolbar. The outlet is needed to be able to add and remove the Road Trip button (and other buttons you'll add along the way).

Follow these steps to add the toolbar that supports the RoadTrip button (needed by the popover) to the Test Drive controller.

1. **In the Project navigator, select Main_iPad.storyboard, and in the View selector, display the Utility area.**

2. **Select the segue from the Master View controller (it is really from the Table View cell, but you can't see that) to the Test Drive controller in the Canvas to display it in the Attributes inspector.**

   Optionally, you could select Push Segue from Table View Cell to TestDrive in the Master View Controller – Master Scene in the Document Outline.

   If the Attributes inspector isn't visible, select it in the Inspector selector.

3. **In the Attributes inspector, choose Replace from the Style drop-down menu, choose Detail Split from the Destination drop-down menu, and enter** TestDrive **in the Identifier field, as I have in Figure 13-11.**

   You'll notice that doing so resizes the view so it can display in the Detail view. That means Test Drive will no longer be displayed in the Master view. If you really want Test Drive to still display in the Master view, you can take that on as your personal exercise.

4. **In the Document Outline (or in the Canvas — as you can see you can use either), select the SeeTheUSA Image View in Test Drive Controller – TestDrive Scene.**

5. **Pin the image view to the edges of the screen with Editor⇨Pin using these four subcommands: Leading Space to Superview, Trailing Space to Superview, Top Space to Superview, and Bottom Space to Superview.**

6. **Drag in a toolbar from the Library in the Utility area and delete the Item button (it's included in the toolbar by default), as I have in Figure 13-12.**

   In the Library, the toolbar item is way down at the bottom of the gallery. Don't confuse the toolbar item with a Navigation bar.

   You're getting there, but now you'll need to connect the toolbar to the outlet in the `DetailViewController` base class.

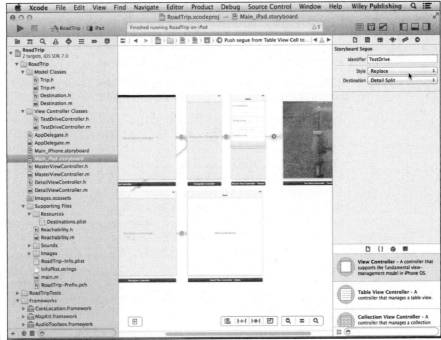

Figure 13-11:
Update the
segue.

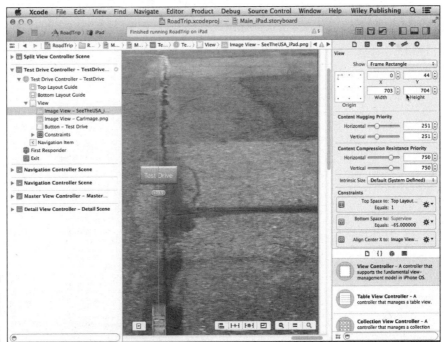

Figure 13-12:
The new
toolbar.

7. Select the Test Drive controller in the Document Outline and open the Connections inspector.

You'd open the Connections inspector as you'd open any inspector: by clicking its icon in the Inspector selector.

8. In the Connections inspector, drag from the Toolbar outlet to the toolbar on the canvas, as I have in Figure 13-13.

You may remember that you added the Toolbar outlet to the `Detail ViewController` base class in Listing 13-4.

Because you deleted the `DetailViewController`'s `detailDescription Label` outlet in Listing 13-4, you'll have to delete it in the storyboard as well. (If you don't, you get a runtime error. Just Control-click the Detail View controller entry in the Document Outline to open the Connections window, as I have in Figure 13-14.) You'll see a yellow warning triangle next to the `detailDescriptionLabel` line in the Outlets section of the window. Simply delete that outlet by clicking the x in front of the `Label - Detail view content goes here` line.

Because you've added the toolbar, you'll have to change the math controlling the route your car takes in the `TestDriveController`.

Update the `TestDriveController`'s `testDrive:` method in `TestDrive Controller.m` with the code in bold in Listing 13-14.

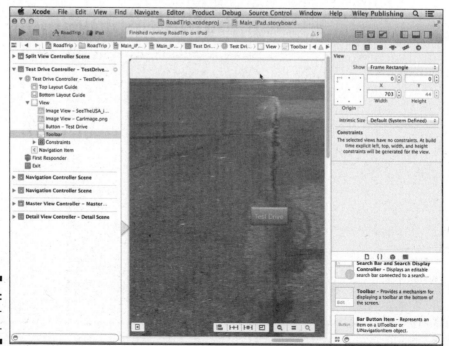

Figure 13-13:
Set the toolbar outlet.

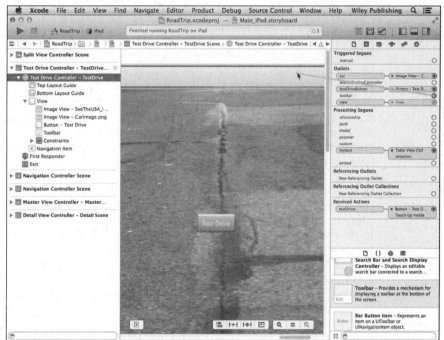

Listing 13-14:   Take the Toolbar into Account

```
- (IBAction)testDrive:(id)sender {

  AudioServicesPlaySystemSound(burnRubberSoundID);
  [self performSelector:@selector(playCarSound)
                      withObject:self afterDelay:.2];

  CGPoint center = CGPointMake(car.center.x,
              self.view.frame.origin.y +
              car.frame.size.height/2
              + self.toolbar.frame.size.height);

  void (^animation)() = ^(){

    car.center = center;
  };

  void (^completion)(BOOL) = ^(BOOL finished){
    [self rotate];
  };

  [UIView animateWithDuration:3 animations:animation
                        completion:completion];
}
```

Adding the button when the view controller is replaced

While all of this gets you close to wrapping up the whole toolbar business, you still need to do one more important thing — and a couple of minor things. The first of these — the important one — I cover in this section. Because you're replacing the view controller with a new one — albeit one from the same base class — the new view controller has no access to the button it needs to display or the popover it needs to dismiss. Fortunately, the folks at Apple provide a perfect place to do that.

When a segue is triggered — which you do when you tap a Table entry — but before the new controller slides its view into place, the storyboard runtime calls the current view controller's method so that it can pass data to the view controller that's about to be displayed. That means that you can pass the button information on to the new view controller before it even gets launched. Then, `prepareForSegue:sender:`, the method you override in Listing 13-15, will both assign the button to be used in `viewDidLoad` (Listing 13-12) and (if necessary) dismiss the view controller as well.

`prepareForSegue:sender:` is a view controller method that notifies a view controller that a segue is about to be performed. `segue` is the `UIStoryboard Segue` object, and it contains information about the view controllers involved in the segue.

Although default implementation of this method does nothing, `UIView Controller` subclasses can override it and pass data to the view controller that's about to be displayed. The `segue` object has properties that point to the source view controller as well as the destination view controller. The segue is the only object that simultaneously knows about both the source and the destination view controllers.

`sender` is the object that caused the segue, but you won't need to use it here.

You add the code to the `prepareForSegue:sender:` method to make the `DestinationController` the `UISplitViewController` delegate and assign the `popOverButton` and `masterPopoverController` properties.

You'll also dismiss the popover when it's present so the user doesn't have to touch in the view to get rid of it.

To do all that, add the code in Listing 13-15 to `MasterViewController.m`.

Listing 13-15: Overriding prepareForSegue:sender:

```
- (void)prepareForSegue:
            (UIStoryboardSegue *)segue sender:(id)sender
        {
  if ([[UIDevice currentDevice] userInterfaceIdiom] ==
                            UIUserInterfaceIdiomPad)
        {
    DetailViewController *currentDetailViewController;
    if ([[self.splitViewController.viewControllers
                                    lastObject]
        isKindOfClass:[UINavigationController class]])
      currentDetailViewController =
        (DetailViewController *) ((UINavigationController
        *)
          [self.splitViewController.viewControllers

        lastObject]).topViewController;
    else
      currentDetailViewController =
        [self.splitViewController.viewControllers

        lastObject];
        if(currentDetailViewController.masterPopover
        Controller

                                        != nil)

        [currentDetailViewController.masterPopover
        Controller

        dismissPopoverAnimated:YES];

    DetailViewController

        *destinationDetailViewController;

  if ([segue.destinationViewController
        isKindOfClass:[UINavigationController class]])
    destinationDetailViewController =
      (DetailViewController *)
        ((UINavigationController *)

    segue.destinationViewController).topViewController;
  else
    destinationDetailViewController =

        segue.destinationViewController;
  self.splitViewController.delegate =
                        destinationDetailViewController;
  destinationDetailViewController.popOverButton =
```

(continued)

Listing 13-15 *(continued)*

```
            currentDetailViewController.popOverButton;
    destinationDetailViewController.
                                    masterPopoverController
        =
      currentDetailViewController.masterPopoverController;
    }
}
```

You start by finding the current Detail View controller because it has the button and popover properties the new view controller needs.

This code appears more complicated than it is. You use the very same logic you used earlier (say, in Listing 13-8) to decide whether you're faced with a Navigation bar or toolbar. That means I first check to see whether I'm running on an iPad. If I am, I get the current Detail View controller by accessing the list of view controllers in the `splitViewController`'s `viewController` array. Fortunately, the `UIViewController` class has a `splitViewController` property to make that easy for me.

I then check to see whether a Navigation controller is in the `viewControllers` array and, if one is there, I get the Navigation controller's `topViewController` (the current view controller); if not, I simply use the controller in the array. (You'll notice a whole lot of casting going on here; I leave it to you to work your way through it.)

```
if ([[[self.splitViewController.viewControllers
        lastObject]
          isKindOfClass:[UINavigationController
        class]])
  currentDetailViewController =
    (RTDetailViewController *)((UINavigationController *)
        [self.splitViewController.viewControllers

        lastObject]).topViewController;
    else
      currentDetailViewController =
        [self.splitViewController.viewControllers
        lastObject];
```

Next, if I see a popover, I want to dismiss it. I check to see whether a popover controller (that's why you had to make the `masterPopoverController` property accessible by moving it into the header file in Listing 13-4) is currently there, and if I see one, I dismiss it.

```
if (currentDetailViewController.masterPopoverController
                                                != nil)
    [currentDetailViewController.masterPopoverController

    dismissPopoverAnimated:YES];
```

Next, I find the new destination controller (the one being transitioned to) using logic similar to the logic I used to find the current Detail View controller.

```
if ([segue.destinationViewController
            isKindOfClass:[UINavigationController class]])
destinationDetailViewController =
  (DetailViewController *)((UINavigationController *)

        segue.destinationViewController).topViewController;
else
  destinationDetailViewController =
                        segue.destinationViewController;
```

Then I simply set the Split View Controller delegate to the new view controller, so it will get the `splitViewController:willHideViewController:withBarButtonItem:forPopoverController:` and `splitViewController:willShowViewController:invalidatingBarButtonItem:` messages.

```
self.splitViewController.delegate =

            destinationDetailViewController;
```

Finally, I assign the `popOverButton` and `masterPopoverController` properties in the new view controller.

```
destinationDetailViewController.popOverButton =
            currentDetailViewController.popOverButton;
destinationDetailViewController.masterPopoverController =

        currentDetailViewController.masterPopoverController;
```

Admittedly, this just dismisses the popover and assigns the properties, but doesn't do anything to display the button. That actually gets done in `viewDidLoad` — which you added earlier in Listing 13-12.

You also can specify the size of the popover window by assigning a value to the `preferredContentSize` property. You should be aware that the actual size may be reduced so that the popover fits on the screen and that the popover does not overlap a keyboard when a keyboard is presented. You can see the code that does that in the `MasterViewController`'s `awakeFromNib` method.

```
- (void)awakeFromNib
{
  if ([[UIDevice currentDevice] userInterfaceIdiom] ==
                                UIUserInterfaceIdiomPad)
      {
      self.clearsSelectionOnViewWillAppear = NO;
```

```
        self.preferredContentSize =
                                CGSizeMake(320.0, 600.0);
    }
    [super awakeFromNib];
}
```

The `awakeFromNib` message is sent to an object that has been instantiated from the storyboard after all the objects have been loaded and initialized. When the message is sent, all its outlet and action connections have been set.

If you decide to ignore the advice in this section and don't dismiss the popover controller, taps outside the popover window will cause the popover to be dismissed. You can, however, allow the user to interact with the specified views and not dismiss the popover, using the `passthroughViews` property (although you won't be doing that here). You'd then have to dismiss the popover yourself.

A Few More Tweaks to the MasterViewController

You're almost, but not quite, done. Right now, when you make a selection in the Table view, it stays highlighted. To fix that, you'll need to implement a Table view method `tableView:didSelectRowAtIndexPath:`. Add the method in Listing 13-16 to `MasterViewController.m` to unhighlight a selected cell.

Listing 13-16:   Deselect the Cell

```
- (void)tableView:(UITableView *)tableView
      didSelectRowAtIndexPath:(NSIndexPath *)indexPath
        {

  [tableView deselectRowAtIndexPath:indexPath

        animated:YES];
}
```

This is a Table View Delegate method that is invoked when the user selects a cell. Normally, you'd launch a view controller here or do something else. (I explain more about this method and other Table View Delegate and Data Source methods in Chapter 20.) But because you're using a segue, the only thing you need to do is deselect the cell that was tapped, which will remove the highlight.

A partner in crime here is the `self.clearsSelectionOnViewWill Appear = NO;` statement you see in the `MasterViewController`'s `awakeFromNib` method I mention in the previous section. If that were set to YES, a highlighted selection wouldn't stay highlighted when a view appeared. I have you deselect it here so you begin to get a feel of how things are connected in a Table view — and that I explain in detail in Chapter 20.

And (a Little Extra) One More Thing

Although tapping the Test Drive cell now replaces the Detail View controller with the Test Drive controller, the gesture recognizer still works. The only problem with it is that now you have both a Navigation bar and a toolbar.

To fix that, you'll need to duplicate the Test Drive controller in the storyboard (select it and then choose Edit⇨Duplicate from the main menu) and give it a different identifier (`TestDriveNavigation`, for example). Remove the toolbar and change the image view origin and size in the Size inspector back to where it was when you started this chapter (origin of $x = 0$, $y = 0$, and height of `1004` — the change in height has to do with the fact that this is now just a view controller without any segues that influence the size). Then change `handleSwipeGesture` in Listing 13-2 to instantiate the new view controller in `MasterViewController.m`.

Delete

```
UIViewController *viewController =
    [storyboard instantiateViewControllerWithIdentifier:

        @"TestDrive"];
```

and replace it with

```
UIViewController *viewController =
    [storyboard instantiateViewControllerWithIdentifier:

        @"TestDriveNavigation"];
```

You should also add the following to `TestDriveController` to keep the popover the right size in Portrait orientation:

```
- (void)awakeFromNib
{
  if ([[UIDevice currentDevice] userInterfaceIdiom] ==
                            UIUserInterfaceIdiomPad) {
    self.preferredContentSize =
                          CGSizeMake(320.0, 600.0);
  }
  [super awakeFromNib];
}
```

Well, that concludes your long and winding tour of Split View controllers. Although it may have been a bit arduous, at this point you have a firm understanding of how Split views and popovers work together — one that you can apply to whatever you want to do in your own app.

Before you do that, however, you'll want to complete the storyboard so you can start adding features and functionality to RoadTrip (besides the Test Drive functionality). You'll also want to change the Detail view that appears when you launch the RoadTrip app.

Don't Forget the iPhone

This chapter was primarily about how to handle the Split View controller used in the iPad user interface. The iPhone doesn't use a Split view, but it does use the `TestDriveController`. In the last section of this chapter, you added another `TestDriveController` scene to the iPad storyboard with a `TestDriveNaviagtion` identifier. This second scene does not need a toolbar, because it is launched with a swipe gesture.

Well, you need that same "toolbarless" scene for using swipe gestures on the iPhone. In fact, the `handleSwipeGesture:` method shown in Listing 13-2 still works fine on the iPhone, so you don't have to do any extra work. It's a bit odd, because it uses part of the iPad storyboard on the iPhone, but it works.

Chapter 14

Finishing the Basic App Structure

*I*n earlier chapters, I've waxed poetic about storyboards but I haven't really (completely) shown you why I find them so appealing. Now it's time for you to experience the reason yourself.

As I say earlier in the book, the storyboard is basically about working with view controllers. You might imagine yourself laying out your storyboard at the beginning of app development, and, in fact, that is how many developers begin. Just as with storyboards for movies, commercials, and games, a storyboard for an app can be understood and discussed by a wide range of people. Developers can recognize the Cocoa Touch components it will use, but potential users, backers, graphic designers, and others can also relate to the simplicity of a storyboard.

Many developers do start with a storyboard, but they often only start with the basics. In an iterative process, they implement the functionality of the basic storyboard and then add another layer of storyboarding and then implement that functionality. This type of iterative development can be very productive because you test each step of the way.

What it does mean, though, is that your storyboard isn't fully designed until you reach the end of app development. How you develop your app is up to you. Do what makes sense to you and don't think that there's a single "right" way to develop your app and your storyboards. (Of course, if you are working on a development team, there may be a single "right" way to keep everyone on the same page.)

In this chapter, I show you how to extend your storyboard to lay out the flow, or the *user experience architecture,* of most of your app — or at least the big pieces of the app, such as the structure for the user to find out the weather forecast for the destination, find events that are happening at the destination, bring up a map, and find a location on a map.

I start by explaining the Weather view controller and then have you move on to complete most of the rest of the view controllers. I also have you replace the Detail View controller that's now displayed at app launch with the Weather controller.

Extending the iPad Storyboard to Add More Functionality to Your App

You start the day's work by selecting `Main_iPad.storyboard` in the Project navigator and showing the Utility area by selecting its icon in the Xcode toolbar's View selector. Next, hide the Project navigator by deselecting it in the Xcode toolbar's View selector (remember, as I explain in Chapter 2, it's a toggle). Doing so gives you a little more real estate onscreen. (If you have an extra-large monitor, though, you can keep the Project navigator open.)

Continuing with your prep work, go ahead and select the Attributes inspector in the Inspector selector bar in the Utility area. Close all the disclosure triangles in the Document Outline to give you a little more room to work in.

Adding the Weather view controller

Here's where the rubber meets the road. To add the Weather view controller — complete with a web view for displaying the weather — you need to do the following:

1. **Select Objects in the Utility area's Library pane and then select a view controller from the pane and drag it onto your storyboard (see Figure 14-1).**

   A new scene is created. (If you're a bit hazy on how storyboards work, check out Chapter 5.)

2. **Select the new view controller on the storyboard.**

   Doing so reveals its attributes in the (already opened) Attributes inspector.

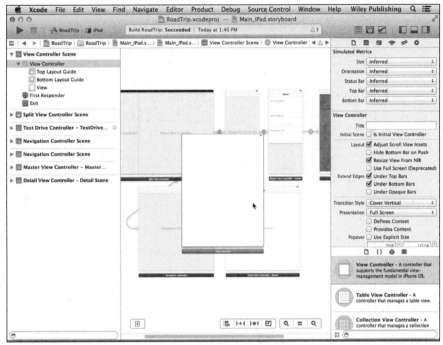

Figure 14-1:
Drag in
a view
controller.

3. **In the View Controller section of the Attributes inspector, enter** Weather **in the Title field, as shown in Figure 14-2. Also enter** Weather **in the Storyboard ID field in the Identity inspector.**

   Be sure to press Return when entering text in a text field in the Attributes inspector.

   The field in the storyboard isn't updated until you press Return, or sometimes until you click in another field *in that inspector*.

   Adding an identifier isn't a requirement, but it's a good habit to get into. For example, you used an identifier in the `handleSwipeGesture:` method in Chapter 13, and you'll need the Weather identifier in `prepareForSegue` later in this book to pass some data to the Destination Controller. As for the Title field, giving anything a title always makes it easier to figure out what's what in the storyboard.

4. **Drag a toolbar from the Utility area's Library pane and position it at the top of the view.**

5. **Delete the Item button (the button that comes by default with the tool-bar when you drag it in from the Library) as shown in Figure 14-3.**

   You did the very same thing for the toolbar you added to the `TestDriveController` in Chapter 13.

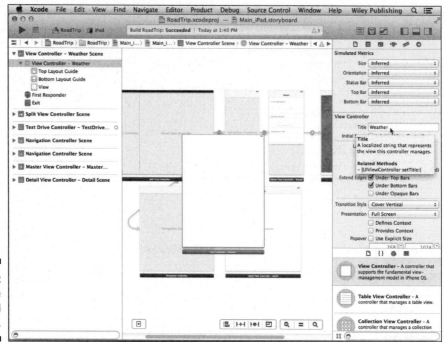

Figure 14-2:
Set the
title and
identifier.

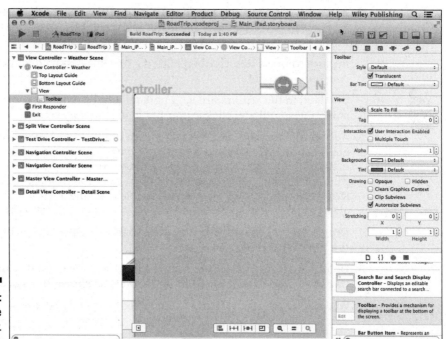

Figure 14-3:
Add the
toolbar.

6. **Select the Weather cell in the Master View controller (it's there under the Table View heading) and Control-drag from there to View Controller – Weather Scene, as shown in Figure 14-4.**

   You can do this either in the canvas or in the Document Outline or both, as you see in Figure 14-4. You may also want to rearrange the canvas so that your new view controller is near the Weather cell while you draw the connection.

   If you haven't done so already, as you work through the cells in the Master View Controller, add an Xcode-specific label to the Table View Cell for each one. It makes your life a lot easier.

7. **Select Replace from the Selection Segue pop-up menu that appears, as shown in Figure 14-5.**

   As I explain in Chapter 5, you use a segue whenever you want to create a transition from one view controller to another. A segue performs the visual transition between two view controllers and supports push (navigation), modal, and custom transitions. All you have to do (as you just saw) is Control-drag from a button or Table View cell to the view controller you want to be displayed.

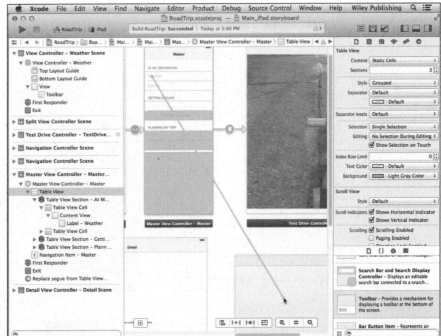

Figure 14-4:
Drag from the Weather cell to the view controller in the Document Outline.

A *push segue* causes the new view controller (with a Back button) to slide into place when the user taps a button; the Navigation bar items are updated appropriately. (See Chapter 5 for more about adding a Navigation controller.)

In contrast to a push segue, a *modal segue* presents the view controller modally, with the transition style you specify, and requires the user to do something (tap Save or Cancel, for example) to get back to the previous view controller. (This requirement that the user *do* something is the modal part of a modal segue.) Segues support the standard visual transition styles, such as Cover Vertical, Flip Horizontal, Cross Dissolve, and Partial Curl.

In addition, segue objects are used to prepare for the transition from one view controller to another. Segue objects contain information about the view controllers involved in a transition. When a segue is triggered, but before the visual transition occurs, the storyboard runtime calls the current view controller's `prepareForSegue:sender:` method so that it can pass any needed data to the view controller that's about to be displayed.

A Replace segue causes the existing view controller to be replaced by a new one.

You'll notice that the view resizes itself. It defaults to a Destination that's the same as the originating view. You'll need to fix that. (The Destination here is the Master view.)

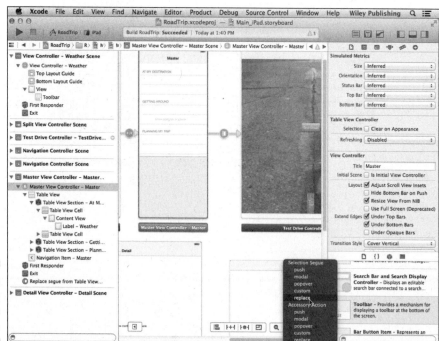

Figure 14-5:
Creating
a Replace
segue.

8. **Select the segue on the storyboard Canvas or in the Document Outline and, back in the Attributes inspector, make sure that *Replace* appears in the Style menu in the Attribute inspector; then enter Weather in the Identifier field and press Return.**

   Again, you won't always use the identifier, but it's good practice to name it so that you can identify it, as shown in Figure 14-6.

9. **If necessary, choose Detail Split from the Destination drop-down menu.**

   Notice that the segue is selected in the Document Outline as well as on the Canvas (it turns from gray to white), and the view controller has resized its view.

10. **Select the Table View cell containing the Weather label in either the Canvas or the Document Outline and, in the Attributes inspector's Accessory field, make sure that the Accessory has been set to None.**

In the rest of this section, I show you how to add the rest of the scenes you need in your storyboard for the RoadTrip app. Some other view controllers in the storyboard aren't launched by segues, and you'll add those as needed.

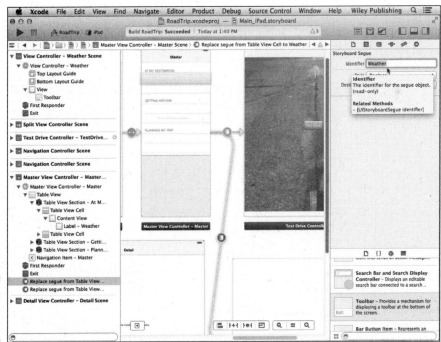

Figure 14-6:
Setting the destination.

Adding the Events controller

The next view controller I have you add is the Events controller, which will display events that you might be interested in at your destination. Interestingly enough, as you'll find in Chapter 16, for the Events controller to work properly, you'll need to have it embedded in a Navigation controller. Fortunately, you have that covered because the work you did in Chapter 13 enables you to handle either a Navigation controller or a toolbar in the Detail View controller's `UISplitViewControllerDelegate` delegate methods.

To add an Events controller, do the following:

1. **Select a new view controller from the Objects section of the Library pane and drag it onto your storyboard.**

2. **In the Attributes inspector, enter** Events **in the view controller's Title field, as well as in the Identity inspector's Storyboard ID field.**

3. **With the new Events view controller selected, choose Editor⇨Embed In⇨Navigation Controller from the main menu, as shown in Figure 14-7.**

   A navigation controller scene is added to your storyboard, along with something called a *Relationship* from `UINavigationController` to `View Controller`. The navigator and related Events view controller are linked by the relationship, but, at this time, they have no other connections to other view controllers.

Figure 14-7: Embedding the Events controller in a Navigation controller.

4. **Select the Navigation controller in the canvas, and in the Attributes inspector, enter** EventsNavigation **in the Title field as well as in the Identity inspector's Storyboard ID field for the Navigation controller so you can find it for the next step.**

   You can see in Figure 14-8 that, in the Document Outline and on the Canvas, the Navigation controller is now identified as EventsNavigation.

   Now you'll want to create a segue from the Events cell to the Navigation controller.

5. **In the Document Outline, select the Events cell in the Master View controller (it's there under the TableView Section – At My Destination under the Table View heading) and Control-drag to the Navigation controller you just added — the one in which you embedded the Events controller and named in Step 4.**

   You can see all the action in Figure 14-9. Note that you may need to rearrange things to connect the table cell to the view controller. After connection is made, you can rearrange things.

   I find it is easier to do this from the Document Outline.

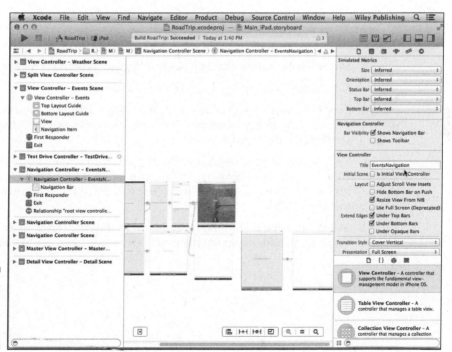

Figure 14-8: Naming the Navigation controller.

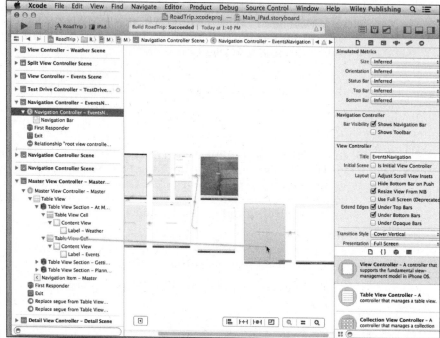

Figure 14-9:
Drag from
the Events
cell to the
Navigation
control-
ler within
which the
Events
controller is
embedded.

6. **Select Replace from the Storyboard Segues pop-up menu that appears.**

   For iPhone, you will use Push rather than Replace.

7. **Select the segue on the Canvas and, in the Attributes inspector, enter** Events **in the Identifier field and choose Detail Split from the Destination drop-down menu.**

   Your storyboard should look like Figure 14-10 when you're done. Figure 14-10 also shows the segue you created in the Attributes inspector. (Note that for iPhone, you will use a Push segue and not use Detail Split.)

8. **Select the Events Table View cell, and in the Attributes inspector's Accessory field, make sure the Accessory has been set to None.**

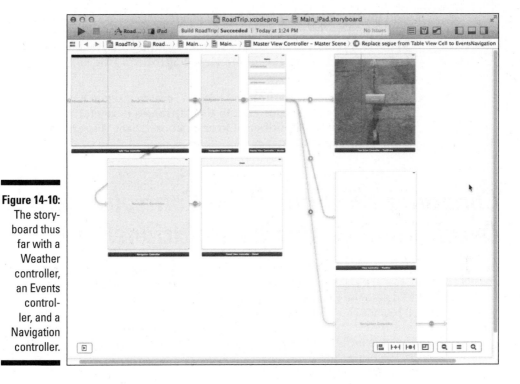

Figure 14-10:
The story-
board thus
far with a
Weather
controller,
an Events
control-
ler, and a
Navigation
controller.

Adding the remaining controllers

The remaining controllers will be added in pretty much the same way, with a little twist when it comes to the Destination controller.

1. **Repeat the steps that you went through when you added the Weather controller to the storyboard in the earlier section "Adding the Weather view controller" to add the Map controller. Be sure to enter** Map **in the view controller's Title and Identifier fields. Enter** Map **in the segue Identifier as well.**

2. **Add the Find controller by repeating Steps 1–5 you followed to add the Weather controller to the storyboard in the earlier section "Adding the Weather view controller." Enter** Find **in the view controller's Title and Identifier fields, respectively.**

   You won't be using a segue for the Find controller. I'll show you a different way to launch a view controller in Chapter 20.

3. **Add the Destination controller by repeating Steps 1–3 and 6–10 (don't add a toolbar) that you followed when adding the Weather controller to the storyboard in the earlier section "Adding the Weather view controller." Enter** Destination **in the view controller's Title and Identifier fields, respectively.**

4. **For the Destination controller, in Step 7, create a segue but make it modal. Select the segue and, in the Attributes inspector, enter Destination in the Identifier field and choose Form Sheet from the Presentation pop-up menu.**

Changing the Split View Controller to a Detail View Controller Relationship

At this point, because it really doesn't do anything, you can delete the Detail View controller object from the iPad storyboard (but be sure not to delete the DetailView controller class files in the Project navigator). You'll replace the relationship between the Split View controller and the Detail View controller with one to the Weather controller. I chose Weather controller arbitrarily here — you could just as easily have replaced it with any of the other view controllers. This is the Detail view the user will see when the app is launched.

The following steps show you how to replace the Detail View controller.

1. **In the Document Outline or on the canvas, select the Navigation controller associated with the Detail View controller (see Figure 14-11) and press Delete.**

   It may be easiest to select the Detail View controller in the Document Outline in order to highlight it. Then you can probably find the Navigation controller right next to it.

2. **Select the Detail View controller in the Document Outline or canvas (see Figure 14-12) and press Delete as well.**

   You'll need to create a new relationship between the Split View controller and the Weather controller.

3. **Select the Split View controller on the storyboard or Document Outline, Control-drag to the Weather controller, and then select Relationship – Detail View Controller from the pop-up menu that appears (as I have in Figure 14-13).**

   The final result of what has been added to the storyboard so far should look like Figure 14-14. I've rearranged things a bit for the sake of clarity. Make certain that everything is named as you rearrange the view controllers. Then you can zoom in and out to see what makes the most logical arrangement.

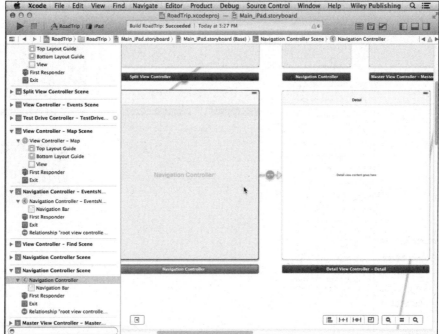

Figure 14-11:
Select the Navigation controller in the Document Outline.

Figure 14-12:
Select the Detail View controller in the Document Outline.

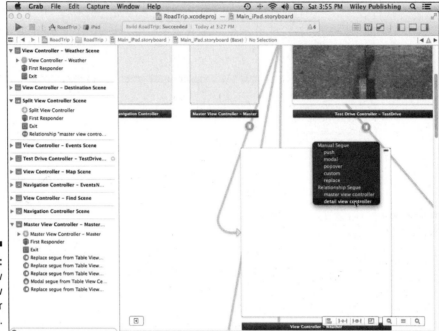

Figure 14-13:
A new
Detail View
controller
relationship.

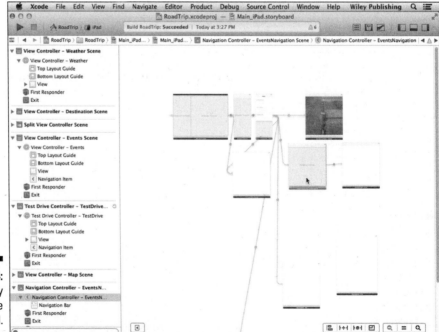

Figure 14-14:
The nearly
complete
storyboard.

You're also going to have to make some changes in `application:didFinish LaunchingWithOptions:`. Add the code in bold shown in Listing 14-1 to that method in `AppDelegate.m`.

Listing 14-1: Updating application:didFinishLaunchingWithOptions:

```
- (BOOL)application:(UIApplication *)application
      didFinishLaunchingWithOptions:
                              (NSDictionary *)launchOptions
{
  if ([[UIDevice currentDevice] userInterfaceIdiom] ==
          UIUserInterfaceIdiomPad) {
    UISplitViewController *splitViewController =
          (UISplitViewController
          *)self.window.rootViewController;
    if ([splitViewController.viewControllers[1]
        isKindOfClass:[UINavigationController class]]) {
      UINavigationController *detailNavigationController =
          [splitViewController.viewControllers
                                            lastObject];
      splitViewController.delegate =
          (id)navigationController.topViewController;
    }
    else
      splitViewController.delegate =
          [splitViewController.viewControllers lastObject];

... the rest of the method
}
```

The change you make here is in how you get the Detail View controller that you will assign as the Split View controller delegate.

As I mention earlier, the Split View controller manages two view controllers, with the last one in its list of controllers corresponding to what's displayed in the Detail view. You check the last view controller to see whether it's a Navigation controller (that contains the Detail View controller) by sending it the `isKindOfClass:` message. This method returns a Boolean indicating whether it is a `UINavigationController`.

```
    if ([splitViewController.viewControllers[1]
        isKindOfClass:[UINavigationController class]]) {
      UINavigationController *detailNavigationController =
          [splitViewController.viewControllers lastObject];
      splitViewController.delegate =
          (id)detailNavigationController.topViewController;
    }
```

If it is a Navigation controller, you need to find its view controller (it's the one that has adopted the `SplitViewControllerDelegate` protocol, implemented the protocol methods, and can become the Split View controller's delegate), which you get by accessing the Navigation controller's `topViewController` property. (It points to the first and only view controller on its stack.) Then you'll assign it as the delegate.

If it's a view controller, rather than a Navigation controller (which it will be because you just made the Weather controller the Detail View controller, and it has no Navigation controller), you just assign that view controller as the delegate.

```
else
   splitViewController.delegate =
         [splitViewController.viewControllers lastObject];
```

If you build and run your project now, it looks like you've taken a step backward; all you'll see is a blank screen — in Portrait orientation no less (unless you've kept the Test Drive controller as the initial Detail View controller). You'll fix that in the next chapter.

Repeat for iPhone

You now need to update the iPhone storyboard file with the same kind of view controllers you just added to the iPad storyboard file. They are as follows:

✔ `WeatherController` with a Push segue (instead of the iPad's Replace segue)

✔ `EventsController` with a Push segue (instead of the iPad's Replace segue)

✔ `MapController` with a Push segue (instead of the iPad's Replace segue)

✔ `FindController`

✔ `DestinationController` with a Modal segue

The iPhone storyboard uses Push segues because you are pushing a new view controller onto the stack when the user touches a cell such as "Weather" in the `tableView` in iPhone's Master View controller.

Part V
Adding the App Content

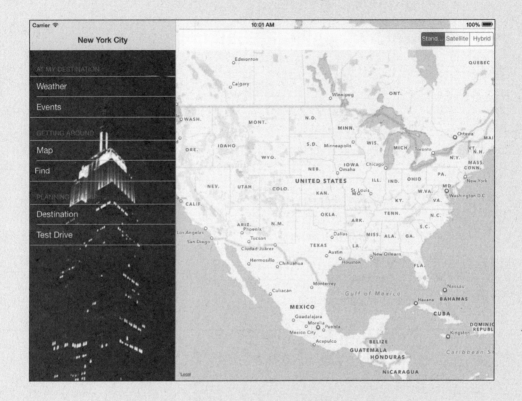

Visit www.dummies.com/extras/iosapplicationdevelopment for more features you can add to your iOS app.

In this part . . .

- ✔ Working with web views
- ✔ Geocoding
- ✔ Finding a location
- ✔ Selecting a destination

Chapter 15

How's the Weather? Working with Web Views

. . . .

In This Chapter

▶ Having your app actually deliver content

▶ Displaying a web page

▶ Understanding the ins and outs of Web views

▶ Encountering some interesting runtime errors

. . . .

Getting the framework (no pun intended) in place for a new app is certainly a crucial part of the development process, but in the grand scheme of things, it's only the spadework that prepares the way for the really cool stuff. After all is said and done, you still need to add the content that the users see or interact with. Content (and functionality) is, after all, the reason they will buy the app.

Now that you have created the storyboard scenes by specifying the view controllers and have spiffed up the Master View controller, it's time to make those new view controllers earn their keep. As I've explained more than once, view controllers are the key elements here. They're the ones that get the content from the `Trip` model object and send it to the view to display. In this chapter, you create a view controller that lets the Weather view know where to get the weather information it needs.

The Plan

You will be adding a custom view controller for displaying the weather, which is actually pretty easy. As is always the case, the view controller will be interacting with a view (actually a hierarchy of views) in a storyboard. There's one view controller and two storyboards — one for iPad and one for iPhone.

What is content? What is functionality?

Hundreds of pages into this book, it may seem a little late to be asking about content and functionality, but it's not. Up to this moment, you've seen the basics of how to put an app together — how to design an interface with storyboards, how to use built-in classes and how to create new classes based on them, and how to work with animation, sound, and navigation. Although content and functionality are the two most basic issues you deal with in starting to build an app, until now, you've needed to become familiar with the tools and features of iOS and Cocoa Touch.

What is the purpose of your app? Is it to show off your development skills just to prove that you can do it, or are you deliberately building a portfolio that can lead to gainful employment in the app world? Have you been tasked with building an app for a specific purpose or client? And is the app supposed to make money?

Don't let the technology get in the way of your content and functionality. Users don't really care about what you need to worry about with view controllers and classes. They want to *use* your app and make it their own. At the 2013 Worldwide Developers Conference, speaker after speaker stressed that the purpose of the major revisions to the interface in iOS 7 was to get the interface out of the way and to focus on the content and functionality of your apps. To paraphrase a saying from the political world, "It's the content, stupid."

But to present the content simply and clearly, you need to do your hard work of coding and designing the interface. So now it's back to that part of the story.

The iPad storyboard

The Weather-related part of the iPad storyboard is shown in Figure 15-1.

The control flow through the iPad storyboard goes like this:

1. The iPad user interface is controlled by an instance of Apple's `UISplitViewController`, which manages a Master View controller and a Detail View controller.

2. The Master View controller, displayed on the left in Landscape orientation, has a relationship to a `UINavigationController`. This relationship is shown as an object in the storyboard file.

3. The Detail View controller, which is always displayed, has a relationship with the custom `WeatherController` that you'll develop in this chapter.

4. You need a navigation controller as a wrapper around the Table view that is displayed in the Master View controller (there is another navigation controller used with the Events controller).

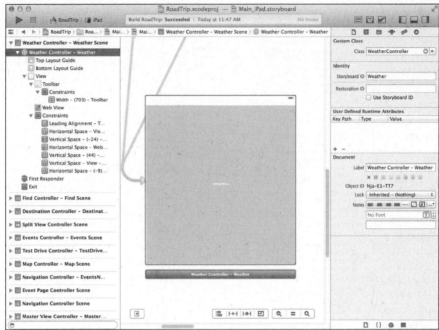

Figure 15-1:
Weather-
related part
of the iPad
storyboard.

5. The first navigation controller has a relationship to your custom `MasterViewController`.

6. The `MasterViewController` manages the Table view that you provide to let the user decide what should be displayed in the Detail view.

7. You'll create a Replace segue to connect the first (Weather) item in the Table view to your weather scene.

8. You'll use a `UIWebView` to display the contents of a web page inside your custom `WeatherController`. Voilà — the user can see a weather forecast.

The iPhone storyboard

The Weather-related part of the iPhone storyboard is shown in Figure 15-2.

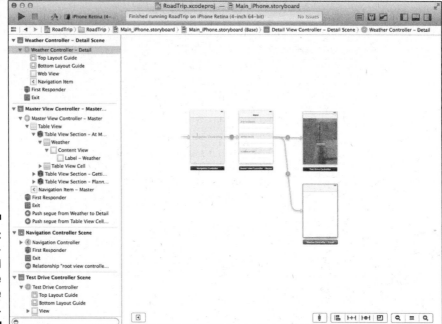

Figure 15-2:
Weather-
related
part of the
iPhone
storyboard.

The control flow through the iPhone storyboard goes like this:

1. The iPhone user interface is controlled by an instance of Apple's `UINavigationController`. The Navigation controller is needed to allow the user to pop (for example, return from) any view controller that is pushed using the Push segue in Step 4.

2. Your `UINavigationController` has a relationship to your Master View controller.

3. The `MasterViewController` manages the Table view that you are using to let the user decide what should be displayed when a table element is selected.

4. You'll connect the first item in your `MasterViewController` to your `WeatherController` using a Push segue.

5. You'll use a `UIWebView` to display the contents of a web page inside your custom `WeatherController`. Voilà — the user can see a weather forecast.

Setting Up the Weather Controller

If the user selects Weather from the Master view in the RoadTrip app, he comes face-to-face with an Internet site displaying weather information. (You'll start with the URL specified in the `Destination.plist`, but you can use any site that you'd like.)

In this section, you add the initial Objective-C code for `WeatherController` class, and then add the logic it needs to get the right URL for the weather from the `Trip` object and send it on to the Weather (Web) view to load.

You'll use the same `WeatherController` class in both the iPad and iPhone storyboard files. Add the `WeatherController` to the iPad storyboard first. After that, you can use the same class in the iPhone storyboard.

Adding the custom view controller

Although you have a view controller defined in the storyboard, it's a generic view controller — in this case, a `UIViewController` — and it's clueless about what you want to display in a view, much less the model it will need to get the data from. In this section, you create a custom controller that *does* know about its view and the model. Replace the generic controller with a custom one. Follow these steps:

1. **In the Project navigator, select the ViewController Classes group and then right-click and choose New File from the contextual menu that appears.**

   Or choose File⇨New⇨File from the main menu (or press ⌘+N).

   Whatever method you choose, the New File dialog appears.

2. **In the left column of the New File dialog, select Cocoa Touch under the iOS heading, select the Objective-C class template in the top-right pane, and then click Next.**

   You'll see a dialog that will enable you to choose the options for your file.

3. **In the Class field of the dialog, enter** WeatherController, **choose or enter** DetailViewController **in the Subclass Of field, make sure that the Target for iPad check box is selected and that the With XIB for User Interface is deselected, and then click Next.**

4. **In the Save sheet that appears, click Create.**

   You've got yourself a new a custom view controller.

Setting Up WeatherController in the Main_iPad.storyboard file

Adding a new custom view controller is a good start, but you still need to tell the storyboard that you want it to load the new custom view controller rather than a `UIViewController`. Follow these steps:

1. **In the Project navigator, select Main_iPad.storyboard and, in the Document Outline, select View Controller – Weather in the View Controller – Weather Scene.**

   The Weather View controller is selected on the canvas.

2. **Open the Utility area and then click the Identity Inspector icon in the Inspector selector bar to open the Identity inspector in the Utility area. Choose WeatherController from the Class drop-down menu (replacing UIViewController) in the Custom Class section, as I have in Figure 15-3.**

   Doing so means that, when Weather is selected in the Master View controller, `WeatherController` will now be instantiated and initialized and will receive events from the user and connect the view to the `Trip` model.

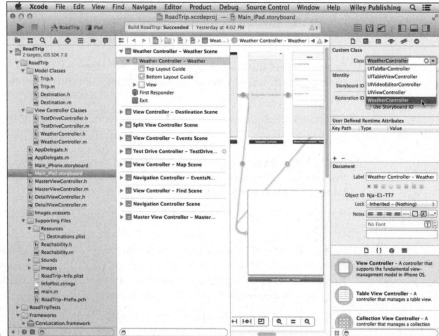

Figure 15-3: Now the storyboard Weather controller is connected to `Weather Controller`.

3. Drag in a Web view from the Utility area's Library pane and position it to fill the Weather controller's view, as shown in Figure 15-4.

In iOS 7, part of the focus on content includes using the full screen. Make certain that the toolbar is translucent so that the Web view can be seen dimly through it when the app runs.

For the RoadTrip app, you want to use a `UIWebView` to display the weather information. This makes sense because you'll be using a website to display the weather.

As I explain in Chapter 4, the `UIWebView` class provides a way to display HTML content. These views can be used as the Main view, or as a subview of another view; wherever they're used, they can access websites.

4. With the Web view selected, use the Editor menu to pin it to the superview by choosing

Editor⇨Pin⇨Leading Space to Superview

Editor⇨Pin⇨Trailing Space to Superview

Editor⇨Pin⇨Top Space to Superview

Editor⇨Pin⇨Bottom Space to Superview

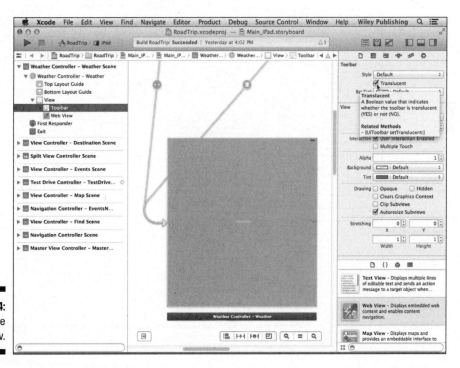

Figure 15-4:
Adding the Web view.

You need to set up two outlets: one to the Web view so that `Weather Controller` can tell the Web view what website to load and a second one to the toolbar so it can place the button there.

5. **Close the Utility area and select the Assistant from the Editor selector in the Xcode toolbar.**

6. **If the `WeatherController.h` file isn't the one that's displayed in the Assistant editor, go up to the Assistant's Jump bar and select it, as I have done in Figure 15-5.**

7. **Control-drag from the Web view (either on the Canvas or in the Document Outline) to the `WeatherController` interface and create an `IBOutlet` named *weatherView*.**

8. **Control-drag from the Web view in the storyboard Canvas (or in the Document Outline) to the `WeatherController` object in the Document Outline and then choose Delegate (see Figure 15-6) from the Outlets menu that appears.**

I'm showing you this to illustrate that you can do all this dragging either on the Canvas or in the Document Outline.

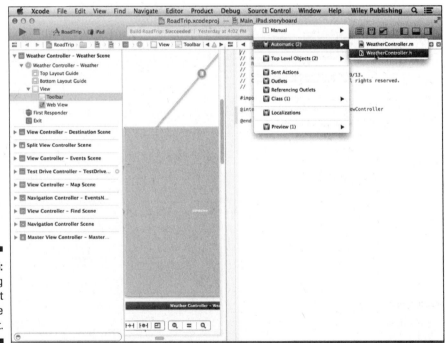

Figure 15-5:
Displaying the correct file in the Assistant.

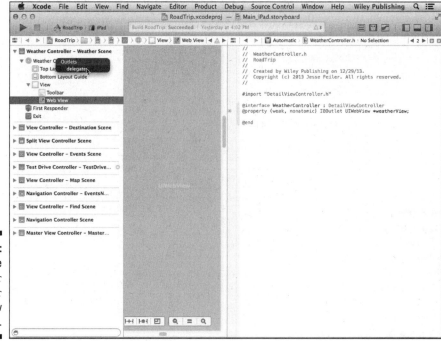

Figure 15-6:
Make the
Weather
Controller
a Web view
delegate.

You must set WeatherController to be a delegate of the view, but you can do so either using code or using the storyboard steps described here. You'll do it in code in the next chapter, so you can take your choice. If, like me, you have a tendency to forget to connect the delegate, you may want to pick one technique to do consistently. (I connect delegates in story-boards as soon as I create the object that's going to be the delegate.)

You still need to connect the toolbar to the `DetailViewController`, the `WeatherController`'s superclass. You take care of that in the next step.

9. **Select the Standard editor in the Editor selector on the toolbar, select Weather Controller in the Document Outline, and open the Connections inspector using the Inspector selector, as I have in Figure 15-7.**

   You could also right-click or Control-click `WeatherController` in the Document Outline to get a similar menu.

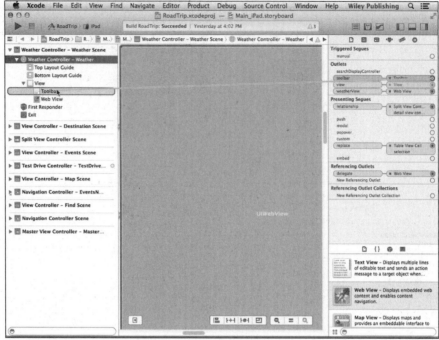

Figure 15-7:
Connecting
the toolbar to
the Detail
View
Controller
base class.

10. **Drag from the toolbar Outlet in the Connections inspector to the toolbar in the Document Outline. (See Figure 15-7.)**

   You have to use the Document Outline because the Web view is on top of the toolbar on the canvas so you can't see it. You didn't need to create the `toolbar` Outlet because it had already been created along with `UIViewController`. The idea here is that you can use the same click-and-drag technique you used to create an outlet to modify which object an existing outlet connects to.

If you were to compile and run the RoadTrip project, you'd see the blank screen displayed at app launch. You could select Weather or Test Drive in the Master View controller (in Portrait or Landscape orientation, mind you), but you'd just see a blank screen if you selected Weather. You'll fix that next.

But keep in mind this is a major step forward. You now have a fully functioning application structure that can, with equal aplomb, use a Navigation controller and its Navigation bar (as you'll see in the next chapter), or simply replace the controller in the Detail view and use a toolbar.

At this point, you have the `WeatherController` class set up and you've arranged for the storyboard to create a `UIWebView` object and set all the outlets (the `toolbar` and `weatherView`) for you when the user selects Weather for the view he wants to see.

Because the `Trip` object owns the data — in this case, the data is provided by the website you're using to display the weather information, but the information about the website is managed by the `Trip` object— you add the methods necessary to the `Trip` model to provide this to `WeatherController`.

Select the Standard editor in the Editor selector on the toolbar and select `Trip.h` in the Project navigator. (If you managed to close the Project navigator at some point in your travels, select its icon in the View selector or choose View⇨Navigators⇨Show Project Navigator to open it again.)

Add the declaration for the `weather` method (the bolded code) to the Trip interface in `Trip.h`, as shown in Listing 15-1.

Listing 15-1:   Updating the Trip.h Interface

```
#import <Foundation/Foundation.h>
#import <mapKit/MapKit.h>

@interface Trip : NSObject

- (id)initWithDestinationIndex:(int)destinationIndex;
- (UIImage *)destinationImage;
- (NSString *) destinationName;
- (CLLocationCoordinate2D) destinationCoordinate;
- (NSString *)weather;

@end
```

Add the `weather` method in Listing 15-2 to `Trip.m`.

Listing 15-2:   Adding the weather Method

```
- (NSString *)weather {

  return _destinationData[@"Weather"];
}
```

All the `Trip` object does here is return the URL that the Web view will use to download the weather HTML page for the site. It got the URL for that site from the dictionary you create in Chapter 11 when you load the `Destination` plist that provides the data for this destination.

The Weather Controller

Now that you have the `Trip` object set up to deliver the data you need, the `WeatherController` needs to pass on to the view to load the web page.

You need to add some #import compiler directives so that Weather Controller can access AppDelegate to get the Trip reference and request the data it needs.

To do that, add the bolded code in Listing 15-3 to WeatherController.m.

Listing 15-3: Updating the WeatherController Implementation

```
#import "DetailViewController.h"
#import "AppDelegate.h"
#import "Trip.h"
```

You're going to need a Back button so add this line to the class extension at the top of WeatherController.m.

```
@property (strong, nonatomic) UIBarButtonItem *backButton;
```

The template provides a viewDidLoad method stub when you create the controller file. You may recall from previous chapters that this is where you want to have the Web view (or any other view) load its data. Add the bolded code in Listing 15-4.

Listing 15-4: Adding to viewDidLoad

```
- (void)viewDidLoad
{
  [super viewDidLoad];
  self.title = @"Weather";
  self.weatherView.scalesPageToFit = YES;
  AppDelegate *appDelegate =
            [[UIApplication sharedApplication] delegate];
  self.backButton = [[UIBarButtonItem alloc]
    initWithTitle:[NSString stringWithFormat:
                     @"Back to %@", self.title]
          style:UIBarButtonItemStyleBordered
         target:self

        action:@selector(goBack:)]; [self.weatherView
      loadRequest: [NSURLRequest requestWithURL:
                    [NSURL URLWithString:
                       [appDelegate.trip weather]]]];
}
```

The first thing you do in Listing 15-4 is set the title to Weather.

The title won't be showing up on the toolbar, however, because this just sets the title in the Navigation bar. I'll use it when I add a Return to *Whatever* button in the next section.

Because what gets loaded is going to be a website, you set `self.weatherView.scalesPageToFit` to `YES`.

`scalesPageToFit` is a `UIWebView` property. If it's set to `YES`, the web page is scaled to fit inside your view, and the user can zoom in and out. If it's set to `NO`, the page is displayed in the view, and zooming is disabled.

I might set it to `NO` when I'm not displaying a web page and the HTML page I created fits just fine and I don't want it to be scalable. You may want to do something else here, of course; I did it this way to show you how (and where) you have control of web page properties.

Next, you create the Back button that will be used to navigate the Web view. As you'll see, you will alternately add and remove this button from the toolbar or navigation bar when there is or isn't a page to go back to. You create the Back to *Whatever* button using the view controller `title`, and return `YES` to tell the Web view to load from the Internet. The `action:@selector(goBack:)` argument is the standard way to specify Target-Action. It says that when the button is tapped, you need to send the `goBack:` message to the `target:self`, which is the `WeatherController`.

```
UIBarButtonItem *backButton = [[UIBarButtonItem alloc]
  initWithTitle:[NSString stringWithFormat:
                             @"Back to %@", self.title]
  style:UIBarButtonItemStylePlain target:self
  action:@selector(goBack:)];
self.navigationItem.rightBarButtonItem = backButton;
return YES;
```

You may want to adjust the title depending on whether you are on an iPad or iPhone. Because there is more space on an iPad, you may want to go with the title suggested here (Back to <title>). On iPhone, you may want to just use the Back chevron and the title or name.

You then create the `NSURLRequest` object that the Web view needs to load the data. To do that, you first create an `NSURL` object (an object that includes the utilities necessary for downloading files or other resources from web and FTP servers) using the URL you get from `Trip`. The code uses this `NSURL` and creates an `NSURLRequest` from it. The `NSURLRequest` is what the `WeatherController` needs to send to the Web view in the `loadRequest:` message, which tells it to load the data associated with that particular `NSURL`.

The `NSURLRequest` class encapsulates a URL and any protocol-specific properties, all the time keeping things protocol-independent. It also provides a number of other things that are beyond the scope of this book but are part of the URL loading system — the set of classes and protocols that provide the underlying capability for an app to access the data specified by a URL. This is the preferred way to access files both locally and on the Internet.

The `loadRequest` message is sent to the Web view, and the Weather website is displayed in the window. This causes the Web view to load the data and display it in the window.

Managing links in a Web view

An interesting thing about the Weather view — or any other view that does (or can) load real web content into your app instead of using a browser — is that the links are live and users can follow those links from that view *if* you let them.

After the user is at the weather website, as you can see in Figure 15-8, the user might want to look at the NWS New York, NY link in the upper-left corner. If the user were to follow that link, though, he wouldn't have a way to get back to the originating page.

Hmm.

To be able to navigate back to the originating view, you need to create another button and label it `Back to Weather` (or whatever the previous controller is) so that the user knows that she can use it to get back to the previous view. Creating this button is pretty easy to do, as you'll see in Listing 15-6.

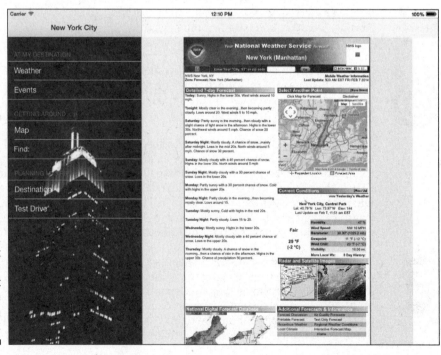

Figure 15-8:
You can select a link (left) to look at National Weather Service info for New York (right) — but you have no way to get back to the originating view.

Of course, I don't want to have that button pop up if the user is at the originating web page because, at that point, there's no going back. So, how do you keep track of who's where in the whole navigational link structure? Here, you're assisted by two Web view delegate methods, `webView:shouldStart` `LoadWithRequest:navigationType:` and `webViewDidFinishLoad:`.

`webView:shouldStartLoadWithRequest:navigationType:` is a `UIWebView` delegate method. It's called before a Web view begins loading content to see whether the user wants the load to proceed.

First, adopt the `UIWebViewDelegate` protocol by adding the bolded code in Listing 15-5 to `WeatherController.h`.

Listing 15-5: Updating the WeatherController Interface

```
#import "DetailViewController.h"

@interface WeatherController : DetailViewController
                                        <UIWebViewDelegate>

@property (weak, nonatomic)
                        IBOutlet UIWebView *weatherView;

@end
```

Remember that when you adopt a delegate protocol, the compiler will then check to make sure that all required methods are in fact there and that all types are correct — so do it!

Next, add the code in Listing 15-6 to `WeatherController.m`.

Listing 15-6: Implementing the webView:shouldStartLoadWithRequest: navigationType: Method

```
- (BOOL)webView:(UIWebView *)webView
        shouldStartLoadWithRequest:
            (NSURLRequest *)request navigationType:
                (UIWebViewNavigationType)navigationType {

  if (navigationType ==
          UIWebViewNavigationTypeLinkClicked){

    if ([[UIDevice currentDevice]
          userInterfaceIdiom] == UIUserInterfaceIdiomPad) {
      if (![self.toolbar.items
          containsObject:self.backButton])
      { NSMutableArray *itemsArray =
              [self.toolbar.items mutableCopy];
```

(continued)

Listing 15-6 *(continued)*

```
        [itemsArray addObject:self.backButton ];
        [self.toolbar setItems:itemsArray animated:NO];
      }
    else {
      self.navigationItem.rightBarButtonItem =
          self.backButton;
      }
    }
  return YES;
}
```

Early on in Listing 15-6, you check to see whether the user has touched an embedded link. (You have to see whether a link is clicked because this message is sent to the delegate under several different circumstances.)

```
if (navigationType == UIWebViewNavigationTypeLinkClicked){
```

Then, you check to see if you're on an iPad or not. If you're on an iPad, you'll be using a toolbar, but on an iPhone, you'll use a navigation bar.

```
if ([[UIDevice currentDevice]
      userInterfaceIdiom] == UIUserInterfaceIdiomPad) {
```

If you're on an iPad and the user has clicked a link, you want to have a Back button (the one you created in `viewDidLoad`) so that the user can get back. Note that I said "have" a Back button and not "add" a Back button. If there's one there, you don't want to add a second. So you look at the items array in the toolbar to see if `self.backButton` is already there.

```
if (![self.toolbar.items
    containsObject: self.backButton])
```

If there isn't a Back button there, add it with the standard code for doing this: you copy the toolbar's `items` array into a mutable array called `itemsArray`. Then you add the Back button to it and replace the toolbar's `items` array with the mutable array.

```
{
    NSMutableArray *itemsArray = [self.toolbar.items
      mutableCopy];
    [itemsArray addObject:self.backButton ];
    [self.toolbar setItems:itemsArray animated:NO];
}
```

Next, add the `goBack:` method in Listing 15-7 to the `WeatherController.m` file. This is the message sent when the Back to *Whatever* button is tapped.

Listing 15-7: Adding the goBack: Method

```
- (void)goBack:(id)sender {
  [self.weatherView goBack];
}
```

Note that you don't need to declare this method in `WeatherController.h` because it's used within `WeatherController.m` for the target-action code in Listings 15-6 and 15-7. The `UIWebView` actually implements much of the behavior you need here. The Web view keeps a Backward *and* Forward list. When you send the `UIWebView` the message (`goBack:`), it reloads the previous page.

Finally, you want to get rid of the Back to *Whatever* button when you're displaying the original page. The code to do that is shown in Listing 15-8.

Listing 15-8:   Implementing webViewDidFinishLoad:

```
- (void)webViewDidFinishLoad:(UIWebView *) webView {

  if ([self.weatherView canGoBack] == NO ) {
    NSUInteger backButtonIndex = [self.toolbar.items
      indexOfObject: self.backButton];

      if (([[UIDevice currentDevice] userInterfaceIdiom]
          == UIUserInterfaceIdiomPad) &&
          (backButtonIndex != NSNotFound)
        {
          NSMutableArray *itemsArray =
            [self.toolbar.items mutableCopy];
          [itemsArray removeObject:self.backButton ];
          [self.toolbar setItems:itemsArray animated:NO];

      }
      else {
        self.navigationItem.rightBarButtonItem = nil;
      }
    }
  }
}
```

The delegate is sent the `webViewDidFinishLoad:` message after the view has loaded. At this point, you check to see whether there's anything to go back to (the Web view keeps track of those sorts of things). If not, remove the button from the toolbar or Navigation bar.

That being said, the Apple Human Interface Guidelines say it's best to avoid creating an app that looks and behaves like a mini web browser. As far as I'm concerned, making it possible to select links in a Web view doesn't do that. The Back button comes close. The choice is up to you.

But if you really don't want to enable the user to follow links (either because of Apple's suggestion that you not make your app act as a mini-browser or if you'd just prefer that your app users stick around for a bit and don't go gallivanting around the Internet), you have to disable the links that are available in the content. You can do that in the `shouldStartLoadWithRequest:` method in the `WeatherController.m` file by replacing the code you added in Listing 15-6 with the code shown in Listing 15-9.

Listing 15-9: Disabling Links

```
- (BOOL)webView:(UIWebView *)webView
  shouldStartLoadWithRequest:(NSURLRequest *)request
  navigationType:(UIWebViewNavigationType)navigationType {

  if (navigationType ==
      UIWebViewNavigationTypeLinkClicked){
    return NO;
  }
  else return YES;
}
```

More Opportunities to Use the Debugger

A couple of runtime errors are easy to get. Two that pop up frequently are `unrecognized selector sent to instance` and `NSUnknownKey Exception`. Although the former error is pretty easy to track down if you actually read the error message, the latter can be a real mystery (it was to me), especially the first time you encounter it. So I want to explain both of them now.

Unrecognized selector sent to instance

The `unrecognized selector sent to instance` runtime error is probably the most common one I get e-mails about; it (understandably) throws many people for a loop. But if you take time to read the error message, you can make sense of it.

```
2013-12-07 19:34:07.166 RoadTrip[1202:12503] ***
Terminating app due to uncaught exception
'NSInvalidArgumentException', reason: '-[WeatherController
goBack]: unrecognized selector sent to instance 0xb7331f0'
```

This error occurs when you thought you created a selector in your code but it's not (really) there.

If, in the `webView shouldStartLoadWithRequest:navigationType:` method, you mistakenly typed `goBack` (without a colon, designating a method with no arguments) rather than `goBack:` (a method with a single argument) when you allocated and initialized the `backButton`:

```
UIBarButtonItem *backButton = [[UIBarButtonItem alloc]
  initWithTitle:[NSString stringWithFormat:
  @"Back to %@", self.title]
  style:UIBarButtonItemStylePlain target:self
  action:@selector(goBack)];
```

and then you ran the app, selected Weather, selected a link, and then tapped the Back to Weather button, what you will see in the Debugger Console pane is

```
2013-12-07 19:34:07.166 RoadTrip[1202:12503] ***
Terminating app due to uncaught exception
'NSInvalidArgumentException', reason: '-[WeatherController
goBack]: unrecognized selector sent to instance 0xb7331f0'
```

You get this error message because you're sending the `goBack` message (not the `goBack:` message) to the `target` — the `WeatherController`. The `WeatherController` *does* have a fully functional `goBack:` method implemented, but it *doesn't* have a `goBack` method implemented — as the debugger so clearly informs you.

Repeat for the iPhone Storyboard

The good news is that you can use the same custom `WeatherController` class in your iPhone storyboard as you used in the iPad storyboard file. You can also reuse the changes you made to the Trip model. You can update the iPhone storyboard file the same way that you did in Chapter 12.

Adding the WeatherController to the iPhone storyboard file

The following steps show how to update the iPhone storyboard file.

1. **Select the** `MainStoryboard_iPhone.storyboard` **file in the Project Navigator.**

2. **Select the generic** `UIViewController` **scene in the Library and drag it onto your storyboard.**

3. **Open the Utility area and select the Identity inspector.**

4. **Change the class name to** `WeatherController` **in the Class drop-down menu, just as you did in Figure 15-3.**

5. **With the** `WeatherController` **scene selected in the storyboard file, select the view in the document outline.**

6. **Change the class name of the view from** `UIView` **to** `UIWebView`.

7. **In the Document Outline, Control-drag from the** `WeatherController` **to the Web view and select** `weatherView` **from the pop-up menu.**

This step connects the `weatherView` outlet in the `WeatherController` class to the instance of `UIWebView` that you'll use to display the weather.

Test in the iPhone Simulator

Run the iPhone app in the Simulator. You should see the web page displayed in Figure 15-9.

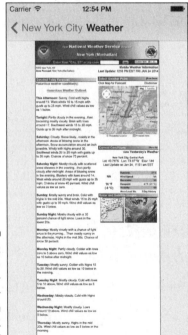

Figure 15-9:
The
Weather
Controller
display on
the iPhone.

Chapter 16

Displaying Events Using a Page View Controller

In This Chapter

▶ Displaying HTML pages in a Web view

▶ Creating page transitions with a `UIPageViewController`

▶ Understanding how Page View controllers work and implementing page turns

*A*fter you have finished this chapter, when the user selects Events from the Master view in the RoadTrip application, he will come face-to-face with a series of pages that describes the latest activities happening at his destination. In this chapter, I'll show you how to use a feature, first introduced in iOS 5, that will allow you to create a view controller that enables a user to "turn pages" in the same way as she can in an iBook.

You will also find out how to use a Web view again to display data, but this time you will download an HTML page stored on my website, rather than connect to the website itself.

The best part of what you discover in this chapter is page-turn transitions. These transitions are implemented by Apple's `UIPageViewController` class — a new container view controller (first provided in iOS 5) that creates page-turn transitions between view controllers. Just as a Navigation controller animates the transitions between, say, the Master View controller and the Test Drive controller, the Page View controller does its thing between two view controllers — in this case, two `EventPageControllers`.

You implement this functionality by adding a `UIPageViewController` to your view controller — `EventsController` — in your code and then creating a view controller (`EventPageController`) for each page.

The `UIPageViewController` needs a Navigation bar. You need it if you want to be able to display the Road Trip button. Because of the way the class is implemented, tapping a button on a toolbar is intercepted and interpreted by the `UIPageViewController` as a page turn. Fortunately, you made it possible for the delegate methods to deal with both Navigation bars and toolbars with equal aplomb.

The Plan

The Events feature actually requires that you add a number of interrelated components to each storyboard file. The components used in the iPad storyboard are shown in Figure 16-1.

The key components for the Events feature include

✔ The "Events" Table view cell in the `MasterViewController`'s Table view.

✔ A Replace segue from the "Events" Table view cell to a Navigation controller that displays a Navigation bar-equipped view controller in the detail view. This bar contains a RoadTrip button used by the user to return from the Events display to the `MasterViewController`.

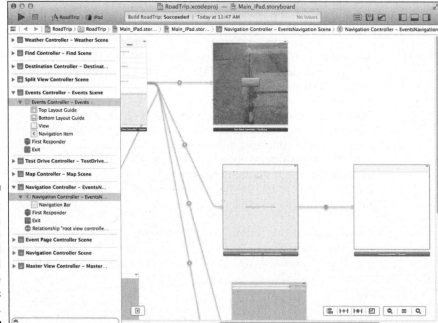

Figure 16-1:
Components used in the iPad storyboard file for the Events feature.

✔ A custom `EventsController` container.

✔ An instance of `UIPageViewController` embedded in the `EventsController` container, responsible for managing transitions (such as page curls) between events pages, where each page is managed by an instance of `EventPageController`.

✔ A custom `EventPageController`, responsible for displaying event information in an HTML web page rendered by an instance of `UIWebView`.

Setting Up the EventsController

In this section, you need to do the same thing you did in Chapter 15 to create and connect the WeatherController object. The way you develop a storyboard is rather formulaic. I review it:

1. Lay out the view controllers you need for the user experience architecture.

2. Add the custom view controller to your app.

3. Tie the two together in your storyboard.

4. Add the code you need to the custom view controller.

After you get into the routine of how to do it, your life as a developer becomes much easier.

You'll also add another view controller to the storyboard (the afore-mentioned `EventPageController`) that will be used by the `UIPageViewController`.

Adding the custom view controller

To add the `EventsController` to the RoadTrip project, follow these steps:

1. **In the Project navigator, select the View Controller Classes group and then either right-click the selection and choose New File from the menu that appears or choose File⇨New⇨File from the main menu (or press ⌘+N).**

   Whatever method you choose, you're greeted by the New File dialog.

2. **In the left column of the dialog, select Cocoa Touch under the iOS heading, select the Objective-C class template in the top-right pane, and then click Next.**

   You'll see a dialog that will enable you to choose the options for your file.

3. **Enter** EventsController **in the Class field, choose or enter** DetailViewController **in the Subclass Of field, make sure that the Target for iPad check box is selected and that With XIB for User Interface is deselected, and then click Next.**

4. **In the Save sheet that appears, click Create.**

You'll also need to create a controller that manages each event page. Follow these steps:

1. **In the Project navigator, select the View Controller Classes group and then either right-click the selection and choose New File from the menu that appears or choose File⇨New⇨File from the main menu (or press ⌘+N).**

   Say hello again to the New File dialog box.

2. **In the left column of the dialog, select Cocoa Touch under the iOS heading, select the Objective-C class template in the top-right pane, and then click Next.**

   You'll see a dialog that will enable you to choose the options for your file.

3. **Enter** EventPageController **in the Class field, choose or enter** UIViewController **in the Subclass Of drop-down menu, and make sure that the Target for iPad check box is selected and that With XIB for User Interface is deselected. Click Next.**

4. **In the Save sheet that appears, click Create.**

Setting up the EventsController in the MainStoryboard

You need to tell the storyboard to load your custom view controller rather than a UIViewController. Follow these steps:

1. **In the Project navigator, select Main_iPad.storyboard and, in the Document Outline, select View Controller – Events in the View Controller – Events Scene.**

   The Events view controller will be selected on the Canvas.

2. **Open the Utility area and then click the Identity Inspector icon in the Inspector selector to open the Identity inspector in the Utility area.**

3. **Choose EventsController from the Class drop-down menu (replacing UIViewController) in the Custom Class section.**

While in `WeatherController`, you added a Web view, but you won't be doing that here. You also created an outlet, but you don't need that here, either. Instead, you'll use a Web view and create an outlet in the `EventPageController`. The `EventPageController` is what you'll need to add to implement a `UIPageViewController`. You do that in the next section.

Adding and setting up the EventPageController in the MainStoryboard

You need a view controller to manage each view within the Page View controller. Although you could've added this view controller when you extended the storyboard, I didn't have you do so because I didn't want my coverage of the topic to get lost among the discussion about segues.

To add the `EventPageController` to the storyboard, follow these steps:

1. **Add another view controller to the storyboard by dragging in a view controller from the Library pane and placing it next to the** `EventsController` **on the Canvas.**

   (You don't *have* to put it there, but doing so hints that a relationship may exist; it also makes it easier to draw that relationship if you want to do so — and you will want to do so in a moment.)

 2. **Open the Identity inspector in the Utility area using the Inspector selector bar, and in the Class drop-down menu in the Custom Class section, choose EventPageController (replacing UIViewController).**

3. **Switch to the Attributes inspector and use its text fields to give the controller the Title of** Event Page. **Then add** Event Page **to the Identity inspector's Storyboard ID field.**

4. **Add a Web view to the** `EventPageController` **by dragging in a Web view from the Library pane and into the Event Page controller.**

   The Event Page view will be a Web view because you'll want it to download and then display an HTML page.

   The `UIWebView` class provides a way to display HTML content and has the built-in functionality to download HTML content from the web.

 5. **Click the Size inspector icon in the Inspector selector to open the Size inspector in the Utility area.**

   Set the X and Y origins to zero and 64 and then resize the Web view to fill the view. The standard for iOS 7 is that views should appear through a translucent navigation bar dimly (iOS 7 takes care of this for you).

In this case, when the iPad split view controller is visible in the master view controller, a navigation bar is shown there (with the title), and I think it looks better to have that space visible in the detail view controller right next to it. Depending on what is behind the translucent bar, the visual effect varies. When it's a map that's scrollable, in many ways each part of the map is the same so placing it behind the translucent bar is fine (and suggested). When you're loading a web page as in this case, you may not know what is going to be seen (the format of the weather page is not under your control, for example), and in a case such as that, I prefer to place the web view lower down so it is not shown behind the navigation bar. That's what happens here: 64 = status bar (20) + navigation bar (44).

6. **Drag in an Activity Indicator view from the Library pane and center it in the view.**

   Because these pages can be large and take some amount of time to download, you want to have some kind of Activity Indicator view to let the user know that the application is still running but busy, as opposed to frozen.

As you can see by looking at the Document Outline in Figure 16-2, both the Web view and Activity Indicator view are siblings — and subviews of the view. It's important that both are siblings, and that the Activity Indicator view is below the Web view in order for it to display. (Remember the Last-One-In-Is-On-Top principle when it comes to subviews.) If that's not the case, rearrange the views in the Document Outline.

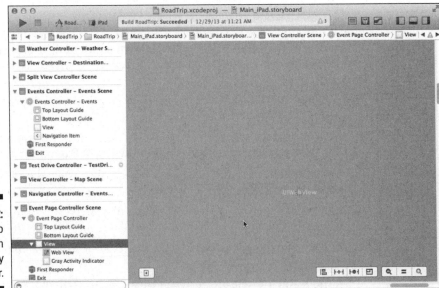

Figure 16-2:
A Web view with an activity indicator.

7. **Switch to the Size inspector in the Utility area using the Inspector selector, and then use Editor⇨Align⇨Horizontal Center in Container and Editor⇨Align⇨Vertical Center in Container to center the activity indicator.**

8. **Close the Utility area and select the Assistant from the Editor selector in the toolbar. If the** `EventPageController.m` **implementation file isn't the one that's displayed, go up to the Assistant's Jump bar and select it.**

9. **Control-drag from the Web view in either the Canvas or the Document Outline to the** `EventPageController` **class extension and create an** `IBOutlet` **(just as you do in Chapter 15) named** `eventDataView`.

10. **Control-drag from the Activity Indicator view to the** `EventPageController` **class extension at the top of the file and create an** `IBOutlet` **named** `activityIndicator`.

11. **Working within the Document Outline, control-drag from the Web view to the Event Page controller, and then select Delegate from the Outlets menu that appears.**

    This will make `EventPageController` the Web view delegate.

Extending the Trip Model

The `EventsController` will need two pieces of information from the `Trip` model: the number of events and the URL for a specific event.

Add the declaration for the two `Events` methods (bolded) to the Trip interface in `Trip.h`, as shown in Listing 16-1.

Listing 16-1:   Update the Trip Interface

```
@interface Trip : NSObject

- (id)initWithDestinationIndex:(int)destinationIndex;
- (UIImage *) destinationImage;
- (NSString *) destinationName;
- (CLLocationCoordinate2D) destinationCoordinate;
- (NSString *)weather;
- (NSUInteger)numberOfEvents;
- (NSString *)getEvent:(NSUInteger)index;
```

But `Trip` isn't going to go at this alone (as it did with `Weather`). It will use an `Events` object (which you'll create shortly). So that `Trip` can use the `Event` object, add the bolded code in Listing 16-2 to `Trip.m`.

Listing 16-2: Updating the Trip Implementation

```
#import "Trip.h"
#import "Destination.h"
#import "Events.h"

@interface Trip ()
  @property (strong, nonatomic)
    NSDictionary *destinationData;
  @property (strong, nonatomic)
    Destination *destination;
  @property (strong, nonatomic)
    Events * events;

@end
```

Until you add the Events class in the next section, you'll see some Live Issues errors.

The EventsController, as you will see, will need to know the number of events and also get the event information.

Add the implementation of methods you need in Listings 16-3 and 16-4 to Trip.m.

Listing 16-3: The Number of Events

```
- (NSUInteger)numberOfEvents {

  return [self.events numberOfEvents];
}
```

Listing 16-4: Get an Event

```
- (NSString *)getEvent:(NSUInteger)index {

  return [self.events getEvent:index];
}
```

To have Trip create the required Events object, add the bolded code in Listing 16-5 to initWithDestinationIndex: in Trip.m.

Listing 16-5: Updating initWithDestinationIndex:

```
- (id)initWithDestinationIndex:
                         (NSUInteger)destinationIndex {
  self = [super init];
  if (self) {

    NSString *filePath = [[NSBundle mainBundle]
```

```
            pathForResource:@"Destinations" ofType:@"plist"];
    NSDictionary *destinations = [NSDictionary
            dictionaryWithContentsOfFile: filePath];
    NSArray *destinationsArray =
            destinations[@"DestinationData"];
    _destinationData = destinationsArray[destinationIndex];
    _destination = [[Destination alloc] initWithDestinatio
            nIndex:destinationIndex];
    events = [[Events alloc]

                    initWithDestinationIndex:destinationIndex];
}
    return self;
}
```

Trip is a composite object that uses other objects to carry out its responsibilities. Whereas you put the Weather logic in the Trip object itself, in this case, you create a new model object to handle the events' responsibilities. That's because handling the events is a bit more complex and deserving of its own model object to encapsulate the logic. Hiding the Events object behind Trip makes things more loosely coupled — a very good thing, which you'll find as you extend and enhance your app. (See Chapter 11 for an explanation of loose coupling.)

Adding the Events Class

If Trip is to use an Events object, you had better create the class. Follow these steps:

1. **In the Project navigator, select the Model Classes group and then either right-click the selection and choose New File from the menu that appears or choose File⇨New⇨File from the main menu (or press ⌘+N).**

   Whatever method you choose, you're greeted by the New File dialog.

2. **In the left column of the dialog, select Cocoa Touch under the iOS heading, select the Objective-C Class template in the top-right pane, and then click Next.**

   You'll see a dialog that will enable you to choose the options for your file.

3. **Enter** Events **in the Class field.**

4. **Choose or enter** NSObject **in the Subclass Of field and then click Next.**

   The iPad and With XIB for User Interface check boxes are dimmed because they are not relevant here — Events is derived from NSObject, and not from any type of view controller.

5. **In the Save sheet that appears, click Create.**

The Events class is the model object that manages the events. Earlier, I said that I'm creating this model object to encapsulate the event logic, and although doing so may seem to be an overreaction here given that the logic isn't that complex, I mainly want to show you how to do that. And in reality, you can imagine that the Events class could be expanded to do a lot more — such as return the location, process events from multiple sources, or even allow a user to add her own events.

To start adding the Events class, add the bolded code in Listing 16-6 to Events.h.

Listing 16-6: Updating the Events Interface

```
@interface Events : NSObject

- (id)initWithDestinationIndex:

          (NSUInteger)destinationIndex;
- (NSUInteger)numberOfEvents;
- (NSString *)getEvent:(NSUInteger)index;
@end
```

This code has three methods: an initialization method and two methods to process the Trip requests.

Next, you need to add a property. Add the code in bold in Listing 16-7 to Events.m to create a class extension with a property. (The basic class extension without the property may already be in your project.)

Listing 16-7: Updating the Events Implementation

```
#import "Events.h"

@interface Events ()
   @property (strong, nonatomic) NSMutableArray *events;

@end

@implementation Events
```

As you can see, Listing 16-6 has an initialization method (which is used by Trip when it creates the Events object). Add the code in Listing 16-8 to Events.m to implement the initWithDestinationIndex: initialization method.

Listing 16-8: Initializing the Events Object

```
- (id)initWithDestinationIndex:
           (NSUInteger)destinationIndex {
  self = [super init];
   if (self) {

     NSString *filePath = [[NSBundle mainBundle]
         pathForResource:@"Destinations" ofType:@"plist"];
     NSDictionary *destinations = [NSDictionary
                 dictionaryWithContentsOfFile: filePath];
     NSArray *destinationsArray =
          destinations[@"DestinationData"];
NSDictionary *data =
       destinationsArray[destinationIndex];
     self.events = [NSMutableArray arrayWithArray:
                            data[@"Events"]];
   }
   return self;
}
```

All this method does at this point is get the array of URLs for the HTML pages I created and you entered in the Destinations plist. It puts these URLs in an array that you create — for more efficient retrieval later. (I make this a mutable array because in the future you may want to allow a user to add his own events.)

The EventsController, as you will see, will need to know the number of events and the event information. You've added the methods to Trip in Listings 16-3 and 16-4, but Trip will actually be getting that information from Events. Add the code in Listing 16-9 to Events.m to implement the method that returns the number of events.

Listing 16-9: The Number of Events

```
- (NSUInteger)numberOfEvents {

  return [self.events count];
}
```

To get the number of events, you return the count of the array.

The EventsController will also need to have a list of the event URLs. Add the code in Listing 16-10 to Events.m to implement that method.

Listing 16-10: Getting an Event

```
- (NSString *)getEvent:(NSUInteger)index {

  return self.events[index];
}
```

To return an `Event`, you return the URL based on the index into the array. This will make more sense when you go through the `EventsController` and `EventPageController` code, which you do next.

The EventsController and Its PageViewController

At the start of this chapter, I promised to show you how to enable users to turn the page between one view controller and another. To implement this cool page-turning stuff, you need a `UIPageViewController`. You create that in the `EventsController` in its `viewDidLoad` method.

To start, though, you need to make the `EventsController` a `UIPageViewController` data source and delegate. (Actually, in this implementation, you won't need to use any of the delegate methods, but it's good for you to know about them.) Add the bolded code in Listing 16-11 (which includes the declaration of another method that you'll use shortly) to `EventsController.h`.

Listing 16-11:   Updating the EventsController Interface

```
#import "DetailViewController.h"
@class EventPageController;

@interface EventsController : DetailViewController
                < UIPageViewControllerDelegate,
                          UIPageViewControllerDataSource >

- (EventPageController *)viewControllerAtIndex:
  (NSUInteger)index storyboard:(UIStoryboard *)storyboard;

@end
```

Now read on to find out about the data source and delegate.

Data sources and delegates

You've used delegates a few times already, such as when you add the code to the app delegate in Chapter 8. A data source is really just another kind of delegate that supplies the data that a framework object needs. When you implement a dynamic Table view, you do that as well, and data sources are also used in many other places in the framework — in picker views, for example, when you select a time or date in the Calendar application.

Data source

The `UIPageViewController` is a new Container View controller for creating page-turn transitions between view controllers first implemented in iOS 5. This means that for every page, you create a new view controller.

The `UIPageViewControllerDataSource` protocol is adopted by an object that provides view controllers (you'll be using the `PageDataController`) to the Page View controller as needed, in response to navigation gestures.

`UIPageViewControllerDataSource` has two required methods:

- ✔ `pageViewController:viewControllerAfterViewController:` returns the view controller after the current view controller.
- ✔ `pageViewController:viewControllerBeforeViewController:` returns the view controller before the current view controller.

Although it is easiest to use a separate page controller for each page, you can actually reuse page view controllers by replacing the data on the page view controller's view with data for the new page. If you are building something along the lines of an ebook with perhaps hundreds of pages, that would be the way to go. With a limited number of pages such as is the case with RoadTrip, separate page view controllers work just fine.

Delegate

The delegate of a Page View controller must adopt the `UIPageView ControllerDelegate` protocol. The methods in this protocol allow you to receive a notification when the device orientation changes or when the user navigates to a new page. In the implementation in this book, you don't need to be concerned with either of those two situations.

The EventsController

Before you add any code, update `EventsController.m` with the bolded code in Listing 16-12.

Listing 16-12:   Updating the EventsController Implementation

```
#import "EventsController.h"
#import "AppDelegate.h"
#import "Trip.h"
#import "EventPageController.h"

@interface EventsController ()
  @property (strong, nonatomic)
    UIPageViewController *pageViewController;
  @property (nonatomic) NSUInteger pageCount;
  @property (nonatomic) NSUInteger currentPage;
@end

@implementation EventsController
```

The `viewDidLoad` method is where most of the work is done. Add the bolded code in Listing 16-13 to `viewDidLoad` in `EventsController.m`.

Listing 16-13:   Updating viewDidLoad

```
- (void)viewDidLoad
{
  [super viewDidLoad];

  AppDelegate *delegate =
            [[UIApplication sharedApplication] delegate];
  self.pageCount = [delegate.trip numberOfEvents];
  self.pageViewController = [[UIPageViewController alloc]
    initWithTransitionStyle:
            UIPageViewControllerTransitionStylePageCurl
    navigationOrientation:
      UIPageViewControllerNavigationOrientationHorizontal
    options:nil];
  self.pageViewController.dataSource = self;
  EventPageController *startingViewController =
    [self viewControllerAtIndex:0
                              storyboard:self.storyboard];
  NSArray *viewControllers = @[startingViewController];
  [self.pageViewControllsetViewControllers:viewControllers
    direction:
        UIPageViewControllerNavigationDirectionForward
    animated:NO completion:NULL];
  [self addChildViewController:self.pageViewController];
```

```
    [self.pageViewController didMoveToParentViewController:
            self];
    [self.view addSubview:self.pageViewController.view];
    self.view.gestureRecognizers =

            self.pageViewController.gestureRecognizers;
}
```

Next, you get the number of events from the `Trip` model so that you know how many pages you'll have:

```
AppDelegate *delegate = [[UIApplication
                            sharedApplication] delegate];
pageCount = [delegate.trip numberOfEvents];
```

Then you allocate and initialize the `PageViewController` and make yourself the data source. I have commented out the delegate assignment because you aren't implementing any of the delegate methods, but here's where you would do it:

```
self.pageViewController = [[UIPageViewController alloc]
  initWithTransitionStyle:
            UIPageViewControllerTransitionStylePageCurl
  navigationOrientation:
      UIPageViewControllerNavigationOrientationHorizontal
      options:nil];
  self.pageViewController.dataSource = self;
```

You're using a `UIPageViewControllerTransitionStylePageCurl` (which gives the appearance of turning a page) and you use a Navigation orientation of `horizontal`, which gives you left-to-right page turning (`UIPageViewControllerNavigationOrientationVertical` gives you pages turning up and down).

You then request the first view controller (I show this method in Listing 16-14 and explain it there), create an array, add the first view controller to the array, and pass that array to the `pageViewController`:

```
EventPageController *startingViewController = [self
    viewControllerAtIndex:0 storyboard:self.storyboard];
NSArray *viewControllers =
        [@startingViewController];
[self.pageViewController setViewControllers:viewControllers
  direction:UIPageViewControllerNavigationDirectionForward
  animated:NO completion:NULL];
```

This array will hold the view controllers that the `UIPageController` manages. You specify the direction as `Forward`. You set animated to `NO` for this transition (setting the view controller array, not the page turning) and you specify no completion block.

Although this approach is pretty simple, you can get way more sophisticated and include features such as double pages and even two-sided pages, and so on. You won't be doing that here.

Next, you add the `pageViewController` as a child view controller, inform the `pageViewController` that it's now the child of another view controller, and make its view a subview so that it's displayed. The idea behind a Container View controller (which the `UIPageViewContainer` and `UINavigationController` both are) is that it manages the presentation of the content from its child view controllers (contained view controllers).

```
[self addChildViewController:self.pageViewController];
[self.pageViewController
        didMoveToParentViewController:self];
[self.view addSubview:pageViewController.view];
```

Finally, add the Page View controller's gesture recognizers to the `EventsController` view so that the gestures are started farther up the chain. (I explain gesture recognizers in Chapter 13.)

```
self.view.gestureRecognizers =
        self.pageViewController.gestureRecognizers;
```

As a supplier of view controllers, you'll be responsible for creating, managing, and returning the right view controller for a page. You'll do that in the `viewControllerAtIndex:storyboard:` method.

Add the `viewControllerAtIndex:storyboard:` method in Listing 16-14 to `EventsController.m`.

You'll see some Live Issues errors until you add the `page` property in the next section.

Listing 16-14:   Adding the viewControllerAtIndex:storyboard: Method

```
- (EventPageController *)viewControllerAtIndex:
    (NSUInteger)index
                storyboard:(UIStoryboard *)storyboard {
```

```
    if ((self.pageCount == 0) || (index >= self.pageCount))
            {
      return nil;
    }
    EventPageController *eventPageController = [storyboard
      instantiateViewControllerWithIdentifier:@"Event
            Page"];
    eventPageController.page = index;
    return eventPageController;
}
```

With Listing 16-14, you're simply doing some error checking to make sure that both pages are available and that the page for the view controller you're supposed to return is available:

```
    if ((self.pageCount == 0) || (index >= self.pageCount))
            {
      return nil;
    }
```

You then allocate and initialize the view controller for that page, setting its page (relative number of the URL to display) so that it knows which event URL to load:

```
    EventPageController *eventPageController = [storyboard
      instantiateViewControllerWithIdentifier:@"Event
            Page"];
    eventPageController.page = index;
```

You have more efficient ways to do this. You could create a cache of controllers that you've created and reuse them as needed. (As you'll see in Chapter 19, that's how I do it with Table View cells.) I'll leave you to explore that topic on your own.

You also need to add the required data source methods in Listing 16-15 to EventsController.m.

Listing 16-15: Implementing pageViewController:viewControllerAfterViewController: and pageViewController:viewControllerBeforeViewController

```
- (UIViewController *)pageViewController:
              (UIPageViewController *)pageViewController
              viewControllerBeforeViewController:
                    (UIViewController *)viewController {
    NSUInteger index =
          ((EventPageController *)viewController).page;
    if (index == 0)
      return nil;
```

(continued)

Listing 16-15 *(continued)*

```
        index--;
      self.currentPage = index;
  return [self viewControllerAtIndex:index
                    storyboard:viewController.storyboard];
    }

- (UIViewController *)pageViewController:
              (UIPageViewController *)pageViewController
              viewControllerAfterViewController:
                    (UIViewController *)viewController {
    NSUInteger index =
            ((EventPageController *)viewController).page;
    index++;
    if (index == self.pageCount)
      return nil;
    self.currentPage = index;
  return [self viewControllerAtIndex:index
                    storyboard:viewController.storyboard];
    }
```

Both of these methods return an `EventDisplayController` initialized with the right page (relative event number) to display. They use the `view ControllerAtIndex:storyboard:` method that you add in Listing 16-14 and indicate which view controller is required by taking the current view controller's page number and then either incrementing or decrementing it appropriately. It then does some error checking to be sure that the page requested is within bounds. If it's not, the method returns `nil`, and the `UIPageViewController` inhibits the page turn.

These data source methods are used by the `UIPageViewController` to get the view controllers that can display the next or previous page, depending on the way the user is turning the page. As mentioned previously, the `UIPageViewController` just manages controllers and the transitions between them. The view controllers that you return operate like the run-of-the-mill view controller you've been using, such as the Weather controller that displays a website.

The next section gives you a look at how these controllers work.

The EventPageController

The `EventPageController` is almost identical to the `WeatherController` that you implemented in Chapter 15.

To follow along in this section, you need to close the Assistant, display the Project navigator, and select `EventPageController.m`.

I have you add the same functionality to this controller as you did to the
WeatherController so that you can select a link and navigate back from
it. You could've created an abstract class — a WebViewController, for
example — that both WeatherController and EventPageController were
derived from, but because the EventPageController is contained by the
UIPageViewController, having an abstract class gets to be a bit more complex.

The EventPageController is what actually displays the event and works
exactly the same as the WeatherController.

First, add the page property, which is set by the viewController
AtIndex:storyboard: method, by adding the bolded code to the
EventPageController.h interface in Listing 16-16.

Listing 16-16: Updating the EventPageController Interface

```
#import <UIKit/UIKit.h>

@interface EventPageController : UIViewController
                                    <UIWebViewDelegate>

@property (readwrite, nonatomic) NSUInteger page;
@end
```

Here's where you make the page (number) a property to enable you to determine which URL to load. You also have the EventPageController adopt
the UIWebViewDelegate protocol.

Add the bolded code to the EventPageController.m implementation in
Listing 16-17.

Listing 16-17: Updating the EventPageController Implementation

```
#import "EventPageController.h"
#import "AppDelegate.h"
#import "Trip.h"

@interface EventPageController ()
@property (weak, nonatomic) IBOutlet UIWebView
        *eventDataView;
@property (weak, nonatomic) IBOutlet
        UIActivityIndicatorView *activityIndicator;
@end

@implementation EventPageController
```

All the work is done in viewDidLoad and the other methods you add. These
methods are the same as the code and methods you added to create the
WeatherController. If you are hazy on what each does, refer to Chapter 15.

Add the bolded code in Listing 16-18 to `EventPageController.m`.

Listing 16-18:   Updating viewDidLoad

```
- (void)viewDidLoad
{
  [super viewDidLoad];
  self.eventDataView.delegate = self;
  [self.activityIndicator startAnimating];
  self.activityIndicator.hidesWhenStopped = YES;
  [self.eventDataView setScalesPageToFit:YES];
  AppDelegate *appDelegate =
              [[UIApplication sharedApplication] delegate];
  [self.eventDataView loadRequest:
    [NSURLRequest requestWithURL:
        [NSURL URLWithString:
                [appDelegate.trip getEvent:self.page]]]];
}
```

Next, add the rest of the Web View Delegate methods in Listing 16-19, just as you do in Chapter 15.

Listing 16-19:   Implementing webView:shouldStartLoadWithRequest: navigationType:, webViewDidFinishLoad:, and add goBack

```
- (BOOL)webView:(UIWebView *)webView
    shouldStartLoadWithRequest:(NSURLRequest *)request
  navigationType:(UIWebViewNavigationType)navigationType {

  if (navigationType ==
                    UIWebViewNavigationTypeLinkClicked) {
    UIBarButtonItem *backButton = [[UIBarButtonItem alloc]
      initWithTitle:[NSString stringWithFormat:
        @"Back to %@", self.parentViewController.
                              parentViewController.title]
      style:UIBarButtonItemStylePlain target:self
                              action:@selector(goBack:)];
    self.parentViewController.parentViewController.
          navigationItem.rightBarButtonItem = backButton;

    return YES;
  }
  else return YES;
}
- (void)goBack:(id)sender {

  [self.eventDataView goBack];
}
```

```
- (void)webViewDidFinishLoad:(UIWebView *)webView {

    [self.activityIndicator stopAnimating];
    if ([self.eventDataView canGoBack] == NO ) {
        self.parentViewController.parentViewController.
                    navigationItem.rightBarButtonItem = nil;
    }
}
```

This code enables you to click a link in an event and then return to the original event page. This is similar to the `WeatherController` functionality, but here you're adding a button to the Navigation bar rather than to a toolbar.

Adding Events Support to the iPhone Storyboard

The Events-related parts of storyboard file for the iPhone is simpler than the one you just did for the iPad, because you don't start with a Navigation controller. The necessary components for the iPhone are shown in Figure 16-3. This figure includes both a Push segue and an Embed segue.

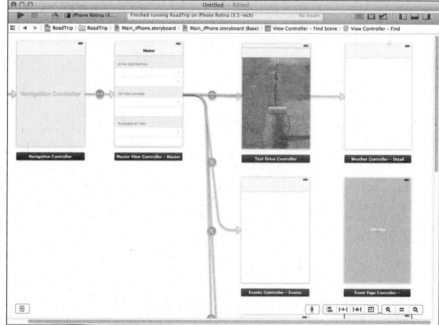

Figure 16-3:
Components used in the iPhone storyboard file for the Events feature.

Your Objective-C code doesn't have to change at all. The key components for the Events feature on the iPhone only require that you add components to the iPhone Storyboard file, connect them to the appropriate Objective-C classes, and connect them to work together. Your small task is summarized in the following. See Figure 16-3 for a diagram of how these components fit together.

✔ You must add a new Events controller to the iPhone Storyboard. This Events controller must be set to use the custom EventsController class.

✔ The "Events" Table view cell in the `MasterViewController`'s Table view must be connected with a push segue to the new Events controller.

✔ An instance of `UIPageViewController` must be embedded in the `EventsController` container. This `UIPageViewController` is responsible for managing transitions (such as page curls) between events pages.

✔ A custom `Event Page` controller must be added to the iPhone Storyboard. It is responsible for displaying event information in an HTML web page rendered by an instance of `UIWebView`. This `Event Page` controller must be set to use the custom `EventPageController` class.

You can assemble this the same way that you added the Events-related component to your iPad storyboard earlier in this chapter, except that you can skip the Navigation controller and connect a Push segue directly to your Events controller scene.

Chapter 17

Finding Your Way

. . . .

. . . .

There's an old saying that there are three keys to a profitable real estate venture: location, location, and location. When it comes to today's mobile devices and the apps we write for them, you can point to the same three keys. Location awareness can allow an app to not only help a user navigate, but it can also open a whole new world of app opportunities. Location-aware apps have the ability to work on their own rather than at a user's command. And that's a major change in our thinking about devices, apps, and ourselves.

When an app is aware of location, your movements can control the app. You can see this in the Reminders app that's built into OS X and iOS. You can enter a reminder for a date and time, but you can also enter a reminder for a place. When you are at that place, the reminder pops up. You don't have to check your calendar or your notes: Once you've set it up, the app takes the initiative. This is the type of interaction that traditional apps such as word processors simply don't have. Even more modern apps such as iTunes don't do this. Yes, they have many automated features, but does iTunes play your favorite song on your birthday? Automatically? (Actually, you can do this with AppleScript fairly easily, but it's not a built-in feature.)

When an app can take the initiative without your intervention, all sorts of new possibilities emerge. For example, to take the reminder example, you can set the reminder to be triggered when you are at a place, but you still have to set it up manually. Apps that work with derived location data are totally doable. If you have a big demo for your terrific new app scheduled for next week, an app can remind you of that demo as you walk by your hair stylist's shop. Many people believe that such connections and inferences are the next great (very great) set of opportunities for app developers.

And much of it all starts with location awareness and mapping.

In this chapter, I show you how to center your map on an area you want to display (New York, for example), add *annotations* (those pins in the map that display a callout to describe that location when you touch them), and even show the user's current location.

The Plan

Your tasks in this chapter are summarized in the following list:

1. First, you define a new custom view controller class, MapController, which will be used to display an instance of Apple's MKMapView. MKMapView is a very useful class because it does most of the hard work involved in displaying maps and allowing users to find their way. You will, however, have to add some code to your MapController class, so that users can control exactly what map data is displayed. In later chapters, you will even allow users to find specific locations — or themselves — on the map.

2. You will add the MapController scene to your iPad storyboard.

3. In your iPad storyboard, you'll use a Replace segue to connect the Map table cell in your MasterViewController to your new MapController. The result will be as shown in Figure 17-1.

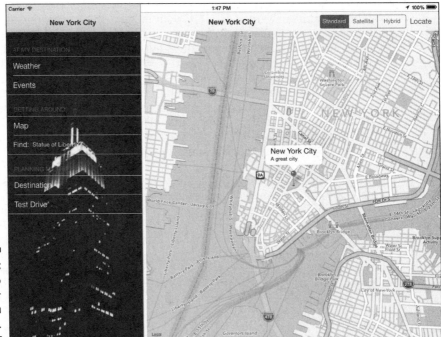

Figure 17-1:
The Map Controller scene on your iPad.

4. You will also need to add Apple's `MapKit` framework to your project, so that the `MKMapView` actually can work.

5. Then you add a `MapController` scene to your iPhone storyboard file.

6. In your iPhone storyboard, you'll use a Push segue to connect the Map table cell in your `MasterViewController` to the `MapController`. The result is shown in Figure 17-2.

Figure 17-2: The `Map Controller` scene on your iPhone.

Setting Up the Map Controller

In this section, you will use the same approach for adding a new view controller that you did in Chapter 16. In this chapter, you will create a new `MapController` class and use it with a new Map controller scene that you will add to your storyboard. Here we go again!

Adding the custom view controller

To add the MapController to the RoadTrip project, follow these steps:

1. **In the Project navigator, select the View Controller Classes group and then either right-click the selection and choose New File from the menu that appears or choose File⇨New⇨File from the main menu (or press ⌘+N).**

   Whatever method you choose, you're greeted by the New File dialog.

2. **In the left column of the dialog, select Cocoa Touch under the iOS heading, select the Objective-C class template in the top-right pane, and then click Next.**

   You'll see a dialog that will enable you to choose the options for your file.

3. **Enter** MapController **in the Class field, choose or enter** DetailView Controller **in the Subclass Of field, make sure that the Target for iPad check box is selected and that With XIB User Interface is deselected, and then click Next.**

4. **In the Save sheet that appears, click Create.**

Setting up the MapController in the Main_iPad.Storyboard

Now that you have a custom view controller, you need to tell the iPad storyboard to load your custom view controller rather than a UIViewController. Follow these steps:

1. **In the Project navigator, select Main_iPad.storyboard and then select View Controller in the View Controller – Map Scene in the Document Outline.**

2. **Using the Inspector selector, open the Identity inspector in the Utility area and then choose MapController from the Custom Class section's Class drop-down menu.**

   Now when Map is selected in the Master View controller, MapController will be instantiated and initialized and will receive events from the user and connect the view to the Trip model.

3. **In the Library pane, scroll back up and drag a Map view onto the Map controller in the Canvas.**

   The MKMapView class provides a way to display maps and has a lot of functionality that I describe later in this chapter.

Starting with iOS 7, views typically cover the entire screen. At the top, the view is dimly visible through tool or navigation bars. This is different from the previous standards in which views were placed below the bars. For views that are scrollable (and map views definitely are), this provides the best user experience. For views that display constrained data such as a formatted data entry form, you can still place the view behind the bars, but you would leave the top part blank. Alternatively, place the view below the bars. Web views are a special case if you don't know what the web page will look like. If you will be displaying a web page that has a title, logo, or other image at the top of the page, consider placing the web view below the bars so as not to obscure the title, logo, or other top image. Or better still, if it's possible, create or use a version of the web page where the top of the web view does not contain critical information.

4. **Open the main disclosure triangle next to Map Controller in the Document Outline (notice that the name changed from View Controller to Map Controller) and then open the sub-disclosure triangle next to View (see Figure 17-3).**

   Notice in Figure 17-3 how the name of the view in the Document Outline is now Map View.

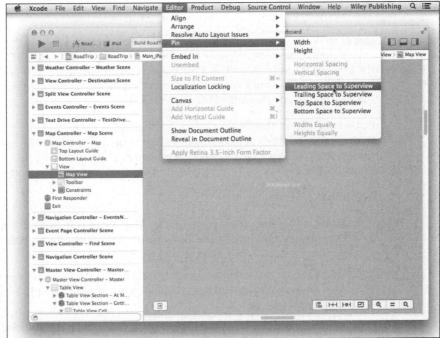

Figure 17-3: Making sure the Web view is sized correctly for the orientation.

5. **With the Map View still selected, choose Editor⇨Pin and pin the top, bottom, leading, and trailing spaces to the superview as you see in Figure 17-3.**

   This setting will result in the map being resized to fill the view as the iPad is rotated.

6. **Open the Size inspector in the Inspector selector, select the Map View, and make certain that it is sized to fill the View. In particular, make certain the X and Y origin points are zero.**

7. **Drag a Toolbar from the Library in the Utilities area onto the Map View and set its origin to 0, 20 in the Size inspector.**

   This places it just below the status bar. Delete the Item bar button item that's part of the Toolbar.

   You still need to connect the toolbar to the view controller in `DetailViewController`, the `MapController`'s superclass.

8. **Select Map Controller on the Document Outline, click the Connections icon in the Inspector selector bar to open the Connections inspector, and then just drag from the toolbar Outlet in the inspector to the toolbar in the `MapController` in the Canvas or the Document Outline.**

   You could also right- or Control-click the Map controller in the Document Outline to open the Connections window and then click and drag from there.

I want to have a nice segmented control in the toolbar to allow the user to select a particular Map type — standard, satellite, or hybrid. Fortunately, the code that implements the Split View Delegate methods that add the Road Trip button won't get in the way of that. It will just insert the Road Trip button on the extreme left of the toolbar.

But what if I want the Type selector to be aligned right (and I do)? All I have to do is add in Interface Builder (or in the code itself) a Flexible Space Bar button item — space that's distributed equally between the other Bar Button items on the toolbar and the segmented control. This is shown in Figure 17-4.

To do that, do the following:

1. **To set up a segmented control (the Map Type selector on the toolbar), drag a Flexible Space Bar button item onto the toolbar in the `MapController`, as I have in Figure 17-4.**

   This item will expand appropriately to make your segmented control aligned right (along with any other button you may add subsequently — look ahead to Figure 17-8).

2. **Drag a Segmented Control from the Library onto the toolbar and place it to the right of the Flexible Space Bar button item (see Figure 17-5).**

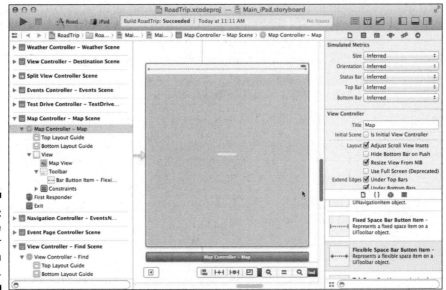

Figure 17-4:
A Flexible Space Bar button item is added.

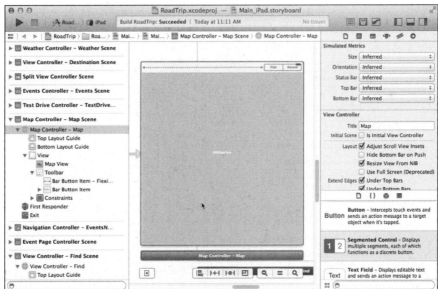

Figure 17-5:
A segmented control on the right side of the toolbar.

3. **With the Segmented Control selected in the Canvas or the Document Outline (it's inside a new bar button item in the Document Outline), click the Attributes Inspector icon in the Inspector selector bar to open the Attributes inspector; in the Segmented Control section, change the number of segments to 3.**

4. Still in the Segmented Control section, make sure that Segment – 0 is selected in the Segment menu, enter Standard **in the Title field, and then press Return.**

The Segment menu should change to Segment – 0 Standard.

5. Now select Segment – 1 in the Segment menu and enter Satellite **in the Title field; then select Segment – 2 and enter** Hybrid **in the Title field.**

Be sure to press Return after each change.

With your Map selector taken care of, it's time to create an outlet so that `MapController` has access to the Map view to center the map and have the annotations display. Follow these steps:

1. Close the Utility area and select the Assistant from the Editor selector on the Xcode toolbar.

If the `MapController.m` file isn't the one that's displayed, go up to the Assistant's Jump bar and select it.

2. Control-drag from the Map view in the Canvas or the Document Outline to the `MapController` **class extension (the private interface at the top of the file) and create an** `IBOutlet` **named** `mapView`**.**

You'll notice a compiler (Live Issue) error (see Figure 17-6) — `Unknown type name 'MKMapView'`.

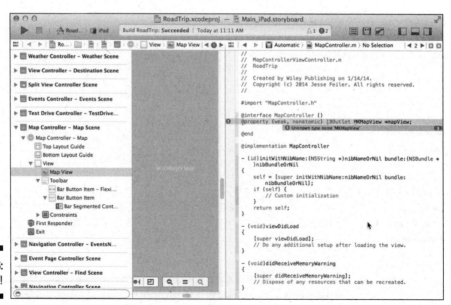

Figure 17-6:
Whoops!

3. **Because you'll be using the** `MapKit` **framework that you added in Chapter 11 and have a property of type** `MKMapView`**, you need to update the** `MapController` **public interface (in the MapController.h file) with the bolded code in Listing 17-1 that follows. (You have it adopt the** `MKMapViewDelegate` **protocol as well.)**

4. **Select and then Control-drag from the segmented control (in this case, it is easier to select and drag from the Document Outline) to the** `MapController` **private interface between the** `@interface` **and** `@end` **statements.**

5. **In the dialog that appears, choose Action from the Connection drop-down menu.**

6. **In the same dialog, leave Value Changed as the selection in the Event drop-down menu.**

   Value Changed is the event that is generated when the user touches a segment to change the selection.

7. **Still in the same dialog, name this action *mapType* by entering** mapType **in the Name field, as shown in Figure 17-7; then click Connect.**

   This action will provide to your code the type of map selected by the user making a choice using the segmented control.

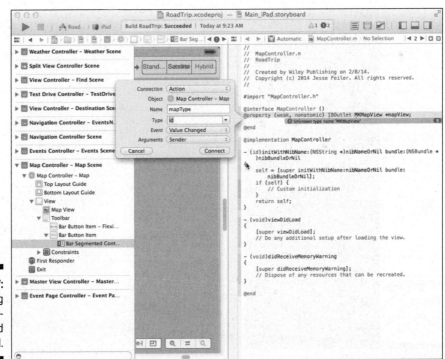

Figure 17-7: Connecting the segmented control.

Because you now have an outlet set up, you'll make the Map controller a delegate in your code as opposed to doing it in Interface Builder as you have been doing previously. Either way is fine. You'll do this delegating business a bit later — in Listing 17-2, to be precise.

Listing 17-1: Updating the MapController Interface

```
#import "DetailViewController.h"
#import <MapKit/MapKit.h>

@interface MapController : RTDetailViewController
                                        <MKMapViewDelegate>
@end
```

Test

Go ahead and run the project.

Presto change-o! If you select the Map entry in the Content controller, you'll see a map centered in the United States as shown in Figure 17-8 (at least you will if you're in the United States). It's as easy as that.

Figure 17-8:
Your first
map.

Cute — and pretty impressive given how little work you've done. The segmented control doesn't count because you still have to implement it, and, as you can see in Figure 17-8, the default width isn't quite big enough, so you'll need to widen it the next time you're in the storyboard.

Furthermore, notice that the status bar at the top of the screen containing the time and battery indicator (as well as the network connection status if it's shown) isn't right. The map view should not be showing through it. I'll show you how to handle that issue later in this chapter.

But first, you need to do some more work to make the map really useful.

This is the general approach that you follow when you add more functionality to your application — add the new controller classes, update the storyboard, and so on.

But you — and your users — want and deserve more than a map centered on the United States. Figure 17-9 shows what you'd like to see on your road trip, rather than the standard Map view you get right out of the box.

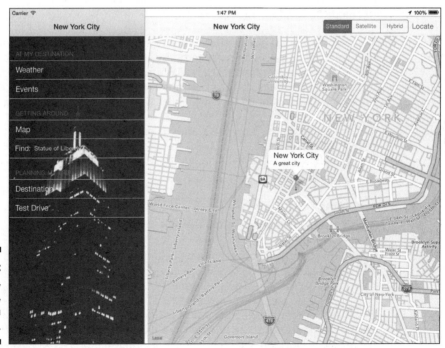

Figure 17-9:
New York, New York, a helluva town.

Putting MapKit through Its Paces

You've done the groundwork for some great map functionality, and now it's time to put the code in place to get that done. Apple's `MapKit.framework` provides all the heavy lifting to make this actually function. `MapKit` enables you to bring up a simple map and also do things with your map without having to do much work at all.

The map looks like the maps in iOS's built-in apps and creates a seamless mapping experience across multiple applications.

MKMapView

The essence of mapping in iOS is the `MKMapView`. It's a `UIView` subclass, and as you saw in the previous section, you can use it out of the box to create a map. You use this class as is to display map information and to manipulate the map contents from your application. It enables you to center the map on a given coordinate, specify the size of the area you want to display, and annotate the map with custom information (by becoming a Map View delegate).

When you initialize a Map view, you can specify the initial region for that map to display. You do this by setting the *region* property of the map. A region is defined by a center point and a horizontal and vertical distance, referred to as the *span*. The span defines how much of the map will be visible and also determines the zoom level. The smaller the span, the greater the zoom.

The Map view supports these standard map gestures:

✔ **Scroll**

✔ **Pinch** (to zoom)

✔ **Double-tap** (to zoom in)

✔ **Two-finger tap** (to zoom out)

In addition, for 3D Flyover maps you can use two-finger gestures to change the viewing angle. You can also specify the Map type — regular, satellite, or hybrid — by changing a single property.

Because `MapKit.framework` was written from scratch, it was developed with the limitations of the iPhone (and later the iPad) in mind. As a result, it optimizes performance on iOS devices by caching data as well as managing memory and seamlessly handling connectivity changes (such as moving from a cellular network to Wi-Fi, for example).

The map data itself is network-hosted, so network connectivity is required.

Although you shouldn't subclass the MKMapView class itself, you can tailor a Map view's behavior by providing a delegate object. The delegate object can be any object in your application, as long as it conforms to the MKMapViewDelegate protocol.

Enhancing the map

Having this nice global map centered on the United States is kind of interesting, but not very useful if you're planning to go to New York. The following sections show you what you have to do to make the map more useful.

To get things started, you need to close the Assistant, show the Project navigator, and select MapController.m.

The current location

What about showing the user's location on the map? That's almost as easy!

In the MapController.m file, add the code in bold shown in Listing 17-2 to viewDidLoad in MapController.m.

Listing 17-2:   Updating viewDidLoad

```
- (void)viewDidLoad
{
  [super viewDidLoad];
  self.mapView.delegate = self;
  self.mapView.showsUserLocation = YES;
}
```

Your additions in Listing 17-2 start by making the MapController the Map View delegate. showsUserLocation is a MKMapView property that tells the Map view whether to show the user location. If YES, you get that same blue pulsing dot you see displayed in the built-in Maps application.

If you were to compile and run the application as it stands now on your iPad, you'd be asked if it were okay to use your current location, and if you tapped OK, you'd get what you see in Figure 17-10 — a U.S. map in Landscape orientation with a blue dot that represents the iPad's current location. (You may have to pan the map to see it; a lag may occur while the iPad determines that location, but you should see it eventually.) Of course, to see it in Landscape orientation, you have to turn the iPad, or choose Hardware⇨Rotate Right (or Rotate Left) from the Simulator menu.

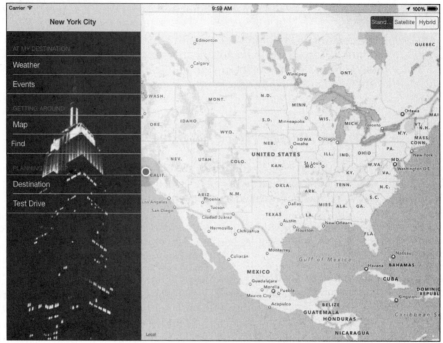

Figure 17-10:
Displaying
a map in
Landscape
orientation
with a user
location.

That's what happens on your iPad. On the Simulator, the story is different.

After launching the application in the Simulator (see Figure 17-11), I've chosen San Francisco by showing the Debug area in the View selector on the toolbar, clicking the Simulate Location icon (it looks like the standard Location icon) in the Debug bar in the Workspace window, and then selecting San Francisco from the menu that appears. I didn't choose New York because later you're going to add some code to shift your map back and forth from the current location to your destination. You can also add more locations (but you don't do that in this book).

You also can simulate the location (with some interesting choices) on the Simulator Debug menu — choose Debug➪Location. Check out City Run for example, or even enter the GPS coordinates for any location (choose Custom Location).

If you don't see the current location, you might want to check to make sure that you've created the `mapView` outlet and connected it to the Map view in the storyboard.

Touching the blue dot also displays what's called an *annotation,* and I tell you how to customize the text to display whatever you cleverly devise — including, as you discover in Chapter 18, the address of the current location.

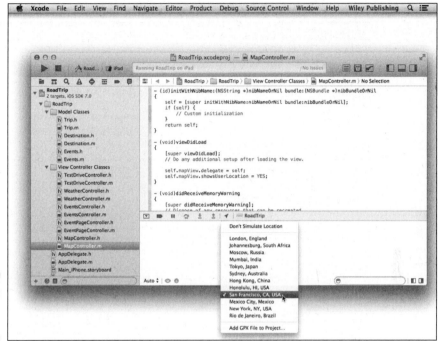

Figure 17-11:
Simulating a
location.

It's about the region

Okay, now you've got a blue dot on a map. Cute, but still not that useful for
the purposes of the app.

Ideally, when you get to New York (or wherever), you should see a map that
centers on where you are as opposed to the entire United States. To get
there from here, however, is also pretty easy. First, you need to look at how
you center the map. To do that, you need to add the method declaration
`setInitialRegion` to `MapController.m`.

First, update the class extension by adding the bolded code in Listing 17-3 to
the class extension in `MapController.m`.

Listing 17-3:   Updating the MapController's Class Extension

```
@interface MapController ()
@property (weak, nonatomic) IBOutlet MKMapView *mapView;
- (IBAction)mapType:(id)sender;
- (void)setInitialRegion;
@end
```

Because the Map controller will get its data from the `Trip` object, as it
should, you have to update the implementation to import the `Trip` class as
well. Add the bolded code in Listing 17-4 to `MapController.m`.

Listing 17-4: Updating the MapController Implementation

```
#import "MapController.h"
#import "AppDelegate.h"
#import "Trip.h"
```

Finally, add the `setInitialRegion` method in Listing 17-5 to
`MapController.m`.

Listing 17-5: Add setInitialRegion

```
- (void) setInitialRegion {

    AppDelegate* appDelegate =
                [[UIApplication sharedApplication] delegate];
    MKCoordinateRegion region;
    CLLocationCoordinate2D  initialCoordinate =
                    [appDelegate.trip destinationCoordinate];
    region.center.latitude = initialCoordinate.latitude;
    region.center.longitude = initialCoordinate.longitude;
    region.span.latitudeDelta = .05;
    region.span.longitudeDelta = .05;
    [self.mapView setRegion:region animated:NO];
}
```

You then need to update `viewDidLoad` to use this method. Add the code
in bold in Listing 17-6 to `viewDidLoad` in `MapController.m` to send this
message.

Listing 17-6: Updating viewDidLoad

```
- (void)viewDidLoad
{
    [super viewDidLoad];
    self.mapView.delegate = self;
    self.mapView.showsUserLocation = YES;
    [self setInitialRegion];
}
```

If you run this now, you see more or less the region you see back in Figure 17-9
(but not the annotations . . . at least not yet).

Setting the *region* is how you center the map and set the zoom level. You
accomplish all this with the following statement:

```
[self.mapView setRegion:region animated:NO];
```

A region is a Map view property that specifies four pieces of information
(as illustrated in Figure 17-12):

✔ `region.center.latitude`: Specifies the latitude of the center of the map.

✔ `region.center.longitude`: Specifies the longitude of the center of the map.

For example, the center of the map would be New York if I were to set those values as

```
region.center.latitude = 40.712756;
region.center.longitude = -74.006047;
```

✔ `region.span.latitudeDelta`: Specifies the north-to-south distance (in latitudinal degrees) to display on the map. One degree of latitude is approximately 111 kilometers (69 miles). A `region.span.latitudeDelta` of 0.0036 would specify a north-to-south distance on the map of about a quarter of a mile. Latitudes north of the equator have positive values, whereas latitudes south of the equator have negative values.

✔ `region.span.longitudeDelta`: Specifies the east-to-west distance (in longitudinal degrees) to display on the map. Unfortunately, the number of miles in one degree of longitude varies based on the latitude. For example, one degree of longitude is approximately 69 miles at the equator, but shrinks to 0 miles at the poles. Longitudes east of the zero meridian (by international convention, the zero or prime meridian passes through the Royal Observatory, Greenwich, in east London) have positive values, and longitudes west of the zero meridian have negative values.

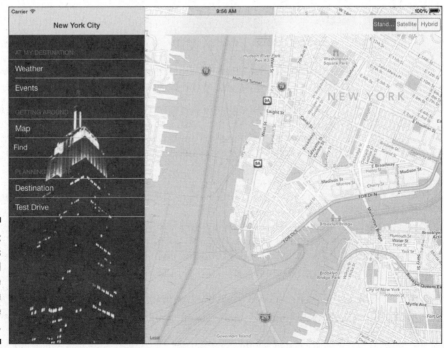

Figure 17-12: How regions work and determine what you see on the map.

Although the span values provide an implicit zoom value for the map, the actual region you see displayed may not equal the span you specify because the map will go to the zoom level that best fits the region that's set. This also means that even if you just change the center coordinate in the map, the zoom level may change because distances represented by a particular span may change at different latitudes and longitudes. To account for that, those smart developers at Apple included a property you can set that changes the center coordinate without changing the zoom level:

```
@property (nonatomic)
                    CLLocationCoordinate2D centerCoordinate
```

When you change the value of this property with a new `CLLocation Coordinate2D`, the map is centered on the new coordinate, and the span values are updated to maintain the current zoom level.

That `CLLocationCoordinate2D` type is something you'll be using a lot, so I'd like to explain that before I take you any further. The `CLLocationCoordinate2D` type is a structure that contains a geographical coordinate using the WGS 84 reference frame (the reference coordinate system used by the Global Positioning System):

```
typedef struct {
CLLocationDegrees latitude;
CLLocationDegrees longitude;
} CLLocationCoordinate2D;
```

Here's a little explanation:

- `latitude`: The latitude in degrees. This is the value you set in the code you just entered (`region.center.latitude = latitude;`). Positive values indicate latitudes north of the equator. Negative values indicate latitudes south of the equator.

- `longitude`: The longitude in degrees. This is the value you set in the code you just entered (`region.center.longitude = longitude;`). Measurements are relative to the zero meridian, with positive values extending east of the meridian and negative values extending west of the meridian.

`CLLocationDegrees` represents a latitude or longitude value specified in degrees and is a `double`.

To center the map display on New York, you send the `setInitialRegion` message (the code you just entered) when the view is loaded in the `viewDidLoad:` method.

The actual values come from the Destinations plist you entered in "Adding the Model Data" in Chapter 11.

Dealing with network failure

But what if the Internet isn't available? The Apple Human Interface Guidelines (and common sense) say that you should keep the user informed of what's going on. By virtue of the fact that you've made the `MapController` an `MKMapView` delegate, your app is in the position to send a message in the event of a load failure, because if a failure occurs, you're notified, provided you implement the `mapViewDidFailLoadingMap:` method. You can respond to a load failure by adding the code in Listing 17-7 to `MapController.m`.

Listing 17-7:   Implementing mapViewDidFailLoadingMap:

```
- (void)mapViewDidFailLoadingMap:(MKMapView *)mapView
                       withError:(NSError *)error {

  NSLog(@"Unresolved error %@, %@", error,
                                   [error userInfo]);

  UIAlertView *alert = [[UIAlertView alloc]
     initWithTitle:@"Unable to load the map"
     message:@"Check to see if you have internet access"
     delegate:self cancelButtonTitle: @"Thanks"
     otherButtonTitles:nil];
  [alert show];
}
```

 Testing this failure business requires disconnecting from the Internet after you have launched RoadTrip. And because of map caching, you might have to pan the map to get the warning. The simplest way to disconnect from the Internet is to turn Airplane Mode on.

Changing the Map Type

`MapKit` supports three Map types — standard, satellite, and hybrid.

The Map type is a Map View property and is represented as an enumerated type, which I have cleverly made the segment numbers in the segmented control correspond to

```
enum {
  MKMapTypeStandard,
  MKMapTypeSatellite,
  MKMapTypeHybrid
};
```

Add the code in bold in Listing 17-8 to the `mapType:` method stub that was created when you added the action in Interface Builder. The code ensures that, when the user selects a new value in the segmented control, it will change the Map type based on the selection.

Listing 17-8:   Updating mapType:

```
- (IBAction)mapType:(id)sender {

    self.mapView.mapType =
        ((UISegmentedControl *)sender).selectedSegmentIndex;
}
```

When the user selects a segment in the segmented control, a *value-changed* event is generated. This is the event (Value Changed) that you specified when you created the action in Step 4 in the "Setting up the MapController in the MainStoryboard_iPad" section, earlier in this chapter.

The segmented control has a `selectedSegmentIndex` property, which contains the value of the selected segment.

I had to do a cast here because the sender is of type `id` — a pointer to an object — which doesn't have a `selectedSegmentIndex` property.

Avoiding the cast

Because I know that the sender in the `mapType:` method is a `UISegmentedControl`, I could have been clever and instead changed the Sender type in the method declaration:

```
- (IBAction)mapType:
   (UISegmentedControl *)
   sender {

   self.mapView.
   mapType = sender.
   selectedSegmentIndex;
}
```

I could've changed the Sender type because you have the option to specify the Sender type when you create the action. (Just be sure you've got the right type.) In fact, I could've changed it by changing the type in the dialog back in Step 6 in the "Setting up the MapController in the MainStoryboard_iPad" section earlier in this chapter, where I first created the action.

Adding Annotations

The `MKMapView` class supports the capability to annotate the map with custom information. The annotation has two parts: the annotation itself, which contains the data for the annotation, and the Annotation view, which displays the data.

Creating the annotation

Any object that conforms to the `MKAnnotation` protocol is an Annotation object; typically, Annotation objects are existing classes in your application's model. The job of an Annotation object is to know its location (coordinates) on the map along with the text to be displayed in the callout. The `MKAnnotation` protocol requires a class that adopts that protocol to implement the `coordinate` property. It can also optionally implement `title` and `subtitle` properties. In that case, that text will be displayed in the annotation callout when the user taps the annotation.

Actually, you already have one class that meets that criteria — `Destination`.

And that's why, when you create the `Destination` class in Chapter 11 (I told you that I would explain this), I have you add the property with the attributes in the way I do. Annotations are required by the protocol to have the properties I have bolded in the following code:

```
@property (nonatomic, readwrite)
                      CLLocationCoordinate2D coordinate;
@property (nonatomic, readwrite, copy) NSString *title;
@property (nonatomic, readwrite, copy) NSString *subtitle;
```

That's it. You already have the properties in place and initialized (see Chapter 12 if you need to review why that's the case).

Also, in Chapter 11, you include some point-of-interest data in your plist. Although in this example, you only have one point of interest (annotation), you can imagine that in a complete RoadTrip app, you'd have quite a few. You want your points of interest to be annotations as well.

You're going to need to go back to the `Trip` object to create the annotations, but first you have to add an `Annotation` class to the Model Classes group by following these steps:

1. **In the Project navigator, select the Model Classes group, and then either right-click the selection and choose New File from the menu that appears or choose File⇨New⇨File from the main menu (or press ⌘+N) to open the New File dialog.**

2. **In the left column of the dialog, select Cocoa Touch under the iOS heading, select the Objective-C Class template in the top-right pane, and then click Next.**

   You'll see a dialog that will enable you to choose the options for your file.

3. **Enter** Annotation **in the Class field.**

4. **Choose or enter** NSObject **in the Subclass Of field and then click Next.**

   Note that the Target for iPad and With XIB for User Interface check boxes are dimmed because they are not relevant here — Events is derived from NSObject, and not any type of view controller.

5. **In the Save sheet that appears, click Create.**

Next, you need to add the code necessary for an annotation.

Add the code in bold in Listing 17-9 to Annotation.h.

Listing 17-9:   Updating the Annotation Interface

```
#import <Foundation/Foundation.h>
#import <MapKit/MapKit.h>

@interface Annotation: NSObject <MKAnnotation>

@property (nonatomic, readwrite)
                        CLLocationCoordinate2D coordinate;
@property (nonatomic, readwrite, copy) NSString *title;
@property (nonatomic, readwrite, copy) NSString *subtitle;

@end
```

I'm using a generic Annotation class to display the points of interest. As you build out the app, you could also include more information about the points of interest and other information, and create a PointOfInterest class. Then you could make it and Destination subclasses of Annotation. In an annotation, you can also have a right and left Callout Accessory view, which display on the right and left side of the standard callout bubble, respectively.

The Callout view is typically used to link to more detailed information about the annotation. Also, you could link to something such as the EventController to display information about a PointOfInterest. Just food for thought.

You need to update the Trip initialization method to create the annotation, but first you have to import the headers you need. Add the bolded code in Listing 17-10 to Trip.m.

Listing 17-10: Updating the Trip Implementation

```
#import "Trip.h"
#import "Destination.h"
#import "Events.h"
#import "Annotation.h"

                  @interface Trip ()
@property (strong, nonatomic) NSDictionary
   *destinationData;
@property (strong, nonatomic) Destination *destination;
@property (strong, nonatomic) Events *events;
@property (strong, nonatomic) NSMutableArray *pois;

@end
```

Now you can add the bolded code in Listing 17-11 to initWithDestinationIndex: in Trip.m. This will turn the point-of-interest data in the plist (the POIs) into annotations (okay, just one) and add the destination as an annotation to boot.

Listing 17-11: Updating initWithDestinationIndex:

```
- (id)initWithDestinationIndex:(int)destinationIndex {
  self = [super init];
  if (self)) {

    NSString *filePath = [[NSBundle mainBundle]
       pathForResource:@"Destinations"   ofType:@"plist"];
    NSDictionary *destinations =
      [NSDictionary dictionaryWithContentsOfFile:filePath];
    NSArray *destinationsArray =
         [destinations objectForKey:@"DestinationData"];
    _destinationData =
       [destinationsArray objectAtIndex:destinationIndex];
    _destination = [[Destination alloc]
            initWithDestinationIndex:destinationIndex];
    events = [[Events alloc]
          initWithDestinationIndex:destinationIndex];
    NSArray *poiData = self.destinationData[@"POIs"];
    _pois = [[NSMutableArray alloc]
                 initWithCapacity:[ poiData count]+1];
    [_pois addObject: self.destination];

    for (NSDictionary *aPOI in poiData) {
      Annotation *annotation = [[Annotation alloc] init];
```

(continued)

Listing 17-11 *(continued)*

```
        CLLocationCoordinate2D coordinate;
        coordinate.latitude =
            [aPOI[@"Latitude"] doubleValue];
        coordinate.longitude =
            [aPOI[@"Longitude"] doubleValue];

        annotation.coordinate = coordinate;
        annotation.title = aPOI[@"Title"];
        annotation.subtitle = aPOI[@"Subtitle"];
        [self.pois addObject:annotation];
    }
  }
return self;
}
```

As you can see, you're creating an `Annotation` for each point of interest (`aPOI`) in the `poiData` array and adding it to a `pois` array you create — an array that will hold all the annotations I want to display on the map. `poiData` is the `POIs` array in the `Destinations.plist` you created in Chapter 11. Note that instead of adding an initialization method to `Annotation`, you're simply assigning the properties directly rather than sending them as parameters in an initialization method.

If you look closely, you can see that I'm adding `Destination` to the `pois` array as well. That way, it, too, will display on the map.

You have to add some new methods to the interface so that `Trip` can return the annotations (and a map title). You also need to update the `Trip` interface. To do that, add the bolded code in Listing 17-12 to `Trip.h`.

Listing 17-12:   Updating the Trip Interface

```
@interface Trip : NSObject

- (UIImage *) destinationImage;
- (NSString *) destinationName;
- (CLLocationCoordinate2D) destinationCoordinate;

- (id)initWithDestinationIndex:(int)destinationIndex;
- (NSString *)weather;
- (NSUInteger)numberOfEvents;
- (NSString *)getEvent:(NSUInteger)index;
- (NSArray *)createAnnotations;
- (NSString *)mapTitle;
@end
```

Now you get to add all the `Trip` methods that will be used by the `MapController`. Start by adding the `createAnnotations` method shown in Listing 17-13 to `Trip.m`.

Listing 17-13: Adding createAnnotations

```
- (NSArray *)createAnnotations {

    return self.pois;
}
```

Even though `pois` is a mutable array, I return it as a basic array because that's all that is needed. `MapController` won't be adding any annotations to it.

You also need to add a method to return the map title. Add the `mapTitle` method in Listing 17-14 to `Trip.m`.

Listing 17-14: Add mapTitle

```
- (NSString *)mapTitle {

    return self.destination.destinationName;
}
```

All that's really left at this point is to add the code to `MapController` to get the annotations and send them to the Map view. The next section walks you through that.

Displaying the map title and annotations

Start by adding the bolded code in Listing 17-15 to update the private interface in `MapController.m`. As you can see, you'll be adding two methods — one to add the annotations, and another to provide the map title. I explain both as you go along.

Listing 17-15: Updating the MapController Private Interface

```
@interface MapController ()
- (IBAction)mapType:(id)sender;
- (void)setInitialRegion;
- (void)addAnnotations;
- (NSString *)mapTitle;
@end
```

With these code additions, you'll display the annotations by sending yourself the `addAnnotations` message in `viewDidLoad`. But another thing I would like to do is display the title of the destination either on the Navigation bar or the toolbar, and I'll do that in `viewDidLoad` as well.

Displaying a title in the Navigation bar is really easy, as you can see in Listing 17-17 — all you need to do is assign whatever you want it to be to the view controller's `title` property. But if you have a toolbar, your task isn't quite as easy. But it does give me a chance to show you a little more about how to work with toolbar items, so that's a good thing.

Update `viewDidLoad` by adding the bolded code in Listing 17-16 to `viewDidLoad` in `MapController.m`.

Listing 17-16:   Update viewDidLoad

```
- (void)viewDidLoad
{
  [super viewDidLoad];
  self.mapView.delegate = self;
  self.mapView.showsUserLocation = YES;
  [self setInitialRegion];
  AppDelegate* appDelegate = [[UIApplication
                                sharedApplication] delegate];
  if ([[UIDevice currentDevice] userInterfaceIdiom] ==
                                UIUserInterfaceIdiomPad) {
    UILabel * titleLabel = [[UILabel alloc]
                  initWithFrame:CGRectMake (0,0,250,44)];
    titleLabel.font = [UIFont boldSystemFontOfSize:17];
    titleLabel.textAlignment = NSTextAlignmentCenter;
    titleLabel.backgroundColor = [UIColor clearColor];
    titleLabel.text = [self mapTitle];
    UIBarButtonItem *titleView = [[UIBarButtonItem alloc]
                            initWithCustomView:titleLabel];
    UIBarButtonItem *flexibleSpace=
    [[UIBarButtonItem alloc] initWithBarButtonSystemItem:
       UIBarButtonSystemItemFlexibleSpace
                                target:nil action:nil];
    flexibleSpace.width = 1.0;
    NSMutableArray *itemsArray =
                            [self.toolbar.items mutableCopy];
    [itemsArray insertObject:flexibleSpace atIndex:
                                [itemsArray count]-2];
    [itemsArray insertObject:titleView atIndex:
                                [itemsArray count]-2];
```

```
      [self.toolbar setItems:itemsArray animated:NO];
   }
   else
      self.title = [appDelegate.trip mapTitle];
 [self addAnnotations];
 }
```

You begin by determining whether you're on the iPad or the iPhone. If you're on the iPad, I make the assumption that you have a toolbar. (You could add the logic to see whether it is a toolbar or a Navigation bar on the iPad if you need to, just as you do in Chapter 8.)

If you're on an iPad, you create a `Label` object with a clear background, a bold system font of size `17`, aligned center, and with a width of `250`. (You could determine the actual size you need by using a number of methods in `NSString`, but that's pretty complicated and outside the scope of this book.) You also send the `mapTitle` message to get the title, which I get to next.

```
UILabel * titleLabel = [[UILabel alloc]
                  initWithFrame:CGRectMake (0,0,250,44)];
   titleLabel.textColor = [UIColor yellowColor];
   titleLabel.font = [UIFont boldSystemFontOfSize:17];
   titleLabel.textAlignment = NSTextAlignmentCenter;
   titleLabel.backgroundColor = [UIColor clearColor];
   titleLabel.text = [self mapTitle];
```

You then create a `UIBarButtonItem` by initializing it with the view (`UILabel`) you just created. This enables you to add virtually whatever you want to the toolbar, as long as it's a view.

```
UIBarButtonItem *titleView = [[UIBarButtonItem alloc]
                        initWithCustomView:titleLabel];
```

Then you create a flexible space of the kind you used earlier in this chapter — doing so adds a space that's distributed equally between the other Bar Button items on the toolbar — so the title will be centered between the Map-type segmented control on the right (which already has a flexible space item in front of it) and the Road Trip button (if there is one) or the left side of the toolbar (if there isn't).

```
UIBarButtonItem *flexibleSpace=
   [[UIBarButtonItem alloc] initWithBarButtonSystemItem:
       UIBarButtonSystemItemFlexibleSpace
                              target:nil action:nil];
flexibleSpace.width = 1.0;
```

You then add the items to the toolbar's `items` array just as you do in Chapter 13.

```
[itemsArray insertObject:flexibleSpace atIndex:
                            [itemsArray count]-2];
[itemsArray insertObject:titleView atIndex:
                            [itemsArray count]-2];
[self.toolbar setItems:itemsArray animated:NO];
```

The `[itemsArray count]-2` index means that you'll add this item before the two existing items (the existing flexible space and the segmented control).

If you are not on the iPad, you just assign whatever you want the title to be to the `title` property of the view controller and it is displayed on the Navigation bar.

```
else
  self.title = [appDelegate.trip mapTitle];
```

With the title taken care of, you send yourself the `addAnnotations` message.

```
[self addAnnotations];
```

Before I get to the `addAnnotations` method you'll need to add, I'll have you finish up the title by adding the `mapTitle` method in Listing 17-17 to `MapController.m`.

Listing 17-17:   Add mapTitle

```
- (NSString *)mapTitle {

  AppDelegate* appDelegate = [[UIApplication
                      sharedApplication] delegate];

  return [appDelegate.trip mapTitle];
}
```

`mapTitle` gets the map title by sending the `mapTitle` message to the `Trip` object — another model responsibility. (This also gives you a chance, as you'll see in Chapter 19, to title the map based on whatever criteria you would like, such as the current location.)

With your title taken care of, it's time to add the annotations. Start by adding the `addAnnotations` method in Listing 17-18 to `MapController.m`.

Listing 17-18: Add addAnnotations

```
- (void)addAnnotations {

  AppDelegate* appDelegate =
              [[UIApplication sharedApplication] delegate];
  [self.mapView addAnnotations:
                   [appDelegate.trip createAnnotations]];
}
```

I make this a separate method because I want to be able to add more annotations after the view is loaded. Although you won't be adding additional annotations here, you take advantage of this method when you implement the `FindController` in Chapter 19 to display locations the user wants to see on a map.

To add an annotation to a Map view, just send the `addAnnotations` message with an array of annotations that have adopted the `MKAnnotation` protocol; that is, each one has a `coordinate` property and an optional `title` (and `subtitle`) method — if it turns out you want to actually display something in the annotation callout.

The Map view places annotations on the screen by sending its delegate the `mapView:viewForAnnotation:` message. This message is sent for each annotation object in the array. Here you can create a custom view or return `nil` to use the default view. (If you don't implement this delegate method — which you won't, in this case — the default view is also used.)

Creating your own (customized) Annotation views is beyond the scope of this book (although I can tell you that the most efficient way to provide the content for an Annotation view is to set its `image` property). Fortunately, the default Annotation view is fine for your purposes. It displays a pin in the location specified in the coordinate property of the Annotation delegate. When the user touches the pin, the optional title and subtitle text will display if the `title` and `subtitle` methods are implemented in the Annotation delegate.

You can also add callouts to the Annotation view, such as a Detail Disclosure or the Info button (like the one you see in many of the utility apps), by using the built-in `MKPinAnnotationView` — you don't have to create your own Annotation view, in other words.

If you compile and build your project, your map is going to proudly display the annotations you added, as shown in Figure 17-13. Notice the Map view is beginning to look more and more like the one back in Figure 17-9.

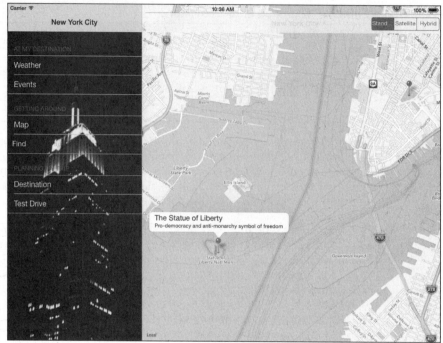

Figure 17-13:
Displaying
an annota-
tion and its
callout.

Going to the Current Location

Although you require the user to pan to the user location on the map if he wants to see it, it's kind of annoying in this particular case unless you're actually coding this in or around New York City. To remove at least that annoyance from your life, I show you how easy it is to add a button to the toolbar bar to zoom in to the current location and then back to the map region and span you're currently displaying.

Add the bolded code in Listing 17-19 to add the button in the `MapController` method `viewDidLoad`.

Listing 17-19:   Updating viewDidLoad

```
- (void)viewDidLoad
{
  [super viewDidLoad];
  self.mapView.delegate = self;
  self.mapView.showsUserLocation = YES;

  [self setInitialRegion];
  RTAppDelegate* appDelegate = [[UIApplication
```

```objc
                              sharedApplication] delegate];
  if ([[UIDevice currentDevice] userInterfaceIdiom] ==
                                  UIUserInterfaceIdiomPad) {
    UILabel * titleLabel = [[UILabel alloc]
                    initWithFrame:CGRectMake (0,0,250,44)];
    titleLabel.textColor = [UIColor yellowColor];
    titleLabel.font = [UIFont boldSystemFontOfSize:17];
    titleLabel.textAlignment = NSTextAlignmentCenter;
    titleLabel.backgroundColor = [UIColor clearColor];
    titleLabel.text = [self mapTitle];
    UIBarButtonItem *titleView = [[UIBarButtonItem alloc]
                          initWithCustomView:titleLabel];
    UIBarButtonItem *flexibleSpace=
    [[UIBarButtonItem alloc] initWithBarButtonSystemItem:
        UIBarButtonSystemItemFlexibleSpace
                                    target:nil action:nil];
    flexibleSpace.width = 1.0;
    NSMutableArray *itemsArray =
                        [self.toolbar.items mutableCopy];
    [itemsArray insertObject:flexibleSpace atIndex:
                                    [itemsArray count]-2];
    [itemsArray insertObject:titleView atIndex:
                                    [itemsArray count]-2];
    [self.toolbar setItems:itemsArray animated:NO];
  }
  else {
    self.title = [appDelegate.trip mapTitle];
  }
[self addAnnotations];
  UIBarButtonItem *locateButton = [[UIBarButtonItem alloc]
          initWithTitle:@"Locate"
          style:UIBarButtonItemStyleBordered target:self
          action:@selector(goToLocation:)];;
  if ([[UIDevice currentDevice] userInterfaceIdiom] ==
          UIUserInterfaceIdiomPad) {
    NSMutableArray *itemsArray =
                        [self.toolbar.items mutableCopy];
    [itemsArray insertObject:locateButton
                            atIndex:[itemsArray count]];
    [self.toolbar setItems:itemsArray animated:NO];
  }
  else {
    self.navigationItem.rightBarButtonItem = locateButton;
  }
}
```

This may look familiar because it's what you did to add the Back button in Chapter 15. When the user taps the Locate button you create here, you've specified that the `goToLocation:` message is to be sent `[action:@ selector(goToLocation:)]` to the `MapController (target:self)`.

```
UIBarButtonItem *locateButton =
    [[UIBarButtonItem alloc] initWithTitle: @"Locate"
    style:UIBarButtonItemStylePlain target:self
    action:@selector(goToLocation:)];
self.navigationItem.rightBarButtonItem = locateButton;
```

Notice that I don't check to see whether this is a Navigation bar or a toolbar. I'm assuming a toolbar, but if you think you may want to someday, for some reason, make this a Navigation bar, I leave this as an exercise for the reader.

Don't forget, to go back to a location you need to choose a simulated location if you are using the Simulator, as you did in the earlier section "Enhancing the map."

Next, add the `goToLocation:` method in Listing 17-20 to `MapController.m`.

Listing 17-20: Adding goToLocation:

```
- (void)goToLocation:(id)sender {

  MKUserLocation *annotation = self.mapView.userLocation;
  CLLocation *location = annotation.location;
  if (nil == location)
    return;
  CLLocationDistance distance =
        MAX(4*location.horizontalAccuracy,500);
  MKCoordinateRegion region =
        MKCoordinateRegionMakeWithDistance
                (location.coordinate, distance, distance);
  [self.mapView setRegion:region animated:NO];

  if ([[UIDevice currentDevice] userInterfaceIdiom] ==
                              UIUserInterfaceIdiomPad) {
    NSArray *itemsArray = self.toolbar.items;

    UIBarButtonItem *locateButton = [itemsArray
                    objectAtIndex:[itemsArray count]-1];
    locateButton.action = @selector(goToDestination:);
    locateButton.title = @"Destination";
  }
  else {
    self.navigationItem.rightBarButtonItem.action =
                          @selector(goToDestination:);
    self.navigationItem.rightBarButtonItem.title =
                                        @"Destination";
  }
}
```

When the user taps the Locate button, your app first checks to see whether the location is available. (It may take a few seconds after the application starts for the location to become available.) If not, you simply return from the method without changing the region. (You could, of course, show an alert informing the user what's happening and to try again in 10 seconds or so — I leave that up to you.)

If the location is available, your app computes the span for the region the user is moving to. In this case, the following code

```
CLLocationDistance distance =
                MAX(4*location.horizontalAccuracy,500);
```

computes the span to be four times the `horizontalAccuracy` of the device (but no less than 1,000 meters). `horizontalAccuracy` is a radius of uncertainty given the accuracy of the device; that is, the user is somewhere within that circle.

You then call the `MKCoordinateRegionMakeWithDistance` function that creates a new `MKCoordinateRegion` from the specified coordinate and distance values. `distance` and `distance` correspond to `latitudinalMeters` and `longitudinalMeters`, respectively. (I'm using the same value for both parameters here.)

If you didn't want to change the span, you could've simply set the Map view's `centerCoordinate` property to `userLocation`, and as I said earlier in the "It's about the region" section, that would've centered the region at the `userLocation` coordinate without changing the span.

When the user taps the Location button, you change the title on the button to the Map title and change the `@selector` to `(goToDestination:)`. You access the button on the iPad in the toolbar `itemsArray` and on the iPhone via the `navigationItem`.

This means that the next time the user touches the button, the `goToDestination:` message will be sent, so you'd better add the code in Listing 17-21 to `MapController.m`. This sets the region back to the Destination region and toggles the button title back to Locate.

Listing 17-21:   Adding goToDestination:

```
- (void)goToDestination:(id)sender {

  [self setInitialRegion];
  if ([[UIDevice currentDevice] userInterfaceIdiom] ==
        UIUserInterfaceIdiomPad) {
    NSArray *itemsArray = self.toolbar.items;
```

(continued)

Listing 17-21 *(continued)*

```
    UIBarButtonItem *locateButton = [itemsArray
            objectAtIndex:[itemsArray count]-1];
    locateButton.action = @selector(goToLocation:);
    locateButton.title = @"Locate";
  }
  else {
    self.navigationItem.rightBarButtonItem.action =
                                @selector(goToLocation:);
    self.navigationItem.rightBarButtonItem.title =
                                             @"Locate";
  }
}
```

Now run your app (and if you're running on the Simulator, choose your default location as explained in the section "Enhancing the map," earlier in this chapter). Because you already have two annotations on the map of New York, you might want to set the Simulator to use a distant location such as San Francisco. That way, you can easily see that the map is working.

You can see the result of tapping the Locate button in Figure 17-14.

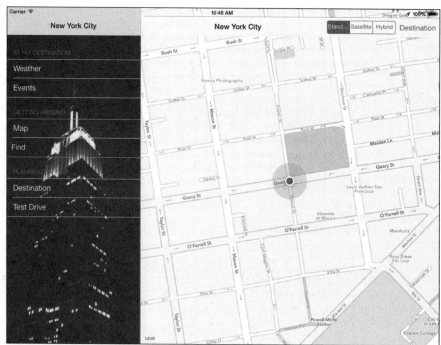

Figure 17-14:
Go to the current location.

Because you have the user location, you might be tempted to use that to center the map, and that would work fine, as long as you start the location-finding mechanism stuff as soon as the program launches. The problem is that the hardware may take a while to find the current location, and if you don't wait long enough, you get an error. You can add the code to center the map to a method that executes later, such as

```
- (void)observeValueForKeyPath:(NSString *)keyPath
    ofObject:(id)object change:(NSDictionary *)change
                              context:(void *)context {
```

This message is sent as soon as the map starts getting location information, but you'll see an initial view and then a redisplay of the centered view. For aesthetic reasons, you really need to initialize `MapController` and `MapView` at program startup — an exercise for the reader.

Fixing the Status Bar

Things are really, really close to being done. There's that status bar issue to worry about. I've saved it for now because although it's really not difficult, it helps to have worked with views and their settings in order to understand it.

In iOS 7, the status bar is transparent, and that's where the issue arises. The issue is that the Web view is showing through the transparent status bar. That's a no-no. It distracts from the status bar information, it destroys the consistency of the iOS interface, and it looks strange to most people.

There are three standard solutions. The easiest is to use a navigation controller to display your content (your main view). A navigation controller has the logic built into it to display an appropriate background for the status bar and to position its content views so that they are not behind the status bar. (This is one of the reasons that the problem doesn't occur so frequently on iPhone apps: they're already using navigation controllers in many cases.)

You also can create a nondistracting background image to place under the status bar and above your view's content.

The most robust solution is to use Auto Layout. So far, you've mostly used Auto Layout for pinning views and embedding them in other views. There's a great deal more to Auto Layout, and here's how you can use it in this case.

First of all, as you can easily find out, the Status Bar is 20 points high. You can go into the Size inspector in the Utility area, and manually set the origin of your top view to 0, 20 so it will be placed below the Status bar.

And next week when Apple introduces an iOS device with a new form factor on which the Status bar is not 20 points high, your app will break. Now there's no guarantee that such as device will be introduced next week, but the odds are pretty good that it will happen (and probably at the most inconvenient time for you).

Start by recognizing that the Status bar is transparent and it's going to be at the top of the screen. (You can hide it for full-screen content, but it should generally not be hidden for a long period of time.) In the case of your Map controller, you have that transparent Status bar at the top of the screen. You want your toolbar below it, and you want your Web view directly below the bottom of the toolbar. (When I say "below" here I mean lower down on the screen and not behind.)

Now that you've recognized that the Status bar is going to be at the top of the screen unless you hide it, here are the steps to position the other views properly.

1. **In the storyboard, open the Document Outline and the Map Controller – Map Scene.**

    You can see it at the left of Figure 17-7.

2. **Notice that you have** `Top Layout Guide` **and a** `Bottom Layout Guide` **inside the scene.**

    They are placed there automatically.

3. **Control-drag from the Toolbar to the** `Top Layout Guide`.

4. **Select Vertical Spacing in the popover that appears, as shown in Figure 17-15.**

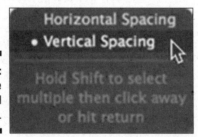

Figure 17-15: Choose Vertical Spacing.

5. **With the Toolbar still selected, choose the Size inspector in the Utility area. In the list of constraints, you'll set Top Space to: Top Layout Guide, as shown in Figure 17-16.**

    That is the constraint that you just created.

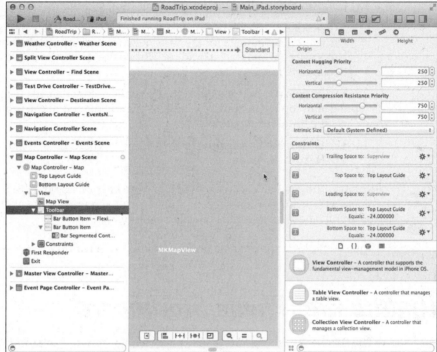

Figure 17-16:
Verify
the new
constraint.

6. **Click the Gear Wheel on that constraint and choose Select and Edit.**

7. **The constraint should have been set as shown in Figure 17-16.**

   Verify that the pop-up menu is set to Equal, the Constant is set to 0, and the Priority is set to 1,000. That is the highest value, and it means that no other constraint can override this one.

8. **If you have any other constraints, use the Gear wheel to delete them.**

   These extra constraints can accumulate as you are experimenting.

9. **Using Editor⇨Pin, pin the leading and trailing spaces to the superview.**

10. **Use the Size inspector to verify that the Toolbar height remains 44.**

    You may want to run the app now to verify that the toolbar no longer overlaps the status bar.

11. **Control-drag from** `Map View` **to** `Toolbar`**.**

12. **Select Vertical Spacing as you did in Step 4.**

13. **Choose Editor➪Resolve Auto Layout Issues➪Add Missing Constraints.**

If the command is grayed out, just verify that you have top, bottom, leading, and trailing constraints for the Web view. If not, make certain the toolbar is selected and then use Editor➪Resolve Auto Layout Issues➪Clear Constraints to try again.

Xcode pins the bottom space to the superview and aligns leading, trailing, and top to the toolbar. The Web view is pinned to the toolbar, which is pinned to the superview.

14. **Verify that the constraints are working by rotating the simulator using the Hardware menu.**

Rotating the simulator is the acid test of Auto Layout. Use the keyboard equivalents as you are working on your storyboard to constantly check that your beautiful landscape layout is equally beautiful in portrait.

You should have the results shown previously in Figure 17-9.

Update the iPhone Storyboard

The iPhone storyboard for maps is very similar to the iPad storyboard. In fact, the quick and easy way to update your iPhone storyboard is as follows:

1. **Select the iPad storyboard file in the Project Navigator.**

2. **Click the mouse on the Map Controller – Map Scene to select it. Make sure that the whole Map Scene is selected and highlighted.**

3. **Copy the Map Controller Scene by choosing Edit➪Copy.**

4. **Select your iPhone storyboard file in the Project Navigator.**

5. **Paste the Map Controller Scene into the iPhone storyboard file.**

6. **Control-drag from the Map item in the Master View controller over to the Map Controller Scene, and choose the Push segue from the pop-up menu.**

7. **Test your new map capabilities in the iPhone simulator.**

8. **Congratulate yourself on a job well done.**

Chapter 18

Geocoding

There are two basic ways of identifying where you are on Earth. You can describe your location in coordinates of latitude and longitude, or you can describe your location in terms of an address. The latitude and longitude coordinates are based on geometry (remember Euclid) and on the assumption that the Earth is a regular sphere.

Addresses are based on history and politics. The geographic coordinates of the city now known as St. Petersburg have not changed over time (yes, I know that continental drift has an effect, but to all intents and purposes, it has been in the same place since its founding by Tsar Peter the Great on May 27, 1703). However, St. Petersburg's name was changed to Petrograd, then to Leningrad, and after that back to St. Petersburg.

Despite the fact that geographic coordinates of a spot on Earth are essentially unchanging and the addresses are subject to change, most people commonly use addresses to describe locations on Earth. Most software that deals with mapping works with geographic coordinates, and it converts back and forth between them and addresses. This process is known as geocoding, and it comes in two flavors: forward and reverse geocoding.

This chapter shows you how to use iOS geocoding tools in your apps.

Understanding Geocoding on the iPad

Converting an address to a set of map coordinates is called *forward geocoding*, whereas converting from a set of coordinates to an address is called *reverse geocoding*. Both forward and reverse geocoding are supported in

Apple's `CLGeocoder` class — which is part of Apple's `CoreLocation` framework. I showed you how to add the `CoreLocation` framework to the RoadTrip project way back in Chapter 11.

The `CLGeocoder` class provides services for converting between a coordinate (specified as a latitude and longitude) and the address of that coordinate. The `CLGeocoder` class also provides services for the reverse: returning the coordinate value for a text string that is the user-friendly representation of that coordinate.

To use a `CLGeocoder` object, first create it and then send it a forward- or reverse-geocoding message.

✔ **Reverse-geocoding:** These requests take a latitude and longitude value and find a user-readable address.

✔ **Forward-geocoding:** These requests take a user-readable address and find the corresponding latitude and longitude value. Forward-geocoding requests may also return additional information about the specified location, such as a point of interest or building at that location.

For both types of request, the results are returned as an array of `CLPlacemark` objects to a completion handler block. In the case of forward-geocoding requests, multiple `placemark` objects may be returned if the provided information yields multiple possible locations.

A `CLPlacemark` object contains, among other things, the following properties:

✔ `location`: Very useful for forward geocoding, which I explain in Chapter 19

✔ `name`: The name of the placemark

✔ `addressDictionary`: A dictionary containing the Address Book keys and values for the placemark

✔ `ISOcountryCode`: The abbreviated country name

✔ `country`: The name of the country

✔ `postalCode`: The postal code

✔ `administrativeArea`: The state or province

✔ `subAdministrativeArea`: Additional administrative area information (such as county)

✔ `locality`: The city

✔ `subLocality`: Additional city-level information such as neighborhood or a common name for the location

✔ `thoroughfare`: The street

✔ `subThoroughfare`: Additional street-level information, such as the building number

✔ `region`: The `CLRegion`

Landmark and geographic information may also be available in the `CLPlacemark` object in the following properties:

✔ `areasOfInterest`: The relevant areas of interest associated with the placemark

✔ `inlandWater`: The name of the inland water body associated with the placemark

✔ `ocean`: The name of the ocean associated with the placemark

To make smart decisions about what types of information to return, the geocoder server uses all the information provided to it when processing the request. For example, if the user is moving quickly along a highway, the geocoder might return the name of the overall region rather than the name of a small park that the user is passing through.

Here are some rather loose rules (Apple's) for using the `CLGeocoder` object:

✔ Send at most one geocoding request for any single user action. That is, don't start another request until the first one has completed.

✔ If the app needs the geocoded location in more than one map location, save and then reuse the results from the initial geocoding request instead of doing another one.

✔ When you want to update the user's current location automatically (such as when the user is moving), issue new geocoding requests only when the user has moved a significant distance, a reasonable amount of time has passed, or both. For example, in a typical situation, you should not send more than one geocoding request per minute.

✔ Do not start a geocoding request if your app is inactive or in the background.

✔ An iOS-based device must have access to the network in order for the `CLGeocoder` object to return detailed placemark information. Although iOS stores enough information locally to report the localized country name and ISO country code for many locations, if country information is not available for a specific location, the `CLGeocoder` object may still report an error.

As you can probably surmise, geocoding is expensive — that's why these rules emphasize caching data and not updating unless it's necessary.

You can use a `CLGeocoder` object either in conjunction with, or independent of, the classes of the `MapKit` framework.

In this chapter, I show you how to add the code to do a reverse geocode. Essentially, you are going to update the `goToLocation:` method to use reverse geocoding to display the address of the current location in the annotation. In the next chapter, you get to do pretty much the same thing in order to set up a forward geocode, although you send a different message and process the placemark differently.

Reverse Geocoding

You'll begin the process of implementing reverse geocoding by adding a new instance variable to `MapController.m` to store a reference to the `CLGeocoder` object. You do all this by adding the bolded code in Listing 18-1 to `MapController.m`. As you'll see later, you'll need that reference to cancel a request.

Listing 18-1:   Updating the MapController Implementation

```
#import "MapController.h"
#import "RTAppDelegate.h"
#import "Trip.h"

@interface MapController ()
@property (weak, nonatomic) IBOutlet MKMapView *mapView;
@property (strong, nonatomic) CLGeocoder *geocoder;

- (IBAction)mapType:(id)sender;
- (void)setInitialRegion;
- (NSString *)mapTitle;
- (void)addAnnotations;
@end
```

Next, you allocate and initialize the `CLGeocoder` and send it a message to return the information for the current location. Adding the bolded code in Listing 18-2 to `goToLocation` in `MapController.m` does that for you.

Listing 18-2:   Updating goToLocation

```
- (void)goToLocation:(id)sender {

void (^clGeocodeCompletionHandler)(NSArray *, NSError *)
         =
  ^(NSArray *placemarks, NSError *error){


    CLPlacemark *placemark = [placemarks
          objectAtIndex:0];
    if (error!= nil || placemark == nil) {
      NSLog(@"Geocoder failure! Error code: %u,
        description: %@, and reason: %@", error.code,
          [error localizedDescription],
                        [error
          localizedFailureReason]);
    }
    else {
      self.mapView.userLocation.subtitle =
          [NSString stringWithFormat: @" lat:%f lon:%f",
          placemark.location.coordinate.latitude,

          placemark.location.coordinate.longitude];
      if ([placemark.areasOfInterest objectAtIndex:0]) {
        self.mapView.userLocation.title =
            [placemark.areasOfInterest
          objectAtIndex:0];
      }
      else {
        if (placemark.thoroughfare) {
          if (placemark.subThoroughfare)
            self.mapView.userLocation.title =
            [NSString stringWithFormat:@"%@ %@",
                        placemark.subThoroughfare,

        placemark.thoroughfare];
          else
            self.mapView.userLocation.title =
            [NSString stringWithFormat:@"%@",

        placemark.thoroughfare];
        }
        else {
          if (placemark.locality) {
            self.mapView.userLocation.title =
```

(continued)

Listing 18-2 *(continued)*

```
          placemark.locality;
          }
          else
            self.mapView.userLocation.title = @"Your
          location";
        }
      }
    }
  }
};

MKUserLocation *annotation = self.mapView.userLocation;
CLLocation *location = annotation.location;
if (nil == location)
  return;
CLLocationDistance distance =
        MAX(4*location.horizontalAccuracy,500);
MKCoordinateRegion region =
        MKCoordinateRegionMakeWithDistance
            (location.coordinate, distance,
        distance);
[self.mapView setRegion:region animated:NO];

if ([[UIDevice currentDevice] userInterfaceIdiom] ==
                            UIUserInterfaceIdiomPad) {
  NSArray *itemsArray = self.toolbar.items];
  UIBarButtonItem *locateButton = [itemsArray
                  objectAtIndex:[itemsArray count]-1];
  locateButton.action = @selector(goToDestination:);
  locateButton.title = @"Destination";
}
else {
  self.navigationItem.rightBarButtonItem.action =
                      @selector(goToDestination:);
  self.navigationItem.rightBarButtonItem.title =
                                  @"Destination";
}
self.geocoder = [[CLGeocoder alloc]init];
[self.geocoder reverseGeocodeLocation:location
      completionHandler:clGeocodeCompletionHandler];

}
```

The code you've added allocates and initializes the CLGeocoder, sends it the message to reverse geocode, and provides it with a completion handler block (just as you did with the animation you did in Chapter 10).

```
self.geocoder = [[CLGeocoder alloc]init];
[self.geocoder reverseGeocodeLocation:location
      completionHandler:clGeocodeCompletionHandler];
```

Sending the `reverseGeocodeLocation:completionHandler:` message is how you make a reverse-geocoding request for the specified location.

This method submits the location data to the geocoding server asynchronously and returns. Your completion handler block will be executed on the main thread. (The main thread encompasses the app's main run loop — apps can add [spawn] additional threads, which is beyond the scope of this book.)

After initiating a reverse-geocoding request, you shouldn't make another reverse- or forward-geocoding request until the first request is completed.

For both types of requests, the results are returned to the completion block in a `CLPlacemark` object. In the case of forward-geocoding requests, multiple placemark objects may be returned if what you submitted results in more than one possible location.

Note that the block is called *whether or not the request is successful*. It's invoked when the `CLGeocoder` either finds placemark information for its coordinate or receives an error. The `CLPlacemark` object, as you previously saw in the "Understanding Geocoding on the iPad" section, earlier in this chapter, will contain placemark data for a given latitude and longitude. Placemark data includes the properties that hold the country, state, city, and so on.

The completion handler is a block that appears in the following form:

```
void (^CLGeocodeCompletionHandler)
  (NSArray *placemark, NSError*error);
```

As you can see, `placemark` contains an array of `CLPlacemark` objects. For most geocoding requests, this array should contain only one entry. However, forward-geocoding requests may return multiple placemark objects in situations in which the specified address couldn't be resolved to a single location.

If the request was canceled or an error in obtaining the placemark information occurred, `placemark` is `nil`.

`error` contains a pointer to an `error` object (if any) indicating why the placemark data wasn't returned.

```
if (error!= nil || placemark == nil) {
  NSLog(@"Geocoder failure! Error code:%u, description:
      %@, and reason: %@", error.code,
        [error localizedDescription],
                 [error localizedFailureReason]);
  }
```

The CLGeocoder can fail for a variety of reasons, such as the service is down or it can't find an address for the coordinate. If the CLGeocoder fails, you get back an error object that can have some useful information. I'll leave it to you to explore the details of the error information on your own.

Although I simply log a message here, you may want to expand the user interface to inform the user what's happening. Doing so isn't important in this case because you can always just leave the annotation as Current Location, but when you start dragging annotations (which you can do, but won't in this book), you might want to develop a plan for what to display in the annotation if the CLGeocoder fails.

If the CLGeocoder is successful, you update the userLocation annotation — provided, as always by the Map view (if you set the showsUserLocation property to YES as you did in Chapter 17) — in the completion handler. user Location is a Map View property representing the user's current location.

As I explain earlier, the CLPlacemark object returned when the block is invoked stores placemark data for a given latitude and longitude. To update what's displayed in the annotation using the information you get back from the geocoder, you start by setting the subtitle using the coordinate in the Placemark Location property:

```
self.mapView.userLocation.subtitle =
    [NSString stringWithFormat: @" lat:%f lon:%f",
        placemark.location.coordinate.latitude,
                    placemark.location.coordinate.longitude];
```

If an areasOfInterest exists in the placemark, you set the title to that:

```
if ([placemark.areasOfInterest objectAtIndex:0]) {
    self.mapView.userLocation.title =
                [placemark.areasOfInterest
            objectAtIndex:0];
}
```

Otherwise, you see whether you have a thoroughfare and use that for the title (along with a subthoroughfare; together they provide the "street address"). Occasionally, however, you may find that a thoroughfare (street) exists, but no sub-thoroughfare (street number). When that's the case, you just display the thoroughfare.

```
if (placemark.thoroughfare) {
   if (placemark.subThoroughfare)
     self.mapView.userLocation.title =
        [NSString stringWithFormat:@"%@ %@",
         placemark.subThoroughfare,
              placemark.thoroughfare];
   else
     self.mapView.userLocation.title =
              [NSString stringWithFormat:@"%@",

         placemark.thoroughfare];
}
```

If no `thoroughfare` exists, you try for a `locality`, and if all else fails, you use a general-purpose location string.

```
if (placemark.locality ) {
   self.mapView.userLocation.title = placemark.locality;
}
else
   self.mapView.userLocation.title = @"Your location";
```

Because the `CLGeocoder` operates asynchronously, the user might tap the button to return to the Destination map before the `CLGeocoder` has completed the request. If that's the case, you'll want to cancel the `CLGeocoder` request. To do so, add the bolded code in Listing 18-3 to `goToDestination:` in `MapController.m`.

Listing 18-3:   Updating goToDestination:

```
- (void)goToDestination:(id)sender {

   [self.geocoder cancelGeocode];
   self.geocoder = nil;

   [self setInitialRegion];
   self.navigationItem.rightBarButtonItem.title =
   @"Locate";
   self.navigationItem.rightBarButtonItem.action =
   @selector(goToLocation:);
}
```

The `cancelGeocode` message cancels a pending geocoding request, which causes the completion handler block to be called.

You cancel the `CLGeocoder` request in this method because although you start the `CLGeocoder` in the `goToLocation:` method, it actually doesn't return the information in that method. It operates asynchronously when it constructs the placemark, gives up, or sends an error. You also set the instance variable to `nil` so that ARC will release the `CLGeocoder`.

But not only might the user return to the Destination map before the geo-coder request completes, he might also leave the Map view entirely and return to the Content controller. This means that you'll want to cancel the request when the view disappears as well, and the logical place to do that is in `viewWillDisappear:`, which notifies the view controller that its view is about to be dismissed, covered, or otherwise hidden from view. In the Map controller, that will happen only if the user taps the Back button to return to the Main view.

Add `viewWillDisappear:` to `MapController.m` with the code in Listing 18-4. (If you added the capability to track user location changes in Chapter 17, `viewWillDisappear` will already be there.)

Listing 18-4:   Overriding viewWillDisappear:

```
- (void) viewWillDisappear:(BOOL)animated {

    [self.geocoder cancelGeocode];
    self.geocoder = nil;
    [super viewWillDisappear:animated];
}
```

After initiating a forward-geocoding request, don't make another forward- or reverse-geocoding request until the first one completes or you cancel it.

Figure 18-1 shows the result of your adventures in reverse geocoding.

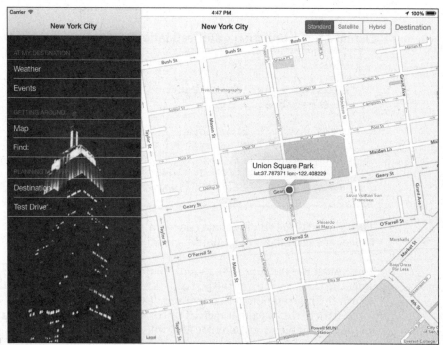

Figure 18-1:
Reverse
geocoding.

Chapter 19

Finding a Location

*I*t's pretty useful when traveling to be able to enter a location and have that display on a map. Although you can do that in many of the map apps currently available, it does take you out of the app you are in. What's more, you can't take that information and then do something with it in your own app, such as display it with all your other annotations.

As I explain in the previous chapter, geocoding allows you to take an address and turn it into a map coordinate. This enables you to add a feature to RoadTrip that allows the user to enter an address, or even just the name of a well-known landmark, and display it on the map. (Reverse geocoding, demonstrated in the previous chapter, allows you to take a map coordinate — your current location, for example — and turn it into an address.) In this chapter, you find out how to enter a location (an address or point of interest) and display it on a map as an annotation.

Setting Up the Find Controller

You already have one piece of the geocoding puzzle in place on your storyboard; I'm talking about the appropriately named Find controller. The trick now is to add the custom controller that will implement the Find features you want.

Adding the custom view controller

To add to the RoadTrip project, follow the same steps you have several times before:

1. **In the Project navigator, select the View Controller Classes group and then either right-click the selection and choose New File from the menu that appears or choose File⇨New⇨File from the main menu (or press ⌘+N).**

   Whatever method you choose, you're greeted by the New File dialog.

2. **In the left column of the dialog, select Cocoa Touch under the iOS heading, select the Objective-C class template in the top-right pane, and then click Next.**

   You'll see a dialog that will enable you to choose the options for your file.

3. **Enter FindController in the Class field, choose MapController from the Subclass Of drop-down menu (FindController is a subclass of MapController with a little more functionality), and make sure that the Target for iPad check box is selected and that With XIB for User Interface is deselected. Click Next.**

4. **In the Save sheet that appears, click Create.**

Setting up FindController in the Main_iPad File

Because FindController's user interface is identical to the Map Controller's, setting up the Find controller in the storyboard is virtually the same as setting up the Map controller in Chapter 17. You do, however, have two choices here. First, you can simply duplicate what you did in Chapter 17 to create the MapController user interface, or you can duplicate MapController in the storyboard and adjust a few values in the Identity and Attribute inspectors.

Personally, I vote for the latter, but feel free to go with the former if you feel the need. Follow these steps to do the latter — for example, duplicate the Map controller and convert the copy to a Find controller.

1. **In the Project navigator, select the iPad's Main_iPad.storyboard file and then select MapController in the MapController – Map Scene in the Document Outline. Then select the MapController scene in the actual Storyboard Canvas.**

   The Map controller on the Storyboard Canvas will be highlighted at the end of Step 1.

2. **Chose Edit⇨Copy and then Edit⇨Paste from the main menu (or press ⌘+C and then ⌘+V).**

   In Figure 19-1, I've moved the duplicate a bit off to the side so you can see it. I've also highlighted the entry for it in the Document Outline.

3. **Delete the old Find controller (I know I told you to add it, but it really was just a placeholder) by selecting it either on the Canvas or in the Document Outline and then dragging the duplicated Map to the old Find controller's place on the Canvas (see Figure 19-2).**

4. **Select the duplicated Map controller on the Canvas or in the Document Outline, open the Identity inspector by clicking its icon in the Inspector selector bar, and then select `FindController` from the Inspector Class drop-down menu, as I have in Figure 19-3.**

5. **Move to the Attributes inspector by clicking its icon in the Inspector selector bar and then enter Find in the inspector's Title field, as well as in the Identity inspector's Storyboard ID field, as shown in Figure 19-4.**

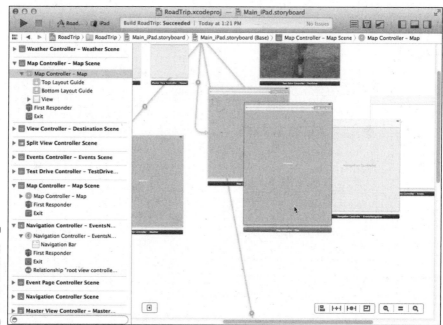

Figure 19-1: The copied and pasted Map controller.

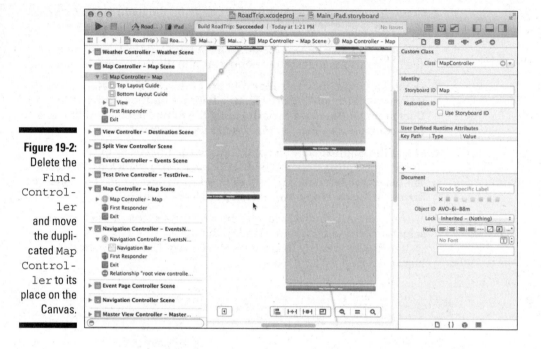

Figure 19-2:
Delete the
Find-
Control-
ler
and move
the dupli-
cated Map
Control-
ler to its
place on the
Canvas.

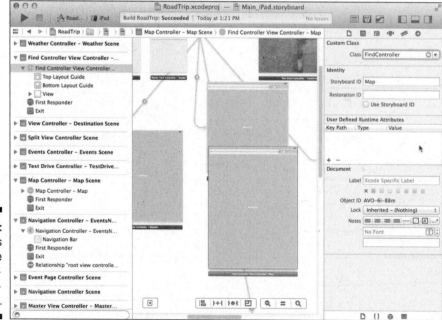

Figure 19-3:
Make this
use the
Find-
Control-
ler class.

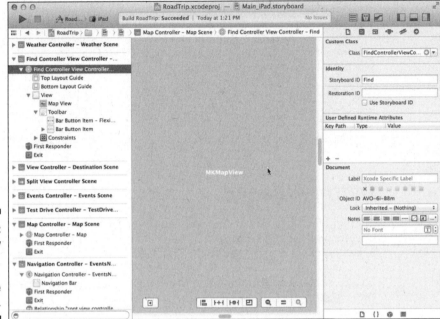

Figure 19-4:
The new
Find-
Control-
ler in the
storyboard.

You'll find that all the required connections to the MapView and toolbar outlets as well as the mapType action are (fortunately or maybe even miraculously) in place.

Implementing the Find Controller

For your geocoding functionality to work, you're going to need to do several things in the Find controller. Most of what you need to do revolves around getting the text the user enters. You'll also have to have the text geocoded and have the geocoded location implemented as an Annotation by the Trip model object, which the Find controller will then add to the map.

Adding the Map View

The Find controller is a subclass of MapController. MapController declares a MapView property for the map that you create in the storyboard. If you declare that property in MapView.h, it is inherited by FindController. However, if as you did previously, you declare it in the MapController class extension, it's not visible to FindController.

You can move the property declaration from the class extension in `Map View.m` to `MapView.h` or you can declare a new `mapView` property in `Find Controller.h`. There are pros and cons to each approach. This type of situation is common as your app evolves and you begin to subclass classes you hadn't thought of subclassing before.

Here is the line of code in question. Either add it to the `FindController` class extension or move it from `MapView.m` to `MapView.h`.

```
@property (weak, nonatomic) IBOutlet MKMapView *mapView;
```

Getting the text

In Chapter 14, you format the Find cell with a label and a Text field. In this chapter, you set things up so that the Master View controller can get the text a user enters and pass it on to the Find controller to, well, find that location.

To access the text, you first need to create an outlet for the Text field. Follow these steps:

1. **Select Main_iPad.storyboard in the Project navigator.**

2. **Select the Master View controller in the Document Outline.**

3. **Select the Assistant in the Editor selector, and if the** `MasterViewController.h` **file doesn't appear, navigate to it using the Jump bar.**

4. **In the Document Outline, open the disclosure triangle for the second Table View section in the Master View Controller – Master Scene to get to the Table View cell.**

5. **Open the Table View Cell to reveal the Content View holding the Find label and text.**

6. **Open that cell's disclosure triangle to display the Text field, and then control-drag from the No Border Style Text field to the Master View controller interface (in the Assistant editor) between the** `@interface` **and** `@end` **compiler directives, and add an outlet named** findText.

   You can see it in Figure 19-5 (actually both steps — naming the property and the finished property are shown simultaneously).

Yes, you could have dragged from the Text field in the cell on the Canvas, but in case you can't find it, this is another way to create the outlet.

A `UITextField` object is a control that displays editable text and sends a message to its delegate when the user presses the Return key. You typically use a `UITextField` object to enable the user to enter small amounts of text and then do something with it — like search for something or add a new contact.

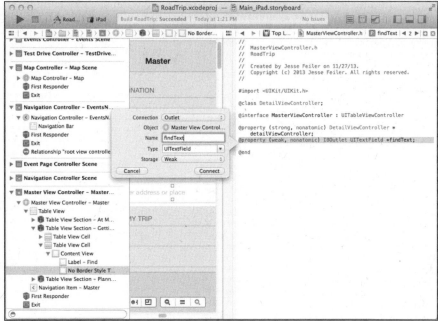

Figure 19-5:
Creating a
`textField`
outlet.

Select the Text field, select the Standard editor in the Editor selector on the Xcode toolbar, and then open the Utility area. You can set a number of Text field properties in the Attributes inspector, as you see in Figure 19-6. Here, I've selected the Appears While Editing option from the Clear Button drop-down menu, I've selected the Clear When Editing Begins check box, and I've selected Go from the Return Key drop-down menu to change what's displayed in the Return key. Go will provide a visual clue to the user on how to get RoadTrip to go find that location.

You may be thinking that, for all this to work, you'd need some kind of Target-Action design pattern that would make sure that some event gets triggered when text gets entered. Otherwise, how would you know when the user has entered some text? Also, how do you get the keyboard to show, and then hide? To answer that, I explain what happens with a `UITextField`.

When a user taps in a `UITextField`, it becomes the first responder (explained in Chapter 4), and the keyboard automatically rises to allow the user to enter text — you don't have to do a thing to make that happen. Although normally you're responsible for scrolling the view if the keyboard will cover the text field — which in this case will only happen when running the app on the iPhone — because the text field is in a Table View cell, scrolling the view is done by the Table view.

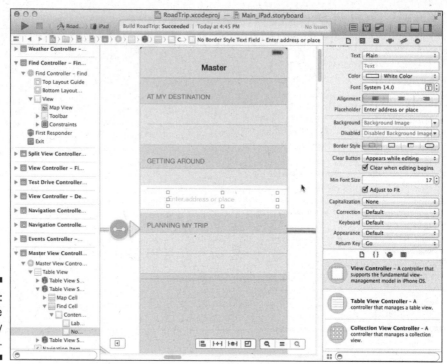

Figure 19-6:
Change the
Return key
to Go.

When the user is done entering text, he taps the Return key — the Return key whose label you managed to change to Go.

When the Go (née Return) key is tapped, the text field determines whether it has a delegate and whether the delegate has implemented a `textField ShouldReturn:` method — one of the optional `UITextFieldDelegate` protocol methods. If the delegate has done so, it sends the delegate the `textFieldShouldReturn:` message. So `textFieldShouldReturn:` is the place to capture the text.

Long story short: To capture the text and send it on to the `FindController`, you need to become the text field's delegate and implement the `textField ShouldReturn:` method. But before you do that, you need to do one more thing in Interface Builder.

You start by making the `MasterViewController` a `UITextFieldDelegate`. Update `MasterViewController.h` with the bolded code in Listing 19-1 to have it adopt the `UITextFieldDelegate` protocol.

Scrolling a view

The way to be notified that the keyboard is about to appear is to register for the `UIKeyb oardWillShowNotification`. That notification is posted by the `UIWindow` class. You pass a block object to the Notification Center and tell it to execute the block when the notification is posted. In that block, you determine the amount you'll need to scroll the view, and you scroll the view by assigning a new frame in an animation block.

Listing 19-1: Updating the MasterViewController Interface

```
#import <UIKit/UIKit.h>

@interface MasterViewController : UITableViewController

        <UITextFieldDelegate>

@property (strong, nonatomic)
        DetailViewController *detailViewController;
@property (weak, nonatomic)
    IBOutlet UITextField *findText;

@end
```

The heavy lifting will be done in the `TextField`'s `textFieldShould Return:` delegate method. The delegate will be passed the Text field being edited as an argument, and the Master View controller (the delegate) will pass that on to the Find controller.

First, you have to update the `MasterViewController` implementation by adding the bolded code in Listing 19-2 to `MasterViewController.m`.

Listing 19-2: Updating the MasterViewController Implementation

```
#import "MasterViewController.h"
#import "DetailViewController.h"
#import "AppDelegate.h"
#import "Trip.h"
#import "FindController.h"

@implementation MasterViewController
```

You'll need to make `MasterViewController` the `textField` delegate. To do that, add the code in bold in Listing 19-3 to `viewDidLoad` in `MasterViewController.m`.

Listing 19-3:   Make the MasterViewController the textField Delegate

```
- (void)viewDidLoad
{
  [super viewDidLoad];
  AppDelegate* appDelegate =
              [[UIApplication sharedApplication] delegate];
  self.title = appDelegate.trip.destinationName;
  UIImageView* imageView = [[UIImageView alloc]
      initWithImage:[appDelegate.trip destinationImage]];
  self.tableView.backgroundView = imageView;

  UISwipeGestureRecognizer *swipeGesture =
  [[UISwipeGestureRecognizer alloc] initWithTarget:self
          action:@selector(handleSwipeGesture:)];
  swipeGesture.direction =
          UISwipeGestureRecognizerDirectionLeft;
  [self.view addGestureRecognizer:swipeGesture];
  self.findText.delegate = self;
}
```

Now you can implement the `textFieldShouldReturn:` delegate method
by adding the code in Listing 19-4 to `MasterViewController.m`.

By the way, you'll notice some Live Issue errors here. You'll need to add the
`findLocation` property to the `FindController`, which you will do in the
"Finding the Location" section, later in the chapter.

Listing 19-4:   Implementing textFieldShouldReturn:

```
- (BOOL)textFieldShouldReturn:(UITextField *)textField {

  [textField resignFirstResponder];

  if ([[UIDevice currentDevice] userInterfaceIdiom] ==
          UIUserInterfaceIdiomPad){
    FindController * findController =
    [[UIStoryboard
     storyboardWithName:@"Main_iPad" bundle:nil]

        instantiateViewControllerWithIdentifier:@"Find"];
    findController.findLocation = textField.text;

    DetailViewController *currentDetailViewController;
    currentDetailViewController =
    [self.splitViewController.viewControllers lastObject];
    if (
       currentDetailViewController.masterPopoverController
          != nil)
        [currentDetailViewController.
                masterPopoverController

        dismissPopoverAnimated:YES];
```

```
      self.splitViewController.delegate = findController;
      findController.popOverButton =

            currentDetailViewController.popOverButton;
      findController.masterPopoverController =
          currentDetailViewController.

            masterPopoverController;

      NSMutableArray* controllers =
        [NSMutableArray arrayWithObjects:
          (self.splitViewController.viewControllers)[0],
              findController, nil];
      self.splitViewController.viewControllers =

            controllers;

   }
   else {
      FindController *findController =
        [[UIStoryboard
          storyboardWithName:@"Main_iPhone"

            bundle:nil]

            instantiateViewControllerWithIdentifier:@"Find"
            ];
      findController.findLocation = textField.text;
      [self.navigationController
            pushViewController:findController animated:YES];
   }
   return YES;
}
```

The first thing Listing 19-4 does for you is to send a message to the Text field asking it to resign as first responder:

```
[textField resignFirstResponder];
```

This has the side effect of dismissing the keyboard.

What you do next is another case where what happens depends on whether your app is running on an iPad or iPhone.

If you're running on an iPad, you instantiate FindController from Main_iPad. storyboard, just as you instantiate the Event Page controller in Chapter 16.

```
FindController * findController =
  [[UIStoryboard storyboardWithName:
      @"Main_iPad" bundle:nil]

        instantiateViewControllerWithIdentifier:@"Find"];
```

You then assign the text from `textField` to the `FindController` `find Location` property (which you'll add shortly to the `FindController`).

```
findController.findLocation = textField.text;
```

You then dismiss the popover if it's present.

```
DetailViewController *currentDetailViewController;
    currentDetailViewController =
    [self.splitViewController.viewControllers lastObject];
if (currentDetailViewController.masterPopoverController
                                                    != nil)
  [currentDetailViewController.
                    masterPopoverController

        dismissPopoverAnimated:YES];
```

Then you assign the `popOverButton` and `masterPopoverController` properties and make `FindController` the Split View controller delegate.

```
self.splitViewController.delegate = findController;
    findController.popOverButton =

                currentDetailViewController.popOverButton;
    findController.masterPopoverController =
        currentDetailViewController.

        masterPopoverController;
```

Then you simply make `FindController` the new Detail View controller in the Split View controller's `viewControllers` property.

```
NSMutableArray* controllers =
    [NSMutableArray arrayWithObjects:
        (self.splitViewController.viewControllers)[0],
                findController, nil];
self.splitViewController.viewControllers = controllers;
```

Note that if it's an iPhone you're dealing with, you instantiate the `Find Controller`, assign the `findLocation` property, and push it on the Navigation controller stack, which causes the view to slide into place.

```
FindController *findController =
  [[UIStoryboardstoryboardWithName:
    @"Main_iPhone" bundle:nil]

        instantiateViewControllerWithIdentifier:@"Find"];
    findController.findLocation = textField.text;
    [self.navigationController
        pushViewController:findController animated:YES];
```

You finally return YES to have the Text field implement its default behavior for the Go-Key-Formerly-Known-As-Return.

If you look back to Chapter 13, this is pretty much the same logic you added to prepareForSegue:sender:. As an exercise, you might want to create a new method that includes the common code.

Disabling cell highlighting

You do have a problem, though. If the user touches outside the label, the cell is automatically highlighted when selected, and it stays selected. The solution is to disable the blue highlight when a cell is selected. To do that, you'll need to do the following:

1. **Select the Main_iPad.storyboard in the Project navigator.**

2. **Select the Master View controller in the Document Outline, open all the disclosure triangles, and select the No Border Style Table View Cell for Find.**

3. **In the Table View Cell section of the Attributes inspector, choose None from the Selection pop-up menu.**

Now you're ready to add the FindController methods.

Finding the Location

In Listing 19-3, you assigned the text that the user entered into the Text field to a FindController property. Now you need to update the FindController interface to declare the property by adding the bolded code in Listing 19-5.

Listing 19-5: Updating the FindController Interface

```
#import "MapController.h"

@interface FindController : MapController

@property (strong, nonatomic) NSString *findLocation;

@end
```

Next, add the bolded code in Listing 19-6 to the FindController.m file to synthesize it and import the header files of the classes you'll use.

Listing 19-6:   Updating the FindController Implementation

```
#import "FindController.h"
#import "AppDelegate.h"
#import "Trip.h"
#import "Annotation.h"


@implementation FindController
```

In my discussion of geocoding in Chapter 18, I point out that `MapController` sends the `CLGeocoder` the `reverseGeocodeLocation:` message to convert a coordinate to an address. The idea now is for you to send the `geocode AddressString:` message to convert an address or point of interest into a coordinate.

This time, however, you go about it in a very interesting way. When the user enters a location she wants to find, you want to create an annotation for that found location and display it on the map. The problem here is that you really don't want the `FindController` (or any other controller) to start creating annotations — that's the `Trip` model's job.

Instead, based on the principles of encapsulation and loose coupling, you'll have the `Trip` object add the found location as additional model data. Therefore, you want the `Trip` object to create the `Annotation` object and send it to the `FindController` to add as a Map annotation.

Although you could create view controller methods to be used by the `Trip` object to add the annotation, a more interesting (and better) way is to use the block design pattern. Blocks actually can make your code less complex, and here's an opportunity for you to see why.

Add the code in bold in Listing 19-7 to `viewDidLoad` in `FindController.m`.

Listing 19-7:   Updating viewDidLoad

```
- (void)viewDidLoad
{
  [super viewDidLoad];
  self.title = self.findLocation;

  void (^addFindLocationCompletionHandler)
    (Annotation *, NSError *) = ^(Annotation *annotation,
                                          NSError *error){
     if (error!= nil || annotation == nil) {
       NSLog(@"Geocoder Failure! Error code: %u,
         description: %@, and reason: %@", error.code,
```

```
                    [error localizedDescription],
                                [error localizedFailureReason]);
      }
      else {
        MKCoordinateRegion region;
        region.center.latitude =

            annotation.coordinate.latitude;
        region.center.longitude =

            annotation.coordinate.longitude;
        region.span.latitudeDelta = .05;
        region.span.longitudeDelta = .05;
        [self.mapView setRegion:region animated:NO];
        [self.mapView addAnnotation:annotation];
      }
    };
    AppDelegate *appDelegate =
                [[UIApplication sharedApplication] delegate];
    [appDelegate.trip addLocation:self.findLocation

        completionHandler:addFindLocationCompletionHandler];
}
```

You get a compiler error when adding this code, but you fix that by declaring the completion handler method in the Trip interface, which is covered in the following section.

You set the title to the string the user entered:

```
    self.title = self.findLocation;
```

You then send the Trip object the addLocation:completionHandler: message. The completion handler is the block you declared. It's defined in Trip, as you'll see, as

```
 (void (^) (Annotation *annotation, NSError* error))
```

That's a block that has no return value and two parameters, an Annotation and an NSError. The block's logic is actually quite straightforward. First, you check for an error:

```
if (error!= nil || annotation == nil) {

  NSLog(@"Geocoder Failure! Error code: %u, description:
    %@, and reason: %@", error.code,
      [error localizedDescription],
                        [error localizedFailureReason]);
}
```

You're passed in an `Annotation` (which will be created in the `Trip` method `addLocation:completionHandler:`), which conforms to the `MKAnnotation` protocol, and you set the region based on the annotation's coordinates:

```
MKCoordinateRegion region;
region.center.latitude = annotation.coordinate.latitude;
region.center.longitude = annotation.coordinate.longitude;
region.span.latitudeDelta = .05;
region.span.longitudeDelta = .05;
[mapView setRegion:region animated:NO];
```

Next, you add the annotation to the map:

```
[mapView addAnnotation:annotation];
```

`addAnnotation:` is an `MKMapView` method that adds an object that conforms to the `MKAnnotation` protocol to the map. This is similar to what you did in `MapController` when you sent the `addAnnotations:` message to add an array of annotations. Doing this, as you see on the map, is additive; that is, adding a new annotation doesn't replace the array you added in `MapController`.

Next, you add the `addLocation:completionHandler:` method (the one that will create the `Annotation`) to `Trip.m`. But first, you need to update the `Trip.m` implementation, so add the bolded code in Listing 19-8 to `Trip.h`.

Listing 19-8: Updating the Trip Interface

```
#import <Foundation/Foundation.h>
#import <MapKit/MapKit.h>
@class Annotation;

@interface Trip : NSObject

- (UIImage *) destinationImage;
- (NSString *) destinationName;
- (CLLocationCoordinate2D) destinationCoordinate;
- (id)initWithDestinationIndex:(int)destinationIndex;
- (NSString *)weather;
- (int)numberOfEvents;
- (NSString *)getEvent:(int)index;
- (NSArray *)createAnnotations;
- (NSString *)mapTitle;
- (void)addLocation:(NSString *)findLocation
     completionHandler:
       (void (^)(Annotation *annotation, NSError* error))

          completion;
@end
```

This code adds the `addLocation:completionHandler:` method declaration, and because one of its parameters is an `Annotation`, you need to add the `@class` statement as well.

`void (^foundLocationCompletionHandler) (Annotation *annotation, NSError* error);` is a type just like `int` or `Find Controller`. It's a block object with the name of `foundLocation CompletionHandler` that has no return value and two parameters: `Annotation` and `NSError`.

I'm going to save `FindController`'s completion block in the `foundLocation CompletionHandler` instance variable. I really don't need to, because, as you'll see, the `addLocation:completionHandler:` has access to it as a parameter. I did it this way to show you how to do that. It took me some time to really get my head around blocks and passing them as parameters, and I wanted to show you how easy it is after you see how it's done. You can use this example as a model for your own apps. I know that it may seem a bit overwhelming now, but I promise you that you'll find yourself using blocks in this way (as I do) as you gain more experience in your own app development.

Add the `foundLocationCompletionHandler` instance variable to `Trip.m` by adding the code in bold in Listing 19-9. Note that because the block is assigned to an instance variable, it goes in brackets at the top of the class extension.

Listing 19-9:   Updating the Trip Implementation

```
#import "Trip.h"
#import "Destination.h"
#import "Events.h"
#import "Annotation.h"


@interface Trip () {  void
          (^foundLocationCompletionHandler)
              (Annotation *annotation, NSError* error);
}

@property (strong, nonatomic) NSDictionary
          *destinationData;
@property (strong, nonatomic) Destination *destination;
@property (strong, nonatomic) Events *events;
@property (strong, nonatomic) NSMutableArray *pois;

}
```

Next, add the `addLocation:completionHandler:` in Listing 19-10 to `Trip.m`.

Listing 19-10:   Adding the addLocation:completionHandler: Method

```
- (void)addLocation:(NSString *)findLocation
                                    completionHandler:
    (void (^)(Annotation *annotation, NSError* error))
                                              completion
        {

  void (^clGeocodeCompletionHandler)(NSArray *, NSError *)
        = ^(NSArray *placemarks, NSError *error){
CLPlacemark *placemark = placemarks[0];
    Annotation *foundAnnotation;
    if (error!= nil || placemark == nil) {
      NSLog(@"Geocoder Failure! Error code: %u",
          error.code);
    }
    else {
      foundAnnotation = [[Annotation alloc]init];
      foundAnnotation.coordinate =

        placemark.location.coordinate;
      foundAnnotation.subtitle =
        [NSString stringWithFormat:@" Lat:%f Lon:%f",
          placemark.location.coordinate.latitude,

          placemark.location.coordinate.longitude];
if (placemark.areasOfInterest[0]) {
        foundAnnotation.title =
            placemark.areasOfInterest[0];
      }
      else {
        if (placemark.thoroughfare) {
          foundAnnotation.title =
            [NSString stringWithFormat:@"%@ %@",
              placemark.subThoroughfare,

          placemark.thoroughfare];
        }
        else {
          if (placemark.locality ) {
            foundAnnotation.title = placemark.locality;
          }
          else
            foundAnnotation.title =
                                    @"Your location";
        }
      }

    }
    foundLocationCompletionHandler(
                              foundAnnotation, error);
  };
```

```
    foundLocationCompletionHandler = completion;
    CLGeocoder* geocoder = [[CLGeocoder alloc] init];
      [geocoder geocodeAddressString:findLocation

          completionHandler:clGeocodeCompletionHandler];
}
```

First (skipping past the block declarations to the bottom of the method for a moment), you save a reference to the block that was sent as a parameter:

```
foundLocationCompletionHandler = completion;
```

You really don't need to save a reference to the block here, but I want to illustrate that blocks are treated like any other variable.

Then you allocate and initialize CLGeocoder just as you do in Chapter 18:

```
CLGeocoder* geocoder = [[CLGeocoder alloc] init];
    [geocoder geocodeAddressString:findLocation
            completionHandler:clGeocodeCompletionHandler];
```

This time, however, you send the geocodeAddressString:completion Handler: message after you initialize the CLGeocoder (rather than the reverseGeocodeLocation:location completionHandler: message you sent in Chapter 18).

This message submits a forward-geocoding request using the text the user entered and describes the location you want to look up. For example, you could specify the string "1 Infinite Loop, Cupertino, CA" to locate Apple headquarters.

In the completion block, you check for a successful completion and then create a new Annotation. When you're done, you call the completion block that the FindController sent you, using the block you had assigned to the foundLocationCompletionHandler variable earlier:

```
foundLocationCompletionHandler(foundAnnotation, error);
```

Finally, if you decide that you don't want the destination and the point of interest annotations you display in the MapController displayed, just override the method that adds the annotations in the MapController superclass:

```
- (void) addAnnotations {
}
```

Making the Map Title the Found Location

In Chapter 17, I show you how to add the map title to the toolbar. In that discussion, I add a method named `mapTitle`, which in the case of the `MapController`, sends a message to the `Trip` object to get the map's title. In the case of the `FindController`, I want to use the text the user entered as the title, so all I do is override `mapTitle`. Add the code in Listing 19-11 to `FindController.m` to display the title as the found location.

Listing 19-11:   Override mapTitle

```
- (NSString *)mapTitle {

    return  self.findLocation;
}
```

If you build and run RoadTrip, and enter **Radio City Music Hall** in the Find field in the Master view and tap the annotation, you should see the screen displayed in Figure 19-7. (Notice I did not go down the road of displaying the Destination and the Point of Interest annotations, but even if you did, you'd still see the Radio City Music Hall annotation.)

Figure 19-7:
Radio City
Music Hall
annotation.

If you wanted to, you could even create a `typedef` for the `addLocation:comp letionHandler:`. The purpose of `typedef` is to assign another name to a type whose declaration is unwieldy. You'd want to use a `typedef` if you were going to have to type `void (^foundLocationCompletionHandler) (Annotation *annotation, NSError* error);` more than once. And while that is not true for RoadTrip, I wanted to show you how to create a `typedef` for a block that you could use in your own projects. Type the following code:

```
typedef void (^addLocationCompletionHandler)
              (Annotation *annotation, NSError* error);
```

Add the instance variable as

```
addLocationCompletionHandler
              addFindLocationCompletionHandler;
```

and then save the block in the new instance variable

```
addFindLocationCompletionHandler = completion;
```

and (finally) call the block in this way instead:

```
addFindLocationCompletionHandler(foundAnnotation, error);
```

Adding the FindController to the iPhone Storyboard

The iPhone storyboard, fortunately, uses the same Objective-C `Find Controller` class that you just defined for the iPad storyboard. But you still have some work to do because you need to add a `FindController` scene to your iPhone storyboard.

One approach is to copy the Find scene from the iPad storyboard file and paste it into the iPhone storyboard file. This will work, but the iPad version has the Toolbar at the top of the view, which is the right answer for the iPad but not for the iPhone.

You should rearrange the view elements in the iPhone version by dragging the toolbar to the bottom of the view and moving the Map view to the top of the enclosing view. Be sure to adjust the location of the iPhone toolbar in the Attributes inspector, as shown in Figure 19-8. You may also need to connect the Master View Controller as the delegate of the text field in the iPhone storyboard.

The Find operation in the iPhone is shown in Figure 19-9.

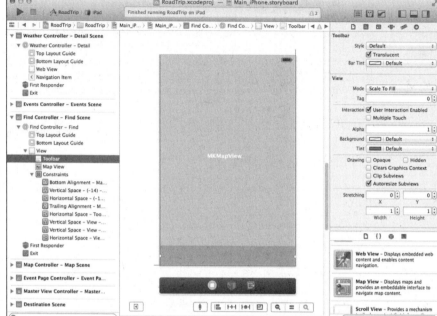

Figure 19-8:
Adjusting
the tool-
bar in the
Find-
Control-
ler scene
in the
iPhone
storyboard.

Figure 19-9:
The Find
function on
the iPhone.

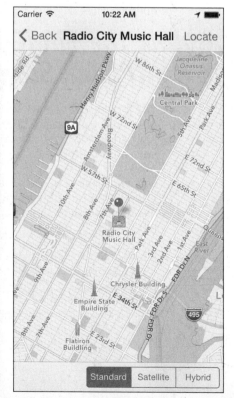

Chapter 20

Selecting a Destination

In This Chapter
▶ Finding an address for a map coordinate and displaying it on the map
▶ Finding the map coordinate from an address and displaying it on the map

*I*n this chapter, you are down to the final parts needed for the RoadTrip app to be complete. Back in Chapter 11, you added multiple destinations to the Destinations.plist, and now it would be nice if the user could select any of the ones you added.

Providing the user with the ability to select a destination is what you implement in this chapter. You also discover more about Table views along the way. I also show you how to work with modal controllers (which present views that require the user to do something) by creating your own protocol.

The Plan

You're going to add a new view controller that manages a modal Table view that allows the user to select a destination — such as New York or San Francisco. Figure 20-1 shows the results for both the iPad and iPhone.

Figure 20-1:
The
Destinations
modal Table
view on
both the
iPad and
iPhone.

Setting Up the DestinationController for the iPad Storyboard

If you've followed along throughout this book, by now you should know the drill. As you might expect, you need a view controller to implement the Selecting a Destination interface.

Adding the custom view controller

Follow these steps to add a new Objective-C `DestinationController` class to the RoadTrip project.

1. **In the Project navigator, select the View Controller Classes group and then either right-click the selection and choose New File from the menu that appears or choose File⇨New⇨File from the main menu (or press ⌘+N).**

   Whatever method you choose, you're greeted by the New File dialog.

2. **In the left column of the dialog, select Cocoa Touch under the iOS heading, select the Objective-C class template in the top-right pane, and then click Next.**

   You'll see a dialog that will enable you to choose the options for your file.

3. **Enter** `DestinationController` **in the Class field, enter or choose UIViewController from the Subclass Of drop-down menu, make sure that the Target for iPad check box is selected and that With XIB for User Interface is deselected, and then click Next.**

4. **In the Save sheet that appears, click Create.**

The Destination controller will be using a Table view, but it won't use a Table View Controller class. That's because I show you how to use a Table view with dynamically generated cells (as well as cell selection handled by the controller) as only one element in the view. This is a handy thing to know if you want to take advantage of the power of a Table view without letting a Table view take over the entire screen.

Setting up the DestinationController in the Main_iPad.storyboard

Now that you have a custom view controller, you need to tell the storyboard to load your custom view controller rather than a `UIViewController`. Follow these steps:

1. **In the Project navigator, select the Main_iPad.storyboard file, and in the Document Outline, select View Controller in the View Controller – Destination Scene.**

2. **Open the Identity inspector in the Utility area using the Inspector selector bar and then choose DestinationController from the Custom Class section's Class drop-down menu.**

   Now when Destination is selected in the Master View controller, `DestinationController` will be instantiated and initialized and will receive events from the user and connect the view to the `Trip` model.

   In Chapter 14, you left this segue style as modal, and I said I would explain a little more about that in Chapter 20. Well, here we are.

3. **Select the segue to the Destination controller on the Canvas.**

4. **Select the Attributes inspector for the Inspector selector bar.**

   A modal dialog requires the user to do something (tap a Table View cell or the Cancel button, for example) before returning to the app.

   When you have a modal segue, you can choose a transition style.

5. **Choose Flip Horizontal in the Transition pop-up menu in the Attributes inspector for the segue.**

   Actually, you can select whatever transition you'd like, but I'd go for Flip Horizontal.

Make sure that Form Sheet is selected in the Presentation pop-up menus. The Presentation choices include

- ✔ **Full Screen:** The modal view covers the screen.
- ✔ **Page Sheet:** The height and width are set to the height and width of the screen in Portrait orientation, with the background view dimmed.
- ✔ **Form Sheet:** The width and height of the modal view are smaller than those of the screen, with the modal view centered on the screen and the background view dimmed.
- ✔ **Current Context:** The modal view is the same style as its presenting view controller. But if the presenting view controller is in a popover, you can use this presentation style only when the transition style is `UIModal TransitionStyleCoverVertical`. If not, you'll get an exception.

After you have the Presentation and the Transition selected in the Attributes inspector, you can get on with formatting the Destination Controller view, which will have a Table view, a Label view, and a very spiffy image as well after you follow these steps:

1. **Select the Destination controller in the storyboard Canvas and then drag in a Navigation bar from the Library.**

   You're going to need someplace to put the Cancel button. Place the Navigation bar at the top of the view.

2. **In the Navigation bar on the Canvas, select the Title (field). Still in the Attributes inspector, enter** Destinations **in the Title field for the selected element (Navigation bar, in this case).**

3. **Drag a Bar Button item from the Library and place it on the left side of the Navigation bar on the Canvas.**

4. **Choose Cancel from the Identifier drop-down menu in the Bar Button section of the Attributes Inspector.**

   You'll use this button to cancel selecting a new destination.

   You don't have to select a tint for the button in the Bar Button Tint section of the Attributes inspector. The app-wide tint color will be used for the button.

5. **Drag an Image view from the Library in the Utility area and place it in the Destination controller on the Canvas so that it takes up the entire view.**

6. **Control-drag from the Image view in the Canvas or the Document Outline to the Top Layout Guide in the Document Outline and select Vertical Spacing.**

7. **With the Image view selected, choose Editor➪Resolve Auto Layout Issues➪Add Missing Constraints.**

If you have any warnings, use Editor⇨Resolve Auto Layout Issues subcommands to fix them. You may need to use Editor⇨Resolve Auto Layout Issues⇨Clear Constraints if you have to start over.

8. **In the Image View section of the Attributes inspector, select Destination Image from the Image drop-down menu.**

   The appropriate image from the asset catalog will be used automatically. You downloaded those images in Chapter 3.

9. **Drag a Label from the Library and add it to the view toward the top of the Image view.**

10. **With the Label selected, enter** Pick a place **in the Text field in the Label section of the Attributes inspector.**

11. **Still in the Attributes inspector, change the style to Text Styles – Headline by selecting the Text icon in the Font field (which opens a window in which you can change the font size) as shown in Figure 20-2.**

12. **Select the label and then choose Editor⇨Size Fit to Content from the Xcode main menu.**

    The label will expand to fit the text.

13. **Change the text color to white in the Text Color drop-down menu.**

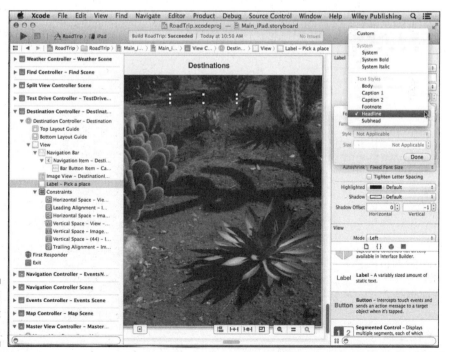

Figure 20-2:
Set the text style.

14. **Position the *Pick a place* label, as shown in Figure 20-3.**

    A word of warning: You need to follow the next set of steps exactly. You can get the look you want in other ways, but this is the most straightforward. The Table view won't be transparent; you'll fix that in `viewDidLoad` in the "Creating the Table View" section, later in the chapter.

15. **Drag a Table view (not Table View controller) from the Library onto the Image view and position it as shown in Figure 20-4.**

    This is the area in which the Table view will display. If you have more selections than can fit in the visible area, the user will be able to scroll the Table view.

16. **With the Table view selected, scroll down the Attributes inspector to reach the View section and then select Clear Color from the Background drop-down menu.**

17. **Still in the Attributes inspector, scroll back up to the Table View section and choose Grouped from the Style menu.**

18. **Enter 1 in the Prototype Cells field (or just use the stepper control to get to 1).**

    Leave these as prototype cells because you'll provide the content for the cells programmatically.

Figure 20-3:
Set the color.

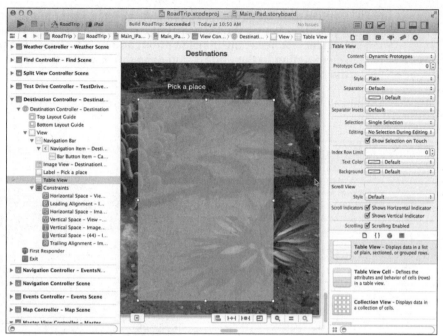

Figure 20-4:
Add a Table
view.

19. **Select the prototype Table View Cell, either on the Canvas or in the Document Outline, and then choose Basic from the inspector's Style menu and enter** DestinationCell **in the Identifier field.**

    You will need to have a reuse identifier (which I explain in the section "Displaying the cell," later in this chapter).

20. **Still in the Attributes inspector, scroll down to the View section and select Clear Color from the Background drop-down menu.**

21. **Select the Table View cell in the Document Outline, open the disclosure triangle, and select the label.**

22. **In the Attributes inspector, scroll down and then choose Clear Color from the Background drop-down menu.**

23. **Close the Utility area and select the Assistant in the Editor selector.**

24. **If the** DestinationController.h **file doesn't appear, select it in the Jump bar.**

25. **Control-drag from the Table view in Document Outline or on the Canvas to the** DestinationController.h **Interface. Release the mouse button, and in the dialog that pops up, enter outlet and** destinationTableView.

26. **Control-drag from the Cancel button in Document Outline or in the Navigation bar on the Canvas to the** `DestinationController.h` **Interface. Release the mouse button, and in the dialog that pops up, select Action in the Connection drop-down menu and enter** cancel **in the Name field.**

When all is said and done, you should see a screen that looks like Figure 20-5.

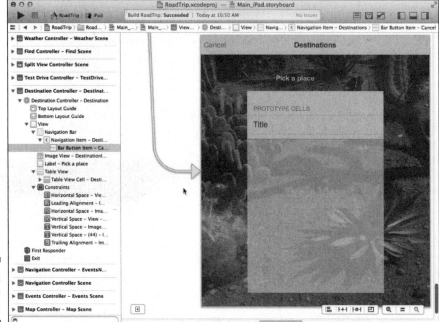

Figure 20-5:
Ready to
code.

Adding a Modal View

Most of the time, the user can control what is happening in the app. You provide the buttons and other interface elements, but the user chooses what to do and what interface elements to tap. Modal views interrupt that user control. They are presented on the screen and, although the user can tap within them, they remain front and center until the user dismisses them. They are used when you want the user to do something or resolve an issue before continuing to use the rest of the app. The device is not locked up because the user can use the Home button to move to another app, but as far as your app is concerned, it's frozen until the modal view is dismissed.

The most common way to manage Modal views is by creating an Objective-C *protocol* that's adopted by the controller presenting the Modal view. The Modal view, when the user has selected an action or Cancel, sends a message to the presenting controller's delegate method. The requesting controller then dismisses the Modal controller. Using this approach means that before it dismisses the Modal controller, the presenting controller can get any data it needs from it. That is the pattern that you will implement here.

You start implementing the Modal view by declaring the protocol and a few other properties you'll need, as well as the protocols the `DestinationController` needs to adopt.

To get things started, add the bolded code in Listing 20-1 to `Destination Controller.h`.

Listing 20-1: Updating the Destination Interface

```
#import <UIKit/UIKit.h>
@protocol DestinationControllerDelegate;

@interface DestinationController : UIViewController
            <UITableViewDelegate, UITableViewDataSource>

@property (weak, nonatomic) IBOutlet UITableView
          *destinationTableView;
@property (strong, nonatomic) id
                  <DestinationControllerDelegate> delegate;
@property (nonatomic, readonly) NSUInteger
          selectedDestination;
- (IBAction)cancel:(id)sender;
@end

@protocol DestinationControllerDelegate
@required
- (void)destinationController:
    (DestinationController *)controller
                            didFinishWithSave:(BOOL)save;
@end
```

The Objective-C language provides a way to formally declare a list of methods (including declared properties) as a protocol. You've used framework-supplied protocols extensively in this book, and now you're defining your own protocol.

You declare formal protocols with the `@protocol` directive. In Listing 20-1, you declared a `DestinationControllerDelegate` protocol with one method, `destinationController:didFinishWithSave:`, which is *required*. Required is the default; if you wanted to declare optional methods, you would use the keyword `@optional`, and all methods following that keyword would be optional. For example, consider this:

```
@protocol SimpleDelegate
@optional
- (void)doNothing;
@end
```

You can have both @required and @optional methods in a protocol. It is common to group them together, but you can intersperse them if you want.

If neither @required or @optional is specified, @required is assumed. However, it is better to be specific about what is required and what is optional. The @protocol DestinationControllerDelegate: statement (at the top) tells the compiler that a protocol is on the way. Like the @class statement, it says, "Trust me, you'll find the protocol." You need this here only because you added this:

```
@property (strong, nonatomic) id
                <DestinationControllerDelegate> delegate;
```

This statement tells the compiler to type check whatever it is you assign to delegate to make sure that it implements the DestinationController Delegate protocol.

You also added the selectedDestination property, which you'll use in the ViewController to determine which destination the user selected. Notice that you have made it read-only because there is no reason for any other object to be able to set it.

You also adopted two protocols from the Cocoa Touch framework, UITable ViewDelegate and UITableViewDataSource, which you'll use to manage the Table view.

Next, you're going to need to update the DestinationController implementation in Listing 20-2 with the bolded code for some header files you'll need to use later.

Listing 20-2: Updating the DestinationController Implementation

```
#import "DestinationController.h"
#import "DetailViewController.h"
#import "AppDelegate.h"

@interface DestinationController ()
@end

@implementation DestinationController
```

Now that you have the plumbing in, you can look at what will go on in the DestinationController.

Implementing a Table View

The functionality in the `DestinationController` is in the Table view. You've worked with Table views before — but those used *static* cells, and all the work was done in the storyboard. Now it's time to branch out on your own and understand what the storyboard was doing for you behind the scenes, as it were.

It's a good thing to know how Table views work, because Table views are front and center in many apps that come with the iOS devices out of the box; they play a major role in many of the apps that you can download from the App Store. (Obvious examples: Almost all the views in the Settings, Mail, Music, and Contacts apps are Table views.) Table views take on such a significant role because, in addition to displaying data, they can also serve as a way to navigate structured data.

If you take a look at an app such as Mail or Settings, you find that Table views present a scrollable list of *items* (or *rows* or *entries* — I use all three terms interchangeably) that may be divided into *sections*. A row can display text or images. It may have an *accessory* such as a disclosure triangle, so that when you select a row, you may be presented with another Table view or with some other view that may display a web page or even controls such as buttons and Text fields. (You can see an illustration of this diversity back in Chapter 4, where Figure 4-6 shows how selecting Map leads to a Map view displaying a map of San Francisco, which is very handy when you roll into town.)

It's worth noting that iOS Table views only provide a single column of data — not the two-dimensional tables that you might build in a Numbers spreadsheet. The OS X Cocoa framework does provide a multi-column `NSTableView` class, but the IOS `UITableView` only supports a single column.

To kick off the Table view creation process, you first need to decide what you want to have happen when the user selects a particular row in the Table view of your app. As you saw with static cells, you can have virtually anything happen. You can display a Web view as you do in Weather or even display another Table view.

In this case, however, the Destination View controller will be dismissed, and the user will find herself in the master view, ready to make another selection.

A Table view is an instance of the class `UITableView`, where each visible row of the table uses a `UITableViewCell` to draw its contents. Think of a *Table view* as the object that creates and manages the table structure, and the *Table View cell* as being responsible for displaying the content of a single cell of the table.

Creating the Table View

Although powerful, Table views are surprisingly easy to work with. To create a Table view, you follow only four — count 'em, four — steps, in the following order:

1. **Create and format the view itself.**

    This includes specifying the Table style and a few other parameters, most of which you do in Interface Builder.

2. **Specify the Table view configuration.**

    Not too complicated, actually. You let `UITableView` know how many sections you want, how many rows you want in each section, and what you want to call your section headers. You do that with the help of the `numberOfSectionsInTableView:`, `tableView:numberOfRowsIn Section:`, and `tableView:titleForHeaderInSection:` methods, respectively.

3. **Supply the text (or graphic) for each row.**

    You return that from the implementation of the `tableView:cellForRow AtIndexPath:` method. This message is sent for each visible row in the Table view, and you return a Table View cell to display the text or graphic.

4. **Respond to a user selection of the row.**

    You use the `tableView:didSelectRowAtIndexPath:` method to take care of this task. In this method, you can create a view controller and push it onto the stack (as the storyboard does in a segue), or you can even send a message to the controller that presented a Modal View controller (or any other object).

A `UITableView` object must have a data source and a delegate:

- ✔ The **data source** supplies the content for the Table view.
- ✔ The **delegate** manages the appearance and behavior of the Table view.

The data source adopts the `UITableViewDataSource` protocol, and the delegate adopts the `UITableViewDelegate` protocol — no surprises there. Of the preceding methods, only `tableView:didSelectRowAtIndexPath:` is included in the `UITableViewDelegate` protocol. All the other methods that I list earlier are included in the `UITableViewDataSource` protocol.

The data source and the delegate are often (but not necessarily) implemented in the same object, which is often a subclass of `UITableViewController`. `UITableViewController` adopts the necessary protocols and even furnishes some method stubs for you. In this case, the Table view is just another object in the `DestinationController` view. I had you do that when creating

DestinationController earlier in the chapter so I could explain the real guts of Table views and because I wanted you to be able to display that Pick a Place label.

There's another way to display a label such as Pick a Place using a UITable ViewController. UITableView has a tableHeaderView property which is a view. You could create a view with the label, one or more images, and maybe another label and then assign that view to tableHeaderView in a UITableView either standing alone as is the case here or situated within a UITableViewController.

Implementing these five (count 'em, five) methods (in the four steps earlier) is all you need to do to implement a Table view.

Not bad.

I already had you adopt the Table View delegate and Data Source protocols in Listing 20-1, so you are already partway there.

Add the bolded code in Listing 20-3 to the DestinationController.m file's viewDidLoad method.

Listing 20-3:   Updating viewDidLoad

```
- (void)viewDidLoad
{
  [super viewDidLoad];
  self.destinationTableView.delegate = self;
  self.destinationTableView.dataSource = self;
}
```

As you might surmise, this makes the DestinationController both the delegate and the data source.

Adding sections

In a grouped Table view, each group is referred to as a *section*.

The two methods you need to implement to start things off are as follows:

```
numberOfSectionsInTableView:(UITableView *)tableView

tableView:(UITableView *)tableView
            numberOfRowsInSection:(NSInteger)section
```

Each of these methods returns an integer, and that integer tells the Table view something — the number of sections and the number of rows in a given section, respectively.

Add the methods in Listing 20-4 to `DestinationController.m` to create a Table view that has one section with the number of rows equal to the number of destinations you have in your `Destinations.plist`. You will get compiler errors that you will fix with code in the next Listing.

Listing 20-4:   Implementing numberOfSectionsInTableView: and tableView:numberOfRowsInSection:

```
- (NSInteger)numberOfSectionsInTableView:
                                (UITableView *)tableView {
  return 1;
}

- (NSInteger)tableView:(UITableView *)tableView
            numberOfRowsInSection:(NSInteger)section {

  NSString *filePath = [[NSBundle mainBundle]
        pathForResource:@"Destinations" ofType:@"plist"];
NSDictionary *destinations =
    [NSDictionary dictionaryWithContentsOfFile: filePath];
  self.destinationsArray = destinations[@"DestinationData"];
  return [destinationsArray count];
}
```

The `numberOfSectionsInTableView:` method is obvious. In the `table View:numberOfRowsInSection:` method, you do what you did in both the `Trip` and `Events` classes — you access `Destination.plist` to extract what you need. In this case, it's the `DestinationData` array, which, to refresh your memory, is an array of dictionaries that have the data for each destination and return the count.

Keep in mind that the first section is zero, as is the first row. This means, of course, that whenever you want to use an index to get to the first row or section, you need to use 0, not 1 — and an index of 1 for the second row and so on.

You'll get an Xcode Live Issue error here because you need to add the new `destinationsArray` property (you'll use this same array later in `table View:cellForRowAtIndexPath:`). In addition, remember that you declared the `selectedDestination` property in `DestinationController.h` as `readonly`. That is fine for the public interface, but you need to be able to set it from within `DestinationController.m`. You can do that by overriding the public property. (This is a very common pattern for a property — `readonly` to the public but `readwrite` within the implementation of the class that declares it.)

To do those things, add the bolded code in Listing 20-5 to `Destination Controller.m`.

Listing 20-5: Updating the DestinationController Implementation

```
#import "DestinationController.h"

@interface DestinationController ()
  @property (strong, nonatomic)
    NSArray *destinationsArray;
  @property (nonatomic, readwrite)
    NSUInteger selectedDestination;

@end
```

Displaying the cell

To display the cell content, your delegate is sent the `tableView:cellFor RowAtIndexPath:` message. Add this method in Listing 20-6 to `DestinationController.m`.

Listing 20-6: Implementing tableView:cellForRowAtIndexPath:

```
- (UITableViewCell *)tableView:(UITableView *)tableView
        cellForRowAtIndexPath:(NSIndexPath *)indexPath {

  static NSString *CellIdentifier = @"DestinationCell";
  UITableViewCell *cell = [tableView
      dequeueReusableCellWithIdentifier:CellIdentifier];
  NSDictionary * destinationData = self.destinationsArray
        [indexPath.row];

  NSAttributedString *attributedString =
        [[NSAttributedString alloc]

        initWithString:destinationData[@"Destination
        Name"]

        attributes:@{ NSFontAttributeName : [UIFont
        systemFontOfSize:17.0f],

        NSForegroundColorAttributeName:  [UIColor
        whiteColor]}];
  cell.textLabel.attributedText = attributedString;
  return cell;
}
```

Walking through Listing 20-6, you see that one of the first things you do is determine whether any cells that you can use are lying around. You may remember that although a Table view can display quite a few rows at a time on the iPad's screen, the table itself can conceivably hold a lot more. A large table can eat up a lot of memory, however, if you create cells for every row. Fortunately, Table views are designed to *reuse* cells. As a Table view's cells scroll off the screen, they're placed in a queue of cells available to be reused.

If the system runs low on memory, the Table view gets rid of the cells in the queue, but as long as it has some available memory for them, it holds on to them in case you want to use them again.

You create a string to use as a *cell identifier* to indicate what cell type you're using:

```
static NSString *CellIdentifier = @"DestinationCell";
```

You recall that this is what you entered in the Identifier field of the Prototype cell in Step 18 in the "Setting up the DestinationController in the MainStoryboard_iPad" section, earlier in this chapter.

It is critical that the `CellIdentifier` and the `Identifier` field of the Prototype cell in Step 18 are the same. If they are not, you won't get the transparent prototype cell you specified in the storyboard.

Table views support multiple cell types, which makes the identifier necessary. In this case, you need only one cell type, but sometimes you may want more than one to accommodate cells with different layouts and formats. For example, if only some cells should have a disclosure triangle, you would probably use two prototypes — one with and one without the disclosure triangle.

You ask the Table view for a specific reusable cell object by sending it a `dequeueReusableCellWithIdentifier:` message:

```
UITableViewCell *cell = [tableView
         dequeueReusableCellWithIdentifier:CellIdentifier];
```

This determines whether any cells of the type you want are available. If no cells are lying around, this method will create a cell using the cell identifier that you specified. You now have a Table View cell that you can return to the Table view.

You have several choices on how to format the Table View cell. Although you're going to be using `UITableViewCellStyleDefault`, you can choose from a number of different styles, listed as follows (the keywords in the Style pop-up menu in the Attributes tab of Interface Builder are shown in brackets):

✔ `UITableViewCellStyleDefault`: Gives you a simple cell with a Text label (black and left-aligned) and an optional Image view. [Basic]

✔ `UITableViewCellStyleValue1`: Gives you a cell with a left-aligned black Text label on the left side of the cell and a right-aligned Text label with smaller gray text on the right side. (The Settings app uses this style of cell.) [Right Detail]

✔ UITableViewCellStyleValue2: Gives you a cell with a right-aligned blue Text label on the left side of the cell and a left-aligned black Text label on the right side of the cell. [Left Detail]

✔ UITableViewCellStyleSubtitle: Gives you a cell with a left-aligned Text label across the top and a left-aligned Text label below it in smaller gray text. (The Music app uses cells in this style.) [Subtitle]

With the formatting out of the way, you then set the Label properties that you're interested in.

You pluck out the name for each destination you've stored by accessing the DestinationName in each Destination dictionary. You do that by accessing the dictionary in the (saved) destinationsArray corresponding to the sections and row in indexPath, which contains the section and row information in a single object. To get the row or the section out of an NSIndexPath, you just have to invoke its section method (indexPath.section) or its row method (indexPath.row), either of which returns an int:

```
NSDictionary * destinationData =
        destinationsArray[indexPath.row];
```

Next, create an attributed string, which can manage both the character strings and attributes such as fonts, colors, and even kerning:

```
NSAttributedString *attributedString =
        [[NSAttributedString alloc]

        initWithString:destinationData[@"Destination
        Name"]

        attributes:@{ NSFontAttributeName : [UIFont
        systemFontOfSize:17.0f],

        NSForegroundColorAttributeName:  [UIColor
        whiteColor]}];
```

Now, use this attributed string to format the cell's text label:

```
cell.textLabel.attributedText = attributedString;
```

Finally, return the formatted cell with the text it needs to display in that row:

```
return cell;
```

Working with user selections

Now you can look at what happens when the user selects a row with a destination displayed.

When the user taps a Table View entry, what happens next depends on what you want your Table view to do for you.

If you're using the Table view to display data (as the Albums view in the Music app does, for example), you want a user's tap to show the next level in the hierarchy, such as a list of songs or a detail view of an item (such as information about a song).

In the case of the RoadTrip app, you want a user's tap to take you back to the Master view and, behind the scenes, create the correct model so that when you tap the Travel button, the right data is there.

To do that, add the final delegate method you need to implement, `tableView: didSelectRowAtIndexPath:`. Add the code in Listing 20-7 to `Destination Controller.m`.

Listing 20-7:   Implementing tableView:didSelectRowAtIndexPath:

```
-  (void)tableView:(UITableView *)tableView
        didSelectRowAtIndexPath:(NSIndexPath *)indexPath
{
   [tableView deselectRowAtIndexPath:
                                indexPath animated:YES];
   self.selectedDestination = indexPath.row;
   [self.delegate destinationController:self
        didFinishWithSave:YES];
}
```

You set the `selectedDestination` property to the selected row. Then you send the delegate the `destinationController:didFinishWithSave:` message with a value of `YES`.

Before I explain the `destinationController:didFinishWithSave:` method, implement the last part of the `DestinationController`. Add the bolded code in Listing 20-8 to the `cancel` method (generated when you created the action) in `DestinationController.m`.

Listing 20-8:   Adding cancel:

```
-  (IBAction)cancel:(id)sender {
   self.delegate destinationController:self
                                didFinishWithSave:NO];
}
```

When the user taps Cancel, the `DestinationController` sends the `destinationController:didFinishWithSave:` message with a value of `NO` to its delegate — which will be the `MasterViewController`. Now you'll go back to the `MasterViewController` and implement the `destinationController:didFinishWithSave:` message.

You also need to have the `MasterViewController` adopt the `Destination` `ControllerDelegate` protocol and declare the `destinationController:` `didFinishWithSave:` method. To do that, add the bolded code in Listing 20-9 to `MasterViewController.h`.

Listing 20-9: Updating the MasterViewController Interface

```
#import <UIKit/UIKit.h>
#import "DestinationController.h"
@class DetailViewController;

@interface RTMasterViewController : UITableViewController
    <UITextFieldDelegate, DestinationControllerDelegate>

@property (strong, nonatomic) RTDetailViewController
          *detailViewController;
@property (weak, nonatomic) IBOutlet UITextField
          *findText;
- (void)destinationController:(DestinationController *)
                controller didFinishWithSave:(BOOL)save;
```

Next, add the `destinationController:didFinishWithSave:` method in Listing 20-10 to `MasterViewController.m`.

Listing 20-10: Adding destinationController:didFinishWithSave:

```
- (void)destinationController:(DestinationController *)
                controller didFinishWithSave:(BOOL)save {

  AppDelegate *appDelegate =
            [[UIApplication sharedApplication] delegate];

  if (save) {
    [appDelegate createDestinationModel:
                        controller.selectedDestination];
    [self viewDidLoad];
    DetailViewController* currentDetailViewController;
    if ([[self.splitViewController.viewControllers
                                        lastObject]
        isKindOfClass:[UINavigationController class]]) {
      UINavigationController *navigationController =
          [self.splitViewController.viewControllers
                                        lastObject];
    currentDetailViewController = (DetailViewController *)
                navigationController.topViewController;
    }
    else
      currentDetailViewController =
          [self.splitViewController.viewControllers
                                        lastObject];
    [currentDetailViewController viewDidLoad];
```

(continued)

Listing 20-10 *(continued)*

```
    if (currentDetailViewController.popOverButton) {
      if (![[self.splitViewController.viewControllers
                                            lastObject]
          isKindOfClass:[UINavigationController class]]) {
        NSMutableArray *itemsArray =
          [currentDetailViewController.toolbar.items
                                            mutableCopy];
        [itemsArray removeObjectAtIndex:0];
        [currentDetailViewController.toolbar
                          setItems:itemsArray animated:NO];
      }
    }
    if ([currentDetailViewController
            isKindOfClass:[MapController class]]) {
      NSMutableArray *itemsArray =
        [currentDetailViewController.toolbar.items
                                            mutableCopy];
      [itemsArray removeLastObject];
      [currentDetailViewController.toolbar
                        setItems:itemsArray animated:NO];
    }
  }
  if (appDelegate.trip == nil)
    [appDelegate createDestinationModel:0];
  [self dismissViewControllerAnimated:YES completion:nil];
}
```

If the user has chosen a new destination, you send the app delegate a message to create that model:

```
[appDelegate
    createDestinationModel:controller.selectedDestination];
```

It determines the selection the user made by accessing the `selected Destination` property you set in the `tableView:didSelectRowAtIndex Path:` method.

As you may recall, `createDestinationModel:` is an already existing method in the app delegate. The `createDestinationModel:` method will actually be creating the model, and I made this a separate method because you'll have to be able to send the `AppDelegate` a message to create a new `Trip` when the user chooses a new destination in Chapter 20. Well, here it is, Chapter 20, and that's exactly what you're doing.

You reload the Master view based on the new destination so you can change the Background image.

```
[self viewDidLoad];
```

You'll also need to update the Detail view.

```
DetailViewController* currentDetailViewController;
if ([[self.splitViewController.viewControllers lastObject]
        isKindOfClass:[UINavigationController class]]) {
  UINavigationController *navigationController =
    [self.splitViewController.viewControllers lastObject];
  currentDetailViewController = (DetailViewController *)
                    navigationController.topViewController;
}
else
  currentDetailViewController =
    [self.splitViewController.viewControllers lastObject];
[currentDetailViewController viewDidLoad];

}
```

You'll need to determine whether the current Detail view is embedded in a
Navigation controller. Then you get the current Detail view and simply send it
the viewDidLoad message, which will cause it to reload all its data.

You also need to take a nuance here into account. If the current view controller isn't embedded in a Navigation controller, that means it has a toolbar. If it
already has a Road Trip button, to keep things in sync, you'll need to remove
the Road Trip button, which will then be added back in when the view
reloads.

```
if (currentDetailViewController.popOverButton) {
  if (![[self.splitViewController.viewControllers
      lastObject] isKindOfClass:
                            [UINavigationController class]]) {
    NSMutableArray *itemsArray =
      [currentDetailViewController.toolbar.items
                                            mutableCopy];
    [itemsArray removeObjectAtIndex:0];
    [currentDetailViewController.toolbar
                        setItems:itemsArray animated:NO];
  }
}
```

And yet another thing: If the current Detail view is a Map view, you'll also
need to remove the Locate button if it's on the toolbar:

```
if ([currentDetailViewController
          isKindOfClass:[MapController class]]) {
  NSMutableArray *itemsArray =
    [currentDetailViewController.toolbar.items
                                          mutableCopy];
  [itemsArray removeLastObject];
  [currentDetailViewController.toolbar
                      setItems:itemsArray animated:NO];
  }
```

If the user hasn't chosen a new destination but no model exists yet (when the user first launches the program, for example, no model exists yet — you'll see how that works in a second), you'll have the app delegate create a model using a default destination. I have arbitrarily chosen the first one.

You then send the `dismissModalViewControllerAnimated:` message, which, as you might expect, dismisses the view controller using the transition you specified in the "Setting up the DestinationController in the MainStoryboard_iPad" section, earlier in this chapter.

If the user has canceled, you simply send the `dismissViewController Animated: completion:` message, and the user finds herself back in the Master view.

But you still have some more work to do.

Previously, you added a `delegate` property to the `Destination Controller`, which it uses when it sends the `destinationController: didFinishWithSave:` message when the user selects a cell or taps Cancel.

The problem is, how do you set that property? Because you use a segue to take care of creating and initializing the controller, how do you assign the delegate property? If you recall from Chapter 19, when setting up `FindController`, you didn't use a segue, so you could assign any property you wanted after you created (but before you added) the `FindController` to the Split View controller `viewControllers` in `textFieldShouldReturn:` (I've bolded where you do that in the `MasterViewController.m` code).

```
- (BOOL)textFieldShouldReturn:(UITextField *)textField {

  [textField resignFirstResponder];

  if ([[UIDevice currentDevice] userInterfaceIdiom] ==
                              UIUserInterfaceIdiomPad){
    FindController * findController =
    [[UIStoryboard storyboardWithName:@"Main_iPad"
                                      bundle:nil]
        instantiateViewControllerWithIdentifier:@"Find"];
    findController.findLocation = textField.text;
  ...
  )
```

Fortunately, you have a way to use a segue and still be able to pass some data on to the view controller that's being instituted by the segue.

prepareForSegue:sender: is a view controller method used to notify the
view controller that a segue is about to be performed. segue is the UIStoryboard
Segue object that contains information about the view controllers involved in
the segue. You've already used prepareForSegue:sender: to dismiss the
popover and assign the popOverButton and masterPopoverController
properties. Now you need to add the code in bold in Listing 20-11 to prepare
ForSegue:sender: in MasterViewController.m. (I've omitted the code
that was already there.)

Listing 20-11: Update prepareForSegue:sender:

```
- (void)prepareForSegue:(UIStoryboardSegue *)segue
          sender:(id)sender {

  if ([segue.identifier isEqualToString:@"Destination"]) {

    if ([[UIDevice currentDevice] userInterfaceIdiom] ==
                            UIUserInterfaceIdiomPad) {
      DetailViewController *currentDetailViewController;

      DestinationController *destinationController =
          (DestinationController *)
            segue.destinationViewController;
      destinationController.delegate = self;

      if ([[self.splitViewController.viewControllers
                                      lastObject]
          isKindOfClass:[UINavigationController class]]) {
        UINavigationController *navigationController =
            [self.splitViewController.viewControllers
                                      lastObject];
        currentDetailViewController =
          (DetailViewController *)
                  navigationController.topViewController;
      }
      else
        currentDetailViewController = [self.
            splitViewController.viewControllers
                                      lastObject];
      if (currentDetailViewController.
                        masterPopoverController != nil)

      [currentDetailViewController.
                  masterPopoverController
                          dismissPopoverAnimated:YES];
    }
```

(continued)

Listing 20-11 *(continued)*

```
    else {
      DestinationController *destinationController =
          (DestinationController *)
                      segue.destinationViewController;
      destinationController.delegate = self;
    }
    return;
  }
  ... // previous code here
}
```

You first check to see whether the segue is the `Destination` segue (see, those identifiers are really useful):

```
if ([destinationSegue.identifier
                    isEqualToString:@"Destination"])
```

If it's the `Destination` segue, you check to see whether the device is an iPad. If it is, you go through the usual logic to find the Detail View (Destination) controller and assign its delegate to `self`.

```
DetailViewController *currentDetailViewController;

DestinationController *destinationController =
                            (DestinationController *)
  [segue.destinationViewController topViewController];
                    destinationController.delegate = self;
```

You then go through the usual logic and find the current Detail View controller and dismiss the popover, if one exists.

```
if ([[self.splitViewController.viewControllers lastObject]
        isKindOfClass:[UINavigationController class]]) {
UINavigationController *navigationController =
    [self.splitViewController.viewControllers lastObject];
currentDetailViewController = (DetailViewController *)
                navigationController.topViewController;
}
else
  currentDetailViewController =
    [self.splitViewController.viewControllers lastObject];
if (currentDetailViewController.
                        masterPopoverController != nil)

  [currentDetailViewController.masterPopoverController
                        dismissPopoverAnimated:YES];
```

If you're on the iPhone, you simply assign the delegate to the segue's `destinationViewController`.

```
DestinationController *destinationController =
            destinationSegue.destinationViewController;
destinationController.delegate = self;
```

Saving the Destination Choice and Selecting a Destination

At this point, if you were to run your project, you would be able to tap the Destination button, choose a destination, and see the data for either New York or San Francisco.

But you're not done yet.

First, if the app is terminated (and I mean terminated, not running in the background and relaunched), the user will find that the destination she selected has reverted to being the default one. You would like RoadTrip to be in position to save, and then restore, the user's destination preference. (In Chapter 11, you see how to default to the *first* destination in the plist. I mention in that chapter that I show you how to allow the user to *select* a destination in Chapter 20, and here you are.)

Start by adding the destinationPreference property to AppDelegate by adding the bolded code in Listing 20-12 to AppDelegate.h.

Listing 20-12:   Updating the AppDelegate Interface

```
#import <UIKit/UIKit.h>
@class Trip;

@interface AppDelegate : UIResponder
                                <UIApplicationDelegate>

@property (strong, nonatomic) UIWindow *window;
@property (nonatomic, strong) Trip *trip;
@property (nonatomic, strong) NSString *
                                destinationPreference;

- (void) createDestinationModel:(int)destinationIndex;

@end
```

Apple provides an NSUserDefaults object — available to any app — that you can use to store user preferences, or any small data values that should be saved by your app. In this section, you use the NSUserDefaults object to save the destination preference, so if the user chooses "San Francisco" the first time they use the app, "San Francisco" will be the location used when the app is next launched.

Data is stored in the user defaults object as a key-value pair. The value will be the `destinationPreference` string (which will be the index of the destination — @"0" or @"1" at this point). The key will be the static `Destination PreferenceKey` that you should now add to `AppDelegate.m`, as shown by the bolded code in Listing 20-13.

Listing 20-13:   Updating the AppDelegate Implementation

```
#import "AppDelegate.h"
#import "Reachability.h"
#import "Trip.h"

static NSString *DestinationPreferenceKey =
                              @"DestinationPreferenceKey";
@implementation AppDelegate
```

You're adding a key (string) that you'll need to use when you save the preference.

What you would like to do is direct the user to select a destination rather than using the default one. I'll have you post an alert to the users that they need to do that. More elegant ways are available to get the users to select the initial destination, but I'll leave that as an exercise for the reader.

Start by adding the bolded code in Listing 20-14 to `viewDidLoad` in `Master ViewController.m`.

Listing 20-14:   Adding to viewDidLoad

```
- (void)viewDidLoad
{
  [super viewDidLoad];
  AppDelegate* appDelegate = [[UIApplication
          sharedApplication] delegate];
  self.title = appDelegate.trip.destinationName;
  UIImageView* imageView = [[UIImageView alloc]
      initWithImage:[appDelegate.trip destinationImage]];
  self.tableView.backgroundView = imageView;

  UISwipeGestureRecognizer *swipeGesture =
    [[UISwipeGestureRecognizer alloc] initWithTarget:self
                  action:@selector(handleSwipeGesture:)];
  swipeGesture.direction =
          UISwipeGestureRecognizerDirectionLeft;
  [self.view addGestureRecognizer:swipeGesture];
  self.findText.delegate = self;

  if(appDelegate.destinationPreference == nil) {
    UIAlertView *alert = [[UIAlertView alloc]
        initWithTitle:@"Welcome to Road Trip"
```

```
        message:@"Please select a Destination from the
                                    Road Trip Menu"
        delegate:nil
        cancelButtonTitle:@"OK"
        otherButtonTitles:nil];
    [alert show];
  }
}
```

As you can see, if the `appDelegate.destinationPreference` property is nil, you'll post the `Please select a destination from the Road Trip` menu alert.

Unfortunately, every time you compile and run your app (or launch it), you'll see the alert because you will never have anything other than `nil` in the `appDelegate.destinationPreference` property.

In Listing 20-15, you fix that problem. At application launch, you'll check to see whether a user preference is saved. If one is, you assign it to `destinationPreference`. If no preference is saved, you leave that preference as `nil`, and the alert to the user to select a destination will be posted by the `MasterViewController`.

Add the bolded code in Listing 20-15 to `application:didFinishLaunching WithOptions:` in `AppDelegate.m` and delete the one line of code that's commented out in bold, italic, and underline.

Listing 20-15:   Updating application:didFinishLaunchingWithOptions:

```
- (BOOL)application:(UIApplication *)application
   didFinishLaunchingWithOptions:
                            (NSDictionary *)launchOptions
{
  ... // previous code here
  self.destinationPreference = [[NSUserDefaults
         standardUserDefaults]
         objectForKey:DestinationPreferenceKey];
  if (self.destinationPreference == nil) {
    NSDictionary *currentDestinationDict =
         @{DestinationPreferenceKey: @"0"};
    [[NSUserDefaults standardUserDefaults]
               registerDefaults:currentDestinationDict];
  }
  else
    [self createDestinationModel:
                   [self.destinationPreference intValue]];
//[self createDestinationModel:0];

  return YES;
}
```

At app launch, you check an `NSUserDefaults` object to see whether an entry exists with a key of `DestinationPreferenceKey` (you added this previously in Listing 20-13):

```
self.destinationPreference =
    [[NSUserDefaults standardUserDefaults]
                objectForKey:DestinationPreferenceKey];
```

You use `NSUserDefaults` to read and store preference data to a defaults data base, using a key value, just as you access keyed data from an `NSDictionary`. In this case, the preference is the destination.

`NSUserDefaults` is implemented as a *singleton,* meaning that only one instance of `NSUserDefaults` is running in your app. To get access to that one instance, I invoke the class method `standardUserDefaults`:

```
[NSUserDefaults standardUserDefaults]
```

`standardUserDefaults` returns the `NSUserDefaults` object. As soon as you have access to the standard user defaults, you can store data there and then get it back when you need it.

`objectForKey:` is an `NSUserDefaults` method that returns the object associated with the specified key, or `nil` if the key wasn't found.

You can add your app's preferences to Settings and then retrieve the values in the same way you are doing here. That is appropriate for settings that you want the user to set directly as opposed to a setting such as the last destination viewed that is managed automatically. Obviously, the first time the app is launched, no data is there, so you create a dictionary with the default value:

```
NSDictionary *currentDestinationDict =
  @{DestinationPreferenceKey: @"0"};
```

Note that you save the value as an `NSString`. That's because the `NSUser Defaults` requires a property list object.

You then send the `NSUserDefaults` object the `registerDefaults` message. This creates a new entry in the `NSUserDefaults` database that you can later access and update using the key you provided in the dictionary.

Because `destinationPreference` is still `nil`, when `viewDidLoad` executes, it will launch the Destination controller.

If a value exists in `NSUserDefaults`, you create the Destination model by sending the `createDestinationModel:` message with the value you had stored — which will be, as you will see, the index of the destination in the Destinations `plist`:

```
[self createDestinationModel:
               [self.destinationPreference intValue]];
```

Note that you use an `NSString` method `intValue`. This method returns the value in a string as an `int`, which is handy because that's what the `create DestinationModel:` method expects.

You also could've made the `currentDestinationIndex` an `NSNumber`. It's an object wrapper for any C scalar (numeric) type. It defines a set of methods that allow you to set and access the value in many different ways, including as a `signed` or `unsigned int`, `double`, `float`, `BOOL`, and others. Also, `NSNumber` defines a `compare:` method to determine the ordering of two `NSNumber` objects.

Using the index number of the destination rather than the name is a common coding practice. You need to be able to quickly go to a specific destination in the array of destinations. Each one has a title and a subtitle for use in displays.

If no `destinationPreference` exists, the user will see a blank Detail view with a default Master view (it looks a little different on the iPhone) and the alert asking her to select a destination. As I said, you have more elegant ways of doing this.

The last step in saving the Destination preference is actually storing `destination Preference` itself, and you do that in `createDestinationModel:`. Add the bolded code in Listing 20-16 to `createDestinationModel:` in `AppDelegate.m`.

Listing 20-16:   Updating createDestinationModel:

```
- (void) createDestinationModel:(int)destinationIndex {

  NSString *selectedDestinationIndex =
      [NSString stringWithFormat: @"%i",destinationIndex];
  if(![selectedDestinationIndex
          isEqualToString:self.destinationPreference]) {
    self.destinationPreference = selectedDestinationIndex;
    [[NSUserDefaults standardUserDefaults]
          setObject:self.destinationPreference
          forKey:DestinationPreferenceKey];
  }
self.trip = [[Trip alloc] initWithDestinationIndex:destina
          tionIndex];
}
```

You start out in Listing 20-16 by converting the `destinationIndex` parameter to a string and comparing it to see whether the Destination preference is the same as the one just selected by the user. (The user may have chosen the same destination again in the Destination controller.)

```
NSString *selectedDestinationIndex =
    [NSString stringWithFormat: @"%i",destinationIndex];
if(![selectedDestinationIndex
        isEqualToString:self.destinationPreference]) {
```

If the destination isn't the same, you assign the new value to the `destinationPreference`:

```
self.destinationPreference = selectedDestinationIndex;
```

and then you save the new value in `NSUserDefaults`:

```
[[NSUserDefaults standardUserDefaults]
    setObject:self.destinationPreference
                    forKey:DestinationPreferenceKey];
```

To store data, you use the `setObject:forKey:` method. The first argument, `setObject:`, is the object I want `NSUserDefaults` to save. This object must be `NSData`, `NSString`, `NSNumber`, `NSDate`, `NSArray`, or `NSDictionary`. In this case, `savedData` is an `NSString`, so you're in good shape.

The second argument is `forKey:`. To get the data back (and for `NSUser Defaults` to know where to save it), you have to be able to identify it to `NSUserDefaults`. You can, after all, have a number of preferences stored in the `NSUserDefaults` database, and the key tells `NSUserDefaults` which one you're interested in.

Next, you create the model passing in the destination index:

```
self.trip = [[Trip alloc]
            initWithDestinationIndex:destinationIndex];
```

Displaying the Destination table

One remaining problem is that the Destination table should appear automatically when the user dismisses the `UIAlertView` — the one that displays the "Welcome to Road Trip" message the first time the app is launched. The best way to handle this is to provide a method that will be called when the Alert is dismissed by the user, and then display the Destination table in that method. Here are the steps to do that:

1. **Add** `UIAlertViewDelegate` **to the** `MasterViewController`**'s comma-separated list of delegates in** `MasterViewController.h`.

2. **Designate the** `MasterViewController` **as the** `UIAlertViewDelegate` **by adding the line of code shown in Listing 20-17 to the** `viewDidLoad` **method in** `MasterViewController.m`.

3. **Add the** `alertView:clickedButtonAtIndex:` **method to** `MasterView`
`Controller.m`. **The simple code shown in Listing 20-18 displays the**
Destination table as desired.

Listing 20-17:   Designating the Master View Controller
as the Alert Delegate

```
- (void) createDestinationModel:(int)destinationIndex {
... // previous code
if(appDelegate.destinationPreference == nil) {
   UIAlertView *alert = [[UIAlertView alloc]
        initWithTitle:@"Welcome to Road Trip"
        message:@"Please select a Destination from the
                                    Road Trip Menu"
        delegate:nil
        cancelButtonTitle:@"OK"
        otherButtonTitles:nil];
   alert.delegate = self;
   [alert show];
}
```

Listing 20-18:   Displaying the Destination Table

```
- (void)alertView:(UIAlertView *)alertView
        clickedButtonAtIndex:(NSInteger)buttonIndex {
[self performSegueWithIdentifier:@"Destination"
        sender:self];
}
```

Testing

You're done. Run your app and test your work.

To test this part of your app, you need to first stop it in the Simulator (or
device) by clicking the Stop button on the Xcode toolbar. Then remove
RoadTrip from the background by following these steps:

1. **Double-click the Home button Hardware⇨Home to display the apps**
running in the background.

2. **Drag the RoadTrip view up and out of the horizontal list of back-**
ground apps. If it's not there, it's not running in the background.

3. **Run your app.**

To test this part of your app again later, you need to first stop it in the Simulator (or device) by clicking the Stop button on the Xcode toolbar. Then remove RoadTrip and its user defaults from the device by following these steps:

1. **Press and hold the RoadTrip icon until it wiggles.**

2. **Click the app Delete icon, the circle with the *X* that appears in the upper-left corner of the icon.**

3. **Press the Delete button when asked if you should delete the app and all of its data.**

4. **Build and run your app again, with the default** `destination Preference` **again set to nil. This gives you a fresh start.**

Adding Destination Support to the iPhone Storyboard

Your goal is to add a Destination scene to your iPhone storyboard in the same way that you added one to your iPad storyboard file. Follow the same directions for creating the Destination Controller scene for iPad storyboard. Steps include the following:

1. **Drag a** `UIViewController` **into the iPhone storyboard.**

2. **Use the Inspector to change the class name to** `Destination Controller` **as well as the Storyboard ID and Title to Destination.**

3. **Drag a Modal segue from the Destination table cell in the** `MasterViewController` **to the** `DestinationController`**. Set the segue ID to Destination.**

4. **Add the Navigation bar, and then place a Cancel button in it.**

5. **Choose the** `DestinationController`**'s cancel action for the Cancel button.**

6. **Add a** `UIImageView` **with an image.**

7. **Add a Label "Pick a Place, Anyplace."**

8. **Add a Table view.**

9. **Set the Table view's delegate and** `dataSource` **to be the** `DestinationController`**.**

10. **Connect the Table view to the destinationTableView property in** `Destination.m`**.**

11. **Format the Table View cell as described earlier in the chapter.**

The resulting layout is shown in Figure 20-6.

The good news is that you don't have to change your Objective-C code at all — the same `DestinationController` code works fine.

Figure 20-6: The Destination scene in the iPhone storyboard.

A Word about Adding Settings

Although space doesn't allow me to show you how to implement settings — for example, letting the user choose whether she wants to hear the car sound when she taps the Test Drive button, or to change the speed of the car — you implement such settings in exactly the same way that you just implemented the Destination preference. You add a setting to `NSUserDefaults` and create an `AppDelegate` property that you check in the car animation messages, for example, before you play the sound. To get even more sophisticated, you could create a `Preferences` class, in the same way you create a `Trip` class, that manages all preferences and uses that rather than the `AppDelegate` to provide Preference data to the rest of your app.

What's Next?

Although this point marks the end of your guided tour of iOS app development, it should also be the start — if you haven't started already — of your own development work.

Developing for iOS is one of the most exciting opportunities I've come across in a long time. I'm hoping that it ends up being as exciting for you.

Do keep in touch, though. Check out my website, www.jessefeiler.com, on a regular basis. There you can find the completed RoadTrip Xcode project as well as any updates.

Finally, keep having fun. I hope I have the opportunity to download one of your apps from the App Store soon.

Part VI
The Part of Tens

Visit www.dummies.com/extras/iosapplicationdevelopment for ten ways to make your app development life easier.

In this part . . .

- ✔ Ten ways to be successful with apps
- ✔ Ten ways to be a happy developer

Chapter 21

Ten Ways to Be Successful with Apps

*W*hen the App Store opened in July 2008, it's safe to say that no one imagined the world of apps we have today. From the launch of the iPhone in June 2007 until July 2008 when iOS 2.0 (it was still called iPhone OS then, but in retrospect we call it iOS 2.0) was released and the App Store opened, the only native apps on the iPhone were written by Apple. Within a year, there were 55,000 apps in the App Store accounting for more than a billion downloads. As of this writing, there are well over a million apps with many billions of downloads.

Particularly with the advent of the iPad and more mature versions of iOS, the world of app development has taken shape. Here are ten suggestions for how you can make money from apps using your own skills and experience as well as what you've learned in this book.

I start with a bonus way to make money. It doesn't count as one of the ten, for reasons you'll soon understand.

Make a Million Dollars in a Week

Take a weekend off, write an app, and watch it become a top seller on the App Store. Yes, and winning the lottery is also a possibility. This does happen, but it's not as common as the other ways listed here.

Build a Portfolio

A resume has traditionally been considered the key to getting a good job or even a temporary position. If you have a handful of apps (three to five) in the App Store, you don't need a resume: You have your work to speak for you. They don't have to be best-sellers, but they should demonstrate what it is that you know how to do.

The mere fact that they're in the App Store will demonstrate that you understand at least the basics of the app review process. You may want a variety of apps or you may want a variety of a specific type of app such as a game. A real-world app may help, so this might be a good time to volunteer for a nonprofit or for a friend or relative's business.

Build App Icons

You don't actually have to build apps, you know. Think about it. As you've worked on the apps in this book, have any parts of the development process really interested you? You don't have to build the whole app yourself. With the understanding of the app development process that you now have, you may want to specialize based on your skills and interests. The next few items suggest areas to focus on.

App icons are a very specific type of graphic design. If you have the ability to synthesize an app into a very tiny image that suggests what the app can do, app icons may be the place for you. This means that you need to understand the rules from Apple for app icons. You also need to be able to quickly and accurately understand what an app does. (And you may need to form this understanding long before the app is written.)

Design User Interfaces

By now, you should have a basic understanding of app design. You've seen toolbars, navigation bars, segues, buttons, and many of the basics (and even some advanced) techniques for controlling an app. Does this play to your strengths? Not every app developer is great at interfaces, so you may find developers who welcome (and will pay for) your expertise. Being able to understand what the main developer is doing can help you be a better user interface designer.

Build Back Ends

Is data management your forte? Or are you into designing web pages that provide data on demand to users? If JSON and http are the acronyms you work with, and if the use of quickly scalable web resources (such as Amazon Web Services) are your game, you've seen in this book how to start integrating them into apps, and you can bring your data management expertise to developers who need someone to help in that area.

Socialize with Apps

Apps and social media are intertwined today. If you have skills in both areas, you have a leg up. Start by looking at the Apple APIs for integration with social media and add a social media app to your portfolio. That's a highly valuable skill.

Talk About Apps with People Who Want Them

There are many business owners who want to have apps built for them. If you know a particular business well, consider helping people in that line of work find the right app developer even if it's not you. Twenty years ago, it seemed as if every business owner wanted a website. Today, they want apps. And, to be perfectly honest, many of them know as much about apps today as they knew about websites 20 years ago. If you can translate from the specific business world to the tech world, and if you are honest and reliable, there are opportunities for you.

Promote Apps

If you have a background or interest in promotion and media relations, your background in apps can help you promote apps and businesses that use them. Knowing the words to use (and which ones to explain) can help you help businesses make their points and get people to download their apps. It's difficult to promote an app if you don't know what it does and how it does it. You now know how apps work.

Provide Support to Users

Many apps are built for a specific company or organization to use to provide services to clients. As is the case with any customer service operation, this process often needs support people who are familiar with the business as well as with the app. A demonstrated ability to understand apps and work on a help desk to support a business's app can open doors to you either where you work now or at a new company.

Fix Bugs

For some developers, a clean build or compile is the end of the road, but you know that it's only the beginning. There's almost always room for code improvements. Even if an app doesn't crash, does it leak memory or behave in unpredictable ways from time to time? For some people, finding these issues is a wonderful multi-dimensional puzzle. If that's you, then there are opportunities waiting for you.

Chapter 22

Ten Ways to Be a Happy Developer

*T*hink of all the things you know you're supposed to do but don't because you think they'll never catch up with you. Not that many people probably enjoy balancing the checkbook or cleaning out gutters, and after all, not flossing won't cause you problems until your teeth fall out years from now, right?

But in iOS app development, those *mañana* gotchas will catch up with you early and often, so I want to tell you about what I've learned to pay attention to from the very start in app development, as well as give you a few tips and tricks that lead to happy and healthy users.

Keep Things Loosely Coupled

A *loosely coupled* system is one in which each of its components has little or no knowledge (or makes no use of any knowledge it may have) of other components. And because loose coupling refers to the degree of direct knowledge that one class has of another, it's not about encapsulation or to one class's knowledge of another class's attributes or implementation, just knowledge of that other class itself.

I explain loose coupling more in Chapter 11.

Remember Memory

iOS does not store "changeable" memory (such as object data) on disk to free space and then read it back in later when needed. This means that running out of memory is easy, and you should use automatic reference counting (ARC) to make the most of the memory available to you. All you have to do is follow the rules:

- ✔ **Rule 1:** Follow the naming conventions. This is really important. Good naming conventions help your code to be self-documenting. Sloppy, lazy, lethargic, sluggish, careless programmers who don't take the time to follow the naming conventions will be dealt with harshly!

- ✔ **Rule 2:** Do not send `retain`, `release`, or `autorelease` messages.

- ✔ **Rule 3:** Do not store object pointers in C structures.

- ✔ **Rule 4:** Inform the compiler about ownership when using Core Foundation–style objects.

- ✔ **Rule 5:** Use the `@autoreleasepool` keyword to mark the start of an autorelease block.

If you follow the rules, all you have to worry about is the retain cycle. This cycle occurs when one object has a back pointer to the object that creates it, either directly or through a chain of other objects, each with a strong reference to the next leading back to the first. Use the `weak` lifetime qualifiers for objects and the `weak` property attribute.

But even if you do everything correctly, in a large app, you may simply run out of memory and need to implement the methods that `UIKit` provides to respond to low-memory conditions, as follows:

- ✔ Override the `viewDidUnload` and `didReceiveMemoryWarning` methods in your custom `UIViewController` subclass.

- ✔ Implement the `applicationDidReceiveMemoryWarning:` method of your application delegate.

- ✔ Register to receive the `UIApplicationDidReceiveMemoryWarning Notification:` notification.

Don't Reinvent the Wheel

The iPhone and iPad are cutting-edge enough that opportunities to expand their capabilities are plentiful, and many of them are (relatively) easy to implement. You're also working with a very mature framework. So if you think that something you want your app to do is going to be really difficult, check the framework; somewhere there you may find an easy way to do what you have in mind.

For example, I once needed to compute the distance between two points on a map. So I got out my trusty trig books, only to find out later that the `distanceFromLocation:` method did exactly what I needed.

Understand State Transitions

The `UIApplication` object provides the application-wide control and coordination for an iOS app. It is responsible for handling the initial routing of incoming user events (touches, for example) as well as dispatching action messages from control objects (such as buttons) to the appropriate target objects. The app object sends messages to its Application Delegate to allow you to respond, in an app-unique way, when your app is executing, to things such as app launch, low-memory warnings, and state transitions, such as moving into background and back into foreground.

You should implement the following `UIApplicationDelegate` methods in your app. Most of these methods are already basically implemented in the code provided by Apple's templates, complete with comments explaining their purposes.

Method	What You Do with It
`application:didFinishLaunchingWithOptions:`	In this method, do what you need to do to initialize your app after it's launched.
`applicationWillResignActive:`	This message is sent when the app is about to move from the active to inactive state. Use this method to do things such as pause ongoing tasks and anything based on a timer (such as a game). Using this method doesn't mean that you will be entering background, but it does mean that your app won't be executing.
`applicationDidEnterBackground:`	This message is sent when your app is going to be entering background. At this point, you need to assume that your app may eventually be terminated without warning, so save user data, invalidate timers, and store enough app state information.
`applicationWillEnterForeground:`	This message is sent when your app has been rescued from background. In this method, reverse what you did in `applicationDidEnterBackground:`.
`applicationDidBecomeActive:`	Your app is now active. You should reverse whatever you did in `applicationWillResignActive:`. You also might want to refresh the user interface.

Do the Right Thing at the Right Time

When it comes to the view controller, you need to be aware of two methods, and you need to know what to do in each method.

The `viewDidLoad` message is sent to a view controller when the view has been loaded and initialized by the system. It is sent only when the view is created — and not, for example, when your app returns from background or when a view controller is returned to after another view controller has been "dismissed."

The `viewWillAppear:` message, on the other hand, is sent whenever the view appears, including when the view reappears after another view controller is "dismissed."

Do view initialization in `viewDidLoad`, but make sure that anything you do to refresh a view whenever it appears is done in `viewWillAppear:`.

Avoid Mistakes in Error Handling

Opportunities for errors abound; use common sense in figuring out which ones you should spend time on. For example, don't panic over handling a missing bundle resource in your code. If you included it in your project, it's supposed to be there; if it's not, look for a bug in your program. If it's *really* not there, the user has big problems, and you probably won't be able to do anything to avert the oncoming catastrophe.

Having said that, here are two big potential pitfalls you do have to pay attention to:

- ✔ Your app goes out to load something off the Internet, and (for a variety of reasons) the item isn't there, or the app can't get to it. You especially need to pay attention to Internet availability and what you're going to do when the Internet isn't available.

- ✔ A geocoder may fail for any number of reasons. For example, the service may be down, a certain GPS coordinate may not have a street address, or the user may access the data before the geocoder has returned.

Use Storyboards

Storyboards are a great way to examine the flow of the app as a whole. In addition, they require you to use less code.

Remember the User

I've been singing this song since Chapter 1, and I'm still singing it now: Keep your app simple and easy to use. Don't build long pages that take lots of scrolling to get through, and don't create really deep hierarchies. Focus on what the user wants to accomplish, and be mindful of the device limitations, especially battery life. And don't forget international roaming charges.

In other words, try to follow the Apple iOS Human Interface Guidelines, found with all the other documentation in the iOS Dev Center website at `http://developer.apple.com/devcenter/ios` in the iOS Developer Library section. Don't even *think* about bending those rules until you really, *really* understand them.

Keep in Mind That the Software Isn't Finished Until the Last User Is Dead

One thing that I can guarantee about app development is that nobody gets it right the first time. The design for RoadTrip (the example app in this book) evolved over time as I learned the capabilities and intricacies of the platform and the impact of my design changes. Object orientation makes extending your app (not to mention fixing bugs) easier, so pay attention to the principles.

Keep It Fun

When I started programming for the iPhone and iPad, it was the most fun I'd had in years. Keep things in perspective: Except for a few tedious tasks, expect that developing iOS apps will be fun for you, too. So don't take it too seriously.

Especially remember the *fun* part at 4 a.m., when you've spent the last five hours looking for a bug.

Index

• *B* •

• M •

• *V* •

• W •

About the Author

Jesse Feiler has designed and managed software for companies and organizations such as the Federal Reserve Bank of New York, Young & Rubicam, Yale University Press, and a wide variety of small businesses and non-profits. He is the creator of Minutes Machine for iPad, an app for managing meetings and minutes (it is available at the App Store). Minutes Machine combines technology with Jesse's real-life experience with organizations such as the Mid-Hudson Library System, the Philmont Village Library, the Plattsburgh Planning Board, Spectra Arts, the Philmont Main Street Committee, the Philmont Comprehensive Plan Board, and HB Studio. He received the Velma K. Moore award for exemplary service and dedication to libraries from the New York State Association of Library Boards.

Jesse is also software architect for the PlattInfo network of walk-up touchscreen kiosks in downtown Plattsburgh, N.Y. In addition to Minutes Machine, Jesse developed the Saranac River Trail app for iPhone, iPad, and iPod touch. It is available as a free download from the App Store.

He has written widely on new technologies and on Apple's OS X (Mac) and iOS (iPad, iPhone, and iPod touch) operating systems. His database expertise covers products such as FileMaker, MySQL, DB2, and Apple's Core Data (which is used in Minutes Machine). Jesse lives in Plattsburgh. He can be reached at his website, www.northcountryconsulting.com.

Author's Acknowledgments

Thanks to my acquisitions editor Kyle Looper, my project editor Linda Morris, and my technical editor Aaron Crabtree.

As always, Carole Jelen at Waterside Productions has been a stalwart supporter and guide through the world of publishers and publishing.

Publisher's Acknowledgments

Acquisitions Editor: Kyle Looper

Project Editor: Linda Morris

Copy Editor: Linda Morris

Technical Editor: Aaron Crabtree

Editorial Assistant: Annie Sullivan

Sr. Editorial Assistant: Cherie Case

Project Coordinator: Phil Midkiff

Cover Image: ©iStockphoto.com/boris64
©iStockphoto.com/chris_lemmens
©iStockphoto.com/AndrewJohnson
©iStockphoto.com/Samarskaya

Apple & Mac

iPad For Dummies,
6th Edition
978-1-118-72306-7

iPhone For Dummies,
7th Edition
978-1-118-69083-3

Macs All-in-One
For Dummies, 4th Edition
978-1-118-82210-4

OS X Mavericks
For Dummies
978-1-118-69188-5

Blogging & Social Media

Facebook For Dummies,
5th Edition
978-1-118-63312-0

Social Media Engagement
For Dummies
978-1-118-53019-1

WordPress For Dummies,
6th Edition
978-1-118-79161-5

Business

Stock Investing
For Dummies, 4th Edition
978-1-118-37678-2

Investing For Dummies,
6th Edition
978-0-470-90545-6

Personal Finance
For Dummies, 7th Edition
978-1-118-11785-9

QuickBooks 2014
For Dummies
978-1-118-72005-9

Small Business Marketing
Kit For Dummies,
3rd Edition
978-1-118-31183-7

Careers

Job Interviews
For Dummies, 4th Edition
978-1-118-11290-8

Job Searching with Social
Media For Dummies,
2nd Edition
978-1-118-67856-5

Personal Branding
For Dummies
978-1-118-11792-7

Resumes For Dummies,
6th Edition
978-0-470-87361-8

Starting an Etsy Business
For Dummies, 2nd Edition
978-1-118-59024-9

Diet & Nutrition

Belly Fat Diet For Dummies
978-1-118-34585-6

Mediterranean Diet
For Dummies
978-1-118-71525-3

Nutrition For Dummies,
5th Edition
978-0-470-93231-5

Digital Photography

Digital SLR Photography
All-in-One For Dummies,
2nd Edition
978-1-118-59082-9

Digital SLR Video &
Filmmaking For Dummies
978-1-118-36598-4

Photoshop Elements 12
For Dummies
978-1-118-72714-0

Gardening

Herb Gardening
For Dummies, 2nd Edition
978-0-470-61778-6

Gardening with Free-Range
Chickens For Dummies
978-1-118-54754-0

Health

Boosting Your Immunity
For Dummies
978-1-118-40200-9

Diabetes For Dummies,
4th Edition
978-1-118-29447-5

Living Paleo For Dummies
978-1-118-29405-5

Big Data

Big Data For Dummies
978-1-118-50422-2

Data Visualization
For Dummies
978-1-118-50289-1

Hadoop For Dummies
978-1-118-60755-8

Language &
Foreign Language

500 Spanish Verbs
For Dummies
978-1-118-02382-2

English Grammar
For Dummies, 2nd Edition
978-0-470-54664-2

French All-in-One
For Dummies
978-1-118-22815-9

German Essentials
For Dummies
978-1-118-18422-6

Italian For Dummies,
2nd Edition
978-1-118-00465-4

Available in print and e-book formats.

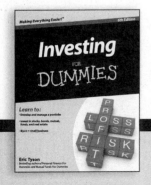

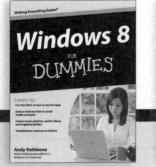

Available wherever books are sold. **For more information or to order direct visit www.dummies.com**

Math & Science

Algebra I For Dummies,
2nd Edition
978-0-470-55964-2

Anatomy and Physiology
For Dummies, 2nd Edition
978-0-470-92326-9

Astronomy For Dummies,
3rd Edition
978-1-118-37697-3

Biology For Dummies,
2nd Edition
978-0-470-59875-7

Chemistry For Dummies,
2nd Edition
978-1-118-00730-3

1001 Algebra II Practice
Problems For Dummies
978-1-118-44662-1

Microsoft Office

Excel 2013 For Dummies
978-1-118-51012-4

Office 2013 All-in-One
For Dummies
978-1-118-51636-2

PowerPoint 2013
For Dummies
978-1-118-50253-2

Word 2013 For Dummies
978-1-118-49123-2

Music

Blues Harmonica
For Dummies
978-1-118-25269-7

Guitar For Dummies,
3rd Edition
978-1-118-11554-1

iPod & iTunes
For Dummies, 10th Edition
978-1-118-50864-0

Programming

Beginning Programming
with C For Dummies
978-1-118-73763-7

Excel VBA Programming
For Dummies, 3rd Edition
978-1-118-49037-2

Java For Dummies,
6th Edition
978-1-118-40780-6

Religion & Inspiration

The Bible For Dummies
978-0-7645-5296-0

Buddhism For Dummies,
2nd Edition
978-1-118-02379-2

Catholicism For Dummies,
2nd Edition
978-1-118-07778-8

Self-Help & Relationships

Beating Sugar Addiction
For Dummies
978-1-118-54645-1

Meditation For Dummies,
3rd Edition
978-1-118-29144-3

Seniors

Laptops For Seniors
For Dummies, 3rd Edition
978-1-118-71105-7

Computers For Seniors
For Dummies, 3rd Edition
978-1-118-11553-4

iPad For Seniors
For Dummies, 6th Edition
978-1-118-72826-0

Social Security
For Dummies
978-1-118-20573-0

Smartphones & Tablets

Android Phones
For Dummies, 2nd Edition
978-1-118-72030-1

Nexus Tablets
For Dummies
978-1-118-77243-0

Samsung Galaxy S 4
For Dummies
978-1-118-64222-1

Samsung Galaxy Tabs
For Dummies
978-1-118-77294-2

Test Prep

ACT For Dummies,
5th Edition
978-1-118-01259-8

ASVAB For Dummies,
3rd Edition
978-0-470-63760-9

GRE For Dummies,
7th Edition
978-0-470-88921-3

Officer Candidate Tests
For Dummies
978-0-470-59876-4

Physician's Assistant Exam
For Dummies
978-1-118-11556-5

Series 7 Exam For Dummies
978-0-470-09932-2

Windows 8

Windows 8.1 All-in-One
For Dummies
978-1-118-82087-2

Windows 8.1 For Dummies
978-1-118-82121-3

Windows 8.1 For Dummies,
Book + DVD Bundle
978-1-118-82107-7

 **Available in print and e-book formats.**

   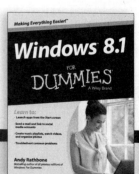

Take Dummies with you everywhere you go!

Whether you are excited about e-books, want more from the web, must have your mobile apps, or are swept up in social media, Dummies makes everything easier.

Leverage the Power

For Dummies is the global leader in the reference category and one of the most trusted and highly regarded brands in the world. No longer just focused on books, customers now have access to the For Dummies content they need in the format they want. Let us help you develop a solution that will fit your brand and help you connect with your customers.

Advertising & Sponsorships

Connect with an engaged audience on a powerful multimedia site, and position your message alongside expert how-to content.

Targeted ads • Video • Email marketing • Microsites • Sweepstakes sponsorship